THE IDEOLOGY OF THE GREAT FEAR

THE JOHNS HOPKINS UNIVERSITY STUDIES
IN HISTORICAL AND POLITICAL SCIENCE
109th Series (1991)

THE IDEOLOGY
OF THE GREAT FEAR

⁊ The Soissonnais in 1789

CLAY RAMSAY

The Johns Hopkins University Press
Baltimore and London

© 1992 The Johns Hopkins University Press
All rights reserved
Printed in the United States of America

The Johns Hopkins University Press
701 West 40th Street
Baltimore, Maryland 21211-2190
The Johns Hopkins Press Ltd., London

Library of Congress Cataloging-in-Publication Data
Ramsay, Clay.
   The ideology of the Great Fear : the Soissonnais in 1789 /
Clay Ramsay.
      p.   cm. — (The Johns Hopkins University studies in
historical and political science : 109th ser., 2)
   Includes bibliographical references (p.   ) and index.
   ISBN 0-8018-4197-6
   1. Soissons Region (France)—History. 2. France—History—
Revolution, 1789. 3. Rumor. 4. Fear—France—Soissons Re-
gion—History—18th century. 5. Peasant uprisings—France—
Soissons Region—History—18th century. 6. Soissons Region
(France)—Militia—History. 7. Soissons Region (France)—
Economic conditions. I. Title. II. Series.
DC195.S56R36   1991
944'.345—dc20   91-17676

To William and Jacqueline Ramsay

❧ CONTENTS

❧ *LIST OF ILLUSTRATIONS*

❧ PREFACE

This study had its genesis in my undergraduate years, when I was introduced to French Revolutionary studies by Professor Jonathan Beecher of the University of California, Santa Cruz. He bore with my fascination for this area for two years—fruitful years for me, and I hope endurable ones for him. At Stanford University, Professor Carolyn Lougee has been a patient and persistent critic and advisor; her efforts contributed vastly to the coherence and final structuring of this text. Professors Peter Paret, Gordon Wright, and later David Bien have also assisted in important ways.

A grant from the Whiting Foundation enabled me to undertake an indispensable second year in France. My thanks go also to staff members of the Archives Nationales, the Archives départementales de l'Aisne, the municipal archives of Compiègne and of Château-Thierry, and the Bibliothèque de Soissons. This work's final stages were generously assisted by a grant for recent recipients of the Ph.D. from the American Council of Learned Societies (funded in part by the National Endowment for the Humanities). At Johns Hopkins University Press, executive editor Henry Tom provided strong and early encouragement, while Miriam Kleiger was a superb copy editor. (Any remaining errors are, of course, my responsibility.) The friendship of Keith Gregory, Steven Kull, and Garey Mills was of great assistance, as was that of Patrick and Suzanna Curry, whose unfailing hospitality in London was a refuge from all things French. The greatest aid, and that most difficult to measure—in assistance, patience, criticism, space, and time—toward the completion of this book came from my wife, Hitomi Tonomura.

My intellectual debts on the French side can never be repaid and remain open accounts. Among these, I must first mention Régine

Robin, whose work during the 1970s on eighteenth-century ideologies remains an inspiration to me; and also Martine Sandor, her student, who passed on to me more of her influence. Through Martine Sandor I met Jacques Guilhaumou, who encouraged me to become the one regularly attending Anglo-Saxon in the late Albert Soboul's Saturday-afternoon advanced seminar of 1980–81 (full though it was of Europeans, Latin Americans, and Japanese). Here I met some of Soboul's last group of younger students: Jacques Bernet, scholar of dechristianization and the editor of *Annales historiques compiégnoises*; Guy-Robert Ikni, specialist in the peasants of the Noyonnais, who guided me one day in the partly unclassified departmental archives of the Oise; and particularly Florence Gauthier, historian of Picard peasants, who in one long and memorable after-dinner conversation led me toward a theoretical standpoint from which I could initiate a critique of Lefebvre's work on the Great Fear.

With the late Albert Soboul himself I had little personal contact, yet perhaps a word of homage is not out of place. Because he has been criticized (both during his life and afterward) as a maker of disciples and an editor of historiographic catechisms, I feel constrained to say that my recollections of him do not fit this mold. The Saturday afternoons of Soboul's last years were, I suppose, badly policed. Perhaps a hundred flowers did not bloom, but three or four banners were visibly hoisted; and in general, I suppose the generation shaped by May 1968 was unamenable to the sort of intellectual control that I had been led to anticipate. I especially recall, for instance, the strong interest evinced for Albert Mathiez's contribution to the history of the Revolution—his comprehension of the sharp, close, and bitter tone of factional struggles at the top, his marked Robespierrism, his voluntarism—a process of rediscovery on the younger historians' part that Soboul wryly called "le romantimathiezisme." Or again, the arguments between (roughly) the more "urban" and the more "rural" historians over the import of dechristianization. I need only recall the uproar that ensued when one speaker went so far as to call dechristianization a "revolutionary error" . . . ! I would not claim that Soboul relished everything in this, only that in the chapel the aroma of incense was distinctly lacking.

Of Soboul himself, I can speak only of a few instants that profiled him for me in a lasting way. One Saturday, a presentation concerning Brazil in the early nineteenth century was scheduled. Noting a certain falling-off in that day's attendance, Soboul upbraided those absent for their narrowness, their neglect of their *culture générale*, and insisted on the importance of knowledges *qui ne font pas carrière* . . .

On another day, in the course of a tumultuous discussion over a tortuous sequence of events in spring 1793 around the trial of Marat, six or seven voices were raised but Soboul's covered them all. He was demanding "la date! la date! la date!" In a peculiar fashion, that moment taught me that in the study of the French Revolution, chronology can be less a matter of days than of hours; that it is not a mere organizational framework, but a pulse: lose the pulse and you are lost yourself. In that same moment I saw Soboul the schoolteacher, reared as a child by other schoolteachers, now surrounded but undaunted by his unruly pupils— and yes, he was sure of the values he had to offer them.

❧ *INTRODUCTION*

From July 20 to August 6, 1789, France was convulsed by the Great Fear, a collective panic that covered two-thirds of the country by transmission from town to town. The Great Fear was provoked by a rumor that underwent numerous local variations, but in substance its message was this: "Thousands of brigands are advancing on your village—they have come to burn the crops in your fields—they have already destroyed a village near you on their line of march—they are only an hour or two away . . . " Those who heard the rumor rang the church bells of the town or village as an alarm. All the able-bodied males of the village gathered together; the municipal officers handed out such firearms as were available. A militia formed, often under the leadership of a noble or an old soldier, and the villagers set out to search their district.

There were no armies of brigands. After patroling the environs for some hours, the militia returned home. The alert came to an end, but the militia did not disband. It retained its guns, selected officers, devised a schedule for watch and patrol, and became an armed presence in its community.

A week or a month later, people came to believe that the rumors that started the Great Fear had been spread by a conspiracy of aristocrats or revolutionaries (depending on one's politics). It was thought well into the nineteenth century that the Fear had begun everywhere on the same day when a prearranged signal was given to agents planted throughout France.

Historically regarded, the Great Fear can be understood as a response to immense political change occurring in a threatening social and economic context. The process of selecting deputies for the Estates-General—unquestionably the deepest-penetrating political event of the eighteenth century—had begun in January 1789. The stated wish of the monarchy that the grievances of every hearth in the land be heard had brought about a participatory tension throughout the country during the ensuing confrontations between the Estates-General and the king. The Tennis Court Oath sworn by Third-Estate and liberal deputies who refused to be disbanded, and the king's dismissal of Jacques Necker, the minister who had urged the convoking of the Estates-General, resonated through France almost as powerfully the event that followed—the fall of the Bastille on July 14, 1789. Meanwhile, the economic crisis affected both cities and countryside; unemployment in the textile manufactures intensified, as did the grain shortage resulting from the poor harvest of 1788. Peasant revolts in the spring in Provence, Dauphiné, Hainaut and the Cambrésis, and Picardy arose from and added to the strain. In such an atmosphere, the fall of the Bastille and the transformation of the Estates-General into a new National Assembly with as yet undefined powers had immense repercussions. The news of July 14 was followed by scattered municipal revolutions in which appointed administrations were overthrown, and by the opening of four new foyers of antiseigneurial revolt, in western Normandy, Franche-Comté, Alsace, and the Mâconnais. The widespread, collective panic of the Great Fear took place in the midst of these overlapping forms of social stress.

Yet these political, economic, and social factors leave much about the Great Fear unclarified. A major prerequisite for the Fear's emergence is still not understood: the shared mentality of its participants. What attitudes and preconceptions gave the Fear its credibility? What was its psychological and ideological setting? These are the questions this study attempts to answer.

This introduction begins with an assessment of the Great Fear's historical importance, and continues with a discussion of some aspects of the phenomenon that remain largely unexplained. The historiography of the Great Fear is considered through an evaluation of the single masterpiece that dominates it, Georges Lefebvre's *La Grande Peur de 1789*.[1] With this background established, we turn to the plan of the present study: its temporal and geographical scope, its interpretive approach to the Great Fear, and its structure and argument.

The Great Fear's Historical Importance

There are two crucial reasons for reexamining the Great Fear. First, the Fear was pivotal to the early political development of the Revolution. Second, the Fear is a window that gives us a panoramic view of attitudes held in common by a wide range of social classes: a whole complex of assumptions regarding the food supply, the credibility of information, and the legitimacy of authority which can be called the "ideology of the Great Fear."

Politically, the Great Fear forced the National Assembly to formally renounce feudalism in the tumultuous evening session of August 4. The Fear vastly amplified Parisians' impression of the peasant revolts in progress in late July, which, while severe, were restricted to four separate regions of France. Many municipalities wrote the National Assembly immediately upon reception of the Fear's rumor. On July 28 the president of the Assembly, the duc de Liancourt, read aloud a letter from the municipal officers and provincial commissioners of Soissons which spoke of four thousand brigands destroying the harvest in broad daylight.[2] More letters—from Vesoul in the raging Franche-Comté, from Quincey in the same province, where the accidental explosion of a barrel of gunpowder in a château had sparked the insurgency—brought news of a rural offensive against seigneurial rights which was difficult to distinguish from the rumors of the Fear. The impact of these letters was heightened by the fact that many of them were read from the rostrum of the Assembly almost as soon as they were received, punctuating the abstract debate on France's constitution and lending that debate an extraneous urgency. Not until July 30 did the Assembly have a functioning correspondence committee to evaluate the mass of incoming reports and digest them for the Assembly.[3] The multitude of reports and the Assembly's fashion of handling them strengthened the impression that France was on the verge of social collapse. This was the atmosphere in which forms of personal servitude, venality of office, and privileges of specific towns were renounced on the night of August 4. As Leguen de Kérengal, one of the most powerful speakers of that night, insisted: "Hasten to give these promises to France; a general cry is audible; you have not a moment to lose; one day's delay will bring new conflagrations; the fall of empires is announced with less fracas. Do you wish to give laws only to a devastated France?"[4] The basic demands of the peasants against the seigneurial system had to be appeased at once. The coalition of radical bourgeois and liberal nobles which produced the night of August 4 hung together because neither group could predict the consequences of an armed countryside. The Fear, which appeared to give the concurrent peasant revolts the status of a unified national phenomenon, forced the Assembly to take drastic measures in order to remain in the van of the Revolution.

It is of equal importance that the Great Fear permanently rearmed the rural population. The royal authorities had systematically disarmed the peasantry, usually at the request of seigneurs seeking to protect their game: the Hainaut and the Cambrésis in 1762 and 1771, Flandre and Artois in 1777, and Normandy and Guyenne in 1785–87 were all stripped of firearms in this way. In the year 1789 itself, villages near Fontainebleau, near Chartres, and in the Thiérache were searched for arms by the mounted police.[5] The creation of militias during the Great Fear undid all this work. After the Fear, the militias persisted: the new municipalities brought to power in towns where upheavals had taken place after July 14 relied on them, while the many old municipalities that had survived judged it less dangerous to regulate the militias than to attempt their disbandment. In these latter towns the militia was a training ground for local revolutionaries and an institution to combat the fading old-regime authorities. The struggles between militias and municipalities snowballed over the autumn and winter, culminating in the nationwide elections of new municipalities in January and February 1790. The major alteration in local power balances which resulted brought about a France politically different from that which had elected the Estates-General in spring 1789; and it was this emerging France, as well as events in Paris, with which the National Assembly had to keep in step.

From the standpoint of attitudes and ideology, the Great Fear inspired a moment—though a moment only—of striking social cohesion. There are a number of cases in which actions of self-defense turned against local nobility after a time,[6] but there is no known case of the rumor being instantly taken by one group as the ruse or provocation of another group within a community. And this at a time when social tensions had reached extreme levels even within small villages! Because of the Fear, municipalities distributed guns to residents with little or no property. Local nobles assumed command of militias whose volunteers' political views were often the reverse of their own. Something about the message of the Fear must have struck a universal chord in French rural society. This universality hints at the nature of the regime that was dying, how it could organize the population through consent as well as coercion, and how it was perceived by its officials and its subjects.

Unexplained Aspects of the Great Fear

On close examination, many characteristics of the Great Fear seem curious or even incredible. At least seven original panics initiated the Fear in different regions of France.[7] As the rumor traveled it gave rise to panics and mobilizations; these often created incidents that set off new panics and mobilizations, which in turn created more incidents, setting off new panics and relaying the Fear in more directions. Relaying panics, and deliberate transmission, together sent currents of the Fear for hundreds of kilometers. However, the importance of deliberate transmission should be noted: panic alone could not have spread the Fear very far. It had to be complemented by prompt, decisive action to warn others, often taken by the authorities. The Fear required considerable cooperation, somewhat analogous to that demanded by an extensive chain letter. But how was such cooperation possible, especially across class lines, in such a period of tension?

In a climate of general suspicion, some of the rumor carriers should have been suspect themselves. The social variety of these messengers is remarkable. George Lefebvre's *The Great Fear of 1789* has a chapter on this subject: it mentions an architect, a doctor, a dancing master, two wine merchants, and a wide range of official personages: parish priests, municipal officers, postmasters and couriers, chiefs of the militia or of the mounted police, royal attorneys, judges, subdelegates of intendants, the military commander of Franche-Comté, and the Parlement of Toulouse. Though people feared strangers, they believed travelers; they believed members of the most hated professions, including an itinerant harvester, a miller, and a dues-collector for the seigneur; if they feared revenge of the two privileged Estates on the victories of the Third, their credulity was ill-placed in nobles, monks, and their innumerable valets who crisscrossed many districts carrying the rumors.[8] Yet, though in some communities one or two derided the rumor, there are no known cases of its being treated as a ruse or provocation.

The Great Fear was a mobilization against "brigands"; but these "brigands" were nonexistent. It has often been argued that the term *brigand* was a euphemism for the very poor, or for the itinerant unemployed, or for wandering beggars (groups that must be distinguished, although they form a continuum).[9] It is certain that to some participants in the Fear, *brigand* meant the poor and uprooted; but it cannot be asserted that this was the word's universal meaning. The Fear was not directed against the poor, because the poor were rarely excluded from the impromptu militias. On the contrary, much of municipal politics in the second half of 1789 sought to undo this rash error. The Fear was not directed against beggars either, because, as will be shown below, the institution of begging had a degree of legitimacy in the rural community.

Lefebvre's detailed geographic study of the Fear's original panics, its currents of rumor, and its points of relay led him to a major conclusion: the peasant revolts and the Great Fear were two distinct sets of events.[10] The Fear did not enter regions that had experienced revolt beforehand. If the Fear was really a fear of the very poor, it would seem logical that the regions where the poor peasants were in active rebellion should have been vulnerable to the rumor. However, the Fear did not penetrate any area recently in revolt.[11]

Finally, there is the question of the rumor's content. Although the identity of the imagined enemies varied geographically, with "foreign troops" making appearances on borders and "foreign navies" along the seacoast, the term *brigand* in all its vagueness seems to have covered by far the most territory. The wide diffusion of this idea is most often explained by France's unity under shared political tension: the fear of an "aristocratic plot" against the Third Estate held the whole country in suspense and so provided a continuous field across which the rumor could race. According to Lefebvre, "the whole Third Estate considered itself under attack because the [supposed] rioters were in the service of the aristocratic plotters and were helped by the foreign regiments in the service of the king and the troops of neighboring rulers brought in by the *émigrés*."[12] But if this was so, why were nobles often made leaders of the improvised militias that set out to find the "brigands"?[13]

I argue that these paradoxes are understandable when viewed against a background of deeply held contemporary attitudes. The startling degree of cooperation evinced across class boundaries during the Great Fear was made possible by consensual notions about the production, sale, and distribution of the food supply (which the "brigands" were supposedly attacking). The credibility of the Fear's messengers came not from themselves but from the social currency of the language of the rumor they disseminated: a currency that can be documented and analyzed. The Great Fear was not a class fear of the poor, because it partook of the old regime's many material and ideological defenses against the danger of sharp class divisions. Nobles could become leaders of impromptu militias whose members had revolutionary sympathies, because old-regime public order and the authorities' repertoire of techniques for its maintenance often involved awkward mixtures of elite leadership and community participation.

Lefebvre's Achievement

Given the historical richness of the Great Fear—its pivotal role in the early Revolution, the questions raised by its size, social composition, and geographical patterns, and the suggestive picture it presents of the ideological workings of the old regime—why is its historiography so sparse? Perhaps because in 1932 Lefebvre answered the questions of the Fear as well as the economic and social approaches could then answer them.

Lefebvre's *The Great Fear of 1789* is a classic that has held its ground for nearly 60 years. Not only has it gone unsupplanted, it has virtually gone unsupplemented. Henri Dinet's painstaking local studies of Poitou and the regions surrounding Paris are the only concentrated work on the Fear since Lefebvre's book.[14] The relative lack of research and writing on the Great Fear is perhaps a consequence of Lefebvre's success in disposing of the traditional problematic associated with the event.

Up to the time that Lefebvre wrote, it was still impossible to dismiss conspiratorial theories of the Great Fear. These theories derived directly from the beliefs of 1790; the Fear seemed so simultaneous an outbreak that it must have begun at a prearranged signal. Because the political outcome of the Fear favored the Revolution and not its opponents, the notion that the panic had been contrived by revolutionaries was the most prevalent conspiratorial explanation. After 140 years of currency, the conspiracy theory was disposed of by Lefebvre's research, which united a rich diversity of local evidence from all over France in one monograph. Lefebvre's book employs numerous archival sources, but primarily it is a synthesis of many local studies—one of the most difficult forms of treatment for any historical subject, but perhaps the only way that the myth of a centrally directed Great Fear could have been exorcised.

Lefebvre implanted the history of the Great Fear in its social context, as well as its political context. As the book's conclusion summarizes, "The Great Fear arose from fear of the 'brigand', which can itself be explained by the economic, social and political circumstances prevailing in France in 1789."[15] Throughout the book, Lefebvre balances different levels of causation admirably, while providing such a wealth of detail that the reader is able to seek alternative explanations. The broadest lines of Lefebvre's argument are encapsulated in the sentence just quoted. The poor harvest of 1788, the increasing numbers of rural poor, and the political stress of the Estates-General combined to form the economic and social causes of the Fear; the tensions around the fall of the Bastille and its aftermath generated a widespread fear of reprisals by nobles, and this fear triggered the general panic. After Lefebvre, the Great Fear could not be treated in a monocausal way.

Lefebvre decided that the description of the Great Fear was a geographical problem. He developed the terminology of "original panics," "currents," and "relays" in which scholars continue to think about the Great Fear. This geographical approach was essential to Lefebvre's goal of deflating conspiracy theories: just as "at once" had to be replaced with a duration in time, "everywhere" had to be replaced with limits in space. The success of the geographical aspect of Lefebvre's book has been formidable. It has made Lefebvre's description of the Fear seem detailed to the point of completeness, and has created a sense of closure in historians.

In this description, Lefebvre proved that the Great Fear had no single point of origin. In fact, he located six (to which Henri Dinet has added a seventh, in Hurepoix). Lefebvre rarely wrote in psychological language, but his discovery of multiple starting points for a single massive event demonstrated that the Fear's unity existed on the psychological level. He distinguished the Great Fear from the "fear of brigands," and his distinction is a purely psychological one:

> The *fear of brigands* appeared for the first time at the end of the winter, reaching its culmination during the second fortnight in July; at its greatest extent, it covered more or less the whole of France. Though it gave rise to the Great Fear it was not at all the same thing and one must make a careful distinction between the two. The Great Fear had its own special characteristics, and these are what they were: until this moment in time, the appearance of the brigands was possible and much dreaded: with the Great Fear it became a total certainty; they were there in the flesh, they could be both seen and heard.[16]

Lefebvre also pointed to the role of autosuggestion in some transmissions of the Fear:

> Finally, one last group of causes relates to the process of autosuggestion. Flocks of sheep moving in the woods or raising dust clouds along the road and in the fallow fields caused many a panic . . . The glow from lime-kilns, the smoke from burning weeds, the reflection of the setting sun in the windows of a château were enough to convince some that the brigands had started a fire.[17]

Lefebvre defined the Great Fear itself as a subjective event, "agreed on" as real by community after community. From this point on the long shoreline of Lefebvre's text, new expeditions to the Great Fear can embark.

These four strengths—the analysis and destruction of conspiracy theories, the grounding of the Fear in a social context, the synthesis of regional information into a satisfying geographical description, and the opening to a psychological understanding of the Fear—give *The Great Fear of 1789* its remarkable staying power. However, two fundamental criticisms must also be made.

The first criticism involves Lefebvre's treatment of the "aristocrats' plot" in the countryside. He puts great emphasis on the fear of an "aristocrats' plot" by the court and the nobility to revenge themselves on the Third Estate, especially after July 14. Part 2 of his book is entitled "The 'Aristocrats' Plot'" and its first four chapters detail (1) the "aristocrats' plot" as unfolded by the Parisian press; (2) the transmission of news of the "plot" from Paris to the provinces, largely by letters from National Assembly deputies; (3) the reaction to the "aristocrats' plot" in provincial towns; and (4) the reaction in the countryside. Lefebvre can amply demonstrate the importance of belief in an "aristocrats' plot" in Paris. The existence of groups of varying sizes in many provincial towns, eager to give local currency to Parisian rumors, is unquestionable. However, the outermost links in the chain of transmission are very difficult to prove. The chapter on the countryside's reaction to the "aristocrats' plot" contains some of the book's weakest lines:

> News of the "aristocrats' plot" spread from town to countryside by the well-known paths but as the peasant never set pen to paper we shall never know what he thought or said about it . . . It would be wrong to believe that people in the countryside accepted the "aristocrats' plot" just because news of it came from Versailles and Paris. The peasants had had some dim forebodings of it as soon as they knew the Estates-General had been called . . . They may have known little about history, but they knew the legends well; they remembered the "brigands" and they never forgot that every jacquerie, every peasant revolt, every ragamuffin rising against the seigneurs, had ended in a blood-bath.[18]

It is most unlike Lefebvre to plead lack of evidence and then go on to fabricate a mentality in this manner, but here he does so. His remarks contain nothing improbable, but as an explanation of the highly improbable Great Fear they are disappointing. It is not a hostility between classes that we must understand, but a brief, bizarre unanimity across class lines against a foe that was imaginary. Subjective factors of great importance for some sectors of the population cannot be unfurled to cover the subjectivity of every sector.

The second criticism accompanies the first: Lefebvre at times identifies the feared "brigands" with vagabonds and the rural poor. This is partly because he must argue against Taine, who took the term *brigands* literally to mean criminals, fugitives from the galleys, and the like.

Lefebvre fights Taine with another literalism, in which *brigands* is taken to mean the uprooted poor. "Today we know that these vagrants were only unemployed workers and peasants driven to despair by hunger," Lefebvre writes in one passage, "but everybody else, the king as well as the bourgeoisie, neither of whom had any more understanding of these poor devils than Taine himself, called them 'brigands' as though they were professional bandits."[19] If Lefebvre had been incognizant of the social uses of language and how a single word can serve as a "wild card" in an ideology, he could be pardoned. In fact, however, he did perceive the social uses of language but did not always take them into account. Early in the book, for instance, he is quite explicit:

> Today it seems surprising that at the end of July 1789 everyone was so ready to believe in "the brigands," but the word occurs continually in contemporary documents. Even the government used it freely to describe both the hordes of beggars and the gangs of petty criminals, those who stole the corn as well as those who rebelled against the seigneurs; indeed the Convention took over the word and applied it to the Vendée rebels.[20]

Lefebvre here is perfectly aware of the multivalence of the word *brigand*, but in much of the book he does not let that fact complicate his analysis of the Great Fear. Absorbed with the task of establishing the social context for this bewildering and unwieldy event, he at times allows the fears inspired by the rural poor in the possessing classes to "stand in" as the basis for the Great Fear itself. Yet the evidence he offers indicates that the rural poor feared the "brigands" too! Essentially, the problem of the idea of "brigands" is the same as that of the "aristocrats' plot": the experience of some sectors of society cannot be used to explain the experience of every sector. The Great Fear was a wide, brief, and common experience, and therein lies the importance of viewing it as an ideological phenomenon.

The Scope of This Study

Lefebvre's accomplishment in *The Great Fear of 1789* was to answer the questions that the social and economic history of his time could pose about the Great Fear. His very success makes it possible to pose other questions that are essentially ideological and psychological. How could people in all walks of life have cooperated so fully in spreading the Great Fear? Why—and how—did the Fear stay clear of regions that experienced peasant revolts? What in the content of the rumor made its messenger trustworthy, no matter who he was? Why were local nobles included in, not left out of, a popular action in defense of peasant communities in the revolutionary year of 1789? These were among the fundamental questions that shaped the present inquiry. I chose the strategy of studying a single region in which the various mass phenomena of 1789 were all represented. I sought an area where the Great Fear was born from an original panic, manifested powerfully, faded away, and was preempted by peasant revolt nearby—all in different zones of the same territory.

These diverse requirements were admirably met by the old intendancy of Soissons—north of Paris, east of Picardy, west of Champagne, south of Flandre and Hainaut—which became in 1790 (with some modifications) the department of the Aisne.[21] The northern edge of the Soissons intendancy was brushed by the spring rebellion centered in the bordering Cambrésis; it experienced the Great Fear only faintly, and the Cambrésis did not experience it at all. The southwest region of the intendancy was the birthplace of two currents of the Great Fear. One current, which originated on the Béthisy plain, spread east to Soissons, south to Château-Thierry, and down the Oise valley into the intendancy of Paris. The other current, which originated in Estrées-St-Denis, traveled west to Clermont-en-Beauvaisis and then northwest as far as Artois. In another corner of the Soissons intendancy—the northern outskirts of Noyon—a group of minuscule villages were not swept up in the Great Fear (which was going on all around them) but attacked a local château instead. In short, the Great Fear in the Soissons intendancy was notable both for its importance and for its absence in certain regions. The Aisne's subsequent behavior in the Revolution was undramatic: neither radical nor rebellious, it took the middle road of vague obedience to Paris. This lack of political idiosyncrasy may make its example suggestive for regions of France that followed a similar line.

In 1789 the Soissons intendancy was under administrative, political, and economic pressure from several directions, and its surroundings are part of its own story. To the south, the Parisian basin was the major pole of attraction for the produce of the Soissonnais—a term that designates the entire intendancy in these pages, just as it did for contemporaries. To the north, Picardy and especially the Cambrésis were far more revolutionary, and the notables of the Soissonnais feared their influence. Beyond Picardy and the Cambrésis to the west were the seaports of Dunkerque and Calais, where much of the grain purchased abroad by the royal government first entered the country. The supply route between these ports and Paris lay through Picardy and the Soissonnais. In the northeast the frontier with the Austrian Netherlands was a powerful presence in the local imagination, which supposed grain to be hemor-rhaging out of France.

The importance of these surrounding regions for understanding the Soissonnais itself led me to a wider use of documents from the Archives Nationales than might be expected in a local study. As the inquiry pro-gressed, it became clear that sources from national, departmental, and communal levels had to be articulated together at almost every step to produce a coherent picture of this diverse and confused period. Tempo-rally, an initial attempt to narrow the evidence to just the months around the Great Fear—broadly, June through August 1789—proved pointless. The attitudes underlying the Great Fear could not be adequately demon-strated using evidence from so narrow a compass; in addition, the Fear's consequences were not entirely manifest until the winter of 1789–90, because it took that long for the revolutionary militias organized during the Fear and the old municipalities to confront each other. Further re-search settled this study into the limits of the calendar year 1789. A few digressions into earlier periods have proven necessary to indicate the roots of certain attitudes and social situations, but for the most part this study examines a very "modern" old regime—that of the final breakup.

This Study's Interpretive Approach

The interpretation presented here has been shaped by three broad influ-ences: first, the "classic" Marxist historiography of the French Revolu-tion; second, analyses of rumor in social psychology and sociology; and third, the thought of Antonio Gramsci. However, none of these three influences is present as a "protagonist" in the pages that follow; the rich documentary base left by eighteenth-century provincial life takes that role instead.

Still, a few admissions are owed the reader. It may as well be avowed at the outset that the tradition, even the "orthodoxy," of Marxist social history that has run from Albert Mathiez through Georges Lefebvre and the late Albert Soboul permeates this study more strongly than do non-Marxist and Anglo-Saxon currents. While I believe that some of the positions taken in the pages that follow are new, my share of archival work in the documents of 1789 has also given me a practical sense of how formidably well grounded the arguments of the old masters really are. I cannot agree with the view that the works of Mathiez, Lefebvre, and Soboul constitute one closed system of interpretation, a "revolution-ary catechism." It seems to me rather that the "classic" interpretation remains an unfinished work in progress. Despite an oft-noted tendency toward economic determinism, the tradition's amazing archival depth gives it an empirical vitality that should not be underestimated, and it contains a far greater number of divergent opinions than is sometimes claimed. These views of mine are due in great part to exchanges with some of Soboul's younger generation of students, whose knowledge of various local archives and trenchant analyses of agrarian struggles have deeply marked this book.

In psychology and sociology the Great Fear has been treated as a classic example of collective panic; it is discussed on occasion (though never in depth) in analyses of rumor. Two sociological works have been of definite aid: Tamotsu Shibutani's *Improvised News: A Sociological Study of Rumor* (1966) and Edgar Morin's *La rumeur d'Orléans* (1969).[22]

Shibutani redefines rumor as an aspect of the social construction of reality. The central question in rumor analysis becomes, what makes the rumor credible?

> The transaction *as a whole* cannot be explained in terms of individual moti-
> vation . . . the problem is to ascertain how a common definition develops in
> spite of the *diversity* of motives . . . Rumor is not so much distortion of some
> word combination but what is held in common.[23]

Accordingly, in the case of the Great Fear the historian must explain why the rumor was plausible to all social classes. This involves the reconstruction of a cluster of attitudes shared up and down society at the end of the old regime—which is precisely the task undertaken in the present study.

Edgar Morin's *La rumeur d'Orléans* introduces two major ideas: first, the "antimyth," that is, the tendency for a conspiracy theory about a rumor to follow a rumor's demise; second, "interclassism," the broad circulation pattern of a rumor through all social strata.[24] Both the "antimyth" and "interclassism" can be observed in the Great Fear, which gave rise to a number of conspiracy theories about itself and which crossed all sorts of class boundaries.

The thought of Antonio Gramsci has been of great assistance in integrating the values and modes of inquiry of sociology with those of history. Since Gramsci's ideas cover an extremely wide range, this is not the place to attempt a synopsis; I have pointed to certain specific debts in the notes. Let me only say that Gramsci's discussions of language have profoundly enriched my own archival reading. They have suggested how historical subjects' uses of words might offer evidence of the most difficult dimension to reconstruct: attitudes, reactions, feelings, assumptions, and the interweaving of all these into a way of seeing.

Structure and Argument

The pages that follow can be described as a search for the "common sense" of the old regime at its close. Few attempts at classification are more difficult than the task of ordering the popular ideas of any society, but to focus on a concrete and spectacular phenomenon like the Great Fear simplifies the task somewhat. I treat the Fear as a nexus of three broad clusters of attitudes: ideas about food, news, and guns—or, to put it more abstractly, agriculture, information, and authority. The Fear sprang up in an atmosphere of intense anxiety over food supplies, was transmitted from place to place as news, and resulted in a newly armed population. Each of these aspects is considered in a separate section. Part 1 examines attitudes toward the food supply (the supposed target of the "brigands") and in consequence toward the entire system of agriculture and provisioning. Part 2 considers the Fear as rumor—the geographic pattern of its transmission in the Soissonnais; the general credibility of rumor and hearsay; how the written and the spoken word were evaluated; in what words news was couched; and what those words meant in contemporary usage. Part 3 treats attitudes toward authority: what "public tranquillity" meant in the old regime and how its character shifted in 1789; to what extent peasant revolt in 1789 partook of the Revolution or utilized older patterns of protest; and how militias, the offspring of the Fear, formed in different communities and created new problems of local power.

In eight chapters, this study develops propositions that can be briefly outlined as follows.

Attitudes toward Food

1. The Soissonnais was characterized by rapid movement toward a capitalist agriculture, but this movement did not include a clearcut breakdown of the traditional triennial scheme of field rotation. Rather, the benefits offered by this system were increasingly monopolized by the richer peasant strata at poor peasants' expense. The triennial system provided both a basis for the concentration of resources into fewer hands, and a palliative for rural social conflict—because rich and poor peasants could unite in rejecting external impositions, for example, on common grazing rights. In the Soissonnais—in contrast to neighboring regions, especially Picardy—the sphere of agricultural production could still be the source of a consensual ideology. The Great Fear's rumor in the Soissonnais projected an attack on agricultural production by outsid-

ers, and the communities' response to the Fear drew on this consensual ideology for its energy and unanimity.

2. Because the Great Fear involved an imagined threat to agricultural production, it was profoundly different from the social unrest associated with grain sales and circulation, and must always be distinguished from it. Market rioting and popular price-setting was an important phenomenon in the Soissonnais—indeed, it was the primary problem facing authorities from early spring to mid-July—but it entirely lacked the rapid communicability of the Fear. Unrest over grain prices was localized by its frame of reference: the opposition between a town and "its" surrounding countryside. Each town used its outskirts as the catchment area for its market supply, both denuding its hinterland of stocks and resupplying that hinterland through the market. Shortages that could not be made good through local requisitioning were met through bargaining with the municipalities of other towns on an "institutional market." Many of the numerous disturbances over grain sales were essentially local conflicts between town and country. In contrast, the Great Fear briefly created a situation in which town and country reciprocally flew to each other's aid.

3. In order to argue that the Great Fear was consensual across classes and overrode urban-rural tensions, the evidence must be examined for the opposing view that the Great Fear was essentially a class fear of beggars, vagabonds, and the rural poor. Despite the hostility toward begging inherent in both royal policies and Enlightenment thought, in local practice, charity given in response to begging remained the fundamental means of poor relief. Municipal and parish authorities counted on begging as a "natural" form of redistribution that would ease demand on their other charitable schemes. While there is little evidence for fear of beggars, there is considerably more for fear of outsiders of varying statuses. Persons far from their home parish, with no one in the community to vouch for their character, were automatically suspect. Even persons of some prosperity and education who were unknown could fall under the same suspicion as, and even be treated similarly to, the unknown poor.

Attitudes toward News

4. Of the six original panics identified by Lefebvre, two began within the Soissons intendancy. Each of these commenced at a point just on the dividing line between forest and arable land, and then spread by moving rapidly away from the forest, through a network of rural parishes, and

thence to the closest town of importance (Crépy-en-Valois and Clermont-en-Beauvaisis). Town authorities officialized the rumor by putting it in writing and relaying it by courier to other municipalities. Thus an informal, rural mode of transmission and a formal, urban mode were active simultaneously during the Fear and gave different kinds of results. Informal transmission did not travel as far, but it involved more of the rural population; formal transmission covered greater distances, but led to responses that were more closely controlled by municipalities. Lefebvre found for France as a whole that the Fear never entered a region that had experienced a peasant revolt in the spring. The Soissonnais example verifies this pattern, while permitting an intimate local look at its workings.

5. An examination of contemporary usages of the term *brigand* reveals a wide spectrum of possible referents—so wide that the word has to be construed as blanketing all groups that might threaten, or simply be external to, the established order. On the other hand, the term *aristocrate* had a clear diffusion from Paris, which can be traced. Picked up by urban groups in touch with National Assembly deputies in July, it emerged into rural language only in October. This suggests that fear of an "aristocrats' plot," so important to Parisians' understanding of events, was not a significant element in the Great Fear as it unfolded in the Soissonnais.

Attitudes toward Authority

6. The development of public order in the old regime is often seen as a steady incursion by the central government into communities' affairs. This study proposes a different perspective, in which the communities (either villages or urban quarters), the legal authorities (of town or bailliage), and the central government (most often represented by troops) were three semiindependent, imperfectly meshing realms that conserved public order in different ways. The Great Fear "invented" an emergency that briefly integrated all three realms under the command of municipalities. The National Assembly sought afterward to preserve this situation by decree as the new revolutionary norm. Thereby it unintentionally created additional strains on old-regime authorities, widening participation in and strengthening the autonomy of local militias.

7. On July 27, the day of the Great Fear elsewhere, villagers in a small district north of Noyon attacked the local château of Frétoy. This took place just a few kilometers from other villages that were fully caught up in defending themselves against "brigands." The château's attackers circulated rumors that were ideologically a world apart from the Fear—

rumors in which the châteaux of the area and the town of Noyon were about to be attacked by royal troops as just punishment for their grain hoarding. The Noyonnais microregion's distinct economic and social characteristics help to explain the revolt, but only in part; the revolt's internal dynamics provide further clues to the consciousness behind it. No clear break existed between old-regime and revolutionary forms of popular activity in July; rather, the revolutionary influence widened and vitalized an already full popular arsenal of tactics.

8. The role of the Great Fear in bringing about the creation of new local militias was more complex than has been supposed. Before the fall of the Bastille, militias were generally viewed by authorities as reasonably pliant tools of the established order, and itendants encouraged them at the village level in the spring of 1789. The Parisian revolution of July 14 was driven forward by an impromptu militia, which put a new light on the institution and raised hesitations on the part of provinical municipalities. Just at this moment the Great Fear arrived, offering an external enemy, the "brigands," and an idea consensus for municipal action to form a militia. With the new militias in existence, the Fear's menace evaporated, leaving all the political problems—of control, officering, breadth of participation, and affinity to revolutionary Paris—that the municipalities had feared. Thus the Great Fear was a conservative-looking catalyst for a radicalizing process. The Fear provided a bridge between subpolitical and politicized mentalities that gave the Revolution much of the early breadth and depth that confounded its opponents.

The Conclusion compares the patterns discernible in the Soissonnais with those suggested by recent studies of a number of other French regions: Burgundy, Provence, the southern Massif Central, Brittany, and others. It considers the possibilities and drawbacks of a "general model" for the Great Fear and suggests alternatives to such an approach. Finally, it reflects on the Fear as the cradle of the new militia, and on the militia's ambiguous place in the development of French nationalism.

PART I

Attitudes toward Food

ONE 𞡀 *CULTIVATION AND*
ITS CONSENSUAL BASE

In the Soissonnais, the Great Fear began at two distinct points: Estrées-St-Denis and St-Martin-de-Béthisy, both minuscule rural communities within eyeshot of a forest's edge. The panic spread from these obscure rural origins across the southern two-thirds of the Soissons intendancy, south into the intendancy of Paris and northwest as far as Artois. The details of the Fear's movements will be examined in a later chapter (chapter 4), but to understand them, we must first understand the rural social medium through which the Fear traveled. The roots of the brief and puzzling solidarity across classes and between town and country, that was manifested on the occasion of the Great Fear began in the community system of cultivation and the perceptions of shared interests which it engendered.

In the spring of 1789, the Soissonnais experienced a lower level of social turmoil than did the Cambrésis and much of Picardy, where April and May saw significant peasant revolts. Peasant bands two hundred to five hundred strong visited the farms of seigneurs, ecclesiastics, and large cultivators and forced them to deliver grain from their stores, usually at a traditional "just price." The revolt reached the gates of St-Quentin and then spilled over the northern border of the Soissons intendancy; Guise and Vervins were nearly swept up in it. The movement went no farther, however, and the bulk of the Soissonnais did not experience it.[1] Instead, the Soissonnais went through numerous local, unconnected disturbances in market towns over grain prices. To modern eyes the difference between these two forms of social conflict seems trivial; but to contemporaries an order of magnitude separated the activity of large peasant bands in the countryside—which only troops or the passage of time could subdue—from disturbances at market, where all the resources of urban order were concentrated and where negotiations between authorities and crowds were a commonplace aspect of old-regime public order.

Four months later, the two regions' situations were reversed. The southern two-thirds of the Soissonnais was in turmoil in late July over the rumors of the Great Fear, while the Cambrésis, eastern Picardy, and the northern part of the Soissons intendancy remained largely unaffected. This paradox had its counterparts elsewhere in France. All the regions that had experienced revolts before July were, or at least bordered on, areas where the Great Fear did not penetrate; many of the regions of revolt were only slightly touched by the Fear.[2] What can be made of this curious pattern? In the Soissonnais, it appears that a social consensus in favor of the community system of agriculture was subjected to less strain than was the case in neighboring regions, and that an understanding of this circumstance can help to explain the widely differing local responses to the crisis of 1789.

From the late seventeenth century to the eve of the Revolution, the divisions sharpened between the upper and lower strata of the peasantry. Rents were structured so that large ensembles were proportionately less expensive than small parcels—a fact that encouraged large tenants to take the lead in concentrating land into bigger holdings. While this process steadily reduced the circumstances of small peasants, it did not entail immediate exodus and proletarianization, for a variety of reasons that will be explored.

A relative ideological accord across classes buttressed the social patterns of cultivation in the Soissonnais of the 1780s. A broadly felt skepticism regarding agricultural reforms and improvements of the physiocratic stamp; the occasional willingness of nobles and members of the bourgeoisie to assist peasants in defending certain communal rights; the widespread verbal condemnation of the largest tenants' ongoing concentration of land; and these tenants' own indifference to pursuing any crop diversification that might have disrupted the traditional cultivation pattern were four major strands in this accord. In brief, the creation of larger units of production and the increasing stratification of the peasantry was proceeding unhindered by the classic triennial framework. The productive limits of that framework were viewed as natural, and these "natural limits" in turn underwrote the social relations through which capitalist agriculture was developing.

It is argued here that this general acceptance of the triennial system and its productive limits added strongly to the resonance and universality of the Great Fear in the Soissonnais. The Fear's fantasy of an overwhelming force from outside assaulting agriculture did not incriminate any group within the community— and considering the ambitions, distrust, and sheer hunger in the air at the time, this fact is remarkable. The Fear's lack of divisiveness should be attributed to the deep ideological resources of the rural order in which it was born.

The Hierarchy of Tenant Farming

The land between the Marne and the Oise is more wooded and more rolling than the grain country of the Beauvaisis. It forms a series of plateaus with transitions whose abruptness disguises the slightness of the changes in altitude. The butte on which old Laon was built is only one hundred meters above its plain, but the impression persists: the "terres de montagne" seem to deserve their name. Despite the ambiguities in its terrain, most of the Soissonnais in the eighteenth century was devoted to cereal production in the conventional threefold division: a third of the land was planted in a "major grain"—wheat, rye, or the two together (*méteil*)—and another third in oats or barley, while the last third lay fallow.[3]

Since medieval times, the existence of ecclesiastical estates had provided space for relatively large scale cultivation. In the first half of the seventeenth century, a gradual but steady rise in rents was sustained by a complementary rise in grain prices. However, after 1650 prices entered a trough that deepened through the crises of the late seventeenth and early eighteenth centuries. During this period, many proprietors converted part of their rents in kind into rents in money, thereby putting the effects of the crisis back on their tenants, large and small.[4] The outcome of this rent conversion was to shape the social structure of Soissonnais agriculture in the following century.

The large farmers—tenants responsible for the largest units of production—were decimated by failures and foreclosures to the point where proprietors could no longer find tenants well established enough to take on major leases. Rents had to stabilize if the great farms were to be rented as ensembles—though rents could continue to rise for smaller parcels rented to middle and poor peasants. Thus rents split into two levels: higher for small tenants, lower for large tenants.

The arrival of the eighteenth century also saw the increasing concentration of land in the hands of rising urban bourgeois, who sought to invest their fortunes in land, office, or both. As far as the purchase of land was concerned, most large peasants were too indebted to compete with bourgeois. However, another path of expansion remained open to large peasants: by rounding out their tenancies, renting additional parcels when they became vacant, they could increase the marketable proportion of their crop. This possibility remained open only so long as rents—for large peasants—did not rise; the split between two levels of rent had to be maintained and widened.

The class of large farmers in the Soissonnais took on solidity and coherence in the struggle against proprietors' efforts to raise their rents. The farmer who accepted a higher lease than his predecessor had paid was regarded as a traitor by his fellows. They might burn his new house or cut his unripe crops at night with a long-handled scythe, which could be swung close to the ground—unlike the short-handled sickle, the legal harvest implement, which left the wheat stalks standing and permitted the communal rights of gleaning (*glanage* and *chaumage*) to be exercised.[5] As a notary described the situation in 1762:

> If one likes, one can regard the proprietors as free to dispose of their farms; but secret reasons constrain other farmers from taking them on . . . a fear of sinister incidents holds cultivators back from taking each others' farms . . . The greatest number are in agreement not to take farms on bordering strips without the farmer's consent, which he often sells quite dearly; otherwise, warnings and arson soon follow.[6]

Even if the new tenant held out, hostility in his community made his tasks far more difficult. As a resident of St-Quentin wrote to the National Assembly in 1789: "Of a hundred people who have evicted their colleagues, I can say that at least four-fifths, if they are not absolutely ruined, have greatly lessened their wealth . . . "[7]

Thus large farmers could legally remain on their lands despite the worst disagreement with a proprietor if they could discourage other tenants from leasing the lands. The law presumed a tacit contract for the next lease (called *reconduction*). No agreement on paper was required. "Thanks to tacit renewal," wrote a Laon lawyer in the 1770s, "a considerable abuse has made the most dangerous progress in the intendancies of Amiens and Soissons. The farmers perpetuate themselves in their farmholds against the will of their lessors."[8] This conflict between farmers and proprietors was still in progress at the time of the Great Fear. In fact, the explanation given by the municipality of Roye for the occurrence of the Great Fear in its neighborhood relied on an incident in which an evicted farmer attacked the crops of his successor.[9]

As the large farming families intermarried over generations, any shift in tenancy became more and more of a "family affair." An extended family council to discuss an important matter was likely to reunite a strong representative sample of the entire local class of large farmers. In this way mutual control was reinforced. With this basis for cooperation, various rented parcels were exchanged among the tenants, and thus the local map was redrawn in a fashion never intended by the proprietors. As the proprietor's surveyor had to be guided by the tenants themselves, the official maps of the property were redrawn to more or less sanction the revisions that the tenants alone had carried out.[10] It was in this fashion that the concentration of agricultural land was carried out by the large peasants rather than by the proprietors.[11]

By comparison, Florence Gauthier's researches in Picardy have shown a more marked seigneurial activity there in purchasing and otherwise concentrating land; however, the territories in question were not farmland but woods. A few of Gauthier's examples can be cited: M. Dumesnil—451 hectares at Fromentiers, 54 percent woods; M. de Berry—267 hectares at Jumel, 66 percent woods; or the marquis de Quevillers—182 hectares, 67 percent woods.[12] As the price of firewood continued to rise throughout the eighteenth century, forested land was one of the best—and least demanding—investments available. Where seigneurs did expand their lands, they often sought to escape the complexities of agriculture altogether. In the Soissonnais the duc d'Orléans was by far the largest landed proprietor, and his apanage's administration of the forests of Compiègne and Retz exemplified this investment policy on a vast scale. Competition with farmers over the creation of large cultivated ensembles was simply not forthcoming from the Second Estate; the class of large tenants was left alone in the field.

Meanwhile, lower levels of the peasantry were suffering the effects of higher rents from proprietors and intensified competition at market from large peasants. A year of poor harvests worked in favor of the big farmer, who sold his still-adequate crop at the higher prevailing price; but it worked against the middle peasant, who needed a greater proportion of his crop to make up his subsistence, had less to sell, yet still had to meet his (higher) rent. This dilemma meant that middle peasants who in good years might be relatively well off had to open sidelines in cartage, firewood selling, and the like. Poorer peasants, often conducting a mediocre polyculture for subsistence on very little land, might sell for rent the grain they would buy again at market a few months later. At the bottom of rural society, seasonal work, local begging, and vagabondage—along with the crucial gleaning and gathering rights—formed the supplement that maintained a tenuous link to the land. The tenacity of the poorest peasants is evident from their willingness to cultivate at tremendous labor the one or two-hectare lots of wasteland that were offered to them increasingly in the 1780s.[13]

As the large peasants consolidated their positions and the rest of the peasantry suffered a gradual degradation, the rents for even the largest tenant holdings began to rise again. The big farmers' own rapidity of accumulation had brought about a shortage of land, and they were forced to compete with one another in order to expand. Consequently, the proprietors again had the opportunity to raise rents. The late 1780s were characterized by this renewal of uniform rent pressure on the whole peasantry.

Despite the concentration of land by large tenants, the evidence for any accompanying technical progress in agriculture during this period is slim. On the plateaus, the large peasant's cultivation differed from the small one's only in the greater extent of sheep raising and in a few economies of scale. The introduction of the "culture of four labors"—a simplification of the annual round of tasks—meant a greater routinization of the laborer's work and less supervision by his employer during sowing to see that the differing yields of various patches of soil were allowed for in the number of seeds allotted. Progress in yield did exist, but it was so slow as to be virtually imperceptible. The most informed judgment is probably Pierre Brunet's: "In 1716 it was estimated that the best lands of the Soissonnais yielded around 15 to 16 quintals per hectare. In the course of the eighteenth century the harvests improved little; one can reasonably estimate that on the eve of the Revolution this yield had only become the average."[14] Aside from a new method of sieving grain before milling,[15] one cannot point to any technical innovation that passed into agricultural practice.[16]

The Belief in Natural Limits

The division of rents into two levels, one for large and one for small peasants, at the beginning of the eighteenth century; the concentration of land by major tenants more than by proprietors; the squeezing out of the middle and small peasantry, without, however, entailing their departure from the land; and the lack of an appreciable intensification or gain in yield: these are the main lines of agricultural society in the Soissonnais in 1789. If we ask how contemporaries viewed this pattern of agricultural production, we are struck to discover that the most widely shared attitude was one of skepticism toward the possibility of producing more.

Fatalism about the size of yield provided a point of agreement, and hence an element of social consensus, in old-regime Soissonnais.

The Soissons Royal Society of Agriculture, almost 30 years old in 1789, was a bastion of this attitude. In 1761 the society had been founded with two bureaus, one in Soissons, one in Laon. The intense jealousy between the two branches was such that one offered an essay prize without informing the other; in fact, during most of their existence they refused to correspond. The members' notions about intensified cultivation were so vague that the Laon bureau gave up the idea of offering prizes to successful cultivators because it could imagine no way to verify that a farmer's results were due to more than the outstanding fertility of his soil.[17]

One writer to the National Assembly dismissed a proprietor's attempt to run his own farm in the following language:

> [Farmers ruin themselves] some through lack of intelligence, others through obstinate determination to introduce a new way of cultivating. I could cite various examples of which I was an eyewitness. At Flez, a dependency of Mouchy-le-Gache, a [proprietor] of Peronne, having evicted various farmers from a considerable tract of land, built and reaped for a certain period, but in the end he was forced to retrench again and certainly not because his balance was in his favor.[18]

Interest in agricultural novelties was seen as a characteristic foible of proprietors, and this social stamp, together with innovators' lack of practical experience, tended to discredit notions of "reforming" agriculture.

At the level of the educated notables, this skepticism about the possibility of greater yields took the form of a certain faith in the permanence of misery. This faith could entwine itself around any number of intellectual frameworks. But let us consider its expression in one contemporary notion, that of a mathematical relation between prosperity, fertility, and population. Notes from a meeting of the National Assembly's committee on mendicancy provide a clear formulation: "The habitual misery of a canton . . . can only derive from the poor quality of the soil, population being equal; or from an excess of population, the extent or fertility of the territory being equal . . . "[19] But—at the level of the local intelligentsia—for instance, Sellier, the director of the Ecole des arts in Amiens—the concept

$$\frac{\text{Fertility of soil}}{\text{Population}} = \text{Prosperity of a district}$$

had a different, more Malthusian meaning. The ratio between fertility and population was fixed. Any surplus in production (natural or due to innovation) would be consumed by the resulting rise in population. Consequently a poor harvest would always return society to the same threshold of misery, unless the new surplus population could be integrated into a growing commerce and manufacture. He concluded: "The surplus of our grains therefore will always be quite a weak resource for the commerce of France. It would be better if in eating all this grain, we could augment our population of which the surplus, if there is one, will procure us a commerce . . . in flax, hemp, oil, livestock."[20] In this way Sellier could combine a progressive approach to commerce with a subsistence mentality regarding agriculture.

For the bureau of agriculture of the Soissonnais's 1787 provincial assembly, there was even a perverse link between fertility and poverty: "The soil's very fertility brings on poverty . . . in the largest part of this province, as in all that are rich and abundant, the people have no property. The land is cultivated by tenants, few in number for each parish, who share the tenure of the whole territory and leave no other means of subsistence to the rest of the inhabitants but the option to serve them . . ."[21] The committee's view that misery was the inevitable complement of wealth also implied that greater wealth, in the form of higher productivity, would only widen the existing rupture in rural life by accelerating the separation of the work force from the land.

Avowals of impotence in the face of the harvest were part of official rhetoric. The bureau of the controller-general's office concerned with food provisioning stated that it had had "no other occupation up to now than the forcing down of prices [for grain]. When will it be occupied with supporting grain prices? God alone can put it in this case by according abundant harvests through His will."[22] Sellier insisted that human efforts had brought about little progress: "From rough observation, I would judge that over 30 years of agricultural improvements we have not augmented the mass of our grains by very much."[23]

Rich and poor had similar mental furniture; the difference often lay in the quality of the upholstery. Whether God or nature was understood as the force that determined good or bad harvests, the intuition of limits was similar. The poor, however, believed with particular firmness that the distribution of fruits was within human powers, and showed their belief by innumerable collective actions to control markets and grain transports. Correspondents of the National Assembly often interpreted popular action in terms of this contradiction between human roles in production and distribution:

The people patiently supported the year of 1788 because it was not abundant in grain . . . But now that the year 1789 promises the people that they
will be happier thanks to the abundance of the harvest, should they suffer
patiently just as they did the year before? This is not to be expected . . .
(Anonymous letter from the area of Coucy, November 1789)

The dearth was great in 1709 and 1740 . . . the peoples did not murmur.
There were no revolts, because they attributed their misfortune to nature . . . (Sellier in Amiens, November 1789)

The people would have supported [high prices] more patiently if they could
blame nothing more than the mediocrity of the last harvest, but everywhere
they have been witness to excessive exportations . . . (Municipality of Abbeville, August 1789)[24]

Social peace went with divine limits, social struggles with human ones.
Perhaps this was another aspect of the resistance to the idea of increased
yields: such increases would have raised the question of who was to
benefit from them and how existing conventions of distribution were to
be adapted.

Communal Rights: Their Erosion and Resilience

There can be no question that communal land and communal rights in
the Soissonnais were under attack. *Vaine pâture*—the use of fallow land
as a commons for grazing—was excoriated by proprietors in terms like
these, addressed (anonymously) to the provincial assembly of 1787:

[The proprietor] has nothing over the other inhabitants beyond the right to
a single mowing of hay; he barely has time to gather it up before his meadow
becomes in an instant the prey of a multitude of beasts of every kind, which
in less than a week strip from the pasture everything of worth. Since the best
grass is eaten away, the meadow does not grow back, except for plants of
little value . . . better for weakening animals by the continual diarrheas they
cause than for offering them nourishment.[25]

Most parish *cahiers de doléances* (grievance lists) from the Soissonnais
have been lost, yet those that remain often speak of seigneurial usurpa-
tion of common land. The parish of Juvigny, within the Orléans apanage,
lost its 60 arpents (roughly, acres) of meadow and 22 arpents of marsh
to the apanage council, which rented them to individuals. Trozy-Loire
rented its communal lands to sustain the cost of a lawsuit against its former
seigneur. "This example is unfortunately all too frequent, for there are

plenty of other parishes in the same case." Urvillers (in the bailliage of St-Quentin, just north of the Soissons intendancy) demanded the suppression of plantings on communal land, "the plantings being made by the seigneurs and for them."[26] The steady invasion of the commons that Florence Gauthier describes for Picardy left signs of its presence in the Soissonnais as well. However, restraining factors can be detected also, and many of these were ideological in nature.

One such restraining notion was the very idea of how land should be valued. In 1788 the Château-Thierry "intermediate bureau," a local branch of the continuing commission set up by the 1787 provincial assembly, sent an agricultural questionnaire to the parishes within its jurisdiction. Its second question read, "How much of the land is undeveloped and unproductive [*en friches et de non-valeur*]?" This juxtaposition of two categories, undeveloped land and land without value, was visibly a source of discomfort to the parishes whose replies have been preserved. The Nogent l'Artaud municipality cautiously replied: "We are not . . . sufficiently educated to be able to determine the quantity very closely; our opinion is that there may be a third of parish lands that are either undeveloped or unproductive; that is to say, lands that are not worth the expense of cultivation." The writers felt the need to define terms that had appeared self-evident to the intermediate bureau. The reply of La Chapelle-sur-Chezy is still more revealing:

- *How much of the land is undeveloped and unproductive?*
  There is none. All of it is productive.

La Chapelle repudiated the notion that land in any form could lie outside the general scheme of agriculture and be "valueless." In its further replies it made clear that its valuation of land was based on a different scale from that which would make plausible a phrase like "undeveloped and unproductive land":

- *Is there an up-to-date land register on paper?*
  It is not known whether the land register is up to date. In general, no one bothers us about those things.
- *If the arable land is divided into three classes and the meadows into two classes . . . [assess your lands by class].*
  The parish lands can only be divided into two classes, mediocre and poor . . . one can count about 8 *charrues* [*charrue* = 30–40 hectares] over the extent of the parish, which has around 25 arpents of arable land, of which the mediocre fields can be evaluated

at 5 livres per arpent, and those of the bottom class at 2 livres 10 sous; as for the meadows, one could certainly divide them into two classes, but it is thought they can all be put at their true value in pricing them at 1 pistole per arpent; there may be about 50 arpents in the parish.[27]

One pistole—that is, 10 livres—per arpent was double the municipality's estimate of its best cultivated land. The value of land that could be worked did not necessarily exceed that of land that did not receive labor. This assessment by the municipal officers of La Chapelle-sur-Chezy is in line with seventeenth-century evaluations noted by Goubert in the Beauvaisis. In the 1645 division of the Ticquet estate, workable land was assessed at 30 to 40 livres per *mine*, 2,551 square meters, and meadowland at more than 100 livres per *mine*; in 1675, two parcels of meadow touching the Oise were estimated at 330 to 400 livres per *mine*, while the richest grainfields of the Tille plain were priced between 60 and 100 livres per *mine*; the division of the Michel estate in 1687 priced the workable land at 50 livres per *mine*, the meadows at 100 to 200 livres per *mine*.[28] Neither the communal lands of the Soissonnais nor those of the Beauvaisis ever matched the quality of the pastures incorporated into these three bourgeois estates, but at a lower level the ratio between prices is similar. Land that could support livestock without impinging on cereal agriculture was seen as crucial, not marginal or unproductive.

The arguments used by small and middle peasants in reply to the questionnaire of 1788 are to be found again on the lips of big farmers and spokesmen of all three Estates in the cahiers of 1789. Barzy-sur-Marne replied to the query "How much land is undeveloped and unproductive?" in these words: "One can count about two hundred arpents . . . in pasture that have a great value for the community. Without them no sod for the vines, no fertilizer, no livestock, and without livestock and fertilizer, no vines, and without vines what would become of the community of Barzy, already so poor?"[29]

Here again the term *non-valeur* is confronted in these phrases that insist on the causative link, through manure, between the communal pasture and the parish's vines. At the time of the spring bailliage assemblies, language that seemed to threaten this link was unlikely to enter either Third- or Second-Estate cahiers in the Soissonnais. The Third-Estate cahier for the bailliage of Château-Thierry advocated using more land for cultivation only if it did not mean less land for pasturage.[30] The secondary bailliage of La Fère produced a single cahier on which all three Estates were agreed, in which enclosures were denounced and *vaine pâture* was defended without reservations:

> That the cultivator be free to cultivate, sow, and harvest as seems right to him, that *vaine pâture* in the meadows after haymowing be retained in this canton, and that the enclosure of meadows for a second mowing be abso-lutely prohibited, since *vaine pâture* in the meadows is a practice followed since time immemorial, and the opposite system could only have been im-agined by narrow and isolated minds; from it would result a decline in livestock by more than half, agriculture would languish from the lack of manure, land rent would not be the same, and finally lands would lose almost half their value.[31]

Here all the same points are made, and more: the physiocrats are evoked and their distance from agricultural practice is derided; the crucial im-portance of manure is asserted, and a new issue is raised: a general reduction in land values that could call the rents of ongoing leases into question. The municipality of La Fère resolved to petition the Keeper of the Seals and other royal ministers if necessary to prevent enclosures on the banks of the Oise, and notified the Guise municipality to that ef-fect.[32]

Local coalitions formed on occasion to defend elements of the com-munal system. The parish of Varesnes, within the jurisdiction of Noyon's intermediate bureau, was able to present a united front against the bu-reau's representative Guenflette when he arrived to preside over the adjudication of detached parcels of common land. Adjudication was a policy supported by the royal administration, in which municipalities rented parcels of communal land to individuals by auction, ending general access and often leading to cultivation. Guenflette arrived in Varesnes on February 16 to find that the hall where adjudication was to take place had been locked. The municipality had refused to call an assembly. Going to the seigneur, he met with the same refusal; he had no choice but to return to Noyon.[33]

The opposition to canal-building proposals likewise revealed the strength that the communal system could summon when threatened. In the Laonnais in the late 1720s, a private entrepreneur proposed to the town to drain neighboring marshlands by means of a navigable canal that would join the Oise. In exchange, he wanted half of the drained land to be ceded to him. The fierce opposition roused by this plan was strongest in the outskirts of Laon, where marsh grazing sustained most poor peasants' livestock. The plan was turned back with the argument that proximate grainfields would become unproductive if the marsh was drained.[34] In Noyon in 1786 Tondu de Muiroger, the son of the local subdelegate to the intendant, proposed a canal project meant to span the two kilometers between Noyon and the Oise. It required the expropriation of the land it would traverse, but de Muiroger presented the draining of marshland as a compensation that would open new agricultural land. Despite royal and episcopal interest that brought about an initial commission, the project died in the face of widespread opposition, best articulated by Margerin, chief clerk for the bailliage court:

> Our possessions, our lands, our houses, our inheritances are seized with a simple promise to pay for them from the profits; under the contrived and specious pretext of draining marshland, our common pastures are expropriated; while the fertility of our lands is eulogized, work goes on to make them sterile by ruining the cultivators . . . the projected reduction in the cost of transporting grain to the docks is not useful in itself and is nothing more than a supposition.[35]

Here Margerin equates "marsh" with "common pasture," valorizing the land in question; he uses the term *sterile* to describe the project's effects on the land; he even insists that the diminution of transport costs is "not useful in itself." This was the language of a lawyer in the parlement and an official of the bailliage. Such discourse was not limited to peasants in parish cahiers; it was common intellectual property.

In any case, the notables of the Soissonnais did not have far to look for the possible costs of aggressive encroachments on communal lands and rights. The spring revolts in Picardy and the Cambrésis were before their eyes. The deputies of all Estates in the Château-Thierry bailliage registered their dismay:

> The deputies of all three orders, children of one family gathered round their Father, draw back with horror from that spirit of dizziness and fermentation that, passing rapidly from insult to injury, from injury to vengeance, has shed the blood of citizens in one of our provinces.[36]

Throughout 1789, Picard villagers retook usurped communal land by force.[37] In the village of Fretin in Flandre on July 25, peasants cut the oats that had been planted in the common marshland. The outlying Amiens *faubourg* of Petit St-Jean seceded from the city to defend the peat and lumber of its communal land.[38] The Soissonnais notables' desire to avoid a comparable degree of turmoil was abetted by their basic agreement with the peasants' view of the communal system.

The Verbal Condemnation of Land Concentration

The techniques of large and small farms were very similar. Larger farms could utilize labor more efficiently and could keep more livestock to produce more manure; but their fixed capital investment per hectare was little different from that of smaller farms, in either quality or quantity.[39] The yield was overwhelmingly determined by the quality of the soil. Perhaps this is why the large farmers' process of land concentration was generally deplored, very seldom defended, and never gave rise to a two-sided argument. In 1789 tenants' concentration came under attack in the cahiers: the Third Estate of the Villers-Cotterets bailliage and all three orders in the Crépy-en-Valois bailliage endorsed articles favoring an upper limit to farm size.[40] The parish cahier of Urvillers agreed: "France must be made to shine like the sun by making all pay taxes and by setting limits to the land of each with his neighbor . . ."[41] For clergy, nobles, and Third Estate to speak with the same voice, proprietors and the bulk of the small peasantry alike must have resented the big farmers' tactics, described here by the intendant's subdelegate at Crépy-en-Valois in 1761:

> This is the ambition of all the big farmers, who seek to add on to the extent of their own farms all the plots of a parish, such that all the small peasants and cottagers find themselves destitute of the resources capable of letting them subsist . . . The big farmer neglects nothing to crush the small peasant and take his plots; he offers an equal and often greater price to the proprietor, who makes no difficulty about dividing the house from the attached land. This ruse usually goes on for the term of one lease, and when the big farmer has managed to starve out all the small peasants and senses that he is the master, he then lays down the law to all the proprietors, who are obliged to rent to him for the price he wants, since they can find no one else able to exploit the land.[42]

Concentration both forced small tenants off the land and narrowed the proprietors' room for maneuver in adjusting rents upward. The question of whether yield might be increased in a more concentrated agriculture was never an issue, nor did the big farmers ever defend themselves in these terms. The self-evident constancy of yields was assumed by all concerned.

The big farmers' land concentration was attacked freely in the cahiers for another reason: by driving the poorest peasants off the land altogether, concentration reduced the size of the fixed labor force. As poor peasants fixed to the land by a house and garden were regarded by proprietors and big tenants alike as the most manageable source of agricultural labor, a poor peasant's loss of a subsistence plot was viewed as the loss of that person's labor to rural society.

It was widely believed that the rural labor pool was dwindling. Sellier, a big-city dweller himself, declared that "emigration to the towns has left the countryside empty of workers, plowmen, and servants."[43] But a depopulated countryside was a social phenomenon that still lay far in the future. It was true, however, that the poorest peasants' ties to the soil were eroding. Those who rented the least land at the highest cost pursued an "impoverished polyculture";[44] they gleaned and made the most of all the "rights of the poor," and occasionally begged around the parish as well. Their wages for working the fields or for spinning wool were impossibly low, taken alone; but such wages were not meant to sustain the full burden of their earners' existences. It was the gradual passing, through concentration, of this wage advantage that was feared as the "desertion of the countryside."

A range of social mechanisms combated this "desertion." One noted by Postel-Vinay is the *surcens*—a word that covered many arrangements, from seigneurial leases in perpetuity to leases given by a creditor to a debtor whose mortgage arrears had invited seizure. This latter type of *surcens* consolidated the tenant's debts while guaranteeing him the use of the land. Postel-Vinay also interprets the mighty alms-giving powers of the ecclesiastical estates as a similar mechanism; however, frequent complaints by notables, curés, and peasants as to the religious orders' lack of discrimination and their generosity to outsiders contradict the notion of alms-giving as a conscious, tenant-directed policy.[45] Another mechanism was the forced "repatriation" of provincials who had wandered into Parisian workhouses (the *ateliers de charité*). There was one such expulsion in late August 1789 and another in January 1790. In at least the latter case, only those "born in small towns and villages" were sent home; those who would have returned to larger towns instead of the countryside were kept in Paris.[46] Such a policy was in full accord with the ideas of the Soissonnais notables who reported on mendicancy to the provincial assembly of 1787: "It is important above all to send back into the countryside those poor attracted into the towns by abundant relief . . . those born in the country, destined for this kind of work, must be subjected to it."[47]

Not only the "ruralization" of the urban poor but also the disemployment of urban workers was contemplated as a means of increasing the rural labor pool. The geographer Expilly presented disemployment as a possible side-effect of a canal scheme: "A great number of men

. . . removed from tilling the fields . . . by jobs in land transport would be returned to the countryside."[48] The notables of the Crepy-en-Valois, Villers-Cotterets, and St-Quentin bailliages hoped that disemployment would result from the taxation of urban property and servants: identical articles in their cahiers proposed to "tax the capitalists, residents of towns, and return useful hands to agriculture."[49]

At an extreme, the use of mounted police for the labor discipline of local beggars might be considered. In a ministerial memorandum urging that the mounted police be instructed to arrest "all beggars, domiciled or not," the argument ran: "The labors of the countryside are about to open, the farmers needed hands to gather a harvest . . . Therefore it is important to motivate with fear those whom nonchalance alone may render unserviceable."[50] In the Soissonnais also, the large farmers demanded for years the application of more police power. Postel-Vinay remarks, "If forced labor was good for the towns, it was impossible in the countryside, and only increased repression could be effective."[51] Not only did labor have to be kept fixed in the countryside, it had to be disciplined by the state as well as by necessity.

The concentration of tenant holdings in the hands of a few big farmers ran counter to all these efforts to keep the countryside rich in dependent labor. Although concentration as a gradual process helped the expanding farmer to stabilize his rents and increase his marketable surplus, the end result would be in no one's interests: not that of the bulk of the peasantry; not that of the proprietors whose rents would be forcibly stabilized; not even that of the large tenants themselves, in that they were destroying the kind of labor they relied on. In consequence, verbal opposition to the concentration process constituted another point of agreement in the ideology of the rural Soissonnais.

The Power of Monoculture and the Barriers to Diversification

The last question concerning agricultural production that we must consider is whether diversification was possible. The Soissonnais's grain monoculture did not, of course, stand alone; it was coextensive with the monoculture of the northern Beauvaisis, the Santerre, and Picardy. Yet its dominance should not be taken for granted. It is legitimate to ask why the traditional crops and rotations persisted during a period of concentration and of intensified pressure on the great majority of peasants. How did a system that kept large and small farms in lockstep continue to retain both the rich and the poor?

Contemporaries divided the Soissonnais into two general kinds of farmland: "mountain lands" and "valley lands." An alluvial plateau sweeps northeast through the Valois and the Soissonnais to the town of Soissons, where it is cut by the westward flow of the Aisne. The southern side of the butte of Laon compares with the plateau in fertility. Further north, the Picard plain commences. The layer of topsoil that makes for easy traction in plowing accepts wheat as a laborable crop; the flat terrain favors large ensembles. The valleys along the Aisne and the Oise, on the contrary, are patchworks of diverse soils and microclimates. Their variety of conditions calls for a variety of crops; in most places, the terrain's narrowness forces small-scale intensive cultivation.[52]

This nuanced plain of the Soissons intendancy can be distinguished from neighboring regions of grainland. Santerre and the Amienois are also alluvial plains, but their deforestation had gone further by the eighteenth century, and hence these regions were more densely peopled. Cambrésis and northern Hainaut form the northern edge of the Picard plain, while the marly soil of southern Hainaut creates a forested region apart. From Lille to the sea, the clay soil, extending to the dunes of the coast, constitutes another break with the grainlands.

This was the view north from the Soissonnais. Westward lay the Beauvaisis, best understood as two regions: the south, with less fertile soil, but offering the opportunities of forest, marsh, and pasture; and the north beyond Beauvais, part of the Picard plain and a true grainland described by Goubert as "without wastes, without communal lands, without meadows, without woods, and without vineyards."[53]

Where then did some degree of agricultural diversification exist in the eighteenth century? One can look to Flandre, where all grains together occupied less than half the cultivated surface. Potatoes, legumes, tobacco, colza, and a variety of fodders were grown on farms where never more than an eighth of the soil lay fallow. The urban markets that supported this intricate system of rotation also supplied the manures that augmented originally unpromising soil: peat ashes, chimney soot, human waste, and lime were all purchased by the farmer, whose manure costs generally ran to one-ninth of his total expenses. This system, late medieval in its origins yet modern in many respects, was so labor-intensive as to require farms smaller than 15 hectares.[54] In the southern Beauvaisis, cattle constituted a significant addition to cereals. Here the clay soil could bear only a "weak" *méteil* (more rye than wheat), and unmixed rye and oats were more likely crops. Yet pasture, riverbanks, commons, and wasteland together comprised 25 percent of the surface (as compared with 7 percent in the northern Beauvaisis). The courtyards and gardens around farmhouses were large—sometimes one and a half hectares—and often contained apple orchards. With both Beauvais and Paris as markets, the southern Beauvaisis was well placed to sell its livestock.[55]

In the Soissons intendancy itself, the valleys of the Marne, the Oise, and the Aisne were axes of mixed intensive agriculture. Vines grown on valley slopes bordered patches of orchard: apple, peach, cherry, pear, and walnut trees. On the left bank of the Oise and the lower valleys of the Aisne, hemp was grown in three successive crops followed by rye. Around Braine, beans alternated with *méteil*; in the sandy valleys north of the Marne, barley or oats alternated with rye. The proportion of fallow land was kept low. Natural pasture made up for the shortage of *vaine pâture*, and while on the plateaus cattle were never more than one-tenth as numerous as sheep, in the valleys their proportion often rose to more than one-fifth. The social complements of this diversification were a high proportion of small farms and a level of peasant proprietorship frequently reaching 40 to 50 percent.[56]

Although these cases of diversification show many differences, a few repetitive features emerge. The most frequent of these is the nature of the soil: clay and sand distinguish diversified regions from the grainlands. Uneven terrain, labor-intensive cultivation, or both made for smaller farms, and in the Soissonnais for a higher rate of peasant ownership. In Flandre and the Soissonnais river valleys, the proportion of fallow land receded almost to the vanishing point as crop rotation gained in sophistication. And for Flandre and the southern Beauvaisis, the strength and proximity of urban outlets supported the cultivator's flexibility; this lack of outlets remained a problem in the Soissonnais, devoid of manufacturing towns and reliant on the single Parisian market.

In general, sheep were the ideal animals for the *vaine pâture*. The way their teeth cropped grass and weeds near the root was acceptable on land whose primary function was to grow grain. But for true meadowland they were disastrous; usually they were kept out of communal pastures. In the Soissonnais, room appears to have remained for more sheep on existing arable land, since larger farmers were able to graze higher "densities" of sheep than smaller ones could. Cattle grazing was a different story, however. For example, in Saconin (a village five kilometers southwest of Soissons, on a tributary of the Aisne but with alluvial soil on its west flank) 10 medium-sized farms comprising 266 hectares among them kept a total of 240 sheep and 20 cows. The single large farmer in the same village, who held half this amount of land (132 hectares), was able to keep 230 sheep—almost as many as the others combined—but had only 13 cows. Without extensive pasture, marsh, forests, or other communal land, cattle ownership remained at a ratio of about one cow per 10 hectares, whatever the size of the farmer's holding.[57]

Consequently, the possibility of diversifying into livestock took sharply different forms in the river valleys, with communal land and pastures but little wheatland, than on the plateaus, with richer soil but much less common land. In the Château-Thierry bailliage, with its extensive wastelands and riverbanks, the subdelegate wrote in 1772 that "the wealth of farmers in the Brie consists in the number of their livestock."[58] Here ownership of animals extended farther down the social scale: the bailliage's Third-Estate cahier even complained that "lumber-cutting in the woods brings a multitude of strangers into the countryside, who often support their animals at public expense."[59] Similarly, in the southern Beauvaisis as early as 1680 laborers were able to keep two or three cows.[60]

Meanwhile, on the plateaus, the largest peasants were squeezing middle and small peasants out of *vaine pâture*. In the Soissonnais the large peasants were disposing of the custom that permitted smaller flocks to be joined to larger ones; in the Amienois they sought to forbid *vaine pâture* to landless peasants ("no farm, no pasture"); in the Hainaut they used the intendant's regulations legally dividing the *vaine pâture* between sheep and cattle to monopolize sheep raising.[61] Although a modification of the triennial system in which a quarter of the fallow land was sown with tares or legumes for livestock had extended from the Paris intendancy through parts of Valois since at least the seventeenth century, the practice never spread farther north. Ultimately, the triennial system in the Soissonnais would pass away only in the nineteenth century with the introduction of the beetroot, whose pulp could be used in a mixed fodder for cattle.[62] In a social context where most peasants were dependent on *vaine pâture* while the largest farmers benefited from it most, where could pressure against the triennial system come from?

For the great farmers, we can compare the costs of two strategies: cornering the free resource of *vaine pâture*, or changing their agricultural practices in any manner that might require capital investment. Such investment was very far indeed from the methods of even farms large and profitable enough to be described as "capitalist." Ninety years later, a major cultivator would recall this agriculture and its financial basis:

> In the old triennial agriculture . . . there were very few advances to make for the enrichment of the soil; no supplementary manure, few laborers; the labors followed each other in a regular pattern and there was no need for

these auxiliary teams of oxen that each year never fail to require the advance of a large capital. The flocks of sheep and cattle renewed themselves by ordinary husbandry; wages were paid largely in kind, with the products of the soil; money wages were paid twice a year, and always after the harvest that had benefited from the work; the tools—all quite primitive—lasted indefinitely and were repaired by the plowwright and blacksmith of the village; overall, in that agriculture one always sold and never bought; the bad harvests did not create crises of cash—one put off the lease payment, all the credit lay in that.[63]

And not only all the credit but also most of the investment lay in the leases, because the tenants, not the proprietors, were concentrating the land. Increasing the size of one's farm was, as we have seen, the only road to partial control over one's rents. Large farms typically benefited from the high market prices of poor harvest years, while middle-sized farms of 60 to 80 hectares, with rents often one-third higher, drew proportionately less benefit. Over the course of the eighteenth century, it was precisely farms of this latter category which most frequently broke up into smaller units at much higher rents.[64] The farmer sought to deploy capital to expand his lands and rise clear of this process.

Large and middle peasants trapped in competitive concentration were fettered to wheat, the crop that transportation conditions and dietary habits made the most commercializable. Efforts toward crop diversification came in fact from the stratum that historians have most often accused of a spirit of routine: the small peasants. Given appropriate terrain, it was the small peasants who practiced a labor-intensive plot agriculture that showed central traits of modern cultivation, including the elimination of fallow land, varied and flexible crop rotations, and specific orientation to urban markets. But hindered by backbreaking rents and dues, and by roads that made it impossible to carry perishable goods very far, such peasants could show stability but not much progress.

Finally, the attitude that rated vegetables as food more appropriate to animals than to human beings should not be underestimated. Even the proposal by Sellier of Amiens to increase vegetable production carried this implication: "By plowing communal land . . . the mass of provisions could be multiplied, above all potatoes . . . peas, beans, lettuce, turnips, carrots and maize, so necessary in years of shortage."[65] The relegation of vegetables to the status of a supplement against famine reflected not only the cultural but also the commercial prestige of cereals.

The cluster of interlocking attitudes described in this chapter can be characterized as follows: "Innovations in farming are ill-advised and not likely to produce improved yields. Traditional culture and the communal usages that go with it have the merit of including the poor, but more importantly they fit the exigencies of nature. However, the land should assure the sustenance of more inhabitants; an upper limit should be set on the size of a single farm. Overall, the existing crops and methods of cultivating them are unlikely to change because they follow the rigorous requirements of the soil."

The currency of these notions by no means assured a backward, routine-oriented peasant mentality, as historians have too often assumed.[66] Such breaks in the triennial system as we have found were due to small peasants' creation of niches outside the competition of the large farmers, where the terrain allowed. However, on wheatland undergoing concentration, the triennial system assumed its full dimensions as the productive organization of all layers of the peasantry, providing for the continued—if increasingly provisional—existence of most, while contributing to the enrichment of a few.

If the productive organization was "founded on nature," how could it be threatened knowingly by any of its members? Attacks on it had to come from outsiders who were either ignorant or evil. The Fear's rumor of brigands attacking standing crops flew as fast as eighteenth-century communications could carry it because it was about the production of food, not about its sale or distribution. A rumor about a disaster befalling production could provoke a unifying response because it announced a catastrophe that might strike everyone equally, great and small. This fact is as significant as the way in which the rumor echoed past military incursions, or how it suggested, by the completeness of the disaster envisioned, nature itself in its freakish, destructive aspect. The "brigands," the "foreign troops" feared in some coastal and border regions, and nature all had this in common: they stood outside the community, confronting it as hostile absolutes.

Of course, in northern regions that experienced more rural conflict than the Soissonnais, the triennial system was also dominant. Its presence did not guarantee social peace. Even within the Soissonnais, cohesion did not always win out over conflict (as we shall see in the Noyonnais). However, differences of degree in the strains placed on the triennial system were highly meaningful in shaping the responses of rural communities in 1789—responses that depended not only on local shadings of social and economic conditions but also on imponderables of personal relations between high and low in the community. The trien-

nial system remained an ideological resource that could buttress a common mentality.

That the rural community regarded its agriculture as a response to
nature's requirements gave it an element of unity and ideological solidarity. The fantasy of malicious outsiders attacking the crop that stood
in the fields mobilized this ideological solidarity and gave it a social
form. For this reason the Great Fear must be sharply distinguished from
the rumors about grain sales and circulation that caused so many local,
limited market riots and blockages of transports. The tension between
town and country over the grain shortage of 1789 should be viewed not
as a contributor to the Great Fear but as a barrier that the Fear was
strong enough to override. To understand this, it is to the realm of grain
sales that we must now turn.

TWO ❧ *THE SALE OF GRAIN AND*
THE MANAGED CONFLICT
BETWEEN TOWN AND
COUNTRY

Over the course of the agricultural year, grain moved out of the sphere of production, marked in the Soissonnais by a degree of relative social consensus, and into the sphere of exchange, characterized by chronic social conflict between sellers and impoverished consumers. This conflict, while troublesome, was so familiar that the old regime had virtually integrated it into its pattern of public order. The sphere of production gave the Great Fear's rumors of "brigands" their basic content: agricultural production was the treasure that communities united to protect from outside assault. The sphere of sale, on the other hand, contributed to the geographical shape of the Fear. Innumerable local polarities between market towns and their immediate hinterlands formed a complex landscape of subsistence and circulation which conditioned the paths along which the Fear traveled.

As a general pattern, both town and country feared each other's incursions. The country feared the town's authority to requisition grain and force its sale at market; the town feared the arrival at market of large crowds of poor rural consumers who could overwhelm the forces of order. In the Great Fear, however, each pole believed the other to be under attack by a mysterious third force. For example, Clermont-en-Beauvaisis had two panics in quick succession: the first caused by rumors of brigandage against crops, and the second by the sight of the peasant militia who were marching toward Clermont under the belief that the town was under attack. When the townspeople learned that the peasants were coming to defend them, they turned jubilant.[1] In the peculiar atmosphere of the moment, urban officials even congratulated themselves on the rapid arming of the countryside. The attorney of the provincial assembly wrote to the mayor of Guise on July 26: "Here we are facing a cruel alarm; we have learned this instant that brigands are cutting the green grain in the department of Crépy . . . it is good that the villagers guard themselves conscientiously, running strict patrols."[2] After the Fear these same officials would remember that a rearmed countryside greatly complicated their task of keeping public order; but for the moment, as Georges Lefebvre wrote, the Great Fear "tightened the bonds of solidarity which linked the town and the countryside around it."[3]

The Great Fear was clearly a phenomenon of interaction between town and country; but during normal times, the sale of grain was the form of interaction that mattered most. In the marketplace— the focal point of tension between town and country throughout the old regime— we can see the antagonism from which the Great Fear was a sort of holiday, momentarily submerging urban-rural tensions and then receding to confirm their existence in a new balance of forces. We can also see the difference between the Soissonnais, a region that experienced the Fear and whose tensions in ensuing months developed largely on town-versus-country lines, and the Cambrésis, where the Great Fear never visited and where the urban and rural poor acted increasingly in concert against the rich.

The Subsistence Crisis in the Soissonnais, and the Supply of Paris

The complexity of the grain trade in the Soissonnais in 1789 defies a rapid summary. The map shown in Figure 2.1 is only a schematic rendering. The long lines of supply for Paris converged on the Oise, the Aisne, the Ourcq, and the Marne. To arrive at points of embarkation, transported grain crossed a number of urban spheres of influence, each with its own market and its own grain-supplying outskirts. Circulation was obstructed everywhere by local officials and popular blockades (*entraves*). These fluctuated with the supply situation from month to month, but the reluctance to let grain pass southward was general.

Viewed from Paris, the intendancy of Soissons was a tributary agricultural region, less rich than the Beauvaisis or Picardy but closer than either thanks to its rivers. In the spring of 1789, however, this province, whose deliveries Paris took for granted, was experiencing a severe shortage of grain. In April the Soissonnais provincial commission (the administrative arm of the provincial assembly established in 1787) convinced

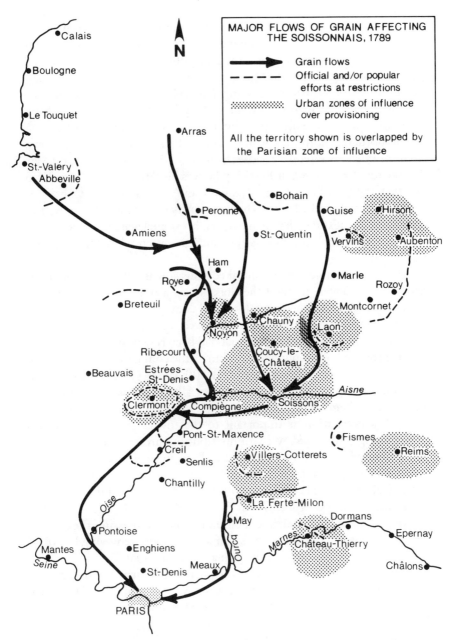

Figure 2.1. Major flows of grain affecting the Soissonnais. (Sources: AN BB30 79, 89; AN Dxxix 34, 41; AN Dxli 2; AN F11 210; AN H 1438; AN 01 485, 486; ADA C14, 913, 927, 941; AC Chauny BB 33; AC Laon BB 46; Dinet, "Grande Peur en Hurepoix," 330–31; Alexandre Michaux, *Histoire de Villers-Cotterets: La ville, le château, la forêt et ses environs* [Soissons, 1886], 86)

the intendant Charles de la Bourdonnaye, comte de Blossac, to prohibit the export of grain from the intendancy.[4] By early May, "border incidents" were taking place. The mounted police of Mareuil boarded an Ourcq canal barge and seized grain that had been purchased by Parisian agents. Farmers with long-standing Parisian markets crossed into the Paris intendancy to load their grain at Lizy-sur-Ourcq. A baker of Nanteuil, just within the Soissonnais intendancy, kept several mills running on the border, sending his white flour to Paris and baking his brown flour for sale in Nanteuil. To close the border effectively, Blossac on May 9 wrote the Paris intendant Bertier, who was his father-in-law: he pointed out that the parishes around Nanteuil and Neuilly-St-Front also furnished the market of Meaux, which was in Bertier's intendancy. Bertier replied on the next day that he had given his subdelegate in Meaux a free hand in the matter—and by this agreement between relatives, the Ourcq was sealed.[5]

At the same time the provincial commission asked Necker, director-general of finances, to send the Soissonnais a portion of government grain. Necker denied the request,[6] but by May 19 he was persuaded that the supply problems of the Soissonnais were serious. He then gave permission for the local sale of grain that had been reserved earlier for Paris, and he promised to supply rice.[7] On June 7 the commission, alarmed that the new grain census showed only 1,600 *muids* (19,200 hectoliters) remaining in Soissons,[8] purchased them all with Blossac's permission and divided them as follows: 600 *muids* were for Soissons and nearby villages (a precaution as important to the town's security as its own provisioning); 800 *muids* were for distribution throughout the province; and 200 *muids* were to be dispensed to Paris in small quantities against only the most pressing engagements. This plan was soon disrupted by the arrival of a special courier from Paris. The city was running short of grain, and "the government was very alarmed . . . in the committee where the ministers had deliberated on the means to assure the subsistence of the capital, one had gone so far as to propose removing by armed force what could be found in the granaries of Soissons."[9]

The intendant set off for Paris at once and returned two days later (the tenth) with a compromise: Soissons was to send Paris 300 *muids* immediately; in exchange, Paris authorized Soissons to make the most thorough searches for grain "at the farms and homes of all individual grainholders." Brayer, who was both the intendant's chief subdelegate and a member of the provincial commission, notified the Laonnais on June 16 that their region was to be the target of this expedition, and reminded them, "You know that for almost two months the carters of your region have not come to Soissons."[10] If Paris broke the embargo of Soissons, Soissons would break the embargo of Laon.

The compromise with Paris of June 9 was viewed in Soissons as a pact that sanctioned the prohibition of "exportation." The Parisian interpretation was that generous concessions had been made to Soissons concerning the town's own urban reserves. The lieutenant of police of Paris certified "a crowd of merchant millers and others from the environs of Paris" to act in the city's name around Villers-Cotterets and Crépy-en-Valois. The Crépy mounted police, for their part, were very active in seizing grain from carters who lacked a certificate from a local municipality; if they claimed to be going to a market at the southern end of the intendancy, their fate was sealed.[11] The provincial commission withheld most of the 300 *muids* it had promised, "forced to conserve what cupidity could not wrest from us."[12]

By mid-July, relentless searches had led to the confiscation of grain sold in advance as early as the preceding winter. The commission wrote, not without satisfaction, to its intermediate bureau in Guise on July 18: "In less than four days of the new dispensation, the look of things has changed. The markets . . . facing Paris, those at Villers-Cotterets, La Ferté-Milon, Neuilly-St-Front, Crépy, and Hauteuil, have been furnished with grain as well as oats . . . [those] grains intended for the capital for which the destination was known have been retained."[13] Nine days before the Great Fear, the local authorities' confidence had begun to return. It appeared to them that they had crossed the worst provisions crisis in two decades without grave mishap.

The Historiographic Debate over the Grain Trade

There is a continuing debate over how best to characterize the realities of the grain market in late eighteenth-century France. The grain market can be seen, according to one's emphasis, as a collection of local autarkies, as an imperfectly realized national market, or as a kind of "metropolitan market" organized around a few major cities—a designation proposed for seventeenth- and eighteenth-century England by Norman Scott Gras.[14]

The concept of local autarky in grain in the eighteenth century was given its definitive form by Ernest Labrousse, and was attacked in 1972 in a famous article by Louise Tilly.[15] Labrousse's argument can be summarized as follows: if there was a national market for grain in France in the eighteenth century, at least no one involved in long-distance transactions made a continuing profit. The wretched patchwork of roads, though supplemented for some regions by river transport, was inadequate to sustain a national trade—quite aside from the question of tolls and seigneurial rights on transport. Labrousse asserted that

> 1790 [transport] prices, reconstituted thanks to the prescriptions of the maximum [of 1793] . . . correspond, after one hundred leagues of transport, to 98 or 109 percent of the price of grain, depending on whether transport took place on a major or minor route; they may have been much higher.
>
> The rise in grain prices, which might have had the effect of lowering the proportional cost of cartage, did not therefore permit, at the end of the eighteenth century . . . profitable operations on grains between zones of usual high and low prices. The prohibitive cost of transport acted after the liberal edicts just as it had before . . . The measures of 1763 and 1764 . . . constitute primarily an affirmation of principle, a declaration of producers' rights, favorable in practice to the holders of large stocks; a glorious doctrinal anticipation with very limited immediate consequences for the mass of the nation, apart from a handful of feudal proprietors.[16]

Labrousse never denied the actual grain movements across France, nor did he greatly concern himself with them during his extensive exploitation of archival sources. He simply noted that widespread profits were inherently improbable. Forty years later, Tilly made a strong show of taking Labrousse to task, but did little in the end to alter his picture. She made the valuable point that "costs were not always rational by modern economic standards, but they were accepted. The evidence shows that grain moved."[17] However, she attempted to demonstrate that "movement toward a formation of a national market" by comparing price series that were extremely long—from 1530 to 1800. The result can perhaps be viewed as showing "the role of Paris as pricemaker, even for Toulouse," but at the end of this glacial movement Tilly's own charts show Toulouse at 24 and Paris at 35 *livres tournois* for a Paris *septier* (156 liters) in 1788.[18] This is precisely what Labrousse meant when he wrote, "But in this period, the 'longue durée' movement and the 'French market' itself are only benevolent abstractions, attenuating the real movement of prices."[19]

Of course there were structural connections among grain prices within a region, especially for countryside already integrated into a city's supply lines. But this integration presupposed the countryside's fertility, accessibility, and political and economic cooperation—the last two typically being engineered by a smaller town within it. Where fertility was absent (as in the case of the *élection* of Reims) or where cooperation was lacking (as with Laon and the Laonnais), mere proximity was not enough. In the case of Soissons and its immediate region, the river Aisne and the city's status as an intendant's headquarters linked its market firmly to that of Paris. Fertility, access, and an administrative seat as a point of leverage accelerated the penetration of Parisian priorities, creating the worst price swings of all. Jean Meuvret pointed out that

> all the markets of small towns or large villages show prices that, in ordinary times, are lower than those of the great centers. This fact is particularly clear in the regions neighboring the capital. On the other hand, when a strong rise supervened, these local prices went up more than proportionally to those of Paris, and when the shortage was at its peak they might arrive at comparable maxima. From this . . . came far stronger oscillations. It was in the country, and often in country rich in cereal production, that the provisioning crises raged with the most intensity.[20]

The Institutional Market: The Examples of Reims and Guise

The Soissonnais fell completely under Parisian sway in abundant or sparse years. Yet contrasts can be found quite nearby, and the *élection* of Reims in the Châlons intendancy was one of them. Its soil was mediocre and provided no more than one-fourth of its inhabitants' subsistence, if we follow pessimistic contemporary estimates. The remainder came mostly from the west and the north: the Soissonnais, Picardy, and the Thiérache. The grain transport charges found by Bernard Vonglis are for short routes only (Châlons to Reims, and Soissons to Reims), but if extended to Labrousse's "one hundred leagues" they add 5 to 11 livres to the original price of the grain. These charges must have doubled the typical prices of abundant years. Reims contained no grain merchants capable of major operations. The sales tax (*stellage*) collected by the archdiocese at market was set at one twenty-ninth of each transaction, and this was high enough to discourage local and outside traders alike, though various means of evasion had become customary. Despite these disadvantages, Vonglis affirms that "at the start of 1789 the prices rose progressively but moderately, while they shot up in neighboring provinces that were traditional exporters." We can confirm this by comparing Reims with Guise in the Thiérache, in normal years one of Reims' own suppliers. When the Guise *jallois* of 86.5 pounds is converted to the 132-pound *septier* of Reims and average monthly wheat prices for February through July 1789 are put side by side, it is clear that prices in Reims lagged behind until May:[21]

	Guise	*Reims*
February	16.7 livres	16.0 livres
March	17.8	17.5
April	18.8	18.3
May	18.3	18.5
June	20.3	20.8
July	23.2	22.6

Not until the previous year's stocks were approaching exhaustion did prices begin to advance more rapidly in Reims than in Guise. Until that point, the absence of traders from outside at Reims's market counterbalanced its paucity of local grains.

While Reims, with inadequate stores of its own, depended on a multitude of small carters for its supply, it was too much of a "consumption market" to support the major resales of grain that might have sustained a real commerce. Vonglis remarks:

> To stay with the specific case of Champagne, we have seen that at the end of the old regime in this province there existed no grain merchant worthy of the name, and consequently no effective commercial structure in this fundamental sector. Up to 1763 this insufficiency can certainly be attributed to the paralyzing effect of royal legislation. But after this date? We have seen that at Reims free trade in grain resulted only in the pullulation of minuscule traders, quite incapable of affecting the market at all. At times of serious crisis, in 1770-71 and in 1788-89, the municipal and royal administrations carried, as they had in the past, the full weight of the crushing burden of provisioning the town in such circumstances.[22]

In a crisis, the municipality of Reims itself turned grain merchant: there was no intermediary available. The municipal officers assembled funds by arranging loans, making drafts on the city's treasury, contributing from their personal fortunes, and arranging subsidies by Church institutions. They would then search for grain outside Reims's traditional catchment area, involving other authorities in the process. These were the practices of most towns in need of provisions.

Dealings of this type, typically conducted at a financial loss, involved cooperation among administrative entities and certainly set a great deal of grain in movement in 1789. They can be described as an "institutional market" not only because institutions and officials were the major participants but also because financial profits were not only rare but socially dangerous if noised about—and because the transactions themselves were official favors that could be traded against future obligations. Thus operations on the institutional market could demonstrate loyalties and

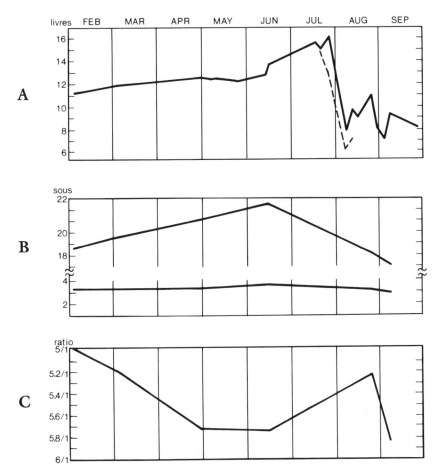

Figure 2.2. Grain and bread prices in Guise, March–September 1789. *A*. Price of the Guise *jallois* of wheat. The dotted line reflects two kinds of discount prices: a July transaction between a Paris Commune agent and the Guise municipality, and the August sales of a rye-and-wheat mixture with low wheat content. *B*. Prices of six-pound and one-pound loaves of bread. *C*. Ratio between prices of six-pound and one-pound loaves. (Source: AC Guise BB 14)

alignments that might come into play again over quite different issues.

To illustrate this, let us examine prices in a single town for which we also know the accompanying events: Guise from February through September 1789. Figure 2.2 shows the price fluctuations of a *jallois* of wheat (in Guise, 86.5 pounds); those of a six-pound loaf of bread; those of a one-pound loaf; and the ratio between the prices of the large and small loaves.

These fluctuations indicate the provisioning policy of the Guise municipality: stabilize the price of the one-pound loaf and protect the smallest consumers; let the six-pound loaf reflect grain prices more closely by letting buyers and sellers work out these prices for themselves. Events in Guise over the same period reflected the vagaries of this policy. On March 12, one week after the ratio between the prices of the six-pound and one-pound loaves had left the five-to-one level (Figure 2.2C), some bakers mutinied and refused to light their ovens. Their punishment was ambiguous: they were forbidden to bake unless the municipality chose to force them to do so. On April 30, the day of an increase in the price of the six-pound loaf (Figure 2.2B), an incipient riot was quelled in front of the mayor's house. One week later, on May 7, the mounted police received the intendant's permission to motivate the countryside into provisioning Guise's market. The plateau in the price of grain for the first three weeks of May (Figure 2.2A) was the happy result of this expedient. By June, however, another tactic had to be found, and Guise resorted to the institutional market. The mayor, a municipal officer, and a third party advanced 3,000 livres to buy grain from Soissons's reserves, planning to be repaid from sales. The rise of June 12 (Figure 2.2A) was due to low supply. The next day the grain from Soissons arrived, but only 21 *muids* had been bought, rather than the 30 intended. According to the municipal officers' figures, Soissons had sold the grain at 13 livres, 10 sous, 7 deniers per *jallois*; Guise would resell it at only 13 livres, 10 sous.[23] Nevertheless, furnishing the market had entailed an immediate rise of nearly 7 percent.

On July 1, Soissons warned Guise not to expect further sales for three weeks. On the twentieth the market at Guise was bare. Then at noon an agent of the Paris Commune named Blémont arrived and sold 50 *jallois* at 15 livres apiece. By a process of farm-to-farm accumulation he had gathered enough grain to fulfill his Parisian mission and to relieve Guise as well. On the twenty-fourth Blémont furnished the market again, but with a split price: 16 livres to individuals and 12 livres to the municipality. The next day was a Saturday: Blémont and the mayor, their cooperation now well-established, went hunting for provisions together: southeast to Marle, then further south to Laon, where they were loaned a small quantity; back to Guise with it "to avoid sedition"; south again all the way to Soissons, where they succeeded in obtaining a larger amount; back to Laon to repay the loan in kind; and thence to Guise again.[24]

Between July 25 and August 7, the Great Fear swept the southern two-thirds of the intendancy, the rye harvest came in, and a wider distribution of arms to the population transformed the Guise "bourgeois guard" into a "national militia." The split prices of August 7 reflected the custom of mixing the new rye with old wheat in differing proportions: the more wheat, the higher the price. Pressure on the countryside was relaxed: farmers were permitted to take home unsold grain on August 10. Grain prices then resumed a climb toward the 10- to 13 livres range, which (according to the municipal register) they reached in neighboring markets; but in Guise the consumers intervened. From August 24 to September 29 the price of grain was "set by the people . . . force having made the law."[25]

The prices of the institutional market had cushioned the general rise but had not curtailed it: the institutional market was indeed an extension of the market proper. The provisioning of Guise in July alone had entailed a complex web of relations, in which the municipalities of Soissons, Paris, Marle, and Laon were all involved, seeking to deal with one another. Order had been kept by and large in Guise by the municipality's skillful use of the mounted police in the countryside and in the market (where they frequently appeared in force, especially in May). Despite the strains of the preharvest period, it was the Great Fear that gave the crowd the means to set prices in Guise. The formation of the new militia upset the authorities' monopoly of force, and it was after the rye harvest, when the crisis might have been expected to ease, that the people in the market implemented their own price controls.

Geography of the Institutional Market

Each town that had its own market and could lay claim to a hinterland particular to it could participate in the institutional market according to its means. Though shortages put stress on towns' spheres of influence and threw the boundaries between hinterlands into flux, in normal times these boundaries seem to have been understood with a fine conciseness. Listen to Massinot, a municipal officer of La Fère-en-Tardenois, corresponding with the commission of the provincial assembly in late April. Massinot divided the immediate surroundings of La Fère-en-Tardenois, at a radius of 5 to 10 kilometers from the town, into three distinct neighborhoods, on which the town had differing kinds of claims: the "lands of Coulanges" to the east, an "exporting region"; "over by La Fère," the southern villages, tied to La Fère-en-Tardenois but already needy; and the independent "parishes on the Soissons side," one of which (Saponay) was virtually on La Fère-en-Tardenois's doorstep, being about an hour's walk away.

Though the district of Coulanges is extensive enough, and fertile enough in grains, here as everywhere else the harvest was slim, and I know that the four or five or six larger farmers who live there have already sold a great part of their grain to the outside . . . the farmers situated over by La Fère[-en-Tardenois] . . . are still more unfortunate . . . a great number of farmers themselves are obliged to buy grain for their subsistence . . . Our resources . . . therefore lie only in those farmers who inhabit the parishes on the Soissons side . . . We have finally convinced to come to our market these farmers who were not coming, being in the custom of going to sell . . . at Soissons . . . Everything is taken on each market [day] by the poor residents of parishes nearest La Fère[-en Tardenois].[26]

The normal supply pattern of La Fère-en-Tardenois had been upset by the crisis. Usually its market was furnished by its eastern and southern outskirts, while its western neighborhood made up part of Soissons's much larger sphere of influence. Now the eastern crop had probably gone down the Marne to Paris, and the town's west would have to feed its south. But this small-town official's way of perceiving the provisioning situation was no different in character from the way those responsible for Soissons, or even for Paris, analyzed their respective predicaments. At the center is the city; around it lies a domain. Greater towns make incursions into the domains of others; smaller towns within a domain require the city's support.

In sparse years the city collected the grain of its surroundings as best it could, and prudently resold it as needed to parishes within its sphere, if possible at a trifle below the current price. Guise did this for the parish of Honnecy in May, and probably also for Vaux-en-Arrouaise in June.[27] Soissons set aside grain in June for just this purpose;[28] and in the same month it passed eight hundred sacks of rye and barley to Noyon, which needed them not for its own provision but for that of its neighboring parishes. If the eight hundred sacks had not been dispatched, wrote the intermediate bureau of Noyon to the provincial commission on June 26, "we [would have been] constrained to interrupt all communication with the country people and expose ourselves to all the consequences of such an extreme position."[29] While a moral economy—a popular consensus over "just prices"—certainly existed in the Soissonnais, what is most striking about it is the degree of its administration from above; and in a sense this is what the "institutional market" was all about.

A town without a grain market could have no place in the institutional market. But for a town without a market to establish one was a disruptive act that invited retaliation. Hirson, a town of about three hundred hearths near the border with the Austrian Netherlands, did just this in spring 1789, thereby seceding from the sphere of influence of Vervins. In January the provincial commission at Soissons had described Hirson as one of the hungriest towns in the intendancy; in May the abbé of Bucilly told the intermediate bureau of Laon: "The markets are not yet absolutely empty, but often there is very little indeed. A new one is being established at Hirson which is drawing grain quite nicely. Those at Vervins and Signy-le-Petit are not being supplied as they were before, not by any means."[30] Tension between the two markets probably existed before August; but by the end of that month the municipality of Hirson requested that the National Assembly send troops to Vervins, declaring:

> The inhabitants [of Vervins] . . . decided a month ago to take up cockades and arms, to make patrols by day and by night; they arrest without distinction, and on their private authority, all people bringing grains to the market of the said Hirson; they seize the said grains with impunity and dispose of them at will or whim, so that the proprietors are deprived of them without compensation . . .
>
> . . . the inhabitants [of Hirson], not knowing how to respond, have hesitated to descend on Vervins as a crowd and fall upon its inhabitants.[31]

Alongside Vervins was Voulpaix, its closest neighbor to the west, whose people stopped northbound grain and dragged it to the Vervins market on August 10 and 24.[32] On September 15 the municipalities of Hirson and 11 other parishes announced to the National Assembly that they had formed a "composite" of all their militia "in order to watch for the public safety, and to effectively oppose the exportation of grain abroad; to leave no room for suspicion, they have given notice of this precaution both by letter and by deputation." Protesting again that "the town of Vervins was the first to permit itself to arrest our carters and fellow citizens" and that "this example was soon followed by its neighbors," Hirson and its allies declared darkly that "the evil is so great that it will hardly be possible to remedy it short of exemplary punishment."[33] The decline of grain prices apparently eased tensions in the autumn.

Though the dispute has a comical aspect from a historical distance, the possibility of violence between the two camps was real. At stake were the control of Vervins over the district of the intendant's subdelegate (then called a "department") of which it was the seat,[34] and of the ability of Hirson to attract provisions to its forested, sparsely populated frontier. These were, in their small way, geopolitical issues, and they had geopolitical consequences on towns' economic and political rank.

The notables of the Soissonnais never stated these truths more explicitly than during the creation of the department of the Aisne in 1790. Soissons, lobbying for Parisian support to transfer its status as administrative seat from the old intendancy to the new department, blatantly emphasized its place in the institutional market. If Laon was to usurp its place, Soissons told the Parisians,

> one would have to remove from Soissons all the public coffers, of which the operations, combined with those of commerce in grain—the only commerce that flourishes there—facilitate and support an annual circulation of over three million [livres], and accelerate by that much . . . the flow of funds into the public treasury. Could one exclude from consideration the need to protect a commerce perhaps unique in the kingdom . . . in the advantages it procures the capital, to which it annually assures a quarter to a third of its subsistence?[35]

Bailly, the mayor of Paris, was a committed supporter of Soissons and spoke the same language:

> The Soissonnais is one of the granaries of the city of Paris . . . it is desirable for the capital that Soissons become the seat of a department. Recall . . . that Soissons furnishes Paris a third or a quarter of its consumption, and that consequently our life depends on Soissons; and if I obtain this for her, which strikes me as just in any case, Soissons will be attached to us as . . . a municipality in our debt.[36]

Nor was Soissons alone in taking this approach; cities throughout the Parisian basin and beyond lobbied in these terms. On the border of the Soissonnais, St-Quentin demanded a department of its own on the basis of its supposed rank in the grain trade.[37] All this activity of course assumed that the hierarchy of the institutional market would ultimately determine events and that a committee in Paris, not a convention of the province's own notables, would decide administrative status. When the National Assembly required the latter course, Laon was able to sway the convention effectively by presenting Soissons as "accustomed to sucking the blood of the province."[38] The majority of delegates voted for Laon: they wanted to separate the administrative control of the department from Soissons's commercial power in the grain trade, and give their own urban spheres more breathing space.

The Institutional Market as "Moral Economy from Above": Necker's Ideas

The term *moral economy* was introduced by E. P. Thompson to describe the ideology behind crowd movements at market, for he explained these movements as the result of something more complex than hunger alone. The moral economy "depended upon a particular set of social relations, a particular equilibrium between paternalist authority and the crowd."[39] The concept of an "institutional market" for grain is meant to describe the primary mechanism for maintaining this equilibrium in the Soissonnais, a mechanism that allowed the "paternalist authority" to move grain at a loss where it was needed, and to close some openings for the crowd's activity while permitting and regulating others. Before the Great Fear, popular action in the Soissonnais included rather less of the price-setting associated with the "moral economy," and rather more of actions intended to assert local interests vis-à-vis "subordinate" towns, or to demand supplies from a higher center.

The institutional market of the Soissonnais was, naturally, a hierarchy. Paris was its distant summit, Soissons its visible, intermediate peak. Below Soissons were all the other towns of the province, arrayed by their relative size, the fertility of their outskirts, their administrative rank, and their historical precedence. While towns might compete, as did Hirson and Vervins, each felt sure of an immediate rural fringe that was its own. Soissons counterposed itself to the entire intendancy as the metropole of a predominantly rural region. Paris counterposed itself in the same way to all the regions that provisioned it. Of course, these statements are platitudes, true for periods later than the eighteenth century as well. But they must be repeated, because they are fundamental to understanding the local nature of the moral economy in the Soissonnais. Each district was involved in a town-country opposition of its own, often different from those of its neighbors. While moral-economic values remained an ideological *lingua franca* that crossed regional and class lines, the specific town-country antagonism in play for the participants in each concrete situation dominated the expression of the moral economy in the Soissonnais.

The administrative action that went with the institutional market was frequently attacked, notably by the physiocrats, as ceaselessly fluid and lacking in clarity or principles. In defense of the institutional market, the words of the royal minister Jacques Necker are worth attending to, not only because he was at the helm in 1789 but also because he believed in administrative fluidity, elevated it to a principle, and equated it with political maturity in the conduct of state affairs.

Necker viewed the art of administration as involving a type of relationship to nature. Just as nature formed the centerpiece of a rural ideology of production, Necker used nature as justification for a way of governing that was profoundly arbitrary—arbitrary both in its staggering injustices and in its sudden, trivial mercies. Nature was paramount, and in his *Sur la législation et le commerce des grains* Necker gave this point all the weight of an undeniable platitude: "It is doubtless beyond an administration's power to foresee all the movements to which grain prices are exposed; for harvests are subject to revolutions against which all the prudence of men is only weakness."[40] Necker used the trump card of nature not to justify inaction, however, but to support the usual flux of administrative activity by claiming that truly significant results should not be expected from it. Necker had a very clear idea of how a perfect royal administrator, "a man whose far-flung intelligence covers all circumstances, and whose supple and adaptive mind knows how to conform his plans and wishes to them," would run the kingdom's grain circulation:

> Such an administrator would now permit, now absolutely prohibit the exportation of grains; perhaps more often he would modify it in different ways, by limiting the places, the times, the circumstances and the quantities . . .
>
> Sometimes, while permitting the free passage of grains within the whole kingdom, he would forbid it in one or two provinces, destined more particularly to the supply of a great city . . .
>
> If extraordinary events agitated imaginations and spread a spirit of discontent, he would watch all the more over the moderation of grain prices.
>
> Finally, for long periods he would not touch this commerce, abandoning its circulation to the industry of merchants; then suddenly he would order purchases and deliveries, if certain specific reasons determined them.
>
> How many other combinations would not escape the vigilant eye capable of thus following the variety of circumstances, to found upon this harmony the greater good of the State?[41]

The passage (far longer in the original) describes the mentality of Necker and most of his fellow administrators well; indeed, it covers much of their repertoire, both national and local. It may even display their image of themselves, cloaked in the translucent modesty of a hypothetical personage.

In all these "extraordinary events," "combinations," and "circumstances," Necker saw both physical nature and social reactions to nature, blended into a single, vague force. Necker describes "human nature" as an immense power, an absolute given, to be ranked with physical nature: "What is force, when it seeks to counter a general sentiment? From this moment on it is no longer force; indeed, each error that forms part of human nature must be treated as a reason." The desires of the people are to be managed in the same way, and for the same reasons, as the forces of nature: "Thus when one desires to make the people's dominant passion submit to a general system, one errs; on the contrary, it is the system that must be combined with this passion; the passion operates as a given in administration; it is the force of the ocean's waves that must be calculated to build a breakwater on the shoreline."[42] These lines summarize the philosophy of local administrators, as shown by their practice. Their use of power deployed very limited resources to divide and regroup overwhelming masses of people, and it relied on the model of the human relation to physical nature to justify itself.

Necker believed that regarding the grain trade no permanent law was possible: "How can the same limits, the same liberty, the same system suit every period, since where grain is concerned different periods have nothing in common? The abundant year ceaselessly recalls the idea of surplus; the year of shortage continually evokes the fear of lacking necessities."[43] Nature was arbitrary; the people partook of nature's arbitrariness; and the administrator's own arbitrariness in now regulating, now easing the grain trade reflected the arbitrariness of natural circumstances. Necker's book was a strong success—not only because it appeared, quite by chance, at the very moment of the "Flour War" in 1775 but also because it encapsulated the wisdom of the elite that dealt on a practical level with subsistence problems.[44]

The Institutional Market and the Town-Country Conflict

The social medium for the flux of administrative action "in response to nature" was the institutional market. The institutional market in turn contained and channeled popular action, because it was founded on the relation between a dominant town and its subordinate countryside. The tension caused by shortages could be translated into intensified pressure on rural supplies, uniting urban rich and poor against rural rich and poor. To sharpen the standing conflict between town and country was not too dangerous a game: the antagonism had such a tradition that even its exacerbation was a kind of stability. Antonio Gramsci's lines written about the cities and countryside of central and southern Italy could apply as well to northern France in 1789:

> In this type of city there exists, among all social groups, an urban ideological unity against the countryside . . . There is hatred and scorn for the "peasant," an implicit common front against the demands of the countryside—which, if realized, would make impossible the existence of this kind of city. Reciprocally, there exists an aversion—which, if "generic," is not there-

by any less tenacious or passionate—of the country for the city, and all the groups that make it up.[45]

In the Soissonnais, irrevocably on the road to large-scale agriculture, the town-country antagonism was especially important . . . to preserve. As we have seen, the widespread reluctance about the emergence of *grande culture* stemmed in part from a fear of an ungovernable mass of poor which would be neither properly urban nor rural. Old-regime administrators were partly conscious of this danger, as their efforts to "repatriate" the newly arrived urban poor to their native villages bear witness.[46]

As the effects of the worst grain shortage since 1770 were compounded by the general political crisis, the limits of the poor's patience seemed nearly reached. Would urban and rural poor join forces to corner municipal elites? Or would turmoil in the countryside direct itself against seigneurs, proprietors, and the largest farmers? Both possibilities seemed realistic; both occurred in various parts of Picardy and the Cambrésis.

In the Soissonnais, however, the town-country conflict held, retaining its form while increasing in intensity. Until the Great Fear, the town poor's desperation was deflected by requisitions in the countryside, official or semiofficial. The mounted police surpassed their orders, controlling grain traffic on their own initiative; they forestalled popular insubordination with their own. As early as January 12, de Latombelle, the royal prosecutor for the Laon bailliage, complained to de Villedeuil, the state secretary of the king's household, that the mounted police were arresting carters for making small purchases at farms; de Villedeuil sent a vague but supportive reply.[47] On April 24 the mounted police brigade of Ferté-Milon seized grain as it was being loaded on a barge to descend the Ourcq canal; the farmer's protest to Paris caused the director-general's office to ask the intendant Blossac to stop the sale of the grain, pending further information.[48] The mounted police acted ahead of, then in cooperation with, local officials to intensify requisitioning: we have already seen the effect of this on prices and public order in Guise. The town's "moral economy" was supported primarily by police activity in rural districts.

The peasant's view of this relationship was fervently expressed in the notes accompanying the parish cahier of Urvillers, a small village six kilometers south of St-Quentin and within its bailliage, its *élection*, and its salt-tax jurisdiction. According to Urvillers, urban domination was absolute; the military and security functions of the town did not justify this domination; and the market regime should be ended and the farmer protected from popular price-setting:

> The town supports the town to oppress the country, that's all. We could defend them by saying that they billet the troops and mount a guard, but they can be deprived of this defense, because one can have troops lodged without being obliged to the town. We have many houses of religious communities that could be filled by billeted troops. One could find some good in that for the king, as he could use the immense wealth that could be better occupied. It's the town that oppresses the whole countryside . . .
>
> All the municipal officers put taxes on many artisan corporations and on sales that involve cash, to the profit of the town hall. This money serves for the attorney . . . To have abundance, it would be necessary to make grain sales free over the whole territory, forbidding any sack-slingers [*porte-sacs*] to put up any obstacles. We hope for every relief in the new redivision, that's why we have deliberated this petition.[49]

In the formula "the town supports the town to oppress the country," the different roles of the municipal officers, the corporations, and the populace—the small consumers, the "porte-sacs"—were noted but not distinguished by the peasants of Urvillers. The town's apparent unity against the countryside dominated their perception of the town's inner structure. And the fact that "porte-sacs" were often poor peasants was effaced for them.

To this rural image of the town-country conflict, we can counterpose an urban image that resembles it like a photographic negative. In 1806 the abbé Hébert wrote an unpublished history of his own town, Château-Thierry. When he described the riots of the 1775 "Flour War," Hébert drew on a comfortable tradition of urban superiority:

> On Tuesday . . . a market day . . . troops of peasants entered by all the gates of the town, each one carrying a stick and a sack. It is said that there were at least four thousand. This army of brigands having entered town, and running through it in disorder, a great number went to the market where they forced grain to be given them at the price they wanted . . .
>
> Some [retired] soldiers who lived in the town . . . and other inhabitants also took up arms and went to support the magistrates . . .
>
> Other peasant troops went off to invade the houses . . . Mme. de Prévôt, wife of a brave officer . . . distinguished herself on this occasion . . . [She] appeared at one of the windows . . . with a pistol in her hand. "Yes," she said, "I have grain; but I will not give it without the presence of a magistrate and two cavaliers from the mounted police; and only to those who present

themselves singly" . . . This short harangue had its effect . . . and they went on . . .

The brigands, in leaving, had announced a new irruption for the following Friday; but for that day precautions were taken. The magistrates had mounted police brigades come from Oulchy, Dormans, Montmirail, and other places. They ordered the bourgeois militia to take up arms . . . Detachments were sent to the far ends of the faubourgs . . .

A multitude of peasants arrived, even more considerable than on Tuesday . . . First they were made to put their sticks down at the outskirts of the faubourgs . . . They could only enter the town by the Bridge Gate, and only four at a time . . . They were conducted in military fashion to the market to provide themselves with grain; and they were brought back the same way to go out by the Bridge Gate.[50]

Gilded by memory, this was the town-country conflict in its Sunday best. The civic virtues displayed on such a day must have animated later retellings. All the townspeople appeared united around the town magistrates. It was a chance for the retired military to demonstrate their valor. The principle of the town's duty to supply the countryside (questions of price aside) was never questioned, not even by Mme. de Prévôt. The country people in departing told the townspeople the date of the next "match." The forewarned municipality prepared the defense of Château-Thierry. The superiority of urban arms was proved, though the countryfolk had no guns in any case. Given that the provisioning context frames all the events in the story, and that the principle of town supply of the countryside in times of need is never questioned, what remains is anything but subversive: a simple trial of strength with a foregone conclusion. Rendered here in myth, this is the pattern of conflict which channeled stress and supported stability.

Managed Town-Country Conflict and the Great Fear: The Contrast between Noyon and Cambrai

In 1789 the ritualized pattern of town-country conflict held remarkably well in the Soissonnais through late July. The rural districts of the Laonnais remained just below the threshold of revolt: the intermediate bureau of Laon wrote the provincial commission in Soissons on June 4 that "the bureau has communicated . . . the apprehensions of numerous municipalities, along with those naturally evoked by the spirit of insurrection that dominates the countryside; several communities have chosen to mount a guard; if they maintain a correspondence with others in this regard, would that not sow alarms?"[51] In these remarks the bureau's language still contrasted "municipalities" to "countryside" and guarded against too rapid a generalization of this conflict.

We can best see the staying power of the town-country framework for antagonism by examining a single town, Noyon, through the correspondence of its intermediate bureau with the provincial commission in Soissons from May 15 through August 21. These documents illustrate the political and administrative interplay characteristic of the institutional market in a crisis period: how intensifying social stress was contained within the institutional market and the managed town-country antagonism it thrived on; and how the aftermath of the Great Fear saw the development of threats to this equilibrium.

On May 15 Noyon's intermediate bureau painted a grim provisions picture for Soissons, claiming to be 50,000 sacks below the town's requirements for the next two and a half months, with a complete absence of small traders at market. In reply, the provincial commission sent 54 *muids* of wheat (not the 100 requested) from Soissons' stores;[52] but at the same time, the intendant Blossac ordered Noyon to supply Chauny, eight kilometers away and part of Noyon's *élection* and diocese, from stores that were originally purchased for the royal government by an agent named Bucquet. This grain had never left Noyon, and a portion of it had been sold on the local market—according to Bucquet's orders, the Noyonnais claimed. The Noyon bureau refused to supply Chauny on the grounds that any movement of grain out of Noyon would cause immediate rioting because the municipality, which controlled all stocks, would suddenly appear to be speculating. In the same breath, the bureau boasted of the relationship of trust it had maintained with the rural districts:

> The public is . . . aware that the quantity of grain required to support its needs, or anything near it, is not to be found in our town, and this knowledge is the reason that the inhabitants of neighboring villages have peacefully let pass the barge loaded with 54 *muids* . . .
>
> Up to now our area has not been exposed to the unwelcome consequences of the brigandage of malcontents who converge to pillage grain from farmers by open force; the reason is that no farmer of this region holds grain beyond his own provisions; but we are informed that the parishes neighboring the towns of St-Quentin and Peronne have experienced some violence . . .[53]

On June 5 Noyon sought another emergency shipment from Soissons, claiming that the royal government had promised one thousand sacks earlier in the spring. The intendant Blossac had already requested a grain census of the Noyon subdelegation; and (though the documents do not allow certainty) it appears that the Noyon municipality had sent an evasive reply, filled with rhetorical images of misery.[54] Noyon's municipal officers must have had some indications that the provincial commission at Soissons was ready initially to meet Noyon's demands for one thousand sacks, because Noyon's municipal officers traveled to Soissons—only to be refused after all. On June 12 Noyon's intermediate bureau made a vehement defense of the town's market policy to the provincial commission:

> If up to now we have had the advantage of not seeing grain prices rise to the level . . . [current] in the surrounding towns, the public owes it only to the sacrifice the municipal officers are making of part of the grain they have paid for, of the grain purchased by them; not to any abundance . . . in our town, as has been claimed, contrary to truth, by certain monopolists who find themselves inconvenienced in their sordid and abominable traffic . . . no one can blame us for the distressing events that may follow—if indeed, we are not personally the victims.[55]

This assertion of "moral-economic" values seems to have had its desired effect. A letter of June 20 from the provincial commission assured the Noyon administrators that they were still held in honor, and that eight hundred sacks of rye and barley were forthcoming. The intermediate bureau noted with satisfaction that "the false reports that have spread in your town about the supposed provisioning of ours" had not been believed by the commission; it had "simply thought that the conduct of certain of our merchants could be suspicious"—a point of no great concern to anyone. However, the bureau did fear that the promised eight hundred sacks might be stopped at Compiègne, where the Aisne and the Oise meet. Without this shipment, Noyon would soon be at a loss to provision its surroundings, and its place in the institutional market would then be endangered.[56]

Since May the municipal officers of Noyon had organized complete control over all stocks of grain within the town, whoever owned them or might claim them. A deputation arrived from Peronne (in the Amiens intendancy) to pick up 160 sacks of grain which had been sold to Peronne by a farmer who had stored them in Noyon: the Noyon municipality turned the group away without difficulty. The next day a mounted police officer and a member of the municipality of Licourt[57] in Santerre came for 300 sacks belonging to a grain merchant named LeCoq. They had a letter from the minister of war ordering the commander of the dragoon detachment posted in Noyon to assist them in carting the sacks away. The Noyonnais did not budge: they declared that they had been entrusted with the grain by the provincial commission, which acted under "royal orders" (i.e., under the intendant Blossac), and that therefore only a direct order from His Majesty could release the grain. This line apparently succeeded: the visitors beat a retreat. If they could have procured a direct royal order, the Noyon municipality would probably have refused that, too, referring the visitors to the baleful gaze of the populace.[58]

Considering the circumstances, the greater part of July passed peacefully in the Noyonnais. The eight hundred sacks of rye and barley from Soissons were received by July 3, and on the seventeenth the intermediate bureau congratulated the provincial commission on the abatement of its provisioning work. Informed rather sourly that the work had not abated, the bureau apologized ("We regret to hear, Messieurs, that your just inquietude over the great business of provisions has not yet reached its term") and went on to other matters: Chauny's refusal to pay two years of (unspecified) taxes that amounted to 17,000 livres.[59]

Up to this point the administrators of Noyon had surmounted an old-regime crisis with old-regime tactics and resources. They had wheedled provisions from the administrative seat; they had brandished the threat of riot when their decisions were questioned; they had bragged of their success in maintaining tranquillity within and without the town; they had refused precise information to the authorities which might have allowed some check on their movements; they had managed both to control and to supply "their" countryside; and they had claimed the authority of the king himself when their control over supplies was challenged. After the Great Fear, the bureau's correspondence provides a different kind of reading. The issue of provisions initially disappeared, which was natural with the arrival of the rye harvest. It was replaced by the issue of smuggling, described as one of the great symptoms of popular rebelliousness—which the Noyon authorities still sought to conceive in town-versus-country terms.

Lefebvre thought that the current of the Great Fear that passed through Noyon originated on the Béthisy plain and moved northward, touching Compiègne and Ribécourt.[60] There is also evidence to indicate that another, simultaneous current originating near Estrées-St-Denis had the stronger effect on Noyon and its surroundings. This geographical question will be discussed in detail in chapter 4. For our present purpose, it is more important to note that Noyon received multiple alarms, armed "all the inhabitants . . . without exception," and passed

the alarm to Chauny. "The inhabitants of our surrounding parishes follow our example," they informed Soissons on July 31, adding that a
"pillage" of the chateau of Frétoy, five kilometers north of Noyon, had
taken place on the twenty-seventh (the very day of the Fear's arrival).
Thus, in one corner of the Noyonnais a minor peasant revolt had
preempted the Great Fear.

One week later, in their letter of August 7, the bureau was no longer
sanguine about "its" countryside, reporting that they had, in obedience
to the provincial commission's orders, sent village syndics copies of the
National Assembly's decree against the sale of untaxed salt and tobacco,
but that "in our department things have gone to such an extreme that
only force could bring a halt to the abuses and the open refusals to honor
the best established rights." The bureau urged that the 40 dragoons
assigned to Noyon be increased to an entire regiment, the complement
that guarded Soissons. "We are obliged to guard ourselves day and
night," they complained, "which is most fatiguing for those persons of
a certain age whose position demands daily and continuous labors and
cares" (a courteous reference to the master artisans in the new militia).
On August 14 the bureau made this summary of the situation: "The
opening of the harvest, which took place in our district almost 15 days
ago, has in fact ended the straits in which we found ourselves for assuring public subsistence, [but] has not ended our fears over the efferves-
cence and dizziness that have overtaken the minds of the country people."[61]

Clearly the fears of Noyon's administrators had not ended but had
only begun with the harvest. The bureau reported that a courier sent
with the National Assembly's decree against salt smuggling had been
pounced on by villagers who refused to release him unless he promised
to stop delivering copies. The bureau also expressed its fears that giving
the peasants permission to hunt would complete their rearmament and
make them far more combative.[62]

Another week passed, and the air of sedition began to enter Noyon
itself. By August 21 the bureau began to grasp that "many causes give us
reasons to fear that we are now exposed to calamities greater than those
which have disturbed us up to this point." They complained suddenly
that the harvest was meager in their stretch of the Oise valley and that
they were already relying on outside suppliers. This may have been true,
but it was also a necessary comment to justify a near-riot, purportedly
over grain, just two weeks after the rye harvest: "Last Friday we were on
the brink of . . . a riot because the market did not hold grains sufficient
to satisfy those there to buy. Apart from that, the people no longer

recognizes either rules or faith; it thinks that everything must bend to its wishes." One may speculate that the local harvest was indeed poor—or that it was adequate, but could not match what might anachronistically be called pent-up consumer demand; or that, just as in Guise, provisions became a rallying point for a display of newly acquired popular strength. From the alarmed bureau's standpoint, the people were closing in: "We are reduced to guarding ourselves against our internal and external enemies."[63]

What had happened? The Great Fear had intervened, and its momentary unity had accomplished what months of privation could not accomplish in the Soissonnais. The tension between town and country had suited the Noyon notables' style of administration, which worked best when hunger was the central issue in the community, but the events of July 27 had overwhelmed the town-country equilibrium. Inside the town, the panic over the harvest had led the authorities to a feverish rearmament that included the lower classes. Outside the town, Noyon had dispatched its troops and mounted police to quell a small island of peasant revolt, while encouraging the rest of its surrounding parishes to follow its example and mount guard. The harvest had been saved from its imagined destroyers, but the countryside now found itself mobilized and better able to reject urban control, and within Noyon the first stirrings against the town's officials were being felt.

What the Noyon bureau feared most was a transformation of the town-country antagonism into a conflict between rich and poor; but only after the Fear did it believe that this prospect could become a reality. In the more volatile Cambrésis, the transformation had already occurred in May. George Lefebvre analyzed it in his *Les paysans du Nord dans la Révolution française*:

> the small peasants, the artisans, and the day-laborers of the countryside
> . . . could have little good to say about the urban municipalities that sought
> to exclude them. Yet . . . the cultivators, inexorably, refused more and more
> to provide day laborers with grain, sending them off to supply themselves in
> the towns; it required no less than the intendant's authority to prevent the
> rural poor from dying of hunger between the granaries and the markets that
> both closed before them. This hostility between townsfolk and rustics did
> not result in a masking of class conflict. At bottom, the farmers did not
> really worry about the town officials . . . they feared much more the com-
> mon people of the towns. However, the poor people of the country had the
> same grievances as the latter; like them, they resented the merchants and
> traders, the municipalities . . . and the big farmers . . . Going to market

each week, they entered into contact with the urban proletariat, and thus the troubles endemic to the towns seemed likely to find a formidable echo in the surrounding countryside. From May on, the proof could be found in the Cambrésis, which, naturally, was the first to tremble: on [May 6], the people of Cambrai rose and seized grain everywhere, paying a price they had fixed; from the eighth, the peasants rose up all round the town's outskirts.[64]

The documents regarding the Cambrai riot of May 6–7 suggest that the town's magistrates were lax about establishing visible control over the granaries within the city, particularly those of religious institutions. When the riot came, they were overly reluctant to employ even the threat of military force to contain it, although (or because) they had a considerable garrison at their orders.[65] After the popular explosion, they sought to shift blame to the lieutenant in command and accused the military of complaisance with the crowd. On the morning of the seventh, they furnished the market so amply and set the price so low that rural small consumers among the purchasers took home what had occurred in Cambrai as a model for their own activity. Many of the forced sales of grain that began on the eighth around Cambrai used the Cambrai price of May 7 as the basis of payment.[66]

In the regions of France where insurrections took place in July, the link between urban unrest and peasant rebellion was clear. In the Norman Bocage, a peasant revolt was preceded by three days of urban rioting in Caen (where the tax offices were attacked) and in four other towns. In Mâcon, the links forged between bourgeois and peasant electors of deputies to the Estates-General in the course of a political struggle against the town's magistracy in March had laid the groundwork for the simultaneous rising of city and country in the days following the news of the fall of the Bastille. In Lyon, the militia returning from the repression of peasant insurgents in Dauphiné were greeted by a riot in their own city. Wherever old-regime order broke down, a degree of *de facto* union between the urban and the rural poor was apparent.[67]

The Soissonnais was one of the provinces where this dreaded union of the urban and the rural poor formed much more slowly. The traditional antagonism between town and country remained a familiar feature of society, a pillar of the old-regime order that included occasional disturbances in its "natural" cycle of events. The institutional market, the grain trade's organizer of last resort, functioned just well enough to keep its social world glued together with a compound of hostility and obedience. The municipalities that visibly defended moral-economic imperatives stayed more or less secure, and in the Great Fear, rural militias marched ostensibly to keep them secure. Only after the Fear did the notables and the common people realize that in a moment of solidarity they had unwittingly created a new balance of forces between them.

THREE

**BEGGING: THE
CENTRAL CHANNEL OF
NONCOMMERCIAL
DISTRIBUTION**

In examining the sphere of cultivation, we have seen that social conflicts
between strata of the peasantry were bounded in the Soissonnais by a
consensus over the basic means and limits of agricultural production. In
considering the sphere of sale and exchange, we have seen that antago-
nistic relations over sale between town and country offered old-regime
authorities certain avenues for control over potentially explosive conflicts between rich and poor. We now turn to the sphere of noncommercial distribution, where it will be shown that on the local level the practice of begging was so closely integrated into the poor-relief efforts of
secular and religious authorities that it comprised the basis of a formally
sanctioned system.

All three of these points are crucial to an understanding of the Great
Fear in the Soissonnais. The consensus over agricultural production
made possible an agreed-upon object that communities could unite to
defend at the moment of the Fear. The managed conflict between town
and country shaped the geography of subsistence that conditioned the
transmission of the Fear. And begging's inclusion in accepted social
practice at the local level was so complete in the Soissonnais that interpretations of the Fear as fundamentally a fear of beggars cannot stand.

Albert Soboul's 1961 description of the Great Fear ("Unemployment and shortages multiplied beggars and vagabonds; in the spring,
bands appeared. The *fear of brigands* reinforced the fear of an aristocratic
plot")[1] is a gloss on Lefebvre which is echoed by the summaries of the
Great Fear in most surveys of the Revolution. The argument that the

Fear was essentially a panic about the mendicant, vagabond poor is well suited to an economistic twentieth-century perspective. Only a localized examination of begging's place in the community and in official practice during the crisis of spring 1789 can begin to break down this established view and open the way to an understanding of the Fear as an ideological phenomenon.

The act of begging was not seen as illegitimate by the people at large or even by many local authorities in the Soissonnais of 1789. Begging was, quite simply, the old-regime form of poor relief, notwithstanding the numerous royal laws against it. Mendicancy was a fundamental channel for the distribution of food, alongside the channel of purchases at market.

We can think of grain as having four possible destinations. The cultivator might use it for immediate subsistence needs; it might form part of a reserve for later use or sale; it might be sold, either at market or surreptitiously (for example, to a Parisian purchasing agent); or it might be given away. The same options applied to purchased grain in the hands of the buyer. In difficult years, and at other times as well, donations of food were indispensable for social peace. These donations were typically structured by the practice of begging rather than by other, more centralized modes of delivering relief. The initiatives against mendicancy that filtered down from the royal level of administration only provided the localities with legal instruments for their control of outsiders, who constituted the true bugbear of old-regime ideology and who were the only actual group for which the Great Fear's label *brigand* was intended.

Begging in Legislation, Social Practice, and Opinion

The contradiction between the legitimacy of begging and its illegality was already very old at the beginning of the eighteenth century. The first royal ordinance against beggars in France was issued by Jean le Bon in 1350.[2] Between 1657 and 1764 eight laws applying to the entire kingdom—and six laws covering either Paris, Paris and environs, or the jurisdiction of the Parlement—succeeded one another, each reshuffling the legal categories "beggars," "able-bodied beggars," "vagabonds," and "gens sans aveu" (literally, "unvouched-for persons").[3] Just as repressive laws against beggars and vagabonds were a tradition, the dilution or reversal of these laws in actual enforcement was a tradition also. After the royal declaration of 1724 that required beggars to be arrested and detained in hospitals, the hospitals themselves continued the customary offering of the *passade*—a coin given to each poor traveler who promised to leave town the next day. In Lyon in the 1730s, the bishop persisted in distributing alms weekly at his palace gates, and the hospitals kept up the same practice.[4]

The material impossibility of the 1724 project for detention of the destitute led to the more modest declaration of 1764, which lacked a single reference to begging and mentioned only "vagabonds and *gens sans aveu.*"[5] However, this declaration was shortly followed by the Council of State edict of 1767, which established workhouses—the *ateliers de charité* for the Paris poor, and the *dépôts de mendicité* for vagabonds in the provinces—new institutions whose rationale really lay in the grandiose earlier policy of confinement (*renfermement*). In the same year, the mounted police were instructed by the controller-general to arrest beggars on suspicion of vagabondage.[6]

Our modern conception of eighteenth-century beggars has been influenced by the artists of that century. They depicted beggars in rags, whose misery was on display to passersby. However, the great majority of the miserable struggled to retain their decency and their membership in civil society, and this struggle of theirs has largely been forgotten. Christian Romon has studied 3,370 Parisian beggars arrested by 99 Châtelet commissioners between 1700 and 1784. A physical description was recorded for each of them at arrest, but only 5 percent were described as being dressed in rags.[7] Yvonne-Elisabeth Broutin, in studying the costumes of those brought to the Rouen workhouse between 1784 and 1789, has noted the numerous English-style overcoats worn by males; this fashionable urban garment had been in circulation for only a few years by 1784 and was just beginning to turn up in secondhand shops. In Rouen, a suspect's lack of a hat or shoes was unusual enough to startle the officials who encountered it.[8]

In Romon's study, 11 percent of the beggars searched by the Châtelet police were actually penniless at the time of arrest, and another 11 percent had just one sou. The remaining 78 percent held amounts that averaged about two livres—not a great deal, but more than the day-wage of a Parisian mason and three times the day-wage of a domestic.[9] This finding implies that the act of begging was a common and accepted response to impoverishment, not a desperate last resort. Gutton's Lyon research showed that in a severe year such as 1771, the percentage of beggars with money in their pockets actually rose as the tide of the economic crisis swept over the respectable poor. Domiciled workers who traveled seasonally often begged along the way in order to bring their small earnings home intact. In Gutton's view, under eighteenth-century conditions "begging constituted an authentic trait in the customs of the poor . . . a quasinormal resource of the modest classes."[10]

At the commanding heights of royal legislation, begging was essentially illegal; in the life of the masses, begging remained an indispensable resource. Between these two realities stood the mounted police. The pattern of actual enforcement of royal laws on mendicancy is a difficult subject; regional variations can be suggested but not yet elucidated. Still, historians have formed two basic interpretations of this enforcement. The first interpretation is that the mounted police sorted through the beggars they apprehended in search of serious criminals and did not regard begging as an offense in itself. The second is that the mounted police were motivated by the bounties periodically offered for arrests, and most often made those arrests for begging which happened to be easiest.

Gutton's work on Lyon supports the first interpretation. Gutton found that in the enforcement of the declaration of 1724 "it is fairly rare to note that a beggar was arrested simply because he begged or fell into the condition of vagabondage." Beggars arrested on suspicion of a second, more serious offense were released if the second offense could not be substantiated. Those beggars arrested for their begging alone were picked up on a few specific and regular patrols, such as the patrol for the highway between Paris and Lyon, or those for the major fairs of the Lyonnais.[11]

This pattern of enforcement may have been particular to the Lyon region in the 1720s and 1730s; Camille Bloch described the situation in the Parisian basin differently, as we shall see below. In any case, the controller-general's and the vice-chancellor's instructions that followed the Royal Council's decree of 1767 urged the police to cast a wider net. From 1767 through 1770, police repression of the traveling poor was apparently vigorous, arbitrary, and mercenary. Olwen Hufton has characterized it this way:

> In 1767 [the government] offered a reward [of three livres] for every beggar arrested . . . The thief and threatening vagrant in small villages were . . . allowed to proceed undisturbed whilst the harmless beggar on the high road, most particularly those labourers who cadged their supper and a night's lodging *en route* to and returning from their seasonal jobs, were apprehended as quick and easy arrests likely to secure a good bonus for the cavalier. When rewards ceased, the numbers arrested fell dramatically as the police lost incentive.[12]

This view of police activity harks back to Camille Bloch, who wrote in 1908 that migrant workers had been the prime victims of mounted police activity in northern France following the declaration of 1724.[13]

However, other social groups also provided easy arrests: invalids, the old, and the very young. These groups were naturally well represented in the hospitals that received entrants arrested either by the mounted police or by their own watchmen. For instance, out of 44 beggars arrested and brought in 1725 to La Charité of St-Etienne in the Lyons intendancy, only 10 were even able-bodied adults: 17 were children and 17 were old or disabled. In the register of entrants for August–December 1724 for the same hospital, there are 28 names, but only 2 of the entrants (both women) were able-bodied adults. The most-represented categories undoubtedly fit best into hospital life: however, they were also the easiest arrests to make.[14]

Still, there is yet another way of viewing the cavalier's basic criterion for making an arrest. Perhaps the very act of traveling, passage itself, was sufficient to throw an individual into an extensive legal pale that shared a long common border with crime, and where numerous actions, begging among them, took on darker significance.

In 1780 a priest of the intendancy of Montpellier protested to the vicar-general of the archbishop of Toulouse about the arrests made by the mounted police: he pleaded for help in seeking the release of "these wretches who are sometimes arrested for having the imprudence to leave a town or a neighboring village without a passport . . . " The priest did not question that those arrested had in fact been begging; he spoke of them as "the poor beggars that are taken for the Montpellier workhouse."[15] However, two recent studies of the workhouse in Rouen suggest that the mounted police arrested strangers on suspicion of begging without the slightest evidence. Marie-Odile Deschamps gives the example of Rose Compiègne, a lacemaker living two kilometers from Dieppe, who was arrested on her way to visit her sick father; she passed through Dieppe in order to buy bread for her father, and also herring that she meant to resell outside the town. She was not caught begging, and she denied any intention of begging. Yvonne-Elisabeth Broutin studied the registers describing 187 persons brought to the Rouen workhouse by the mounted police between June 1784 and July 1789. She found that only 21 were recidivists, while 162 were (supposed) first offenders. What is more, "the persons arrested nearly always denied begging. A great number of records carry the comment 'no other charges' . . . Therefore, one finds . . . an overwhelming majority of persons arrested according to criteria that are difficult to elucidate, since none of these persons were caught in the act, and practically all of them insisted they had not been begging."[16]

Broutin mentions the case of one Guillaume Hamel, who traveled from lower Normandy to the area of Rouen in order to rent a small farm, and was arrested on his return trip. Broutin cites Hamel's letter to the curé of his village—written by himself in an elegant hand, and studded with Latin tags. Hamel understood clearly why he had been arrested: "In returning home I had the misfortune to be arrested by cavaliers of the mounted police, because I had not taken the precaution of providing myself with a passport and certificate."[17]

Broutin rightly finds that this evidence "stimulates us to question what criteria of appearance led the mounted police to suspect a person."[18] But are not these criteria obscured today precisely by the twentieth-century assumption that an individual's outward marks of well-being or poverty were paramount to the observing eyes of eighteenth-century police? The evidence suggests instead that signs of being a stranger to the territory—such as a variant accent, or even an expression of perplexity before a crossroads—may have been more important. The "passport and certificate" that police might arbitrarily require were demanded less as a proof of one's station in life than as a substitute for a local witness who could speak for one's character. For the common people, the testimony of a local witness was the authentic source of identification for official purposes: any document was a makeshift in comparison.

So much for the cavalier's understanding of his work. But how did the higher levels of government and public opinion classify the poor? Their categories seem to have derived from three crude oppositions: between the domiciled poor and the homeless poor; between the "true poor" and the "false poor"; and between the "good poor" and the "bad poor." These three oppositions tended to converge, as we shall see, with the two latter, moral oppositions overlapping the first, material one.

At the time of the 1767 Royal Council decree, when the controller-general Averdy decided to tighten by administrative fiat the repression of begging, his instructions to the intendants distinguished between domiciled and nondomiciled beggars, in order to avoid the overcrowding of prisons and workhouses. As a guideline he proposed that beggars arrested within two leagues of home be warned and released—though he certainly meant that anyone caught begging should be apprehended. He then classified the objects of police action into three distinct groups:

The mounted police should arrest few vagabonds and beggars at a time; perhaps their actions even should be directed more against disabled beggars than against healthy ones, because since the first do not have the ability to work it is more difficult to stop them from begging, while if the healthy beggars see the disabled ones arrested they will be far more frightened . . . But [the mounted police's] principal and most immediate patrols should target these troops of beggars who wander the countryside and force con-tributions from the farmers. Since domiciled beggars are least to be feared . . . perhaps it would even be best for you to await new orders before having them arrested.[19]

Averdy clearly intended the mounted police to arrest beggars who trav-eled in groups and threatened isolated farmers—and also the disabled, those poor for whom work could no longer provide even the illusion of self-sufficiency. The domiciled poor who begged near home were to be, if possible, broken of the practice through example; but as a question of public order they were insignificant. In 1768 the vice-chancellor in-structed the mounted police to arrest poor people found begging within only half a league of their homes, instead of two leagues as before: reports of available capacity in the prisons and workhouses occasioned this new regulation, which proved short-lived. The instruction defined the domiciled beggar as a person who has remained in one place for six months, begs only on occasion, has some visible means of support (prop-erty or a trade), and, perhaps most importantly, "can have himself vouched for on the spot by persons worthy of trust."[20] To have oneself acknowledged—this was the proof of one's membership in society.

The distinction between the domiciled and the traveling poor, founded on the mechanics of public order, mingled with the pseudomor-al distinctions "true poor"/"false poor" and "good poor"/"bad poor." Resident poor were "true poor" in that the causes of their poverty were known to their communities. With their circumstances understood and their conduct monitored, these were also usually "good poor." Home-less, traveling poor might be "false poor"; no local person could testify about them or their condition, so their self-descriptions might be false; in any case, they were out of place, far from their parishes of origin, and this constituted an evasion of public order in the old regime. A widely read treatise on begging expressed the problem as follows in 1779:

If one considers who these importunate and dangerous beggars are who infest our roads, who besiege our towns and country districts, one will see that almost always they are men foreign to the region that they annoy. The poor reduced to begging by true misfortunes hardly ever leave the region of their birth to become wanderers and vagabonds. In this shameful class one ordinarily sees only those men who have entered it through laziness, through libertinage, to evade paternal rule or the authority of the laws, or sometimes even to escape punishment . . . Such is the idea that one may form of this hideous troop to be seen wandering our countryside, made up of men and women united by caprice and libertinage more often than by legitimate ties.[21]

This passage asserts flatly that those who beg outside "the region of their birth" do so out of immorality alone, thus formalizing one of the practical criteria of the mounted police. The same thought can be discerned in a 1770 instruction from Turgot, then intendant of Limousin. He too distinguished "willful begging occasioned by libertinage and love of idleness [from] the true poor, each in the parish where they make their homes."[22]

The domiciled beggar's virtually statutory place in society in the 1780s is well known, but something of begging's strength as an institution can be seen by how much longer it survived, and its moral attribution along with it. Lefebvre in his study of the department of the Nord found the small town of Estaires in 1790 supporting ten or so professional beggars "often from father to son"; 3 beggars and 2 citizens "laborers and beggars" on the list of donors (!) to the 1790 patriotic contribution at St-Rémy-Chaussée; and 4 beggars on the property rolls of Sainghin-en-Weppes in Year X (1801-2).[23] The sixth report of the National Assembly's Committee on Mendicancy in January 1791—the one that dealt specifically with begging as a legal offense—treated the distinction between the domiciled and the homeless poor with the utmost clarity as an anchored social dichotomy that future legislation would have to accept:

The domiciled beggar should be considered as committing an offense against society to which a momentary error of idleness, of sloth, has carried him, but which he was not forced to by necessity, since as a domiciled person he has a right [under the future system] to the aid of the municipality . . . [and] to the voluntary assistance of his fellow-citizens, who, if they know him to be honest and laborious, will not leave him in absolute need. The begging outsider can only be viewed as having committed an offense through necessity, since the assistance of the place where he finds himself does not belong to him by right, no one knows him, and his current condition prejudices people against his love of work and his morals . . . [24]

The committee's understanding of the situation could not be made plainer. The local pauper who begs has, in the eyes of the community, committed only a slip; his or her morality is known to all, and if it is decent the beggar can expect not only the official aid planned by the committee but the informal help of the neighborhood. The stranger who begs has the misfortune of being in the wrong place, where the authorities cannot offer aid (save by arrest and nourishment in prison), and where the citizens will presume the stranger to be immoral on the sole evidence of poverty. The committee recognized this as a prejudice, but the forcible return of beggars to their home parishes was still central to its proposed legislation.

The ideological link between traveling light and behaving evilly remained current into the Directory but was transposed into more republican terms. Alan Forrest has unearthed reports by deputies addressed to the Council of Ancients in Year VIII, in which vagabonds where characterized as messengers interlinking Vendée rebels, refractory priests, and *émigrés*.[25] And as for the acceptance of domiciled beggars, the custom left enough roots that statutory recognition of the beggar was readopted by the Restoration in 1818.[26]

In the Soissonnais of 1789, charity elicited by begging was the fundamental means of poor relief. The measures taken by the clergy and municipal officers worked with begging, not against it, and even Montlinot, the inspector of the workhouse who began by rejecting mendicancy, accepted by 1789 its place in the old-regime order of things. It now remains to concretely examine how Soissonnais authorities thought and operated as they sought to provide subsistence in communities where begging was legitimate, though travel was suspect.

The Grain Census of Ribemont: The Integration of Begging into Municipal Calculations

Our first example is drawn from Ribemont, a village on the left bank of the Oise, in the *élection* and diocese of Laon, and about 15 kilometers northwest of that town. Ribemont was a large village of about 240 households and hardly more than one street.[27] Like most towns of northern France, in May 1789 it was engaged in the painful exercise of the grain census (*recensement*). Municipal officers went from house to house, inspecting and accounting for all private stocks of grain. The accumulated totals gave the municipality an indication of whether the townspeople could survive until the rye harvest in late July, or whether the municipality should enter the institutional market and negotiate an emergency shipment from Laon or Soissons. Of course, the presence of beggars from the villages around Ribemont and beyond was sure to make these calculations more difficult.

The municipal officers chose to include beggars in their overall count; indeed, they set aside a special column of the census for them. Their own final totals showed beggars at 35.8 percent of all persons accounted for (379 out of 1,058). Grain census records are rarely amenable to quantitative analysis, but those of Ribemont in May are unusually well organized.[28] The register is in six pages. The first page is ruled in five columns, titled as follows: (1) "Name"; (2) "Quantity"; (3) "Deficit"; (4) "Surplus"; and (5) "Persons." The recorders visited the 35 households listed on the first page. For each, they noted the amount of grain on hand, how much this amount exceeded or fell below that needed for the household's subsistence until harvest, and the number of people who lived there. But this approach, which regarded each household as an independent unit, rapidly led the recorders into anomalies. Some households were supported by others, which gave rise to tallies like this: "Claude Brancourt—quantity: 0; deficit: 0; surplus: 0; persons: 3." Therefore, the recorders added a column headed "Observations—beggars" beginning on page 2 as a safety valve for ambiguity. To add up grand totals, they integrated column 5 ("Persons") of page 1 with column 6 ("Beggars") of the following pages, perhaps because they felt that their first page of households noted about as many extra dependents as properly domiciled persons. It is clear that they began with the poor and worked their way toward the more prosperous; the last name on the list ("Monsieur Berenger") was a great provider (450 *quartels* of surplus, 100 people in column 6).[29] "Observations—beggars" consequently includes both individuals on the margin of a given household and beggars clustering around larger establishments.

From the grain census it is simple to establish classes of consumers as the Ribemont magistrates perceived and divided them.[30] These classes are shown in Table 3.1.

These figures show two majorities in Ribemont in time of shortage: households with some grain, but in no position to aid others outside their immediate circles ("grain deficit" + "enough grain" = 63.6 percent); and all the households unable to meet their own needs ("no grain" + "grain deficit" = 81.5 percent). For the municipality, preserving order depended on encouraging the cohesion of the majority of small grainholders so that the second majority, that of the hungry, would not form.

The census makers did not apply a consistent rule of thumb for estimating normative consumption until harvest. So much is certain, for the normative consumption per person can be calculated for all 179 households. The lowest figure is 1.1 *quartels*, the highest 9 *quartels*; but

Table 3.1   Consumer Households as Tallied by Ribemont Magistrates

	Where Listed		
	Page 1	Pages 2-6	Total
Households with	*No. (%)*	*No. (%)*	*No. (%)*
No grain	18 (52.9)	42 (29.0)	60 (33.5)
Grain deficit	14 (41.2)	72 (49.6)	86 (48.0)
Enough grain	2 (5.9)	26 (17.9)	28 (15.6)
Surplus	0	5 (3.4)	5 (2.8)

81 { 60 (33.5), 86 (48.0) } pages, grouping: 81 spanning No grain and Grain deficit; 64 spanning Grain deficit and Enough grain.

Source: Grain census record of Ribemont, [May 1789], ADA C938.

these are rare deviations: the great cluster is around 2 to 4 *quartels*. Table 3.2 shows the averages for all the classes of consumers, with the differences between pages 1 and pages 2-6 indicated.

The recorders began with a notion of three *quartels* per person, but after the first 35 houses they were ready to lower their sights. Grasping the situation intuitively, probably counting off for children (who ate less), for assistance from relatives, for all the varieties of informal aid, they sought to impose economies; but they dared not impose them on the trifling margins that the majority of small grainholders enjoyed. So it was the normative consumption of the poorest that decreased the most—by half a *quartel*, compared to a quarter from small grainholders.

If we examine the 15 households with beggars noted in column 6 over pages 2-6, we find that the numbers of beggars varies sharply from one household to the next (Table 3.3). The 15 households listed with "beggars" comprise 10.4 percent of the 144 households on pages 2-6. No household with a surplus was listed without beggars. Three were listed as actually being in deficit with two extra people each, perhaps relatives. Seven of the 15 households had sufficient grain; of these 7, 5 were listed as feeding between 2 and 4 additional people, while the curé's household was listed with 6 and 2 other households with 16. It appears plausible that the houses claiming 2 to 4 people provided the names of those they supported, while those with 6 or 16 gave the officials a rough figure to represent their "beggar load," thus avoiding being classed as surplus holders. The five surplus holders' figures for column 6 (16, 50, 16, 16, 100) clearly pertain to the ancient art of crowd counting.

For the municipal officers of Ribemont, begging was a social fact, and they thought they would be likely to go amiss in their provisioning calculations without careful accounting of this fact. For each donor, they

Table 3.2 Normative Consumption per Person

	Where Listed	
Households with	*Page 1*	*Pages 2–6*
No grain	3.00 quartels	2.44 quartels
Grain deficit	3.26 quartels	2.95 quartels
Enough grain	3.25 quartels	3.04 quartels
Surplus	—	3.47 quartels

Source: Grain census record of Ribemont, [May 1789], ADA C938.

estimated the size of the surrounding cluster of recipients, and integrated these clusters into the overall problem of distribution. Households that supported 2 or 3 other persons went into the same category as those that supported 50 or 100. Though large-scale charity, practiced by the few "rich" in the community, must have been semipublic in nature, the grain census put it on the same terms as the small charity of many others. What counted was begging as a whole: a dimension of economic activity like any other.

Informal Charity in the Laonnais: Begging and Parish Poor Relief

In May 1789, the provincial commission in Soissons pressured the intermediate bureau of Laon to demand a parish-by-parish census of the poor from the curés of the Laonnais. With figures at hand, the commission hoped to persuade Necker to approve the creation of an English-style "poor tax," in which municipalities would collect a contribution from each parishioner for the parish's registered poor. At the least, the commission meant to require each beggar to carry a certificate from the curé of his or her parish; the certificate would state a local limit on the beggar's wanderings which the mounted police would enforce.[31]

The intermediate bureau of Laon received word of the coming questionnaire on May 5; it was to be accompanied by requests to municipalities for their grain censuses. The bureau feared the raising of hopes for assistance and wrote the commission at once "to warn of the dangers that might result—above all if these benevolent intentions are not fulfilled by obtaining a decree from the Council."[32] The commission replied by insisting that the questionnaire be distributed and declaring its certitude of Necker's eventual support. The intermediate bureau began distributing the questionnaire on May 12 and had received almost all of

Table 3.3   Ribemont Households for Which "Beggars" Were Listed

Name	Quantity	Deficit	Surplus	Persons	Beggars; Observations
[Illegible]	12	0	0	3	4
Pierre Dupont	8	4	0	3	2
Quentin Detranchant	24	0	28	6	16
J.-L. Duquenois	36	0	0	7	16
[Illegible]	8	10	0	7	2
Duerot fils	6	0	0	2	2
Louis Clement	12	0	0	4	2
Alex. LeClerc	30	0	0	6	3
M. le curé	20	0	0	2	6
Jos. Degieux	16	4	0	9	2
M. Latour fils	80	0	80	14	50
M. Latour père	25	0	45	4	16
Nicolas Malezieu	18	0	0	6	4
Charles Fouchet père	24	0	80	7	16
M. Berenger	150	0	450	20	100

Source: Grain census records of Ribemont, [May 1789], ADA C938.

the 184 extant replies before the month's end. La Millière (*maître des requêtes* and intendant of finances) quashed the commission's project in a letter of May 20 informing the commission that Necker had already written over its head to Blossac, intendant of Soissons, holding him to the status quo concerning beggars and the police. La Millière added that Blossac had assured Necker in response that the mounted police were at work arresting "those who demand alms with insolence."[33]

It is impossible to know how many curés did not respond to the circular, because the intermediate bureau sent it out with such reluctance that we cannot be sure of its full distribution. However, the subdelegation of Laon (to which the bureau's district corresponded) was equivalent to the diocese of Laon (345 parishes) minus the *doyennés* of Aubenton and Guise (64 parishes). This would give 281 parishes for the subdelegation and thus (always assuming complete delivery) about one hundred unanswered copies.

The curés who received an official questionnaire could only wonder how official it was. It derived its authority from the provincial commission—and from the commission's speculation on future approval from Paris. The Laon intermediate bureau had distributed the questionnaire reluctantly and late. Understandably, the curés answered the circular in a mixed spirit of worry, hope, and calculation. In interpreting their replies, we must seek to exploit both the suggestiveness of their individual comments and, where possible, the quantitative data that the questionnaire gathered. Taken together, the comments and the figures give a remarkably concrete picture of how some curés improvised charity in their parishes.

There are several obstacles to a quantitative approach. Ideally, we would compare the curés' absolute numbers for their parish poor with parish population figures.[34] But this comparison can be validly made in only 16 out of 184 cases.[35] Many curés offered no statistics. Others offered numbers of persons rather than numbers of hearths (*feux*), the old-regime census unit. The contemporary administrator's rule of thumb when faced with this problem was to divide the stated number of persons by four. We could do the same. However, those curés who gave figures frequently gave two numbers: one of households, one of old and ill people. We know from the lists of those curés who chose to give names that they entered some poor individuals twice: once in the old-and-ill category, and once as members of poor households. We must allow the possibility that some curés who gave figures followed the same practice.

However, all 184 letters can be studied quantitatively to learn how curés responded to the questionnaire: whether they answered it, hedged on it, refused it, or forwarded it to the officers of their municipality (Figure 3.1).

The majority of curés who responded cooperated fully with the questionnaire. Even though nearly two-fifths of the curés withheld full cooperation, the curés were more helpful than the municipal officers. Half of the 24 responding municipalities refused all or part of their cooperation. These findings would suggest that local authorities, municipal and clerical, were reluctant to collaborate in a scheme going beyond their own locality.

Curés who mistrusted the questionnaire tended to give it a public airing, the results of which reinforced their first impression. "I read aloud the letter you have honored me with," wrote the curé of Aippe. "I showed it to M. the baron and the community, who pointed out the word 'tax' in the second article of your letter and who required me to ask you: whether the intermediate assembly would pay the costs of this fine charity to the poor; or would it be at the community's expense?"[36] He insisted on his willingness to answer the questionnaire after details were provided—but the commission's scheme would fall through before he would have to make his word good.

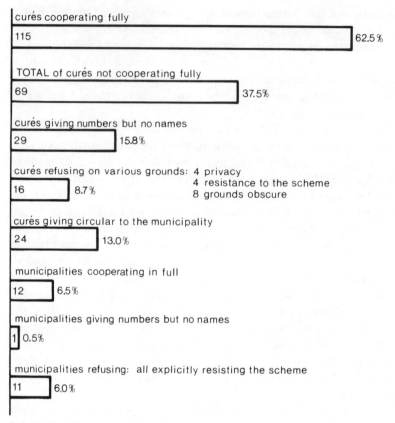

Figure 3.1. Types of questionnaire responses received from the curés of the Laonnais, May 1789. (Source: ADA C 937-940)

There is an implicit consensus running through the 184 letters that some analysis, however rough, had to be made of parish conditions if charity were to be administered. This analysis often meant picking out the poorest families in an already poor village. Those curés who described their processes of selection showed a notable unity as to method. They spoke of dividing their parishioners into three classes:

1. Those who could give;

2. Those who needed to receive; and

3. Those who must not be asked to give lest they insist on receiving.

Those curés who worried about their parishes expressed their concern in language like that of the curé of Brie-Fourdrain, who wrote: "Made up of about four to five hundred communicants, of which two or three are begging . . . it happens that a third of my parishioners are in misery, and I dare say a misery greater than the beggars suffer; the other two [thirds] can manage without assistance, and in this second class I see no more than twenty people who could give."[37] The curé of Folembray explained why he had referred the questionnaire to the municipality: "This list [of the poor] necessarily requires that one distinguish the parishioners beforehand into three classes: first, those who will be aided, second, those who will aid, and third, those who without being poor enough to be aided, are not well enough off to aid the others. Well, this discussion is so delicate that it seems more appropriate for my ministry not to enter into it."[38] At least these matters were often too delicate to discuss in public.

It was essential that the curés' analyses remain private in order to avoid accusations of favoritism. If the analysis were to be made publicly, it would be better done by the town's secular authorities, who were qualified to handle the resulting dissension. "It would be very difficult to give an exact list of the needy, because the greatest number [here] are all part of the same class, and it would have to include more than half the inhabitants, otherwise one would hear nothing but complaints and murmuring from those who are not registered, especially since they would be obliged to provide for the mass of poor, though poor themselves," wrote Chalonnier, the curé of Yviers.[39]

Curés also expressed concern that the cultivators of the land rather than its owners were bearing the expenses of charity. The curé of Etreau-Treaupont and Gergny advocated a fourfold division of all those not so poor as to require charity. His categories were the rich, the well-off, those who had their provision and were naturally generous, and those who could not afford to give. However, he insisted that "no one is unaware that it is the richest who usually refuses the most to contribute to public charges."[40] The curé of Fay-le-Noyez-sur-Fontaine observed, "It would be more to the point to ask landed proprietors than to extract it from the farmers, since they are overwhelmed with beggars from morning till evening."[41] "A tax for poor relief should in all justice be a charge on rich proprietors," echoed the municipal officers of Mouy.[42]

Only 3 of the 184 replies mentioned a local bureau of charity, and these replies were all written by unusually civic-minded and systematic curés. Two of these, Henry of Doeuillet and Joffet of Vervins, cooperated fully with the questionnaire. Henry of Doeuillet put forward a plan for combining one-third of his church's tithe with the returns from the annual auction of grazing rights on the communal land, thus providing the church treasury with an income of 340 livres per year. A third, anonymous curé turned the questions over to the municipality of La Fère, which refused to answer them until they were told who would pay for the reforms in view. Joffet of Vervins and the unsigned curé of La Fère were both town priests who operated a donation system in which charitable ladies solicited contributions. Both complained that the system could not sustain the pressure of the high price of grain and the increasing number of poor.[43]

Eight replies mentioned a nearby abbey, either favorably or unfavorably, as an element in the community's resources. Two curés complained, but only one was explicit: "M. the *religieux* of St-Denis in [Ile-de-] France [whose border was not far from Craonne] who have all the tithe and a very fine farm which must yield them nearly five thousand livres every year do not make any great efforts at charity," wrote Lefevre, the curé of Concevreux.[44] Whether or not the abbot was in residence was not clearly reflected by a difference in generosity. Managers on the spot often included charity in their general good husbandry, insofar as it eased relations with the community that provided a pool of seasonal labor.[45] Maules of Chambry was suspicious of abbeys on the principle that "where there are many poor there must be many rich," but was not more specific.[46] The other six curés had nothing but praise for the abbey in their vicinity. The curés in the region around Craonne agreed in worrying that a poor tax would spell the end of the abbeys' contributions; one municipality even urged the provincial commission to break up the clusters of poor that charitable abbeys attracted:

> to stop the poor strangers attracted from all the neighboring villages at least four leagues round by the continual alms that they receive from the abbeys of Cuissy and Vauclair, without distinction between the needy and the others, who form crowds by their comings and goings and absorb more than double what would be sufficient to assist those of the parish. [The municipal officers] therefore demand . . . that the others be sent back each to their own parish . . . so that only the truly needy will be there.[47]

In their eyes the poor of their own parish were the "true poor" and outside poor were the "false poor."

Near the manufacturing town of St-Gobain and the forest village of St-Nicolas-au-Bois, abbeys gave charity to local suppliants whom the curé had furnished with tickets. A Benedictine at the abbey of St-Nicolas-au-Bois wrote, "The abbey refuses neither bread, nor wine, nor money, nor medicine to those who are provided with a ticket from the curé." In fact, the curé had referred the questionnaire to the abbey.[48] Complaints about the abbeys faulted their indiscriminate distributions, yet, since the parish framework for distribution was the only one recognized by either curés or municipal officers, their "reforms" would have locked each abbey's resources in to the sole needs of whichever parish could claim them.

In the absence of an organized bureau of charity or a local abbey, curés tended to gather charitable resources by private arrangement with a very few notables. There were sound social reasons for this method. For one thing, it reconciled the egalitarianism of the curé with the elitism of the notables. A great many of these curés would have concurred with the inimitable phrase of Maules of Chambry, "Where there are many poor there must be many rich."[49] On the other side, charity offered the wealthy an ethical way to display their wealth.

Montlinot, the inspector of the Soissons workhouse (to whose works we shall turn below), described the phenomenon well: "There are men, more generous than enlightened, who assemble at their door at fixed hours, with an ostentation that is at least indiscreet, a certain quantity of poor."[50] For charity to be a modest vehicle of personal display, it had to meet certain requirements. It had to be personal; it had to be local. Charity needed the religious context that the curés' involvement reinforced, and it had to be absolutely voluntary: a pious, generous gesture. The provincial commission, however, was a secular body: response to it, instead of to the poor in person, carried the odium of fulfilling a legal requirement—the very opposite of *noblesse* (or *richesse*) *oblige*.

Added to these social and psychological advantages was the lower cost of feeding the poor by improvised means. If a donor had an oven, the baker could be bypassed. As the syndic Hubert had pointed out to the curé of Etreau-Treaupont: "To buy bread from the baker is to buy bread at the highest price and to furnish the indigent with a bread that is less substantial . . . he [Hubert] consequently offers . . . to purchase grain in concert with the principal inhabitants, to have the bread rolled and baked in his own house, to furnish gratis the wood needed for the oven."[51] The notables who could hit upon arrangements of this nature deserved certain privileges, such as a voice in answering the commission's questionnaire. Lerdun, the curé of Beaurieux, felt that "the manner in which persons are requested in my parish to relieve the unfortunate, which I have proposed in diverse circumstances to the best-off persons, imposes on me a kind of obligation not to put them under contribution unless they have been notified in advance."[52]

These improvisations between curé and notables corresponded, however badly, to the ideal of each parish feeding its own poor; but this approximation broke down frequently in practice. If the proprietors of rural land resided in town, they exercised their generosity there, where they could be seen doing it. On the underside of society, in bad years beggars had to cover wider areas in order to eat, straying farther from their own parishes, where improvisation had already broken down, entering new regions, imposing themselves upon notables who had no claim on them, making largesse impersonal.[53] Thomas, the curé of Charme, reported the first dilemma: "In Charme . . . there is only one tenant, whose farm is no more than two *charrues* [40 hectares]; the rest of the land, small as it is, is leased to farmers in the outskirts of La Fère, who offer nothing to the unfortunates of the parish."[54] He pleaded against a poor tax, yet submitted a complete census of his poor. Curés who had resources in their notables often feared that these big donors would be wiped out by the strain of beggars from 'outside'—and the more complete and paternal charity was, the more it attracted strangers. Godefroy, the curé of Richecourt, reported: "I have no poor person in my two little parishes of Richecourt and Chevresis-les-Dames, they consist only of two châteaux, three farms, a mill, and several houses for servants, nonetheless we are overwhelmed with poor strangers, it costs me alone about 30 sous . . . per day, and a great deal of bread per farm . . ."[55] In truth, the parish as a geographic unit was no longer dominant in the economic life of either the rich or the poor. But psychologically it was very real. It remained an entity that organized people's understanding of their location. Consequently, the parish was the only geographical unit around which either curés or secular administrators might devise some "system" of charity.

In the course of improvising charity, curés had to face the fact that mendicancy sustained some of the parishioners whose welfare most worried them. To say that they fully accepted mendicancy would be an overstatement, but they implicitly relied upon it in numerous situations simply as a means of distribution. And if something like the questionnaire forced them to, they would virtually declare their reliance upon mendicancy. Their letters did not amount to an overt defense of begging.[56] But in the world of the parish, begging presented some advantages, and the ones the curés cited most frequently are summarized in the seven points that follow:

1. *People too young, too old, or too disabled to work could still beg to contribute to their households.* Seldom did a curé identify a beggar by name in these letters—an act that could make one of his parishioners an object for the mounted police. However, the curé of Neuville in his census of the parish poor placed crosses next to the names of those who begged: four boys between 10 and 14 years of age, and one 12-year-old girl.[57]

Because they begged for their fathers, they were blameless. Gobert of Clacy recommended: "If his work does not suffice because he has several children not yet old enough to work, let him send out those among them who can go ask for a few pieces of bread in his neighborhood and round about . . . the one father of a family marked on my list, with a wife and seven children, has survived up to now—I don't say without trouble— sending no more than one of his children out to beg and only in the parish and at six or seven houses."[58] Thus begging could have a redeem- ing context that gave it a bit of the value of work itself.

2. *Parishioners preferred to feed beggars who were fellow parishioners. This preference was a force for parish charity.* Curés conceived of "their" beggars as holding places that would otherwise be filled by beggars from out- side. Berthand of Rozoy-sur-Serre observed that "if [the project of the commission] does not take place in the province of Champagne at the same time, the wise dispositions of Soissons will be of little use to us because we are overwhelmed by the poor of the Reims diocese . . . "[59] Godard of Brissi passed on the decision of his municipality: "Here is their position . . . The prosperous inhabitants will take up a collection to cover the deficit [of 30 to 40 livres of revenue for the poor], always assuming that mendicancy does not bring to their doors the poor or vagabonds of other villages, and it is only in this case that we will sub- mit . . . to the arrangements."[60] To the extent that some parishioners gave and others received, the ideal of each parish taking care of its own was maintained. Whether or not this receiving took the form of mendi- cancy was a secondary issue.

3. *If parish poor begged outside the parish, they were "self-supporting"— from the viewpoint not only of their own households, but of the entire commun- ity.* No curé would ever have uttered the preceding statement, yet some came close enough. Hezette of Bouffiguereux agreed to take on "a poor woman rather advanced in age" if, as the result of the commission's actions, "assistance is refused her elsewhere."[61] As the outspoken Gobert put it: "It is a . . . maxim here with us that the public good is preferable to that of the individual. For that matter, no one here seeks to do harm to individuals, since what is demanded for the needy is to leave them the way free, the way of begging that has served them up to now."[62]

4. *If inter-parish begging were suppressed, intraparish begging alone might solve the curé's problem.* Flamant, the curé of Cevry, explicitly pro- posed it: "I [know] that it would be better to permit the poor of each parish to beg in their parish and not elsewhere, so that begging from village to village would be entirely and absolutely destroyed."[63] Dugnet of Parfondeval estimated that for his listed poor (three households and

two invalids): "Six hundred livres would be sufficient to help them live . . . Above all if one left them the freedom to beg over the extent of the parish. But if they were the only ones who had the right to beg in the village, they would not require other assistance; they would have it in abundance."[64] Beggary (regarded as a kind of "system") had already opened so many doors that year that if the "poor strangers" could be kept out of them the parish poor would be sustained.

5. *Alms are alms, whether given via the palm, the priest, or the poor tax.* As discussed above, for the richer donors, giving alms to beggars could be an act in which selfish and unselfish pleasures were exquisitely mixed. The curé of Gany and Pargan passed on the word that "the municipal officers whom it was my duty to consult claim[ed] that a new tax . . . would unsettle people's minds, arrest the course of charities, and do more harm than good; one likes better to give alms of one's own free will than to be forced to it . . ."[65] Clearly, charity remained alms, whatever form it took. Chaffaux of Boury spoke of nourishing the poor "with all the more pleasure because we know to whom we give . . ."[66] According to Gobert, the curé who sought contributions for the poor begged no less than the poor themselves: "As to the needy who are kept at home by their great age . . . It is for their pastors to procure them their needs, if these are unmet . . . or to beg for them."[67] Giving was not seen as an obligation and was resented if it was made into one. Consequently, an organization might rationalize charity but might also simply end it.

6. *Feeding beggars was cheaper (if less decorous) than feeding the poor.* We have already heard the curé of Etreau-Treaupont's discussion with the syndic about eliminating the baker as a middleman. In some parishes this arrangement could not be made formally, but in the informal exchange between beggar and donor it took place anyhow, with the corresponding economies made. Noël, the curé of Dizy, made this analysis:

> It appears to me that this tax will notably harm the class that gives alms and that which is in need of receiving them.
>
> In my parish there are 40 poor at 5 sous each per day . . . 300 livres per month to divide among 30 houses, which (one carrying the other) would pay 10 livres per month.
>
> With bread at 3 sous per pound, each poor person would receive only seven quarter-pounds of bread of the worst quality per day, while presently they receive at least two pounds of the best quality, which does not cost even 4 sous per two pounds to those who give . . .
>
> Among the begging strangers, there are some who are not in need, and for sufficient reason one gives to them rather than refusing, and in giving

to them it still costs less than the tax of 5 sous for each poor person . . . Everything considered, living in the country . . . I think that it is appropriate to let alms and begging go as they will, the end does not look far off.[68]

7. To suppress beggary energetically in the conditions of May 1789 was an invitation to revolt. Throughout the letters runs the conviction that wiping out mendicancy was impossible. This view was expressed sometimes with regret, sometimes with horror at the very idea of the attempt. Chalonnier, the curé of Yviers, wrote, "Our municipality charges me with informing you . . . that forbidding the poor to go beg their bread, at this critical moment, would deprive them of a very great resource . . . "[69] The municipal officers of Mouy were more definite: "If you knew as we do the degree of fermentation presently in the minds of these unfortunates, you would judge that the remedy would be worse than the disease, and that to desire at this moment to strip these wretches of the liberty that they have had up to now of asking for relief in the surrounding district would determine them on a general revolt . . . "[70] Begging was an institution that, in times of scarcity, contributed to the maintenance, rather than the disruption, of public order. It was an indispensable part of practical class relations in the countryside.

The Ideas of Leclerc de Montlinot

The workhouse of Soissons—the institution that represented the royal government's effort to combat mendicancy—was headed by Leclerc de Montlinot. Originally a canon of St-Pierre in Lille, he became a bookseller and a journalist in Paris and was sent to Soissons by a *lettre de cachet* after 1773. Appointed by Necker in 1778 to his post as inspector of the workhouse, he became what Alan Forrest has recently called him: "a well-known advocate of Enlightened reform and the author of some of the most eminent tracts on the whole subject of charity to be published in the last years of the Ancien Régime."[71]

However, the evolution of Montlinot's thinking over his years of administering the workhouse deserves scrutiny because of its remarkable reversal: from fierce opposition of, to frank apology for, begging as a social institution.

In 1779 Montlinot won the essay prize of the royal society of agriculture of Soissons with his answer to the query "What are the means for destroying mendicancy . . . ?" His essay breathes rationalism and the work ethic from every page.[72] In the scheme proposed, each beggar would be arrested and interrogated. If a native, he would be imprisoned and kept on bread and water while the director of the prison sought work for him. If he knew no trade, he would be kept in prison until he chose one and then frugally supported during a short apprenticeship. The poor mainly needed discipline and regimentation. "Idleness is the gangrene of the soul; one must hardily put to it the iron and the fire . . . Those who have seen the rooms of soldiers in garrison know what order and economy can do on a fixed budget." In addition, a constant surveillance of the poor would be organized: in each neighborhood a "respectable bourgeois," the poor inspector, would have two "visitors" drawn from the working class for his eyes and ears; inspectors-general chosen from the "prosperous class" would oversee districts of five or six neighborhoods each. The role of the priest in this system would be minimal: "Parish curés will not be charged in any way with the distribution of alms . . . their function is to solicit the rich on behalf of the unfortunate. Our divine Master made alms a principle, but he never gave them."[73]

This fantasy of rigor melted slowly in the heat of administrative experience. Rigor led Montlinot to attempt the compilation of statistics, and the figures on his charges led him to some bald truths. From 854 residents of both sexes in 1786, he counted 256 with some specific trade, but 294 "day-laborers without places or resources."[74] He perceived the role of land concentration in forming the wandering population, and began to suggest that they be offered uncleared land in France or even in Africa. At the same time, his opinion of the energy and character of the hardened vagabond rose; he found they made the best "trusties" for rooms of 15 to 20 inmates: "The provosts were almost always chosen [he wrote in 1786] from the class of vagabonds, who had height and a few years of [army] service . . . it takes nerve to have an order executed, and experience of subjection to orders to know how to obey."[75]

By 1789 Montlinot had fully rejected laziness as a cause of mendicancy. "One can be surprised . . . that these [writers] nearly always conjoin the words of laziness and begging . . . Professional vagabonds . . . lead an active life: it takes planning to avoid the mounted police, energy to make forced marches, and audacity to travel at night amongst a thousand dangers . . . " Montlinot now saw in these "professionals" the objects of future transportation who would form the advance guard of French colonization in Africa. As for beggars over 50 years of age, he described them frankly as the shells of extracted surplus labor:

The trades, agriculture not excepted, devour in less than 30 years the living machines they commandeer . . . no state . . . should claim to be able to destroy this type of mendicancy, always self-renewing, which has its root in the great institutions of society . . . Society consumes the poor, therefore, like a commodity [*denrée*] . . . If the remedy was not inherent in the evil itself, if nineteen-twentieths of people without property did not die before their time, the weight of these wretches could not be borne by the administration . . .

For this structural cause of mendicancy Montlinot saw no remedy. Beggary itself he was now prepared to accept as an institution; further, he dismissed the rationalizing approach altogether, in favor of the sentiment of compassion—the one force for amelioration that society could afford. "Mendicancy acquired through labor can only be administered by universal commiseration . . . it alone, ever active, seizes upon the objects before its eyes; it feeds itself on tears and melancholy . . . the heart opens and drinks long drafts of this sweet benevolence familiar to sensitive souls." Thus beggary was no crime unless it disturbed the peace, and the beggar "does not trouble public order except when, in the country, he disquiets the cultivator who does not owe him hospitality." However, the beggar was owed assistance by the farmers of his own district.[76]

Eight years of administering the workhouse had brought Montlinot far. His original determination to fight begging by organizing the poor's existence had evolved into a belief that begging was an indispensable condition of society's supply of labor.

We close this chapter with the spectacle of the inspector of the royal workhouse approving openly of begging itself, and of the informal system of local charity in which it played a fundamental role.

This chapter's emphasis on local charity should not be misunderstood as seeking to evoke any nostalgia for paternalism. Nor is any suggestion meant that charity was effective; the unceasing movement of displaced countryfolk across France during this period testifies to its impotence. However, it is asserted that this informal system had a profound ideological import, and that while it accomplished little in the way of actual social solidarity it remained an object of belief and "common sense" for rulers and ruled alike.

Figure 3.2 suggests a schema for the informal system of charity described in the preceding pages.

The schema shown in Figure 3.2 centers on the village's municipality and its curé. On roughly the same social plane were the municipalities of

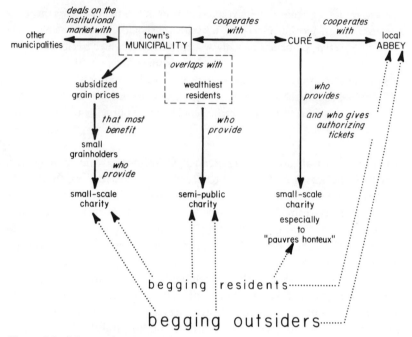

Figure 3.2. Schema of parish charity.

other towns, as well as the nearest abbey—included here not because an abbey was close by in the majority of cases, or because such an abbey could be assumed to be charitable, but because of the presence of an abbey fitted into the ideological construct by which contemporaries represented their society to themselves as a humane and Christian one. The town's wealthy residents, often themselves composing the municipality, provided backing for its dealings on the institutional market; in negotiating with its counterparts, the municipality managed to bring home grain that could be sold at a subsidized price. This price was often not particularly low, even in the context of a shortage, but it did represent a shield against unabated future increases behind which middling artisans and peasants could provision themselves and their intimates. They were thus kept from fusion with the truly poor, their neighbors and social inferiors. Both the small grainholders and the best-off residents gave alms to beggars, though on very different scales.

Like the municipality, the curé also stood at the center of a nexus of relations. He provided a small amount of charity himself, especially to the "embarrassed poor" (*pauvres honteux*), those who could not or would not beg and were judged morally deserving. He provided information on his parishioners to the municipality; and given the presence of a local abbey, he often supplied parishioners with tickets that entitled them to the abbey's alms. In the background of this intensely local system of charity stood the outsiders, who (in the view of the local authorities) sought to mingle with the local poor in each of their niches, to catch with them the runoff of this or that rivulet of assistance.

The ultimate distinction in the ideology of this system was between those poor known to the community and those who were strangers. For the poor who were known, begging was seen as fundamentally legitimate, a right that was justified by their labor, a form of distribution that kept them in personal relations of dependence and that (like many of the practices described in chapter 1) played its part in keeping their labor within the community. For the poor who were unknown, begging had no relationship to labor that the community could validate; they were perceived as "out of place." But this perception by the community did not focus on the external poor alone; rather, the perception included the external poor in a much wider category: "outsiders." As we have seen, "outsiders," even those who drew the attention of the police, were quite varied socially. Which people were designated outsiders depended on the designators' locations, perspectives, and points of view. For this reason, the fear of "outsiders" was eminently ideological, in the classic sense of masking social classes from consciousness.

PART II

Attitudes toward News

FOUR 𝕖 *THE COURSE OF*
THE GREAT FEAR IN
THE SOISSONNAIS

On July 27–28, 1789, the Soissons intendancy was rocked by the contagious panic of the Great Fear. Nationally, the Great Fear had at least seven points of origin; two of these were in the Soissons intendancy. One panic began on the plain of Béthisy, between the Oise and the town of Crépy-en-Valois (Figure 4.1). From Béthisy the Fear spread west to Soissons and then south to Château-Thierry; towns along the Oise relayed the panic southwest to the Seine; and from Compiègne the Fear traveled north toward Guise, fading away as it approached the Cambrésis. Another panic started in Estrées-St-Denis and moved east to Clermont and the Beauvaisis, then north to cover western Picardy and part of Artois.

While we cannot determine the exact circumstances in which the Soissonnais's two original panics were born, the geography of each is clear. Each panic arose in a place where forests and arable land lay side by side in sharp contrast. The original panics engendered strong, spontaneous rural alarms that soon washed into the closest towns. In the towns, the Great Fear was converted into the different "currencies" of urban society: the interchange among social groups regarding public order; the interchange between town and country; and the interchange among towns.

In all three of these urban interchanges, the crucial factor was the militia. Who would compose it, and how would it be led? How would it combine—or would it?—with garrisoned troops and mounted police? Was it safest to keep it in town, or to send it out to search the countryside? Should it go to assist other towns, and if so, which ones? All these

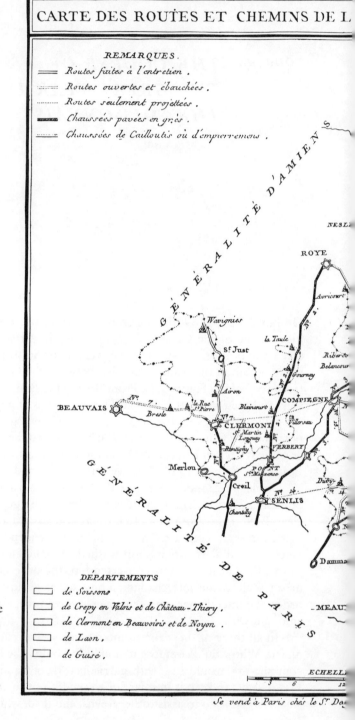

Figure 4.1. The roads of the Soissons intendancy in 1788. (From R. Hennequin, *La formation du département de l'Aisne en 1790* [Soissons: Société académique de Laon, 1911], p. 38)

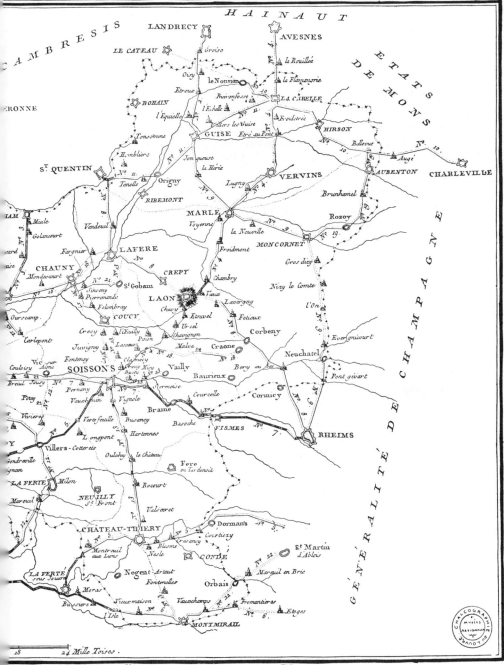

Graveur de M.ʳ le Comte d'Artois, rue S.ᵗ Louis aux marais. N.° 77.

83

questions had to be resolved on the spot by the authorities, often under urgent pressure from townspeople and rural neighbors.

Towns' responses were varied and do not fall into a ready typology. Towns received the Fear's rumor at different levels of intensity; their municipal officers showed differing degrees of resource; and in some towns new or renovated militias were already on an active footing. Broadly though, on the morning after the Great Fear, the towns of the Soissonnais were facing the future with one of three sorts of community organization. Some of them had passed through the panic without creating any new institutions—neither a militia nor a permanent committee. Others had created something new, but in a fashion closely controlled by the existing authorities, often through cooperation between local nobles and the upper bourgeoisie. Still other towns now had new, unpedigreed institutions that were sure to seek identities for themselves in the weeks to come, and were likely to find them in the Revolution.

Some towns did not sit neatly in any of these categories, and often it is their experiences that tell us most: hence the depth of detail in what follows.

The Original Panic at Béthisy

The panic that sparked most of the Great Fear's activity in the Soissonnais began on the plain of Béthisy, at the southern edge of the forest of Compiègne. The precise event or perception that gave rise to the rumor of brigands cannot be known for certain, but three stories of such an event have come down to us—each a reasonable explanation in itself, and each distinct from the other two.

According to the chevalier Ferrand, a retired infantry captain who directed the defense of Beaulieu-les-Fontaines (between Roye and Noyon), the lieutenant of mounted police at Roye dispatched couriers to gather information after the Great Fear had run its course and no brigands had appeared. Two possible causes of the rumor had been garnered:

> . . . he had learned that a troop of poachers hunting in the forest of Compiègne had revolted against the royal gamekeepers, that in the same district a farmer who had been evicted by another had avenged himself by cutting the green grain on two *journeaux* of land.
>
> [These causes had aroused the multitude] in the belief that there were ill-intentioned people sent out to ravage the whole standing harvest of the province and then put everything to fire and sword.[1]

A third cause is known to us through the investigations of the lieutenant of mounted police for Senlis. Receiving word of brigands at Pont-Ste-Maxence, he rode toward that town and learned on the way that "a quarrel between peasants returning from the fête at Rivecourt and some poachers had misled the neighboring inhabitants and made them believe these individuals had the intention of destroying their harvests."[2] Though all three stories are based on hearsay, each is inherently plausible. Confrontations between poachers and guards were frequent; severe reprisals by evicted farmers against those who breached custom and took up lost leases were a normal feature of rural life.[3] Peasants returning from Rivecourt might well have taken the ferry at Verberie to cross to the left bank of the Oise in the evening, which would have placed them in the southwest corner of the Compiègne forest; and there they might have encountered poachers in semidarkness, with unpredictable results.[4] However, there are no grounds for choosing any one story over the other two; nor can we conflate the stories on the mere assumption that they must have had a sole source.[5] The precise origin of the panic in one social incident cannot be finally determined; but the geography of the terrain where the Fear originated is well known to us.

The villages of St-Pierre-de-Béthisy and St-Martin-de-Béthisy are within eyeshot—one kilometer—of the southern fringe of the forest of Compiègne (Figure 4.2). This fringe represents both an agricultural and a geological boundary: the northern edge of the Valois's alluvial plateau. Beyond this limit, grain cultivation not only ceases but is no longer possible. The forest soil is sandy and argillaceous, and to live on it or from it required a way of life distinct from that practiced only a short walk away.[6] In social terms, the forest of Compiègne was a royal preserve, zealously guarded by the corps of the Maîtrise of Streams and Forests. To the landless peasant or impoverished artisan, the forest was a cornucopia attainable only with risk—a seemingly inexhaustible source of game and forage, of fuel to be burnt or sold. The proof of the forest's attractive power can be seen in the explosion of its popular use from August 1789 onward. Gaspard Escuyer, a local historian and a resident of Compiègne in 1789, recalled that time 30 years later: "That portion of the people . . . abandoned itself to an immoderate joy at the sole hope of benefits [from the Revolution] . . . Already this beautiful forest . . . was open to daily incursions and to a sort of brigandage; already people went there in crowds and troops that overawed the guards, and each person indiscriminately cut what suited them."[7] In mid-October, Versailles dispatched an army regiment solely to protect the forest; on November 23 the sharp complaints of the Maîtrise prompted the Compiègne

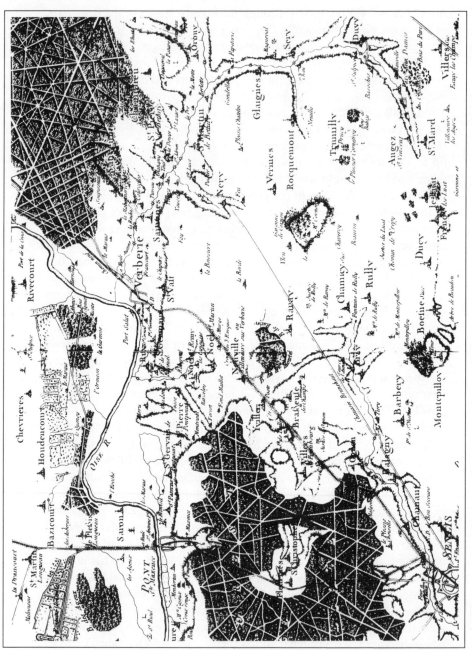

Figure 4.2. The northern Valois. The Compiègne forest is in the northeast corner, the Halatte forest in the southwest. (Detail of

municipality to send its militia to police the forest; the Maîtrise complained again on December 15 and 28; and on January 13, 1790, a skirmish took place involving troops, militia, mounted police, and the inhabitants of villages near Compiègne who were hunting in large groups.[8]

Though we cannot know the actual incident that precipitated the Great Fear in the Soissonnais, we can distinguish the geographic point of tension that brought it forth. To live on the plain of Béthisy was to live with an acute contrast between arable land and woods, each of which meant a different way of survival for the poor. The night of July 26–27, 1789, came not only at the worst phase of the food shortage that had so far dominated the year (no less than had political events) but also at a peak of anticipation for the rye harvest that would commence in a week's time or less. In space, people felt the tension between surviving sociably in the world of cultivation, or surviving outside the pale through forage; in time, they felt the tension between a terribly present hunger, and the promise of an abundance to which one could virtually count the hours.

The Great Fear arrived in the town of Crépy-en-Valois at 8:30 on the morning of July 27, carried from the parish of St-Martin-de-Béthisy, eight kilometers away (and perhaps from several other parishes as well). Here the Fear found its first urban relay—and Crépy proved to be a potent one. Unusually for the Soissonnais, the town had already organized a militia on July 22, only five days earlier. The communal archives cite "incursions of the ill-intentioned and brigands, the example of the capital and of surrounding towns" as major reasons for forming a militia.[9] The strains Crépy had undergone in the preceding weeks suggest additional causes. In late June the Crépy market had been unable to withstand both local and Parisian pressures and had been in severe distress.[10] Crépy's own mounted police brigade had taken unauthorized measures to interdict grain transports heading for the Ourcq canal and Paris. By mid-July the situation had eased, but not without severe searches of local farmers and the expropriation of grain pre-sold to Parisian dealers.[11] Finally, no one in Crépy could have been unaware of the comte de Puysegur's efforts to concentrate troops in a tight ring around Paris: the Saintonge infantry regiment, expected to billet in Crépy on July 11, arrived and then marched south the same day to Dammartin; the Dauphin infantry, expected on the fourteenth, bypassed Crépy in its haste to make for Dammartin also.[12] Extreme tension over provisions and an awareness of events in Paris had already led the municipality of Crépy to arm some trusted residents.

The surest, through sparsest, source for the Fear in Crépy is the brief comment in the minutes of municipal deliberations:

On Monday, July 27, on the word given us by the municipality of St-Martin-de-Béthisy as well as various individuals from the adjoining country, that bands of brigands are spreading through the countryside to cut the green grain, we have believed it necessary to take up arms on the spot and form a permanent committee at the town hall, in order to establish the necessary order for the course of action that must be followed; in consequence we have named to form the said committee M. le Parquier, president; MM. Boitel and Mahieu, *religieux*; MM. Pambry, Magnier, Pommeret, De Varu, Lefebvre, Darey, town magistrates; and Laurens, mayor.[13]

From this we know that the Fear reached Crépy through a municipal channel and through various informal ones. The content of the rumor Crépy heard matched that of the rumor most frequently reported throughout France, for which the Great Fear is still famous. The municipality responded by arming the militia with the weapons available (on July 22 it had already deplored the lack of arms and had sent a representative to the duc de Gesvres, military governor of the province).[14] It also took the shrewd step of forming a permanent committee to its own liking—including two canon priests and a number of its own magistrates. Since the municipal officers of Crépy were appointed by the duc d'Orléans as a privilege of his apanage,[15] they were likely to face demands from merchants and artisans for a permanent committee that would include delegates to the bailliage assembly for the Estates-General. The best way to head off such demands was to rapidly form a permanent committee that would ratify the municipal officers' decisions.

Dambry, member of the Crépy committee, wrote a letter on the day after the Fear that was printed in the July 30 *Journal de Paris*:

Messieurs,

Yesterday, the twenty-seventh of this month, at half past eight, the frightful report that a countless multitude of brigands were cutting the green grain on the fields of Valois, between Verberie and Crépy, spread here and seemed to be confirmed by the letters of several municipal syndics. This unheard-of villainy—of which . . . all were more apprehensive than persuaded—caused a troop of six thousand armed men to assemble in Verberie in a few hours, composed of citizen militias and of calvary detachments in garrison in the towns of Pont, Compiègne, Senlis, and Crépy.

Happily this was only a false alarm that owed its cause to the quarrel of a dozen peasants who, squabbling in the middle of a grainfield, had so frightened the farm laborers that they had the tocsin rung in all the parishes around, exciting by their despair so great a terror that the unhappy peasants deserted their cottages and came from everywhere to take refuge in the neighboring towns.[16]

Henri Dinet is correct to advise caution in using this evidence: he points out that "the newspaper's editor probably 'worked up' the content of the message."[17] Nonetheless, certain confirmations can be noted. The content of the rumor—brigands attacking standing crops—is affirmed again. The scene of the rumor is "between Verberie et Crépy"—an axis that runs quite parallel to the southern edge of the Compiègne forest. Most interesting is the information that militias and mounted police brigades converged on Verberie. While the number of "six thousand armed men" need not be taken seriously, the directions of activity are significant. From Crépy to Verberie, the militia skirted the Compiègne forest; from Compiègne to Verberie it did the same, except that the armed citizens moved between the western edge of that forest and the left bank of the Oise. The path from Pont to Verberie ran along the left bank also, and someone traveling to Verberie would have seen the northern edge of the Halatte forest to the right. As one proceeded from Senlis to Verberie, the eastern fringe of the Halatte would have been on the left, the expanse of the Valois plateau to the right. Of course, sharp detours into the center of the plain may well have been taken. However, each of the four paths suggested by the letter follows a dividing line between forest and arable land which was also a social division between the world of cultivation and the world of foraging, hunting, and smuggling.

On July 29, the permanent committee of Crépy wrote its Parisian counterpart, responding to the news that an anonymous placard had been posted at the Palais-Royal which read: "The mayor of Crépy-en-Valois proposed that the commune wear the [revolutionary] cockade; one St-Georges, recently ennobled, opposed it, and the wearing of it is forbidden. We denounce the authors of this crime of treason to the nation. Dated Crépy, July 25." The permanent committee denied that such a motion had been made, and declared that on the day of the Fear the militiamen of Crépy had pinned on the cockade and that "M. de St-Georges was the first to pick it up and to traverse the countryside with a detachment of bourgeois." The committee demanded that the *Journal de Paris*, which had reported the placard, print a clarification.[18] The committee was determined to defend its reputation as an effective coalition of the local bourgeoisie and the liberal nobility, and it put forward Crépy's response to the Great Fear as a symbolic model of this coalition in action. In harmony with the requirements of such a coalition, the committee furloughed the members of its militia the day after the Fear, "after the information received regarding the calm that reigns in the environs," seeing no reason to "vainly fatigue the inhabitants, who each have their own work to do."[19] While this may have been a popular decision, was it popular with all? In the merchant milieux, where tension about the minimal role offered their members can be discerned from the beginning of 1789 in the preparations for the Estates-General,[20] this denial of any opportunity to cut a figure may have been sharply felt.

A final aspect to consider is Crépy's activity in warning other communities. Crépy appears to have sent warnings in only two directions: northeast and south. In the north lay Villers-Cotterets and Soissons, both strategic reserves for the maintenance of order: Soissons as a garrison and the intendant's seat; Villers-Cotterets as the local seat of the Orléans apanage, with its own foresters and estate guards. To the south of Crépy lay the great part of the region that the "brigands" might attack: the grainfields that covered the Valois and beyond. Georges Lefebvre found that the Great Fear reached Dammartin and Meaux (well into the intendancy of Paris) on the twenty-seventh, only hours after its arrival in Crépy in the morning;[21] but it is unclear whether the Fear was relayed from Crépy, from Senlis, or along rural channels. For Villers-Cotterets and Soissons, however, the evidence points to prompt action by the permanent committee of Crépy. A letter of the twenty-seventh from Soissons to its deputy the duc de Liancourt, then president of the National Assembly, indicates that its first word of the Fear was from a Crépy courier who had ridden the 38 kilometers by 1:30 in the afternoon.[22] His passage was recorded in Villers-Cotterets: "A courier, arriving from Crépy and going to Soissons to seek help, announced in passing that the grain was cut down the previous night at Béthisy, and that the terrible reapers were moving toward Villers-Cotterets, Pierrefonds, and Attichy."[23] The mention of Pierrefonds and Attichy is intriguing, as both towns are near the eastern edge of the Compiègne forest. This would suggest that the "danger zone" was perceived as continuous, from Béthisy, near the southwest corner of the forest, to Attichy, near its northeast corner. If the "brigands" could not be contained, an arc of farmland extending from Senlis and Dammartin in the south to Soissons itself in the east would be laid open to attack.

Villers-Cotterets and Soissons

The municipal archives of Villers-Cotterets were lost in World War I, but remaining evidence suggests that in that town the Fear was primarily an occasion for the municipality to seek troops from the garrison at Soissons. An 1886 study by a local antiquarian indicates that four thousand "brigands" were expected and that "the municipality went into permanent session"—which seems to imply that no additional members were included in this Orléans-appointed group. The municipality "finished by deciding to send a courier to Soissons; he left about four o'clock in the afternoon and arrived about six o'clock." Since word of the Fear from the Crépy courier had probably arrived at about 11:30 that morning, this timing suggests slow, even reluctant activity. Clamecy, the mayor of Soissons, replied to Villers-Cotterets that its "infantry regiment barely sufficed to guard the town and its outskirts, and that he could only offer 25 hussars who were leaving at once in pursuit of brigands," but that he was writing to the president of the National Assembly for troops. On August 1, five days after the Fear, the Villers-Cotterets municipality asked the comte de Barbançon (master of streams and forests for Villers-Cotterets, and royal captain of the hunt for Louis XVI) to intervene with the War Ministry and procure 25 dragoons, supposedly to aid the militia—of which this is the first mention—in keeping order at the market, and to "assure the harvest." On the eighth the municipality repeated the request, and in mid-August it got its wish: dragoons took the patriotic oath in Villers-Cotterets on the twenty-sixth.[24] This succession of events is tantalizing. When was the militia formed? Before the Fear, as in Crépy; or as a consequence of it? The insistent request for troops, coupled with silence regarding any movement of militia during the Fear, suggest that the municipality avoided forming a militia as long as it could.

We know little of the Fear at Pierrefonds, except for Soissons's word that a messenger from Pierrefonds had arrived in Soissons. Dinet believes that the original panic near Béthisy may have sent waves northeast (traveling through or around the forest) and may have reached Pierrefonds without a town acting as intermediary.[25] Attichy, a little northeast of Pierrefonds, may have been an independent starting point for the Fear in the Soissonnais. Dinet, unable to link it to any relay, considers it an original panic. Attichy's municipal deliberations for August 1790 show that the mayor of 1789, Guibert, told a general assembly that he had been menaced with legal action to recover the costs "of renting post horses for the searches of July 26, 1789."[26] If the date is accurate, the twenty-sixth would seem too early for rumors relayed from the opposite corner of the Compiègne forest to have sparked the Fear in Attichy. Unfortunately, we cannot be sure of Guibert's memory. We can only speculate that Attichy's mounted police brigade could have made the town a relay for rural fears, as was Crépy-de-Valois.[27]

Four couriers arrived in Soissons from its west in rapid succession on the afternoon of July 27. The best account of the Great Fear's arrival is the letter that Soissons notables sent to the duc de Liancourt-Roche-foucauld, the town's noble deputy to the National Assembly and the current president of the Assembly on the same day:

> Monsieur le Duc,
>
> Perhaps you are already informed of the frightful event that has brought us to the depths of despair; a courier, arriving from Crépy at half past one, tells us that a troop of brigands cut down the grain last night on the plain of Béthisy. Presently, at six in the evening, couriers have arrived from Villers-Cotterets, Pierrefonds, and Attichy, toward which the troop is advancing at this moment; it is cutting down the grain in broad daylight. These brigands are said to number four thousand; we have only 25 hussars who are about to leave in their pursuit; the infantry regiment can only guard the town and its outskirts. You see, Monsieur le duc, the need we have for cavalry and light troops; we count on your goodwill to put under the eyes of the King and the National Assembly the situation in which we find ourselves, the consequences of which will be more terrible than those from the scourge of the hail that we endured last year.
>
> With respect we are,
>
> Monsieur le duc,   Your humble and very obedient servants, the
>   deputies composing the provincial commission,
>   the intermediate bureau and the municipality.[28]

The importance of this document is unfortunately enhanced by our lack of Soissons's municipal archives for the revolutionary period, which were destroyed in Napoleon's 1814 campaign.[29] The letter stands as evidence for two important points. First, the rumor's content had not been altered by its travels during the day; the Soissons notables clearly had no difficulty in reconciling the four different messages they had received. All the messages seemed to show the "brigands" in implacable eastward movement toward Soissons's own rural environs. Second, there is no mention of raising a bourgeois militia—perhaps no surprise in a request for regular troops, but still an intriguing omission. In Soissons even more than in most other towns of the intendancy, the town's oligarchy thought in terms of troops when it thought of public order, and it is worthwhile to examine why this was so.

Like Crépy-en-Valois and Villers-Cotterets, the seat of the intendancy was run by municipal officers selected by the Orléans apanage. Notables in Soissons could be divided into three interest groups. The first group had ties to the Orléans apanage and to its appointed municipality; lacking any wider social base, they tended to rely on garrisoned troops that could be requisitioned to maintain public order. The second group lacked both ties to the apanage and a voice in affairs proportionate to their economic importance. This "outer circle" of merchants and lawyers had something to gain by seeking the support of classes below them; serving as officers of a militia might suit their aims perfectly. The third group was the provincial commission, whose members represented not only Soissons but the whole intendancy. They sat in Soissons and had the ear of the intendant Blossac. Their property and that of their peers needed protection from rural unrest, and the dispatch of troops from Soissons could meet their purposes. What we know of Soissons's response to the Great Fear at the official level suggests an attempt to reconcile all three interests.

The abiding friction between those bourgeois who had the apanage's patronage and those who did not surfaced in the preparations for the Estates-General. On February 12 a meeting of delegates from Soissons's parishes, corporations, and guilds quickly turned into a nomination session for new municipal officers. The mayor, Clamecy, was absent from this meeting, and the three magistrates present split among themselves; delegates made nominations and voted on them.[30] De Limon, the duc d'Orléans's intendant for the apanage in Valois, was authorized by the apanage council to go to Soissons "unofficially" and discreetly reassert control. He reported back on May 17; the council decided to leave the current officers in place until the Estates-General promulgated a new plan of municipal government.[31]

The tension between apanage and non-apanage bourgeoisie may have kept the municipal officers worried about the risks of mounting a bourgeois militia to police Soissons. Yet without a militia, troops would be necessary, and the deputies of the Soissonnais provincial commission had other uses in view for the troops stationed in Soissons. On June 4 the commission wrote the comte d'Egmont:

> The riots, the crowds, the pillages . . . in nearly all parts of the province have put us in the position of making the minister sense the need of granting the

military support that we requested . . . all the intermediate bureaus have
told us their fears of seeing the next harvest exposed to the devastations a
blind and hopeless populace will think permissible; fears founded on threats
that are already strongly pronounced . . .

It is a most indispensable necessity to establish, with troops that are in the
Soissonnais, a cordon that will embrace all points of the province in a
fashion that makes all the malevolent expect a vigorous resistance, and that
tranquillizes the cultivators.

The commission had its own scheme for deploying troops, in which the
Swiss regiment of Reinach would be divided into squads and dispersed
into the countryside; the artillery detachment of the military school at
La Fère sent northwest to Chauny and Noyon; the cavalry of the Royal
Bourgogne sent farther northwest "to the Roye and Montdidier side";
"and the Thiérache . . . guarded by the sergeant of one's choice."[32] This
plan (shelved in Paris) amounted in substance to a defense of the river
Oise against unruly elements from Picardy. On June 22 the Swiss regiment departed: Versailles needed it in St-Denis as part of its concentration of force around Paris. Four days later, Soissons's municipal officers
asked the intendant to order the garrisoned hussars to patrol the town
daily from 5:00 A.M. to 1:00 P.M.[33]

Leroux, whose history of Soissons was written within living memory of the Revolution, states: "The whole population of Soissons took up
arms spontaneously on July 25 [*sic*] on the news brought by an express
courier from Crépy-en-Valois, that brigands had cut down the grain . . .
This arming was the origin of the National Guard, which replaced the
old town militia, dead of decrepitude, and absorbed into its midst the old
companies of Archery, the Arquebus, and the Town."[34] Although a proper National Guard certainly formed eventually, it was not an immediate
outcome of the Fear. We have already seen that the notables' letter to
Liancourt-Rochefoucauld insisted on the need for regular troops, while
saying that some of those available had been reserved for urban duty.

On August 1 the provincial commission wrote its affiliate bureaus in
Noyon and Guise, explaining Soissons's actions during the panic:

Everywhere it was said that the brigands were cutting down the green grain.
Everywhere people armed and formed into troops. Everywhere prompt aid
was demanded; military troops and armed citizens left Soissons on the night
of July 27–28 and went to all the places where it was said that the devastations were being committed . . . With calm reestablished, our citizens believed it prudent to form, on the capital's example, a permanent committee,

the members of which have been associated with the municipal officers. The bourgeois militia is going to take up arms.[35]

The provincial commission put the emphasis on the response of Soissons to the alarms to its west, though in justifying the town's behavior after the fact, the commission universalized the Fear, which was not really "everywhere." The question of a militia was phrased in terms of a revival, not a new creation.

We know that sometime between July 27 and August 5 a permanent committee was formed "under the presidency of our municipal officers";[36] and a printed circular from the committee dated August 5 has survived. It may have been widely distributed, since it is preserved in the Laon municipal archives. It is addressed to "proprietors," and alerts them as follows:

> The first and most pressing object of our solicitude being to assure the preservation of the harvest, the Committee has given a first ordinance for the formation of a mounted patrol composed of bourgeois volunteers, joined to the hussar detachment quartered in Soissons, that [can] proceed to any given district. It would seem indispensable for the farmers and cultivators . . . to patrol their territories, and . . . to alert the mounted police or the patrols of such measures as may be necessary.[37]

Here is evidence of a cavalry militia (or at least a willingness to create one), but conjoined with royal troops. It appears that when the Fear arrived the regular infantry were put in charge of protecting the town proper. The energies of Third-Estate mobilization were channeled into the countryside, wherever the harvests were believed to be in danger. When the panic subsided, the notables cautiously began the task of creating revolutionary institutions—a militia and a permanent committee—that would remain tame. This pattern also occurred (with variations) in other towns where municipalities sought to contain and master the formidable social forces seeking expression.

The village of Venizel, four kilometers east of Soissons, appears to have received the Fear directly from Soissons, not via the countryside. On July 28 the village received a letter written at 2:00 A.M. from Soissons's town hall. The church bells were rung to convoke the inhabitants, and the letter was read to the assembly. Soissons instructed Venizel to stop anyone passing through the neighborhood with a scythe or sickle in hand. The assembly armed four villagers and authorized them to make arrests and convey suspects to Soissons. Venizel passed the Soissons letter on to another village, and urged it to pass the word in turn.[38] Venizel received the panic from above, from its urban authorities: its recorded response shows unusual police measures, but no general arming of the population.

Château-Thierry and the Marne

The Fear was transmitted to Château-Thierry by a courier direct from Soissons: its dispatch could not have been more official. No evidence has come to light that the Fear was disseminated along the road connecting the two towns. It may be that the Fear was of little importance in the region between Soissons and Château-Thierry. Certainly the Fear was not significant east of Soissons. Braine, 15 kilometers eastward, provides an indication. Its communal archives have survived and do not mention the Fear. A militia was formed only on August 17, "to conform to the king's declaration."[39] The lack of a written record does not prove that the Fear did not occur there, but three weeks' pause before any mention of a militia does suggest that this was so.

In Château-Thierry the response to the Fear was full-scale, and yet it appears that the "brigands" were thought to be some distance away, in the direction of Crépy and Villers-Cotterets. Our information comes from two quite different sources: the duc de Gesvres, the military governor of Ile-de-France, who mentions the activity of Château-Thierry's lieutenant of mounted police; and the abbé Hébert, the author of an unpublished history of Château-Thierry written during the Empire. The two accounts agree on little except for the direction from which the perceived danger was thought to be coming.

The duc de Gesvres resided in Gesvres, 21 kilometers south of Crépy. The Fear arrived in his village, but he did not bestir himself personally: "M. Leger, second lieutenant of the mounted police of Château-Thierry . . . headed the brigades." The duc described the forces searching for the "brigands" as "the mounted police brigades marching at the head of the inhabitants" and said that they proceeded almost to Verberie, finding only two beggars near Crépy who had been discharged from the workhouse at St-Denis and told to withdraw 30 leagues from Paris.[40] If the mounted police of Château-Thierry were accompanied by some of its inhabitants, the latter must also have been mounted, for the distance they covered was some 50 kilometers, not counting the return trip.

The abbé Hébert does not mention the mounted police at all, possibly because their response to the news was to mount at once and ride toward distant parts. Hébert's interest lies in the doings of his fellow townspeople, which he renders in the mock-heroic style for which the subject provides such a temptation. Briefly, his account is this:[41] On July 28 a courier from Soissons rode into Château-Thierry with the news that 2,500 brigands were drawing closer. They had cut the grain in the fields near Senlis, and then between Senlis and Soissons; soon they would be near Château-Thierry. The mayor ordered the tocsin rung and sent couriers to Montmirail (in the south) and Dormans (east along the Marne). The male inhabitants armed themselves with farming implements and a few firearms and formed into troops, led by the traditional bourgeois guard, the arquebus company. This assemblage left town by the north gate, on the road to Soissons. Then the gates were closed, the streets were barricaded, and lookouts mounted the church towers.

The impromptu militia made for a patch of forest north of the town "that was said to be the enemies' rendezvous." They beat the bushes without success and returned to the main road. Encountering a miller's boy, they asked him "which way were the brigands." He told them that the brigands were at Bouresches, a village six kilometers west of Château-Thierry and well out of their current path (Figure 4.3). So the militia made an about-face and returned to town.

Back in Château-Thierry, the militia chief sent a scout on horseback toward Bouresches. Soon the scout returned; "he had not gone all the way there, but he had seen the houses of Bouresches all in flames." The tocsin was rung again and the panic redoubled. The bourgeois guard marched out of Château-Thierry again, this time by the south gate. They stopped in the village of Essômes to raise reinforcements. They mobilized most adults in Essômes: some (including women) marched west toward Bouresches, others stood guard on Essômes's outskirts, and the remaining women crossed the Marne with the children and livestock. This last group was spotted by Château-Thierry's sentinels in the church tower. The tocsin was sounded a third time, with the cry "There they are; they are crossing the river beyond Essômes; they are in the plain; they are cutting down the grain; they are bringing in herds; they are spreading on all sides." The men left behind to defend Château-Thierry rushed out, only to encounter women, children, and cattle of Essômes. Soon afterward, the main force returned from Bouresches empty-handed: "What our people had taken for a fire set to the village was the reflection of the sun's rays on white walls and roofs thatched with new straw."

What the abbé Hébert's account shows us is the direction of the perceived threat (the "front") and the geography of a reserve area to be secured (the "rear") in the minds of the people in and around Château-

Figure 4.3. Château-Thierry and the Marne valley. The Bouresches forest is in the top center. La Ferté-sous-Jouarre is at the lower left. (Detail of the Cassini *Carte de France* [1744–60], Library of Congress, Washington, D.C.)

Thierry. The "front" was evidently to the north and west, which implies that the supposed path of the "brigands" remained what it was for Soissons: a sweep across the grainlands of the Valois. The young miller who pointed toward Bouresches, west of Château-Thierry, suggests that the Fear communicated informally on the popular level shared roughly the same geography as the Fear communicated officially between municipalities. Château-Thierry sent couriers to warn Dormans, about 20 kilometers east along the Marne; Montmirail, the same distance to the southeast; and La Ferté-sous-Jouarre, 20 kilometers to the southwest. The "rear" to be secured for Château-Thierry appears to have begun on the south bank of the Marne.

Château-Thierry warned La Ferté-sous-Jouarre with an official letter, delivered by special courier. This letter cited the letter from Soissons to Château-Thierry, with little embellishment: " . . . we have just received a letter from the Soissons municipality . . . a very considerable troop of brigands is spreading over the plains around Villers-Cotterets, Crépy, and Pierrefonds, committing frightful disorders and cutting down the green grain . . . These brigands . . . may be on our necks at any moment."[42] Montreuil-aux-Lyons, a village on the road to La Ferté, received a letter also—and soon a warning from La Ferté, which probably perceived Montreuil as being within its sphere of influence. The Montreuil municipality wrote back on July 31: "We have profited from these two letters to stay on our guard and run patrols in our territory. We accept with pleasure the aid that you are good enough to offer us; if, on the other hand, it so happens that we can be useful to you, we will fly to your aid."[43] The tendency of armed towns to form alliances between their militias, which later became widespread enough that the National Assembly forbade it, was present from the day of the Great Fear.

The village of Grandchamp (now known as Tancrou) is 8 kilometers northwest of La Ferté-sous-Jouarre and 11 kilometers northeast of Meaux. Meaux appears to have warned first Grandchamp (probably on July 28), and then La Ferté (on July 29). Far from panicking, Grandchamp called a general assembly and concluded that "it would be best to wait before putting ourselves on the defensive." Meaux's town clerk had assured a local resident that Meaux had already sent messengers to Crépy for a closer look: "The persons dispatched to the spot have reported that the harvest workers had cut down grain on the farmers' land, despite the said farmers, because they had refused to feed them." The municipality of Grandchamp asked La Ferté to send over any further news with the masons who traveled to work at Grandchamp each morning. If the uncertainty was not dispelled by the next day, two local people had volunteered to go to Crépy for news.[44] Grandchamp's calm suggests that informal transmission of the rumor was weak or nonexistent here, and that the matter was regarded as one that larger towns already had in hand.

South of the Marne, Jouarre received the Fear from La Ferté-sous-Jouarre late on the night of July 28. Earlier that day, Coulommiers, 13 kilometers farther south, took steps to defend itself; Dinet speculates that Meaux could have warned Coulommiers the previous day. We have already noted that lukewarm response to the Fear in Grandchamp; Jouarre's municipal officers conferred with a few notables and armed only 24 men.[45]

While the transmission of the Fear did continue along the Marne and south of the river, a loss of intensity is evident. It seems likely that official relays of the rumor between municipalities were more important here than informal, popular transmission, which lacked the vibrancy we have seen in the northern Valois. Lefebvre believed that Meaux received the Fear from Crépy and Villers-Cotterets, and that the panic then traveled west along the Marne; he seems to have been unaware of Soissons's message to Château-Thierry.[46] Popular channels matched or bested official channels in speed and emotional impact southward along the Valois plain to Meaux, but official channels were stronger from Soissons to Château-Thierry and along the Marne.

The Southern Oise Valley

So far we have followed the Great Fear along the best-paved roads of the Soissons intendancy, and along administrative channels that were equally well maintained. We now return to the local Fear's original panic on the Béthisy plain (Figure 4.2), in order to follow another strand of its transmission. From Verberie, the Fear descended the Oise, crossed out of the intendancy of Soissons, and spread through the northern part of the Paris intendancy. Though this chapter is limited to the Soissonnais, an exception must be made for the southern Oise valley, which was geographically and economically inseparable from it.

Verberie, within the bailliage of Crépy-en-Valois, had been faced with an especially acute grain shortage throughout the spring. Situated where the northern edge of the Valois plain meets the Oise, it was part of a strategic grain supply area, dominated by Paris but frequently encroached upon by Compiègne and Clermont.[47] Verberie's communal archives discuss only provisioning difficulties up to July 24.[48] In mid-June, Verberie purchased grain *en grenier*, or "in the crib" (without the required public purchase in market) from a farmer near Nery, a village just three kilometers southwest of St-Martin-de-Béthisy, where the local Fear would originate. This mild incursion into the territory of Crépy-en-Valois did not succeed. The Crépy mounted police brigade spotted the grain in movement toward Verberie on July 22 and seized it, leaving it under the guard of the people of Nery. Armed inhabitants of Verberie, led by their provost and fiscal attorney, marched to Nery, but a "rather lively brawl" was avoided when the intendant's subdelegate for Crépy granted Verberie possession of the grain on condition that it not be sold or disposed of. Verberie's river access meant bad supply relations with its immediate neighbors; any grain moving toward Verberie was suspected to be leaving the region.[49]

As the Fear's rumor crossed the Soissonnais, the name of Verberie went from town to town: it was a place inundated by "brigands." An impressive number of mounted police brigades and town militias hurried to Verberie on July 27. According to Dambry, a member of the Crépy permanent committee, the Fear brought six thousand armed men to the village.[50] While the figure of six thousand is almost certainly exaggerated, a startling number of armed persons must have been active in the vicinity on July 27—perhaps a number approaching some people's idea of the "brigands" themselves. In Verberie's general assembly on July 28, the syndic's first concern was to ensure the payment (and the continued goodwill?) of all the troops and mounted police who had come to the rescue. A small militia of 15 men—more like a constabulary—was created to patrol Verberie from 8:00 P.M. to 4:00 A.M. The militiamen's cockades and arms had to be deposited at the guardhouse each morning.[51]

Pont-Ste-Maxence, 10 kilometers west of Verberie and also on the Oise, was a major river port and grain depot. Pont was an intersection between land and water transport; a major road ran north and south through Pont, connecting Peronne and the grain of Picardy with Senlis and Paris. Pont's own supply situation was wretched in proportion to its importance in the grain trade. By the end of June, according to a military report, Pont's market sold only "regulation grain"—grains, usually rye and barley, mixed according to a municipal plan of rationing.[52] When the Third-Estate electors of Paris took control of the capital after the fall of the Bastille, one of their first acts was to send grain commissioners to Pont.[53] By late July, Pont was dependent on Paris for its own emergency provisions.[54]

Although 350 dragoons had arrived in Pont from Metz on June 24, the municipality of Pont still thought the situation serious enough to reorganize the traditional militia sometime before the Great Fear. We know of a second reorganization on July 25, which refined the division of the militia into companies and the town into patrol districts.[55]

The Great Fear arrived in Pont from Verberie early on the morning of July 27. Though Pont's municipal deliberations are silent on the panic, we know from other sources that the dragoons rode for Verberie at once, messengers were sent south to Senlis, and women and children fled west to Creil, the next town downriver.[56] The intensity of the Fear in Pont may be gauged from the fact that Senlis believed in the early morning of July 27 that the "brigands" were sacking villages near Pont at that moment.

The Great Fear in Senlis must be understood in the context of events in Versailles, because the Senlis militia was formed under the aegis of Louis XVI. In the town of Versailles on July 17, three days after the fall of the Bastille, a spontaneous meeting of young men conceived the project of a militia that would serve as an honor guard, protecting the king on his visits to the capital. The Versailles municipal officers feared any militia and immediately consulted with the royal household. However, Louis approved the idea when the duc de Guiche broached it. The next day a Versailles general assembly created the militia and elected as its officers nobles closely associated with the municipality.[57]

This agreeable outcome inspired the young duc de Lévis, a noble deputy for Senlis to the National Assembly, to gain Louis's permission for new militias throughout his bailliage. The Senlis bailliage was an extensive territory, reaching from Pont in the north down the Oise to Pontoise, and southward toward Paris. The revolutionary Parisian militia was in a process of consolidation under the wealthiest and most respectable officers. Unvouched-for persons found armed in the streets were being disarmed and expelled from Paris. The duc de Lévis feared that those displaced would collect into groups and harass the Senlis region. His letter to Pontoise, written on July 18, described the danger in terms of "outsiders," and his letters to other towns of the Senlis bailliage were similar:

> Monsieur, I have just received the king's order to have the bourgeois militia of Pontoise armed at once.
>
> As there is no state secretary for war, nor one for the provinces, the king had me come to him and commanded me to rush these orders to all the municipal officers of the Senlis bailliage, beginning with those of Pontoise, since this town is menaced by pillage from a group of bandits who are in Poissy and St-Germain at this moment and who have hung two honest citizens.[58]

The king's intention is to register all the domiciled persons above 16 and below 50 years of age, who by numerous and frequent patrols will prevent disorder, and [who] will be authorized to disarm the unvouched-for persons [*gens sans aveu*] who are the sole authors of all the excesses committed in Paris and its environs.

You will distribute the arms at your disposal to the most respectable bourgeois, and the others will use their own arms; through these wise precautions the reestablishment of order has been managed in Paris. At this moment in Versailles, the bourgeois militia is being organized on the same principles. It seems to me also, Monsieur, that: the greatest precautions must be taken for the markets' security, because as you know this is where riots usually start; it is necessary for the militia to be divided into several companies, so that in case of alarm each one will know its post; also, several night patrols and squads of guards for the gates will be required.

In this way you will avoid the frightful misfortunes that menace the environs of Paris, due to the number of ill-intentioned people that have been expelled from the capital.[59]

The Senlis municipality received a letter like this one, accompanied by another to the same effect from the Third-Estate deputy Blanc (also the mayor of Senlis). With such sponsors, it was natural that the Senlis general assembly of July 20 created a militia marked by cooperation between the nobles and the bourgeoisie, and made the duc de Lévis its titular chief. As Verberie and other towns would do later, Senlis made the cockade the distinctive mark of the militia and removed it from general circulation—at least on paper. The assembly then debated the question of where to obtain arms. A representative from nearby Chantilly proposed a militia association between the two towns, in which Chantilly would provide the guns. This idea fell flat, partly because the Senlisiens felt that Chantilly should be subordinate to Senlis, and partly because some of the arms that Chantilly was generously offering had been borrowed from Senlis and never returned. In the end the militia officers decided to ask Paris for aid in reconstituting an arsenal—a favor that the electors and La Fayette usually refused.[60]

Grain stocks dwindled and tensions heightened in Senlis from July 20 until the day of the Great Fear. The rumor arrived in Senlis—informally, it seems—early on the twenty-seventh:

At seven in the morning the alarming report spread through the town that brigands in very great numbers were cutting down the green grain on the plains near Pont-Ste-Maxence and that they were pillaging the inhabitants of the countryside.

The most rapid precautions were taken, the inhabitants in general took up arms, the posts were reinforced, and a detachment of cavalry of the bourgeois militia, with M. de la Bruyères, lieutenant of mounted police, at the head, rode posthaste to Pont-Ste-Maxence to investigate whether these reports had foundation. Tranquillity was reestablished in the town with the arrival of two couriers, one dispatched by the municipal officers of Pont, and the other by M. de Bruyères.[61]

On July 28, with the Fear over, a major market riot erupted. It was contained by the Royal-Bourgogne cavalry, without aid from the new militia. The poor of Senlis and the villagers who relied on its market apparently put the Fear's opportunity for mobilization to good use. The regular troops were still keeping order alone, which shows that the Senlis municipality preferred to direct the militia into the countryside, not to use it in a risky confrontation with fellow townspeople. The Royal-Bourgogne commandant was outraged: when the riot ended he went at once to the town hall and demanded that 50 militiamen be detailed for market duty.[62]

On the twenty-ninth, the Senlis authorities initiated an elaborate system of correspondence with parishes within about a 15-kilometer radius, forming a network of mutual aid with Senlis firmly at the center. Verberie, Pont-Ste-Maxence, Creil, and Chantilly were all included.[63] This decision was of a piece with Senlis's role as seat of a bailliage and its ambitions for the future: in 1790 it petitioned the National Assembly to be named the seat of a new department to be drawn around it.[64]

Dammartin, 18 kilometers southeast of Senlis, could have received the Great Fear's rumor from Crépy-en-Valois or Senlis, or both. Dammartin's letter to La Fayette makes clear that the rural Fear at the village level was acute, though brief, in the southern Valois. On the twenty-seventh, the same day that the Fear began around Crépy and Verberie, the municipal officers of Dammartin could already write: "The widespread report that the green grain was being cut down has been destroyed. It is true that it came about through the effect caused by some drunken scamps and roisterers who threatened to perform this maneuver. The report ran from one village to the next; each sounded the tocsin and alarm was in everyone's hearts."[65]

The Fear traveled down the banks of the Oise with great vivacity all the way to the Seine. Beaumont-sur-Oise, like Senlis and Pontoise, had formed a militia at the instigation of the duc de Lévis on July 19. The two top officers (one a *chevalier*, and the other a farmer with military experience) were elected; all other officers were appointed by a permanent council.[66] On the day of the Fear, an agent of the Paris electors, one Laubeypine, was in the region. His July 28 letter to the *Courrier* (the newspaper of Gorsas, the future Girondin), gives a vivid picture of rapid and not entirely disorganized activity at the height of the Great Fear:

Yesterday, Monsieur, at eleven o'clock in the morning, arriving at Beaumont-sur-Oise on the way to Chambly, I was stopped by several people who urged me to go no farther. Beaumont, Chambly, and all the places around were being assailed, they told me, by a considerable troop of brigands who had already cut down more than 1,200 arpents of grain.

Encouraged rather than intimidated, I walk to Beaumont on foot; everywhere I find disorder and desolation. Everyone cries, "To arms." A detachment of the Trois-Evêches dragoons is already on horseback. The commandant has his soldiers' pistols and carbines given out to the citizens who are unarmed. I hurry onto the bridge where the detachment and the citizens have gone; I find already there several cannon in good condition. Every village for two or three leagues around has sent requests for aid. All the mounted bourgeois have joined with the dragoons, or have gone off in pursuit. A rider arrives with a letter that asks for help for a village three leagues off.

Now I am recognized as a native of Chambly. Everyone presses me to mount this man's horse and go home, to unite Chambly's forces with those of Beaumont. I leave at once; but there I find a still greater desolation. No one is left but the old, some women, and sobbing children. I take my arms; I quickly join the brave men who have rushed in a tumult to the highest ground in the area; I find them in good order, commanded by M. Dubillot, under the orders of M. the marquis Dubelloy, *maréchal-de-camp*. Detachments are sent off in all directions: I myself leave on horseback with a gamekeeper.

We never discovered anything; when we arrived at one place where we had been told the supposed vagabonds were doing damage, we were sent off to another. Finally, after five hours of riding and searching, we had not managed to find out anything, and doubtless there was nothing that resembled the alarm that had been spread, at the same time and the same moment, for 10 leagues all around.

. . . One woman especially struck me; she was at the head of the peasants of her village; she had fixed a shoemaker's knife on the end of a stick, which she seemed disposed to make use of if need be . . .

I arrive at last in Beaumont, and now I find it completely calm; a strong and sure guard has taken control of all the streets of the town. Chambly, and all the surrounding places, remain on the alert. All the villages have so ordered themselves that at that first signal all the inhabitants will rapidly mobilize.[67]

Laubeypine's description is revealing, despite its literary flourishes. It shows us the intensity of the Great Fear in this locale: near Beaumont, Laubeypine was warned that the "brigands" were virtually at hand. We see Beaumont's disposition of forces: the cavalry in garrison were requisitioned by the municipality for the defense of the town proper, not dispatched to meet the "enemy." With the troops kept on hand, the arming of civilians within the town was acceptable. The countryside was patroled by mounted bourgeois detachments. Thus the militia was divided, with one segment under military direction and the other sent away from the town. The noble-bourgeois alliance appears in the leadership of the Chambly militia, where a marquis presided and a *laboureur* acted as staff officer—like the *chevalier-laboureur* pair in Beaumont. Finally, the entire narrative creates an impression of relative discipline, and this impression is perhaps more accurate than the traditional one, derived from later memoirs and testimonies, of panic and bravura. The capacity of communities to put themselves rapidly on a paramilitary footing was very real at the end of the old regime. This fact should be remembered, because it played a part in the techniques of popular protest and was assimilated into the revolutionary militias that soon rivaled municipal governments.

The Northern Oise Valley

From Verberie southward along the Oise, the Great Fear was keenly felt. Its northern movement up the Oise gradually lost intensity and here was contained, there was overshadowed by other events (Figure 4.1). In Compiègne the Fear was less significant after the July 18 capture of the intendant of Paris within the town. In Noyon the Fear arrived at a moment of local peasant mobilization. In Chauny the Fear was apparently contained by the municipality's speedy requisition of troops from the artillery school in nearby La Fère.

The previous week, Compiègne had been agitated by the capture of Bertier de Sauvigny, the intendant of Paris, whose whereabouts had been unknown since July 15. Bertier had been responsible for the provisioning of the troops that encircled Paris. After the Bastille fell, the troops withdrew from Paris at the king's orders, and Bertier seemed to ruminate over the situation. He traveled incognito through his intendancy: west to Meulan, then east through Pontoise and St-Denis to Meaux. On July 17, he crossed into the intendancy of his son-in-law Blossac and was in Soissons that evening visiting his daughter. The next day he rode west to Compiègne, in his own intendancy.[68] Here he was spotted; and the townspeople, who had been much aroused by the news of the Bastille, massed at the sound of the tocsin. The municipality was forced to put Bertier under protective guard on July 20.[69] The electors dispatched a body of mounted militia to recover him, and on the return trip a Compiègne detachment accompanied them southward as far as Verberie.[70] The stir caused by these events, and their sharply political, polarizing character—for the population had pressured the authorities into taking a revolutionary step—may have robbed Compiègne's response to the Great Fear six days later of some of its vigor.

It seems most probable that Verberie communicated the Great Fear to Compiègne by dispatching a courier on the paved road that ran north through the forest. Compiègne's municipal archives are silent on the subject; we only know that on August 7 Verberie received a letter from Compiègne "concerning the day of the alarm, last Monday, July 27." We also have the word of a member of Crépy-en-Valois's permanent committee that Compiègne sent a cavalry detachment to Verberie. These are our only indications that Compiègne experienced the Fear. We know that Compiègne had a traditional bourgeois militia in working order, because on July 6 the municipality ended night watch duty, seeing it as no longer necessary. A new "national militia" was not organized until August 20. Hence there is no evidence of Compiègne being thrown into much confusion by the Fear.[71]

Both Lefebvre and Dinet have written that the Great Fear spread up the valley of the Oise, via Ribécourt to Noyon.[72] However, other evidence suggests that the panic around Noyon may have been related to the strand of the Great Fear which originated near Estrées-St-Denis. The Estrées-St-Denis panic was distinct and will be discussed in its own right later in this chapter.

In Noyon on July 27, the rumor of brigands destroying crops in the fields arrived a few hours after the (accurate) news of a peasant invasion of the château of Frétoy, about eight kilometers to the north (Figure 4.4). In Noyon's experience the Great Fear was overshadowed by local peasant protest, as letters from the Noyon intermediate bureau to the Soissons provincial commission reveal:

[July 31, 1789]
Doubtless you are already informed of the different alerts that we have been obliged to undergo, in order to parry any surprises and to put our-

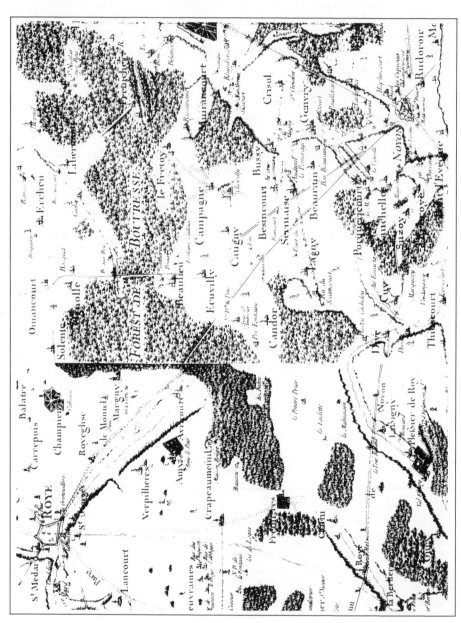

Figure 4.4. Roye and Noyon. Beaulieu and Frétoy are in the northeast corner. (Detail of the Cassini *Carte de France* [1744–60], Library of Congress, Washington, D.C. This eighteenth-century atlas, a collection of segments engraved over 15 years' time, lacks the accuracy of fit between segments that is expected in modern maps.)

selves on a defensive footing. All the inhabitants of our town, without exception, are under arms and mount guard. The inhabitants of our surrounding parishes follow our example. Monday at nine in the morning the château of Frétoy was pillaged. The pillagers' chief was arrested and brought to our prison by the detachment of dragoons; he is a veteran with 14 sous, 6 deniers of pension. The inhabitants of Carlepont, Bailly, and Ourscamp brought us the same day another bad subject who was arrested in Ourscamp abbey.

[August 7, 1789]
Our inquietudes have been no less cruel than yours; all the difference there is between you and us is that the false alarms given us came after an event which alone was capable of making us regard them as real . . . in the morning of the day when the false reports of the devastated harvests were being spread, a considerable troop of peasants, with a veteran at their head, arrived in Frétoy with drums beating; once in this parish they broke down the doors of the château [and] pillaged the grain to be found there . . . [73]

There is no mention of any courier bringing the Fear's alarm from another municipality. A letter of the chevalier de Ferrand in Beaulieu-les-Fontaines, halfway between Roye and Noyon, implies that the Fear was spreading from Roye westward:

. . . Monday the twenty-seventh . . . at one in the afternoon, there came to the village of Beaulieu near Noyon, a dependency of the marquisat of Nesle, where I live, a countryman on horseback to warn us that a troop of evildoers that he said amounted to 15,000 men were ravaging the country by cutting down all the green grain and burning all the places where they passed; that all the villages and even the town of Roye . . . were in arms.

Ferrand assembled the inhabitants of Beaulieu and marched west, away from Noyon.[74] This would suggest that the Fear around Beaulieu, though only 10 kilometers from Noyon, was part of the general alert on the Picard plain, not the Fear in the Oise valley.

Why was the Great Fear around Noyon overshadowed by the militancy of peasants in the neighborhood? While a definitive answer cannot be given, the distinctiveness of the Noyonnais should be noted as a factor. Its agricultural practices presented characteristics that marked it off from the grainland on both sides.[75]

The Noyonnais is hilly country, ill suited for large-scale grain cultivation. In the eighteenth century it supported a polyculture of striking variety: along with wheat and hemp, hillside vineyards were peppered with fruit and walnut trees.[76] The terrain and the crops favored small parcels, and small parcels accommodated peasant proprietorship. The classic practice of triennial rotation was breaking down under a variety of pressures, and the intendant's subdelegate at Noyon, Tondu, estimated that only one-third of the parishes still followed it.[77] The importance of cash crops undercut the cultivation of grain for subsistence; an average local grain crop sufficed for only three-quarters of the year. Labor-intensive polyculture created a severe dependence on the Noyon market for grain and bread, and in a year of shortage like 1789 the Noyon market was under pressure from Parisian and regional forces. In the grainlands with their large farms, begging provided inadequate but real relief in this crisis; but begging thrived on the division between large and small peasants, and in the Noyonnais this division was less developed. A sharp grain crisis acting on a small peasantry with a relatively high proportion of owners; rural communities that were not dominated for a few large farmers—these may have been the essential ingredients of peasant protest in the Noyonnais.

The Great Fear arrived in Chauny, another 17 kilometers northeast of Noyon along the Oise, sometime during July 27. We do not know whether it was relayed by Noyon or communicated informally. The municipal officers immediately requested aid from La Fère, with its arsenal, garrison, and artillery school. The next morning a detachment of 60 soldiers arrived, with orders that they be fed at Chauny's expense. A general assembly ratified the daily payments for the new arrivals and for the dragoons already garrisoned in Chauny, and the municipal officers announced that two of their number were off to La Fère to receive 350 rifles "to arm the inhabitants and put them in position to resist the insults that menace us." Yet the municipality was in no hurry to form a militia. On August 16 it received the National Assembly decree on militias from its Third-Estate deputy Le Carlier; on August 23 it was still scrutinizing the roll, making the militia more exclusive.[78] It would appear that Chauny had the means to handle the Fear within a military framework, avoiding the spontaneous formation of a citizen militia. As for La Fère, it sent a proposed militia constitution to the royal household, which approved it on August 11.[79] La Fère thus acted rather like the towns of the Senlis bailliage which created their militias under royal aegis, and this was probably due to the influence of La Fère's military establishment.

Laon and the North

The Laonnais and parts of Picardy (the Thiérache and the Vermandois) comprised the north of the Soissons intendancy. According to Lefebvre, the Great Fear "carried on through Chauny, La Fère, Ribemont and Guise and entered the Thiérache where it appeared in Marle and Rozoy, in the Serre valley and in Vervins" (Figure 4.1).[80] The presence of the Fear in these towns cannot be disproved (with the possible exception of Guise); however, this chapter brings no support to Lefebvre's statement. It seems rather that the Fear was notable by its absence, and that the task of explanation here is to understand why it faded away in the north.

La Fère is 21 kilometers west of Laon and 21 kilometers south of St-Quentin. St-Quentin lay just within the Amiens intendancy. Lefebvre notes that the Great Fear "moved no further into Flanders and . . . did not penetrate the usually stormy provinces of Hainaut and the Cambrésis."[81] St-Quentin was on the rim of this area of silence.

St-Quentin had been governed by its own patriciate since medieval times, and its traditional militia retained a certain vitality. Through the grain troubles of early spring, St-Quentin relied on its own forces and refused offers of troops from d'Agay, the intendant in Amiens. Then came the explosive riots of May 6–7 in Cambrai. The countryside between Cambrai and St-Quentin teemed with bands of peasants exacting grain from large establishments, whether ecclesiastical, noble, or common. When a riot at St-Quentin's own market got out of control, the town magistrates reversed themselves and requested troops from Amiens.[82] But they also sought to make the militia more visible: they instituted a mandatory Sunday parade, presumably to overawe the populace. This parade was taken very seriously, and the ranking military officer in town reprimanded merchants who sought to be excused for mere business reasons.[83]

Most remarkably, after May St-Quentin abandoned its grain relations with the hinterland. In mid-June the town declared itself unable to provide for the adjoining 20 parishes, and these parishes took the unusual step of forming a committee to go to the port of St-Valéry, some 250 kilometers away, to arrange their subsistence.[84] In this northern region, the rural and urban revolts of May preempted the Great Fear of July as the stage-setting event: the moment that created a context that would last through the year. The crucial division between rich and poor had widened to the point where society had, so to speak, no surface smooth enough for the Fear to travel across.

In the Soissonnais, the privileged orders as well as the notables of the Third Estate in March viewed Picardy as a source of contagion.[85] The sense that in the north public order had already broken down made it an unlikely direction to send couriers bearing a vague but powerful tale of chaos.

Guise, 27 kilometers northeast of St-Quentin, was part of the Soissons intendancy, but in May it lay within the same radius of troubles as did St-Quentin. By May 11 the municipality of Guise had borrowed a detachment of 70 artillerymen from La Fère. It was the understanding of the Soissons provincial commission that

> at Guise there is an organized, habitual assemblage of two hundred armed men . . . These men go from farm to farm, using open force to have themselves given grain at half the current price.
>
> . . . a number disguised themselves in an alarming fashion to go in a troop to demand grain from the farms, even having the audacity to declare that they came to seize the grain on the king's authority.[86]

The first indication of the Great Fear in Guise appears on the morning of July 31, when the mayor received a letter from the provincial commission written at the moment the Fear arrived in Soissons. At 2:00 P.M. the news of the king's recall of Necker arrived in Guise. The municipal officers reacted with enthusiasm, planning to invite the citizens to illuminate their houses. Putting all the news together, they apparently decided that a militia was in order, because they called a general assembly at 3:00 P.M. We have the record of the mayor's remarks on this occasion, and so have the luck to know what he thought were the cogent reasons for proposing the burden of a militia. His discourse reflected the events of May, not the Great Fear rumor current in the lower part of the intendancy; and he added tangential concerns about the open sale of smuggled salt and the breaking down of tax collection:

> The assembly is doubtless aware that for some time troops have formed of audacious men who, listening to the laws of conscience no more than they respect those of honor, have acted as if they were persuaded one might attack with impunity the properties of the state and individuals; that, full of these false and pernicious principles, they have allowed themselves excesses of every kind; that [they have gone] in force to the country homesteads closest to this town, not to seek their sustenance—which they did not lack— but to pillage and squander what pity and charity had reserved for misery and the requirements of the needy; that at other times they have not feared

to appear in the town itself to . . . publicly sell . . . merchandise prohibited
until now by the regulations, to mistreat and insult the commissioner assigned to collect excise taxes, and to upset the established order . . . [87]

Here we are far from the "brigands cutting down the green grain" that
terrified the Valois. Not the fields, but the houses and granaries of
farmers are menaced, just as they really were in May. The mayor lumps
the "attroupements d'hommes audacieux" together with other signs of
insubordination. In towns seized by the Fear, there was no time to make
such verbal amalgams; the felt reality of the brigands was too strong.
What is more, the Guise authorities themselves believed in August that
the Fear had passed them by. On August 7 the intermediate bureau for
the Guise *élection* put it succinctly to Soissons: "We have been free so far,
Messieurs, of the inquietudes and alarms occasioned by false reports
about brigandage and the destruction of green grain . . . "[88] The distinction between the Great Fear and what Guise had experienced was clearcut to them. However, the absence of the Fear in this region did not
preclude the creation of a vigilant militia: on August 6 the Guise militia
were "invited" to halt all persons, "of whatever estate and condition they
may be," who did not wear the revolutionary cockade.[89]

In Laon, 24 kilometers south of Guise, there was no popular rumor
of "brigands" destroying crops. On the contrary, there was an entirely
different theme in these closing days of July: a report that a shipment of
arms was on its way to Laon or perhaps was already within the town. On
July 25, two days before the outbreak of the Fear in the Valois, this was
the concern that seized the municipality's attention:

Regarding the reports circulating that several days ago arms, gunpowder,
and other munitions of war entered into the bishop's palace, M. Gobers,
doyen of the cathedral, had requested the municipal officers to have an
investigation made of the buildings, cellars, granaries, and other places
forming part of the said palace; the matter being taken in deliberation,
messieurs have decided that to satisfy M. the doyen, bring the alarming
reports to a halt . . . and avoid any kind of disorder to which such reports
might give occasion, this visit will be made today by the firemen's company . . . [90]

The municipal officers of Laon were selected in part by the Orléans
apanage. They provided the focus for the town's moderate party, while
the commune, at which the corporations of trades and professions were
represented, was more radical. On June 30, the commune forced the

municipality to communicate the "eyes-only" letters it had received from Laon's deputies at the National Assembly; on July 17 the commune staged a town meeting that became a virtual rally in support of revolutionary Paris.[91] The development of a dual authority was already underway, and this made the municipality reluctant to consider revamping Laon's decrepit militia.

Though the diocese's fears were misplaced, an arms shipment was in fact coming to Laon. Seventeen crates of guns were traveling by wagon—13 of them to the merchant Godoy in Paris—and the municipality got wind of their passage through Laon a day beforehand. The mounted police rode north on the Marle road, intercepted the wagons, and escorted them to Laon on August 1, where the municipality impounded them and did not release them until September 3.[92]

Yet national events were forcing the municipality to grapple with the question of a militia. On July 31 the municipal officers decided to delay discussion of the topic until their meeting with the electors of Estates-General deputies on Sunday, August 2. In the meantime they agreed to write to their counterparts in Soissons for advice: "How does the bourgeois militia serve alongside regular troops, and which of the two . . . has the command . . . [?]" The questions that bothered them would trouble towns throughout France for the rest of the year: how to avoid (or, for some people, create) a situation of dual power. At this stage, however, the Laon authorities were fortunate in having the support of the electors. The August 2 meeting decided unanimously not to arm a militia—which would be "perhaps dangerous to execute, since the town was enjoying the most perfect tranquillity."[93] Though Laon did communicate with Soissons, and went through an alarm of sorts at the end of July, the very different content of the rumor that stirred Laon does not meld well with the Great Fear as experienced by other parts of the intendancy.

There is a bit of evidence that Laon passed the Great Fear's rumor on to the countryside. In Parfondeval, a village of 160 hearths 40 kilometers northeast of Laon, the syndic received "an edict from the commune of electors of Laon" that worried him enough to call together the other members of the municipality on July 30. The language of the register is ambiguous, but it could indicate that the Laon commune was industriously spreading the Fear's rumor in its *élection*.

> . . . after the syndic had said he had notified all the members of the municipal assembly of this parish to be present in the usual assembly room the following noon, and only Sieur Ponce Brice and Pierre Quaneaux were

there . . . to hear the reading of a letter from the commune of electors of
Laon, advising what course to take relative to the disastrous enterprise
being committed by a disastrous troop of brigands in the act of despoiling
the grains in our area which have been found destroyed, and advising on the
means to conserve our own; and at that moment arrived master Duguet the
priest, Claude Foquet, Louis Douce, members of the said assembly; we
deliberated that the syndic should be given a commission to go to Rozoy to
find out precisely what was going on, in case it appeared necessary to
commit some person to guarding our [grain] during the night, and in this
case authorizing the syndic to invite and name those he judges appropriate,
referring ourselves to his prudence in this regard.[94]

That some members arrived late does not suggest an overpowering urgency, which the informal transmission of the Great Fear would have
caused. Those present decided to send to the closest town for more
information, another sign that the Fear's rumor had arrived through
official channels. Assuming that the news from Rozoy was bad, Parfondeval would post a single night watchman—again, not a desperate response. If the Great Fear did travel to the eastern corners of the
Thiérache, it came via official relays and lacked resonance.

Clermont: The Original Panic at Estrées-St-Denis

The Soissons intendancy's westernmost *élection*, Clermont (today Clermont-en-Beauvaisis), was separated from the main body of the intendancy by a strip of territory that connected the intendancies of Paris and
Amiens. Within this *élection* another of the Great Fear's original panics
materialized. The panic that began at Estrées-St-Denis was larger and
more influential than the panic that started simultaneously on the
Béthisy plain; the Clermont current covered western Picardy and the
Artois, reaching Amiens and Arras before the end of July 27.[95] It is
treated somewhat briefly in this study because its main effects lay outside
the Soissonnais. The timing and rumor content of the Clermont and
Valois currents were identical, which led Lefebvre to think that the two
were really one. Further work by Dinet has shown the absence of a
connection, however; instead, it appears that the Estrées-St-Denis panic
flowed west while the Béthisy panic flowed east. Their synchronism
must be ascribed to the imminence of the harvest in both places. Like St-
Martin-de-Béthisy, Estrées-St-Denis bordered on a wood (Figure 4.5),
and the incident that sparked this current of the Fear partook of the same
tension between cultivation and forage as in Béthisy.

Figure 4.5. The Clermontois. Estrées-St Denis verges on the Bois de Remy in the east; Clermont is in the west. (Detail of the Cassini *Carte de France* [1744–60], Library of Congress, Washington, D.C.)

We have already seen how Clermont and Compiègne blocked off grain transport to the market of Pont-Ste-Maxence. Clermont's rough provisioning regime created early the right sort of strain between town and country for a flamboyant appearance of the Great Fear. On June 5 Clermont's royal attorney ordered that Picard grains must be brought to market in Clermont and not taken further south, under pain of a three-thousand-livre fine.[96] In two weeks' time, an anonymous letter purporting to speak for surrounding parishes found its way to the attorney, assuring him that a pillage of Clermont's grain stocks followed by arson was in the offing if he did not desist. The municipal officers mobilized part of Clermont's (traditional) militia to begin a night watch on June 20. After the fall of the Bastille, Clermont took the Parisian warnings about "an infinite number of unvouched-for persons chased out of the city" very seriously, since the road from Paris to Amiens ran through its walls. In a general assembly the municipal officers renounced their own exemptions from militia duty, engaged others so privileged to follow their example, and established a new militia with more members but a satisfying class composition.[97]

The Great Fear awoke Clermont on the morning of July 27, and its telling should be left to Clermont's provost of mounted police, Duguey. There are many reasons for quoting his letter to the intendant of Soissons in full. Duguey offers the rarity of a skeptical, "morning-after" account, written by a police professional to his superior. The provost had taken no extravagant steps that required a defense, and he could write in a style that eschewed political coloring. Consequently, this document can be called one of the first interpretations of the Great Fear. As such it was useful to Lefebvre, who quoted it and agreed with its conclusions.

I have the honor to render you an account of a most extraordinary alarm that we had yesterday, which unfortunately must have extended quite far, to judge by the effect it produced here.

Sunday evening some poachers had a fairly violent row with some estate guards on the land of Estrées-St-Denis, four leagues from here. The inhabitants of this parish, who along with those living in the country have the fixed idea that one would come cut their grain, seeing from a distance the uproar between the poachers and guards, imagined that ill-intentioned people were coming to ravage their fields. They sounded the tocsin, assembled all the inhabitants, and the neighboring parishes did the same—so that yesterday at seven in the morning I received a first dispatch, announcing to me that a band of two hundred persons were presently on the land of Sacy-le-Grand, busy cutting down grain.

I gave orders on the spot to the Royal Bourgogne detachment to prepare their horses, and to the mounted police as well. While I readied myself to ride, other dispatches arrived from different directions—from Lieuville, from Estrées-St-Denis—telling me that everything was ravaged there. I was at the point of putting the messengers in jail because none of them had seen the offense and it was all still hearsay. In riding through town I saw what terror can do once it has seized people's minds. There was no one left save crying women fleeing with their children, carrying all their effects, and others who closed up their doors and their shutters and got ready to do the same.

Now at the head of the detachment, I ran across the town militia under arms, carrying rifles, meat skewers, axes, whatever they could find; all the wives and women crying and grieving—and it was just at this moment that someone came to announce that four thousand of these vagabonds were arriving in Clermont from the direction of Nointel. I could argue all I wanted that this was impossible; no one wanted to believe me.

I immediately left town with a detachment of 17 cavaliers, myself included, along with about 10 mounted bourgeois; the militia stayed assembled in the town. When I was just two or three lengths of musket-shot from Clermont, I met the hunt captain of M. the duc de Bourbon, who galloped up to tell me that there was nothing; that he had sent men with pikes out in different directions, but no grain had been cut, *and that the rumor had started with the row between poachers and guards*, and the trooping together of neighboring parishes that had been seen from far off in the fields.

I returned rapidly to calm people down, and that gave me no trouble; but while everyone was rejoicing, another alarm supervened when the news came that someone had seen bands coming from the Paris and Beauvais directions. At once everyone believed themselves lost; they reassembled as best they could to await the enemy. I soon learned that it was the neighboring parishes for three leagues all around coming to save us, armed with pitchforks, hatchets, etc.

I cannot, Monsieur, give you any idea of such a spectacle, nor of the tumult that it occasioned. The citizens of Clermont took up a collection on the spot to reimburse some of the countryfolk for the loss of their time and for their good will toward the town. Two or three hundred of these auxiliary troops, after having thoroughly refreshed themselves, went off to hunt in the forest of La Neuville, where people had already begun to hunt several days ago. They killed so much large game that it is being sold publicly in the villages.

The town of Beauvais had also sent to our aid a detachment of two hundred men of the bourgeois militia, with their cannon. They arrived as far as the village of Bresles, accompanied by soldiers, where they learned that it was a false alarm. Then they were content to send two deputies here to let us know of their goodwill.

I forgot to tell you, Monsieur, that when I reentered the town with my detachment I met a messenger from M. Legrand, the postmaster at St-Just, off to Paris to announce that everything had been ravaged in the Beauvaisis. I found this act quite imprudent, and I had the man taken to the town hall, where I urged M. the municipal officers to write on the spot to the Paris permanent committee to reassure them and to prevent such a piece of news from carrying trouble into the capital.[98]

The appeal of this document for the twentieth-century historian is transparent. It begins with causes and moves on to effects; it distinguishes a general cause (widespread harvest anxiety) from a specific cause (the poaching incident). The writer's claim to have been skeptical seems convincing. By pinning the original panic on a conflict between gamekeepers and poachers, the document supports a social interpretation of the Great Fear. It also shows the Fear's participants taking fright of each other, a phenomenon that was fundamental to Lefebvre's explanation for the Fear's immense size. All these points provided tools for Lefebvre in his work of disassembling the conspiratorial theories about the Fear.

Though Duguey refers to it by name only once, the Clermont municipality's activity shows clearly through his letter. The mobilized militia he encountered as he prepared to leave town was the municipality's doing. The detachment of Beauvais militia that turned back as the rumor subsided probably came in response to an urgent dispatch from the municipality. The Great Fear suited the municipality's outlook and preparations, for Clermont had already coordinated the militia that was simply evoked by the panic in other communities.

Note also that what began in *braconnage* ended in *braconnage*: the uproar set off by a poaching incident died down into widespread poaching in the forest west of Clermont. The threat of "brigands" had led to the distribution of weapons to peasants; now these peasants used them for an activity that was a form of "brigandage"—from the standpoint of the upper classes.

Lefebvre was the first to discover that the Great Fear did not penetrate areas that had recently experienced peasant revolt. Except in the Dauphiné, where the peasant mobilization of the Fear provided the basis for peasants' action on their own account, he concluded, "Between the agrarian revolts and the Great Fear, there is so little interdependence that the two do not coincide . . . "[99] In the smaller sphere of the intendancy of Soissons, this phenomenon can be observed in the difference between the south, agitated only by market disturbances, and the north, on the periphery of a spring rural upheaval in the Cambrésis and Hainaut.

The Soissons intendancy was not only fertile ground for the Fear, it propagated it far and wide. Two original panics took place in the intendancy, and the resulting alarms traveled through the Beauvaisis, western Picardy, and Artois, while Soissons's own anxieties resonated in the National Assembly. Yet the Fear covered at most two-thirds of the intendancy, and within that territory it often changed complexion, as a close reading of the local documents can demonstrate.

The original panics of Béthisy and Estrées-St-Denis had a single character: they arose at the border between forest and arable land, where contrasting ways of life—in times of shortage, even ways of survival— were juxtaposed. The geography of both original panics embodied the consensus that made the Great Fear. This consensus was the shared physical and psychological space of cereal agriculture itself, abiding within the disintegrating triennial system. It contained widening divisions between classes, but also deep ideological reserves that could briefly unify the rural world against the specter of malicious outsiders.

The Great Fear had two modes of transmission: a popular, informal mode, predominantly rural, relying on the sound of the tocsin, rippling outward across rings of parishes; and an administered, formal mode, initiated by municipalities, relying on roads and couriers, proceeding from urban point to point. The formal mode has left almost all the historical evidence, so naturally it looms large to us. It is important to realize, however, that in places where formal transmission got ahead of informal transmission—as in the hinterland of Château-Thierry—the Great Fear met with only a lukewarm response. The sole word of urban authorities on this matter was considered by villages with much deliberation and reluctance, as it was on any other matter. Further, while formal transmission spread the rumor in a linear way to distant points, it was informal transmission that truly filled the landscape with alarms and defensive activity and gave the Fear its profundity as a formative political experience. The importance of the formal mode of transmission really lies in the municipalities' willingness to give the Great Fear their imprimatur and to amplify it with their own resources. The modern attitude toward "rumor control" was expressed only by Duguey, the provost of the mounted police in Clermont, who actually arrested the courier of the

St-Just postmaster for saying that the Beauvaisis was devastated. Duguey was not politically placed to understand why a municipality would put itself at the head of a spontaneous coalition against enemies of the entire community.

No municipality did what Duguey did, saying to alarmed citizens that what they feared was impossible. Still, many municipal officers responded to the Great Fear with mixed feelings. The Fear's invitation to unity, in itself welcome, immediately posed questions of organizing armed force and hence of power-sharing. The ability to organize towns-men for self-defense was a patrimony from preceding centuries. Though its mechanisms might be rusty, the social habit of rallying against intruders was not. Would the old-regime municipalities be skillful enough to retain this patrimony and the legitimacy that accompanied it, or would it pass into new hands?

In some towns—Villers-Cotterets and Chauny, for example—the question could be avoided by resorting to regular troops alone, and no doubt that option would have been seized upon in many more localities had it existed. Towns such as Clermont and the towns of the Senlis bailliage, which had controlled the reorganization of their traditional militia before the Fear struck, found themselves in a viable position. But in many other towns, once the Fear had swept the community strongly, demands for a new militia of the "national" type became hard to resist, especially since something of the sort had just formed spontaneously and was unwilling to fully disband. At this point, municipal officers might attempt to pour the old wine of a traditional militia into the new bottle of a national one, staffing the new militia with the old officers and putting a noble at its head; however, this procedure succeeded best if implemented before or during the Fear.

Especially in towns of the Valois—Crépy, Senlis, Beaumont, Chambly—the militias of July showed an ostentatious alliance between the upper bourgeoisie and the more-or-less liberal nobles of the area. On the night of August 4, this alliance would be made in the National Assembly, and then its costs to the old regime—expressed in the personal concessions made by noble deputies—would be (as it were) estimated. But at the end of July on the local level, the costs of a noble-bourgeois coalition were unclear and the benefits to the municipalities undeniable. Not lease of these was the diversion of the bourgeois themselves, out into the rural districts where they could be involved in the managed conflict between town and country, while any troops that were not light calvary remained in town to oversee the population (as happened in Soissons and Beaumont). Of course, to reap these benefits the municipal officers had to continuously control the militia's arms (checking them in and out of the town hall), its leadership (watching over officer selection), its symbolism (making the cockade an exclusive badge), and above all, its numbers (applying not just a property qualification but personal knowledge of each domiciled inhabitant).

The municipalities' last alternative was to give in and establish a true "national militia," as they were called—one without links to old-regime militia structure, with broad recruitment and untested officers. This was rightly felt to be the most dangerous course; we have seen St-Quentin and Laon (largely outside the Fear's reach) struggling to avoid it. To found a national militia was to create half the basis for dual power in the town. Paris had demonstrated that only two things were required to overthrow an old-regime municipality: a united, permanent committee of Estates-General electors, and a national militia. Part 3 of this study will show how the authorities' fears and the citizens' ambitions worked out in practice.

Tracing the geographic movement of the Great Fear reveals in detail how the "news" of the rumor traveled and how people reacted to it. But it cannot tell what the "news" really was. Though we know the formula of words that encapsulated the rumor, only superficially do we understand what the words meant then. We are aware of their dictionary meanings, but not of the range of usages to which eighteenth-century people put them. The study of word usage is especially important for the socially volatile circumstances of 1789, when so many words, acts, and signs carried high symbolic charges. Contemporaries' heavily loaded language has naturally become obscure to us, and historians often prefer to describe it as "exalted" or "intoxicated," rather than to pursue its exact sense. Chapter 5 seeks to analyze the Great Fear's semantic content, how the rumors' meanings were plural rather than singular, and how those meanings could pass from low to high company and back again.

FIVE ❧ THE SEMANTICS OF THE GREAT FEAR

The people of 1789 spoke a fascinating language. Whether it permitted them to understand each other is debatable, but certainly it let them concert vast activities together, the Great Fear among them. A whole book could be devoted to the political vocabulary of 1789; here we can only explain a few of its aspects. One of these aspects is not even verbal, but cannot be dissociated from verbal messages: it is the clanging of the tocsin that summoned the parish to hear and act upon the Fear's news. A second aspect is the notion of news itself, as best we can grasp it through the contemporary usages of the words *nouvelle, bruit,* and *rumeur.* A third and most important aspect is the interpretation of words frequently met with in documents that are—to the modern way of thinking—politically opaque. *Brigand* is chief among these words and remains the term with which the Great Fear is historically associated. But equally significant are the usages of *peuple* and *aristocrate*: *peuple* for its semantic similarity to *brigand* in breadth and multiplicity of meaning, and *aristocrate* as an index of belief in an "aristocratic plot" that was central to Lefebvre's explanation of the Great Fear.

Why do these problems of language deserve their own chapter?

If the dimension of language were excluded, this study's attempt to explain the Great Fear would end, in a sense, at the physical aspects of the rumor's transmission—the couriers, the roads, the actions of authorities, and the other details discussed in chapter 4. These aspects comprised only the outer shell of the Great Fear. The heart of the Fear was the phenomenon of credence. Examining the language of 1789 gets us only a little closer to this phenomenon, but the precious indications that it offers are worth the effort.

One cannot study language or discourse without negotiating a welter of ideas about the relationship between language and society—that area in which the late Michel Foucault has been the most creative recent exponent. It is consequently necessary to sketch here, very briefly, a few assumptions accepted in this study. These deal with three areas: first, the Gramscian concepts of ideology and language that were touched upon in the Introduction; second, the value and limitations of (primarily French) attempts to mate linguistics with French Revolutionary history over the last 20 years; and third, the specific methods employed in this chapter.

As George Rudé has observed, "every writer in the social sciences—I am thinking in particular of Marx, Mannheim, Lukacs, Clifford Geertz—uses the term [*ideology*] in his own manner, some (since Marx's *German Ideology*) seeing it as a form of 'mystification' or 'false reality', others defining it strictly in terms of a structured set of values or political beliefs, others again favoring a more elastic approach in which myths, 'attitudes' and what the French call *mentalités* all have their part."[1] In the thought of Antonio Gramsci, ideology is not so much a coherent set of ideas that can be ascribed to one side in a conflict, as it is a basic conceptual frame indistinguishable from the grand lines of the society to which it belongs. For Gramsci "the material forces would be inconceivable historically without form, and the ideologies would be individual fancies without the historical forces."[2] A society's ideology is a frame wide enough to be generally shared, even by opposing forces. Gramsci sought to clarify this meaning of ideology and distinguish it from other meanings in the following passage:

> It seems to me that there is a potential element of error in assessing the value of ideologies, due to the fact (by no means casual) that the name ideology is given both to the necessary superstructure of a particular structure and to the arbitrary elucubrations of particular individuals . . .
>
> One must therefore distinguish between historically organic ideologies, those, that is, which are necessary to a given structure, and ideologies that are arbitrary, rationalistic, or "willed." To the extent that ideologies are historically necessary they have a validity which is "psychological"; they "organize" human masses, and create the terrain on which men move, acquire consciousness of their position, struggle, etc.[3]

This study attempts to work with such a "terrain" concept of ideology. In speaking of an ideology of the Great Fear, the intent is to delineate a "psychologically valid" world-view in which the rumors that sparked the Fear were highly plausible: that is, an environment of credence, a "terrain" on which the Fear could be acted out.

Gramsci's concept of language runs parallel to his concept of ideology. Language, another complex creation involving the entire society, acts—very imperfectly—as a unifier:

> It seems that one can say that "language" is essentially a collective term which does not presuppose any single thing existing in time and space. Language also means culture and philosophy (if only at the level of common sense) and therefore the fact of "language" is in reality a multiplicity of facts more or less organically coherent and coordinated. At the limit it could be said that every speaking being has a personal language of his own, that is his own particular way of thinking and feeling. Culture, at its various levels, unifies in a series of strata, to the extent that they come into contact with each other, a greater or lesser number of individuals who understand each other's mode of expression in differing degrees, etc.
>
> . . . An historical act can only be performed by "collective man," and this presupposes the attainment of a "cultural-social" unity . . . Since this is the way things happen, great importance is assumed by the general question of language, that is, the question of collectively attaining a single cultural "climate."[4]

Since groups and even individuals use the same words to refer to varying realities, language itself can be seen as eminently political—in fact, as a kind of vast, unwieldy coalition in which some terms tend to be divisive, while others represent patches of common ground. A semantic unity is always incomplete and always in process of attainment. Hence when masses of people participated across classes in the Great Fear, the agreement to act in common was also necessarily an agreement on terms, and these particular terms deserve study as clues to the historical act itself.

This chapter's approach to words owes a debt to French historians who have worked since the 1960s on problems of Revolutionary vocabulary—among them Jacques Guilhaumou, Annie Geffroy, and especially Régine Robin.[5] Their studies have thrown light on such difficult areas as the meanings of *féodalité* and related terms, the manifold uses of *roi* and *peuple* in the speeches of Saint-Just, and the carefully crafted political mummery of Hébert's *Père Duchesne*.[6] Equally important, at their best these studies have shown precisely what can be gained from linguistic analysis of a text, and what must be drawn from the broader historical context in order to interpret that text.

Seated before the gleaming dashboard of a powerful methodology, one sometimes forgets that a method is basically a way of arranging questions, rather than of arranging answers. Régine Robin acutely remarked in 1973, "The pitfall for linguistics in history is to have attributed to it the same role and the same function as statistics in economics."[7] There is nothing in the analysis of discourse that can override the requirement, and the risk, of interpreting both the results of the linguistic research and the texts in their original settings. While analysis of discourse can tell us something about the "internal economy" of an ideology, it cannot of itself explain the integration between an ideology and its society.

Linguistics in history has a second problem, which is a natural companion to its tendency toward scientism: at times it is unreadable. Jacques Godechot has expressed the problem this way: "The more that so-called scientific works of history use jargon, the less they will be read and the more a 'history of amateurs' will develop."[8] Even specialized historical writing still retains its precious capacity for being understood with little recourse to a specialized vocabulary. The historian who works with an ancillary discipline must confront the difficulties of conserving this intelligibility.

This chapter does flourish a linguistic apparatus, but it makes no truth claim beyond that regular to historical writing—that is, to interpret a set of sources in a way that supports scrutiny. Contemporary occurrences of certain terms have been collected from the primary sources that form the basis of the study as a whole. The majority of occurrences come from archives—administrative correspondence, municipal deliberations, petitions, and other documents. A smaller proportion are drawn from the press of 1789-91 and the proceedings of the National Assembly. A majority of the occurrences are from the Soissonnais; a minority are from Picardy, the Cambrésis, Hainaut, and Paris and its environs. None of the occurrences precedes the late 1780s; the great majority date from 1789, but some later ones have been admitted.

For each term, occurrences are classified according to the case system of the linguist Charles Fillmore. Fillmore works in the field of linguistic universals: the study of those characteristics common enough to all languages that they can be used to describe language in general. He has developed a set of eight cases (reminiscent of Latin cases) to describe the function of a noun within its sentence.

Fillmore defines the eight cases as follows:

1. Agent, the instigator of an event;
2. Counteragent, the force or resistance against which an action is carried out;
3. Object, the entity that moves or changes or whose position or existence is under consideration;
4. Result, the entity coming into existence from an action;
5. Instrument, the stimulus, means, or immediate physical cause of an event;
6. Source, the place from which something moves;
7. Goal, the place to which something moves; and
8. Experiencer, the entity receiving, accepting, experiencing, or undergoing the effect of an action (similar to the classical dative).[9]

In sections of this chapter, Fillmore's case system serves as a framework for a thematic discussion of the terms under consideration. Numbers and percentages are generally relegated to the notes; in some instances they are omitted where they show no noteworthy pattern. The intent is to integrate linguistic analysis into an interpretation and to present that interpretation, rather than a "result."

Before examining words relating to the Great Fear's message, however, it is essential to look at the situation in which that message was often disseminated: an impromptu assembly summoned by the tocsin.

The Tocsin

The tocsin was a sharp, rapid way of pealing church bells which informed the community to gather near the church because something was afoot. While the tocsin was in essence an alarm, it was used for so many different reasons that we cannot assume its hearers could guess what it meant on a given occasion, as the range of examples in this section is meant to demonstrate. People responded to the tocsin by coming to find out why the tocsin was ringing. As we saw in chapter 4, the tocsin communicated both within a village and between villages; in rural districts it was a more thorough communicator of the Great Fear than were the couriers who rode from town to town.

The tocsin allowed the transmission of urgent news to large numbers of people by collecting them in one place. In the context of the eighteenth century, it was efficient; the custom persisted in great part due to its utility to the authorities. At the same time, it was of course quite dangerous. To pass information on to the community, one had to partially mobilize it, and the tocsin was audible beyond the community as well. Consequently, authorities used the drum in day-to-day situations: a crier would walk drumming through the streets and repeating a message (for example, the date and time of a coming general assembly). With both drum and tocsin, however, the essence of the authorities' problem was that they had to address the community as a community, as a physically congruent whole. It was not customary or practical to impart a message to the community as a multitude of disparate individuals. The low level of literacy meant that the use of broadsides or even printed handbills, aside from being slower and more costly than public announcements, would lead to the assembly of groups in which some read aloud to others. In short, the notoriously volatile eighteenth-century crowd was, as often as not, duly convoked by the authorities.

Given the importance and the risks attached to the use of church bells, it is surprising that local authorities did not quarrel over it more often. In the Soissonnais there is some evidence of rivalries between curé and syndic over control of the bells,[10] but in normal circumstances municipal use was confined to Sunday after services and apparently presented few problems of coordination. In 1789, however, from late July on, many towns had to face the question of whether control over the tocsin could be shared between the municipality and a new institution, the "renewed" or "national" militia. In Enghien-Montmorency, just north of Paris, the cautious municipality decided on July 22 that the reported danger of unvouched-for persons expelled from Paris justified the creation of what it still chose to call a "bourgeois guard." The guard's statutes stipulated that the door to the belfry staircase be flanked by two sentries whenever the guard was on duty. To raise an alarm, a militiaman had to fire a shot in the air. His companions on duty would hasten toward him, and together they would hunt up the syndic, who then might decide to ring the tocsin. These stringent regulations did not suffice—Enghien's municipal officers were overthrown by a revolutionary faction in early August[11]—but they vividly illustrate the concern that municipalities felt about controlling their communication lines.

In market riots or grain seizures, members of the crowd sometimes entered the belfry and rang the tocsin, with two results: the crowd swelled greatly, and the forces of order arrived on the scene. In Essonnes, about 30 kilometers south of Paris, on July 25, carters from Provence stopped during the afternoon. While the carters ate, local folk perceived that grain was hidden beneath wine barrels on the three carts. Some rang the tocsin to gather more people to help seize the grain. The municipal officers emerged from their houses to see what was the matter, but could do no more than oversee the forced sale of the grain at a fixed price of 24 livres per *septier*.[12] In Poissy on July 7, a group of women surrounded a grain cart caught in a rut while others sounded the tocsin "several times running to amass the people"; the racket alerted the mounted police brigade and a detachment of Swiss troops stationed in Poissy, who dispersed the crowd with the promise that grain would be delivered from the neighboring market of St-Germain-en-Laye.[13] On August 10 a group of residents of Voulpaix, in the northeast corner of the Soissons intendancy, organized a militia on their own initiative. The same day they seized grain moving north toward La Capelle and brought it to Vervins, the closest market town. Once the grain was sold, they deposited the receipts with Vervins's court clerk and rang the tocsin. Before the assembled people, the Voulpaix militia demanded that the municipal officers of Vervins mount guard with them. They prevailed: probably constrained by the crowd, the officers joined patrols for three nights.[14] Many such examples could be recounted. The crowd's use of the tocsin, though unauthorized, was hardly stealthy or surreptitious. Rather, it was meant to summon both the people at large and the authorities, whose participation was inevitable and expected. The ringers' aim was to convoke the community as a whole by surprise and gain concessions from unprepared officials or police.

This element of surprise also entered into the authorities' calculations in using the tocsin. When the commandant of the Valenciennes garrison had to deal in late August with a case of excessive fraternization between his soldiers and rowdier elements of the Third Estate, he used the tocsin with careful timing:

> The soldiers together with the townspeople ran through the town all night, sword in hand, until their drunkenness made them drop in the streets.
>
> The danger was urgent that if they were allowed to emerge from the condition of stupor in which the debauch had left them, their rage would recommence . . . I took advantage of the gathering of magistrates and captains of the national militia at the town hall and offered them the services of the small number of sober soldiers that I had, together with the militia and all the officers; the tocsin was rung, drums were beaten, and while the "nationals" yanked drunks from cabarets I left with some mixed detachments to go into the villages and gather up the soldiers.[15]

This dawn tocsin, timed to coincide with the onset of a wretched collective hangover, was smartly executed in the event; but note that the commandant would not have dreamed of attempting it a few hours earlier.

Since the tocsin mobilized all sides of any social situation, its use had to be well concerted.

In conflicts between village and seigneur, the tocsin was a device to ensure the widest possible participation in acts entailing legal risk. In Chatou, near St-Germain-en-Laye, the village organized on May 11 to demolish a wall the seigneur had built across a road used constantly by the community. The tocsin was rung and most villagers assembled; Chatou's two *messiers* (field watchmen) walked through the surrounding country, encouraging stragglers to attend; in the village, doors were knocked on and people summoned out to enhance unanimity. The syndic and the clerk were put at the head of the procession that marched to the seigneur's wall and began to dismantle it. When the mounted police brigade of Nanterre arrived, it sought to identify persons who had made themselves prominent enough in the affair to be punished as examples to the rest. The brigadiers were told that "the whole parish had worked without exception, each forced by the others [*contraint les uns par les autres*]."[16] In Chatou's case, the tocsin was one of a set of ploys intended to give the demolition of the wall both unanimity and officiousness.

Finally, control of the tocsin was crucial in any struggle between an old-regime municipality and a group determined to replace it. Brie-Comte-Robert, in the southeastern environs of Paris, was an unusual example of full municipal revolt within days of the fall of the Bastille. At a meeting of municipal officers in the mayor's house on Sunday, July 19, one Cousin, the duc de Penthièvre's *fermier du droit de minage* (official measurer of grain at the market), leaped up and tapped his right pocket significantly: "I have in here, he said, the powers of the Nation and of the Assembly of the Hôtel de Ville of Paris. I want and intend the assembly to be held today, at two o'clock, at my house or at the town hall . . . and I intend the municipal officers to be excluded." An uproar commenced. Cousin had the message of a general assembly drummed through the streets. The assembly, packed with Cousin's supporters, reorganized the militia under his command. The mayor and the bailiff fled to Paris to ask the capital's revolutionary authorities for aid. To give the new militia its baptism of fire, Cousin rang the tocsin violently at nine o'clock that evening and kept patrols running until just before dawn.[17]

Incidents such as these vividly suggest the implications that must have run through the minds of municipal officers at the moment of the Great Fear. They would first ask themselves whether a situation had arisen in which the tocsin was likely to be rung—by someone. If this were the case, they wanted to be the ones to ring it. Once the tocsin was rung, the community would be on its feet. At that point it might well be best to go on and arm the inhabitants, so long as it was done under municipal authority; not to arm them could mean losing sway over the assembly.

Words about News: *Bruit, Rumeur, Nouvelle*

In our day, we think of *news* and *rumor* as two opposed terms, with *news* having overtones of truth and *rumor* overtones of falsehood. In 1789 this way of thinking was still in the process of formation. An examination of usages of the words *bruit, rumeur,* and *nouvelle* can help us to distinguish the stage this process had reached. Word-of-mouth news, while somewhat disreputable, was a potent, living reality. According to Lefebvre, "if we except the Assembly's debates, of which the deputies' correspondence gave a glimpse, up to August news came only . . . through private letters and word of mouth."[18] The people of the villages and small towns had their "official channels" of information—the spoken words of familiar intermediaries: the curé; the notary; the syndic; the clerk; and also the notably prosperous, who were usually connected, formally or informally, with the municipality. The municipal officers thought of themselves as controllers of rumor, though the slim means at their disposal had fostered approaches that certainly did not resemble modern notions of "rumor control."

The vitality of word-of-mouth news takes on clearer definition when we examine usages of the words *bruit, rumeur,* and *nouvelle* in 1789, because it becomes evident that news as content was inseparable from the activity of spreading and reacting to news.

Bruit

The term *bruit* had a flavor comparable to that of the modern English term *rumor,* carrying overtones of triviality and scurrility, and also suggesting a need for—and the possibility of—control. When the municipality of Laon decided in late July to search the cellars of the bishop's palace for arms,[19] they did so "to satisfy M. the doyen, and bring an end to the alarming *bruits* that one is pleased [*que l'on se plaise*] to spread on this subject . . . "[20] This phrase encapsulates two assumptions: that to act on a *bruit* is a way to control it; and that someone is spreading the *bruit* intentionally (and perhaps even with a certain gusto). In the sources, *bruit* is most frequently encountered in Fillmore's object and instrument cases. It was either acted upon in a sentence ("to go check that the *bruits* that one spread were not false") or given an instrumental sense, providing the immediate stimulus for an event ("It's on these *bruits* that the people have come to rise up here . . . ").[21]

Typically, the word *bruit* was connected with some form of the verb *répandre* (to spread).[22] Users seem to have chosen between employing the reflexive verb *se répandre*, which implied that the *bruit* "spread itself" ("the *bruit* is spreading that . . . ," "the false *bruits* that are spread," "a frightening *bruit* had spread");[23] or introducing an agent to do the work ("the *bruits* that one spread . . . ," "those who spread this false *bruit*").[24] The use of *on* ("one") as the most general agent possible offered a sort of conspiracy theory without conspirators, which readers or listeners might interpret according to their own lights.

When *bruit* was put in the instrument case, it was usually shown affecting popular action—but not always. Official behavior could also be described as triggered by a *bruit*. The phrase "on the *bruit*" was frequently employed to introduce a *bruit* as the immediate cause of an event. Here are three examples:

> The inhabitants of Compiègne, having been informed that M. Berthier de Sauvigny, intendant of Paris, had arrived in this town, arrested him on the *bruit* that the capital was making a search for him . . . (Municipal officers of Compiègne)

> They said that the town of Etampes was in the greatest fermentation and the liveliest alarms, on the *bruit* that had spread that it was proposed to remove from it, for the subsistence of the capital, the little grain and flour that was left to it . . . (Minutes of the electors of Paris)

> . . . This indictment had been drafted, through zeal as well as fear, on some *bruits* that were a bit too vague, coming from the inhabitants of this canton. (Duc de Gesvres)[25]

"On the *bruit*" was a verbal link connecting activity and word-of-mouth information.

Of course, *bruits* were qualified by adjectives that denigrated or legitimized them. "False *bruit*" appeared frequently, but only after the activity around the *bruit* in question had died down. On August 9, 1789, after the Great Fear's rumors were known to be false, a royal proclamation spoke of "ill-intentioned people . . . who begin by sowing false *bruits* in the countryside . . . " At the other end of the social scale, country curés in Hainaut imploring clemency for their neighbors after a collective act of defiance in their village claimed that "they let themselves be borne along, each by the others, through blindness, error, and the false or exaggerated *bruits* that one is pleased to spread among them . . . "[26] But these *bruits* were not described as false by their nature as *bruits*, as orally delivered news; they had turned out to be false in the process of running their course.

Bruits could also be "frightening," "alarming," "injurious," "slanderous," or "infamous," but there were fewer qualifiers in use that could mark a *bruit* as the product of low society. In the National Assembly a Third-Estate deputy, arguing against local officials' practice of taking into protective custody persons who had gained the enmity of a crowd, insisted: "The only public clamor that can authorize an imprisonment is that which pursues the guilty party at the moment he is passing by when he has been seen committing the crime. If by 'public clamor' one understands a *bruit populaire*, vague suspicions, what citizen can then count on that public and personal liberty that we are charged to defend?"[27] *Bruit populaire* is just the coin the historian might expect more of, but does not find in wide currency. On the other hand, *bruit public* crops up more often, with its connotation of a common, if plebeian, resource:

> The parish of Voulpaix, deprived up to the approach of the harvest of the victuals necessary for its subsistence, or forced to procure them at exorbitant prices, has believed on *bruits publics* that the excessive dearness of grain, or its shortage, result from nocturnal sales and exportations. (Municipal officers of Voulpaix)

> This intendant has governed this province up to the moment of his escape— which, following the *bruit public*, our municipal officers have qualified as an "absence" . . . (Militia officers of Amiens)

> . . . he said that he knew, according to the *bruits publics* and even from nearly all the villagers roundabout, that at the château of the village of Ecluse there were several small cannon and a great number of muskets . . . (Testimony of a tax collector for the *eau-de-vie* excise, near Douai)[28]

In the expression *bruit public*, the *bruit* came into its own as a medium of rapid communication, almost a utility that happened to be available to the humblest. This implication recurs in another frequent expression, *voix publique*: the "public voice" ("Once this project was known to Sieur Dorimont through the *voix publique*, he trembled . . . "),[29] which likewise weakens the class character that could be attached to *bruit*. This sense of *bruit* as a medium of transmission explains, for example, the apparent redundancy of a sentence from the Soissons provincial commission, which couples *bruit* with *nouvelles* in the same awkward phrase: "Certain frightening *nouvelles* which had no foundation and which, on false *bruits*, were propagated at the same moment in a number of towns and parishes of our province and the neighboring provinces, invited all the citizens to [take] precautions that one believed to be as pressing as they were necessary."[30] Here *nouvelles* are the content, and travel on *bruits*, which serve as vehicles. The meaning of *bruit* took in both the matter and the process of word-of-mouth dissemination.

Rumeur

The term *rumeur* seems to have been resorted to less frequently than *bruit*, and to have carried worse connotations.[31] *Rumeur*, like *bruit*, had the secondary meaning of "noise," thus lying on a spectrum that included *murmures*, a favorite old-regime euphemism for popular unrest. *Rumeur* was used to describe situations more extreme than those covered by *bruit*:

> . . . in the evening, a *rumeur* arose in this place which occasioned gatherings that did not break up until daylight the next day, and which threw a fright into Argenteuil. (Municipal officers of Argenteuil)

> September 6 at about nine o'clock at night, M. Sambrenau de St-Sauveur came to warn me that there was *grande rumeur* among the populace, who said that if the hussars were not made to leave, they would set fire to the house where they were lodged and massacre them afterward. (Lieutenant of hussars, Château-Thierry)[32]

By the same token, *rumeur* was a strong enough term that officials used it to explain situations where they had bowed to outside pressure. In the first and third examples below, *rumeur* is a counteragent:

> Clermont-en-Beauvaisis . . . decided on a decree on August 3 to protect the tax collectors, but did not announce it, held back by the *rumeur populaire*. (Clerk, controller-general's office)

> Since assurances were given us by MM. the military chiefs that the regiments would make no opposition to reestablishing the price of bread on the old footing for the townspeople, we took the resolution to do so . . . ; but, warned the next day that this resolution had excited a new *rumeur*, we consequently believed we had to suspend its execution . . . (Municipal officers of Douai)

> . . . the said officers of the committee . . . were brought to authorize the said searches, only because of the gravity of the circumstances and the importance of the denunciations . . . and they [acted] as if forced by the *rumeur publique* to combat their private opinions . . . (Officers of Douai militia)[33]

Along with the strength of the term *rumeur* came a pronounced class accent. "Rumeur populaire," "*rumeur* among the populace," "some *rumeur* in the lowest class of the people," appear as qualifiers for this dangerous force. While the meaning of *rumeur* overlapped that of *bruit*, when they were used to refer to the content of word-of-mouth news, the activity associated with *rumeur* was different. *Rumeur* signified that early stage of popular unrest often called *fermentation* by old-regime officials.

Nouvelle

In both modern and eighteenth-century parlance, *nouvelle* is usually— and properly—translated as "news." In 1789 also, *nouvelle* meant a piece of news, assumed to be true unless the noun was somehow qualified ("chimerical *nouvelle*," "*nouvelles* . . . that had no foundation").[34] Compared to *bruit* and *rumeur*, *nouvelle* had fewer connotations of oral delivery and was more likely than the other two to describe printed or written information. For instance, in these comments by Gorsas on the veracity of the Paris press, *nouvelle* was the central term:

> The permanent committee has had a placard posted by which it invites MM. the printers to print nothing but authentic *nouvelles*. The author of the *Courrier* . . . has always taken, and . . . will take great care to give nothing but authentic *nouvelles*, and he will make it a duty to note those that could be dubious.[35]

This is not to say that *nouvelle* was used only for written news; it was used for orally delivered news also ("give the *nouvelles* to one another," "one of these orators . . . finally cried out the terrible *nouvelle*").[36] However, *bruit* and *rumeur* were by and large confined to the oral realm, while *nouvelle* was not.

Nouvelle had a presumed veracity that gave it power in a sentence. In almost half of the occurrences collected, *nouvelle* was employed in Fillmore's agent case.

> But the *nouvelles* that come to us each day from the provinces press us to deliberate. (Duport, National Assembly)

> The *nouvelle* of a reprieve from execution of the guilty persons who had been arrested committing disorders in this province has encouraged the ill-intentioned. (Comte d'Esterhazy, Valenciennes)

> We should not dissimulate from you the fright produced in our fellow-citizens by the *nouvelle* hurriedly reported in this town, Tuesday afternoon, by some travelers . . . (Municipal officers of Etampes)[37]

Nouvelle was coupled with the verb *répandre* far less often than were *bruit* and *rumeur*. Instead, verbs describing transmission of *nouvelles* were more likely to suggest a relatively orderly, point-to-point delivery: *donner, annoncer, recevoir, rapporter,* and *imprimer* (give, announce, receive, report, print) characteristically occur.

We have already noted the relation between *nouvelle* and *bruit*, in which *bruits* are a medium, providing currents that circulate *nouvelles* ("frightening *nouvelles* . . . which, on false *bruits* were propagated.")[38] The two terms could also be used together in such a way that *bruits* indicated false reports while *nouvelles* indicated correct ones, as in this example from the correspondence of the royal household:

> The same *bruits* spread at the same time almost everywhere in the kingdom, without the source being discovered, even now; in truth they were accredited by the *nouvelles* coming from several places where the bandits had committed great excesses, but in the greatest number of provinces, the terror was without any foundation . . . [39]

Note that the "bruits" are "répandus" (spread), while the "nouvelles" have "venues" (come). In fact all the reports, true or false, received by the royal household arrived from the proper sources: the local authorities.

For a *nouvelle* to *se répandre*, like a *bruit*, implied its degeneration. In this example the Parisian journalist Desmaisons coupled *nouvelle* and *se répandre* to explain a current of the Great Fear that touched Paris directly:

> On Monday evening there were lively alarms. They were excited by a *nouvelle* augmented by fright. A troop of day laborers had offered their services to a farmer whose crop was ready to harvest. Since the latter had refused to give them the price they demanded, the spirit of anarchy carried them to threats. They claimed they were going to cut his grain in spite of him and ruin his harvest. The frightened farmer called for aid. The *nouvelle* grew as it spread [*se répandit en s'augmentant*]. The tocsin was rung in all the adjacent parishes. The fright was communicated to St-Denis and soon to Paris. The troop of workers became an army of vagabonds. The specific threat was taken for a threat of general destruction of the harvests.[40]

Desmaison's explanation is similar to that of Duguey, the sensible provost of mounted police in Clermont-en-Beauvaisis quoted at length in chapter 4. A limited, concrete incident is augmented through fear to vast proportions; no conspiracy need be supposed in order to understand the panic. In Desmaison's language, *nouvelle* stands for the factual core, which is then *répandu*, changes its form, and is converted into a spurious fright (*frayeur*).

Nouvelle was distinguishable in meaning from *bruit* and *rumeur*; it consistently signified a piece of information rather than a process of information. While *bruit* and *rumeur* both connoted a process of circulating news which involved many participants, *nouvelle* was used for news transmitted along more controllable channels. This distinction represents only a pattern, not a rule; nevertheless the pattern indicates that the modern division between news and rumor was gradually emerging.

Nouvelle was used in ways that implied separate roles for disseminators of information and recipients of information. In the use of *bruit* and *rumeur*, these roles lost all definition: to hear information, to pass it along, and to act in response to it tended to fuse into one sequence, often carried out by *on* (one), an anonymous or collective persona. *Bruit* meant both the content of a word-of-mouth news item, and the "grapevine" as an information medium: *rumeur* meant the content of a word-of-mouth news item, and connoted an ominous rapidity in the transmission of that content.

Eighteenth-century words about news tended to evoke ranges of activity linked with news; content, process, and response formed a continuum. Old-regime "rumor control" focused on the response end of this continuum. Rather than dispensing counterinformation to damp down a rumor, authorities sought to be the first to respond to it. When they believed a rumor to be false, they might organize a highly visible, demonstrative investigation (for example, sending the Laon fire brigade to the bishop's cellar), which paradoxically tended to affirm the role of rumor in public life. If the authorities were uncertain whether the rumor was true or false, then official activity based on the rumor was often the option they preferred, because it at least put them at the forefront of events. The active, participatory nature of the news that reached the general public in 1789 goes a long way to explain the promptness of action shown by many local authorities in the Great Fear. Not only did the Fear have great credibility—or, put another way, social acceptability—to old-regime officials, but those officials also acted in a fashion that they believed fairly prudent whether the Fear might turn out to be true or false. Thus the Great Fear was to a considerable extent a massive exercise in "rumor control," according to the lights of the old regime.

Three Words of 1789: *Brigand, Peuple, Aristocrate*

The remainder of this chapter is concerned with three words that are salient to the problem of the Great Fear. The meaning of the word *brigand* is essential to the question, who was the enemy in the mind's eye of rural society during the Great Fear?

An examination of the many meanings of *brigand* reveals a similarity—in vagueness and in semantic extension—to other eighteenth-century terms, *peuple* foremost among them. *Peuple* is then considered in comparison to *brigand*, and the implications of the similarity are explored.

Finally, the word *aristocrate* is examined because of the importance in Parisian thinking during July and August 1789 of the idea of an "aristocratic plot." Georges Lefebvre made the "aristocratic plot" the centerpiece of his explanation of the Great Fear. Does the evidence in the Soissonnais for the currency of this idea justify granting it a fundamental role in the region?

Brigand

Brigand is surely one of the vaguest words of 1789. The term was so ambiguous that its meaning in any given case was almost a reflector of the assumptions of the speaker or writer and the situation of the moment. Its interpretation by historians has always tended to falter at this ambiguity. At times, though not consistently, the great French social historians of the Revolution identified the "brigands" of the Great Fear with actual social classes: artisans and peasants for Mathiez, the urban and rural unemployed for Lefebvre, beggars and vagabonds for Soboul.[41] Each of these identifications can indeed be supported by contemporary examples, but other identifications could be supported as well.

The source materials for this study have yielded 110 occurrences— 99 of *brigand* and 11 of *brigandage*. The great majority of these cases come from known situations and social contexts. Thus it has been possible to classify many of these occurrences by a probable referent. There are 20 cases where *brigand* or *brigandage* apparently refers to peasants in revolt; 12 where participants in disturbances over grain seem to be intended; and another 12 dispersed among four more categories: robber bands (5 cases), foreigners (2 cases), poachers and other forest types (2 cases), and urban crowds in revolt against tax collection or active in other affairs unrelated to subsistence (3 cases). This much accounts for 44 of the cases. Of the remaining 66, · 41 refer to the (nonexistent) "brigands" of the Great Fear—that is, "brigands" as destroyers of harvests and sackers of villages—and 25 occurrences are too unclear, ambivalent, amorphous, or exceptional to fit into any category. Overall, in 66 of 110 cases, *brigand* and *brigandage* either signify the Great Fear's "crimes" ("crimes" that never took place and that could have found support in no sector of society) or are used in a rhetorical and indeterminate manner.

Brigands as Peasants in Revolt. In these 20 cases *brigand* and *brigandage* function precisely as simple euphemisms for a social class. Because *brigandage* refers to the act, not the actor, its usages are often straightforward. D'Agay, the intendant of Amiens, writing of the May revolt in the Cambrésis, simply stated that the participants were "the collected inhabitants of a number of country parishes estimated at seven to eight thousand men . . . who . . . have already committed a number of *brigandages* . . . " D'Agay counterposed *brigands* to higher strata of the peasantry: "the honest peasants who will risk valuable lives against *brigands* who, knowing the parish forces, will always take measures so as not to be repulsed . . . "[42] Of course, the "brigands" knew the forces of each parish because they inhabited those parishes.

When *brigand* was used in this social context, the existence of leaders was frequently mentioned:

> One of the chiefs of these *brigands* persuaded the inhabitants of Fretin that they were owners of this village's marsh. (Royalist journalist, 1790)

> They broke down the doors of the château, pillaged the grain they found there, drank wine and liqueurs, and pilfered various effects; this troop of *brigands* was disposed to continue in their exercise of violence, had their leader not been arrested . . . (Intermediate bureau of Noyon, August 1789)[43]

The use of *chef* (leader) was a borrowing from the robber-band meaning of *brigand*. Just as inhabitants of a village were verbally separated from that village's rebellion by applying the label *brigand* to the rebellion's participants, so the participants themselves were verbally separated from the rebellion's purpose by the emphasis on a supposed leader.

Brigands as Grain Rioters. It is of considerable interest that these 12 occurrences include 6 of the 11 occurrences of *brigandage*. If the use of *brigand* implies a need to rename those persons and groups involved in socially threatening behavior, then the use of *brigandage* suggests a milder need to simply condemn that behavior without masking the identity of the participants. The weaker terms *malveillants* (the malevolent), *populace*, and even *malheureux citoyens* (unfortunate citizens) are used to name the perpetrators of *brigandages*. *Brigandage* also stands on its own, as in "these *brigandages* were committed everywhere at the same time" or "this odious *brigandage* transpired under the eyes of the timid and cowardly mounted police."[44]

Another noteworthy pattern is the use of *brigands* to supplement more prosaic culprits. In the remark of a Parisian elector that "these [grain] convoys . . . were exposed in those days of trouble to the pillage of *brigands*, and even of the inhabitants of the places they passed through," *brigand* is used like a polite cough before the real information is conveyed.[45] Troubles over grain were common enough that the use of *brigand* in this context may have smacked of hyperbole even by contemporary standards.

Brigands as Robber Bands, Poachers, Foreigners, or the Seditious. When *brigands* was used in the sense of "robber bands," it designated much smaller groups of persons than it did in other social contexts. In place of hundreds or thousands, we find groups of two dozen:

> I have just been informed that a group of *brigands*, 15 in number, are traveling by night and falling upon farmsteads—especially, isolated ones— where, by violence, by assault and battery, and by breaking doors and windows, they put the farmers to contribution and demand money from them; otherwise they are threatened with arson. (Provost of mounted police, Paris intendancy)
>
> . . . there are some *brigands*, 20 to 24 in number, near the village of Veneux, who made attacks in the forest of Fontainebleau. (Mounted police of Fontainebleau)[46]

It is possible that these examples represent the professional use of *brigand* by the police, and that more extended uses were part of "civilian" vocabulary.

Brigand in the sense of "robber" was also used to describe an individual's slide into criminality. On July 15, the municipal officers of Walincourt in the Cambrésis petitioned the National Assembly for clemency to villagers who had forced the local seigneur and abbey to sell them grain at a low, fixed price. The legal pursuit of the case by the mounted police had alarmed participants to such a point that "they live wandering in the woods, abandoning the care of their families." The officers added, "To this alarming circumstance is joined the fear that persons whom we knew to be honest may become *brigands* to procure themselves the essentials . . . ."[47] This is one of just two references I have found to any process of becoming a "brigand." Such a reference must draw an explicit connection between "brigands" and people of another social status, and these connections are very rare.

The three remaining social contexts—references to foreigners, poachers, and urban revolt unrelated to provisions—have only seven examples among them. There is a recognition of a process of becoming a "brigand" in the remark of Laon's attorney for the Maîtrise of Streams and Forests that "there is often no more difference or interval between a poacher and a *brigand* than the next opportunity."[48] Neither of the two references to foreigners as "brigands" are contemporary with the Fear. One came from a militia near the northern border, "the frontier with the Austrian Netherlands, in which people are armed everywhere, and from which one may well fear the incursions of bandits or *brigands*, above all in the current circumstances."[49] The other is from Montjoie, a royalist journalist, in 1791, recalling the Great Fear: "No one thought that France could produce so many monsters; one wanted to think that they were foreigners for the most part . . . ."[50] No contemporary evidence of a fear of foreigners or foreign troops has been found for the Great Fear in the Soissonnais, though both were part of Fear rumors elsewhere in France.[51]

The three *brigand* references to urban rioters that are not concerned with grain remind us of the contrast in numbers with robber bands. They speak of "two thousand armed *brigands*" and of "swarms of *brigands*."[52] Might the use of large numbers and superlatives with *brigand* have clued in the listener or reader that a social group was being referred to obliquely?

Brigands of the Great Fear. Before examining how *brigand* was used in references to the Fear, it is worth noting that Duguey, the provost of mounted police of Clermont-en-Beauvaisis whose report of the Fear was quoted in chapter 4, eschewed the term *brigand* throughout. The words he preferred are instructive (emphases are added):

> The inhabitants of this parish, who . . . have the fixed idea . . . that *on* [one] would come cut their grain . . . imagined that *gens malintentionnés* [ill-intentioned people] were coming to ravage their fields . . .

> . . . I received a first dispatch, announcing to me that a *bande* of two hundred *personnes* [persons] were presently on the land of Sacy-le-Grand, busy cutting down grain.

... someone came to announce that four thousand of these *vagabonds* were arriving in Clermont ... I could argue all I wanted that this was impossible; no one wanted to believe me.

... another alarm supervened when the *nouvelle* came that someone had seen *bandes* [bands] coming from the Paris and Beauvais directions.[53]

Duguey's use of *vagabonds*, along with two uses of *bande*, show how his thoughts ran. In his report he took the position that the Great Fear was inherently improbable. It was improbable to Duguey because the menace to public order in the countryside that he expected was groups of vagabonds or very poor peasants, and in his experience vagabonds simply did not come in groups of four thousand. Entire districts in rebellion came in those magnitudes, but the couriers of the Fear reported no sign of rebellion. Duguey seems to have rejected the term *brigand* because he could not tie it to any group in the population and it therefore had no value for him. He did use the equally vague *gens malintentionnés* (ill-intentioned people), but only in the context of describing the peasants' state of mind in Estrées-St-Denis.

In occurrences of *brigand* whose context is the Fear's panic itself, two motifs emerge: the "brigands" as destroyers of the harvest, and the "brigands" as arsonists of communities. Of the 15 occurrences that depict destroyers of the harvest, 11 come from persons responsible for public order. "Brigands" are often characterized by officials as a "troupe," an "attroupement," "bandes," "une troupe considérable," or "une troupe forte considérable ... " Despite the appearance of large numbers (four thousand "brigands" in the letter of the Soissons notables to the National Assembly) these frequent occurrences of the word *troupe* attempt to locate the "brigands" in the authorities' familiar world of rural disorder. Something of the same conception is shared by a member of the Paris district of St-Jacques, who wrote a proposal to the municipality's military committee on July 28 for controlling the "brigands" in the Paris intendancy:

One would probably arrive at the destruction of the *brigands*, or at least their dispersion, by forming a guard corps in each principal inn of the places of passage, and even in those away from the roads, because as these ferocious beasts cannot after all live from the damage they commit on the plains, they will always find themselves in the absolute necessity of approaching villages, where they will be arrested without fail ...

These scoundrels are ill-dressed for the most part, and have no passports;

they will be easily arrested on the roads when hunger chases them from their dens.[54]

All this is evidence for a loose conception of the "brigands" as hungry vagabonds—but primarily in the town-dweller's mind. The hunger of the "brigands" coexists, against all logic, with the image of the "brigands" as destroyers of food: the part of the picture that originated in the rural wellsprings of the Fear.

In the Soissonnais, arson was not part of the image of the "brigands" in documents contemporaneous with the Great Fear. The only local evidence found for such an idea comes from the 1806 manuscript history of Château-Thierry by the abbé Hébert. According to Hébert, "Clamecy, the mayor of Soissons, apparently informed that there had been a fire at Coincy a little while before, of which the cause was unknown . . . wrote . . . that the environs of Soissons were full of *brigands*. What was more, it was asserted that the comte d'Artois had been seen at the head of these *brigands*, and that he had had fires started wherever he passed."[55] Neither the emphasis on arson nor the mention of nobles can be found in other documents. The regional emphasis on the destruction of harvests, as opposed to the destruction of communities, was overwhelming. Some reports from other regions and in the Parisian press did involve fire:

> Several couriers have announced to us that a considerable number of *brigands* or "troop against the nation" are spread through different provinces, that they pillage and rob the towns and villages and set fires wherever they pass, [they] said this troop was more than 50,000 men . . . (Gendarme near Mamers, July 24, 1789)

> The *bruit* spread that the *brigands*, after having sacked Nemours and burned Château-Landon, were coming to burn Toury . . . (Paris journalist, August 1789)[56]

However, this conception of the "brigands," with its echoes of an invading army, played no part so far detected in the Great Fear as seen in the Soissonnais.

Socially Vague Usages of *Brigand*. Among the occurrences that cannot be classified socially with any confidence, some exhibit an intriguing trait: a tendency to set off "brigands" against a reference to an existing class or group. Here is the opposite of the type of usage that employs *brigands* as a euphemism for an actual class: instead, these usages distinguish an actual class by marking it off from the "brigands."

This device could be used for different purposes. The term *brigand* could separate grave offenses from less serious ones (committed in real life by the same persons):

> There are complaints on all sides about enterprises carried out against persons and property by the *brigands* wandering the provinces, and about the obstacles that are put up everywhere to the free circulation of provisions. (The deputy Dupont, a curé of Lille, in the National Assembly on August 5)[57]

In royalist usage, *brigand* could double the reader's impression of the disorder left by the disturbances that had actually taken place:

> It was natural that the court, alarmed on one hand by the appearance of so many *brigands*, and on the other by the popular insurrections, would determine on employing public force. (Montjoie, 1791)[58]

Finally, here is the duc d'Aiguillon speaking in the National Assembly on the night of August 4:

> It is not only the *brigands* who, arms in hand, want to enrich themselves in the midst of calamities; in several provinces the entire *peuple* form a sort of league to destroy the châteaux, ravage the land, and above all to seize the archives where the titles to feudal properties are deposited.[59]

D'Aiguillon was of course referring to the peasant revolts of preceding weeks and relabeling the participants; but he did not do so by saying "the *brigands* are a fiction," though by August 4 the Assembly knew that many earlier reports of brigands had proved false. Instead, he said "not only the *brigands*, but . . . the entire *peuple*," keeping the term *brigand* in his vocabulary as a prelude to proposing measures of conciliation with the "peuple."

Brigand in a Royalist Theory of Conspiracy: Montjoie. The use of *brigand* by the royalist journalist Montjoie merits a brief separate discussion. Montjoie wrote about the Great Fear in 1791, two years after it occurred. He took as his intellectual project the development of a conspiracy theory large enough to embrace the entire revolution as it had unfolded up to that time. This is what makes his use of *brigand* interesting, because the term, which would seem perfectly suited to the requirements of conspiracy theory, actually gave him considerable trouble. Its ambiguity tended to shift from the convenient to the unmanageable; and at times real "brigands," at other times nonexistent ones, wander through his text.

Montjoie's intellectual reliance on the idea of a conspiracy is absolute. He knows this and even celebrates it in these words:

> If one loses sight, in the course of my story, of what I am about to say on the preexistence of a plan of revolution, one will understand nothing of either the various scenes that have taken place, or of the movements to which the principal actors have lent themselves . . .
>
> In admitting on the contrary, as a truth, that the design of the new edifice was sketched out [in advance] . . . everything becomes explicable; the events arrive in the foreseen order, they are only the natural and necessary effects of a cause one knows: the means astonish; but when one perceives the end to which the characters are tending, one watches them with interest as they travel the different routes that lead to it.[60]

According to Montjoie, the hidden general staff of the Revolution worked with two "plans" that had the same goal. Montjoie alternates these "plans," generally using whichever does less violence to the facts at hand. In one plan, panic would be spread so that respectable townsmen would take fright and arm themselves. In the other plan, hordes of paid "brigands" would be released throughout France in order to achieve the same result. "To produce so prodigious an effect, it was necessary to cover France with *brigands*, it was necessary to exaggerate their number and their excesses, it was necessary to show them at the capital's gates and to flood the streets with them."[61] Montjoie uses both "plans" in parallel while trying to circumvent overt contradictions.

With the first "plan," the plot to spread panic, Montjoie put the emphasis on Paris as the central point from which "fraudulent tales" radiated: "Numerous bands of scoundrels, starting from Paris as from a common center, spread along the roads, traversed the towns and villages, stopped nowhere, made the tocsin sound everywhere, announced foreign troops and hordes of *brigands*, carried arms, and sowed bribes as they passed."[62] Where there were no emissaries, National Assembly deputies corresponded with their local agents. This piece of Montjoie's argument took into account the known fact that the "brigands" had turned out to be nonexistent.

The second "plan," the plot to unleash actual "brigands" on France, relied heavily on the notion of a "famine pact," which by 1789 had been in circulation for many years.[63] According to Montjoie, the large sums that Necker had requisitioned to buy grain abroad had been manipulated to create secret funds, augmented by the high price gotten at resale, and the whole paid out secretly as "the brigands' share."[64] The plotters' artificial famine both created discontent and raised money to hire agitators. In this aspect of Montjoie's argument the "brigands" are real again.

In Montjoie's writings, the identity of the "brigands" is not only vague, it is utterly lacking in importance. Even the question of whether they existed or not—much less who they might be—is irrelevant, because either way they served as a device to the same end for the same masters. However, these masters remain unknown. Montjoie refrains from outlining a concrete conspiratorial structure (Orléanist, for instance) in which actual personalities would have specific places: "If it had been necessary for M. d'Orléans to encourage the capital's insurrection by his presence, it would also have been necessary that he be present at the same time at all points of the kingdom, for everywhere in the same period the people rose up as in Paris, through hidden intrigues and invisible hands."[65] To devise a conspiracy theory that met the magnitude of the situation, the roles assigned to the "brigands" had to be as hazy and multifarious as those assigned by contemporary language in general.

Brigand Viewed by Fillmore Case. Divided by Fillmore case, occurrences of *brigand* form a simple pattern. Roughly half the occurrences have *brigand* in the agent case; the remaining half are scattered among the seven other cases without one clearly predominating. *Brigand* is an active subject in the agent case, linked with verbs such as *marcher, répandre, exiger, menacer, couper, faucher, forcer, briser, ouvrir, piller, voler,* and *incendier* (march, spread, demand, threaten, cut, reap, force, break, open, pillage, rob, burn). If the occurrences are ordered by date and those from the peak of the Great Fear (July 27–August 4) are separated from all the rest, the pattern holds for both Great Fear and non-Great Fear occurrences; but the tension of the Fear days is reflected by an exaggeration of the pattern (Table 5.1).

The Fillmore cases to note are the agent case, which rises sharply due to the impact of the Great Fear, and the object and instrument cases, which drop noticeably. This is not an alteration but a heightening of the basic pattern. *Brigand* was a word often used to signify persons out of the control of other forces; in the Fear, *brigand* was only used in this manner more distinctly. Linguistically, the Great Fear was not an aberration but rather a tensing up of the same speech patterns normally present in a more relaxed form.

Brigand was a portmanteau word, a "wild card" in old-regime ideology. Like another portmanteau word, *féodalité* (feudalism), it had an amazing breadth of application, "as if [in the words of Régine Robin]

Table 5.1 Occurrences of *Brigand* during the Great Fear and at Other Times, by Fillmore Case

Fillmore Case	All Occurrences except *Those of* July 27–August 4 (N = 70)		Occurrences of July 27–August 4 (N = 29)		Percentage Difference
	No.	%	No.	%	
Agent	30	42.8	16	55.2	+12.4
Counteragent	7	10.0	3	10.3	+0.3
Object	17	24.3	5	17.2	−7.1
Result	1	1.4	1	3.4	+2.0
Instrument	7	10.0	1	3.4	−6.6
Source	5	7.1	3	10.3	+3.2
Goal	3	4.3	0	0.0	−4.3
Experiencer	0	0.0	0	0.0	——

Source: These contemporary occurrences of *brigand* were collected from the primary sources that form the basis of this study as a whole.

one were handling a signifier able to include the maximum of elements that are negative and, as such, to be rejected."[66] However, unlike *féodalité*, a term that contested the existing state of things, *brigand* was a term integral to the old regime. The word *peuple* provides a closer comparison. Both *brigand* and *peuple* blurred distinctions and confounded groups below a certain murky social threshold: the threshold of *honnêteté*, or respectability. *Brigand* did this in the sense of illegality and exteriority regarding the society and its norms. *Peuple* did the same thing, but within legality and on the interior of the society. The same persons, groups, and classes were at times alluded to as inside the pale (*peuple*) or outside the pale (*brigands*). In some cases *brigand* and *peuple* designated the "outside" and the "inside" as social spaces, without intending to pick out actual groups at all. A closer look at how *peuple* was used will make the comparison clearer.

Peuple

Like *brigand*, the word *peuple* in the language of 1789 was a whirlpool of crosscurrents. Mirabeau justly observed that the word "lends itself to anything."[67] Its four basic meanings were as follows: It could signify (1) the people of the nation (*le peuple français*), or (2) in the plural, the

peoples of all the regions of France ("the king is father of his *peuples*");
it could indicate (3) a low social class, but with the greatest vagueness
("*le peuple* will recognize its errors sooner or later"; "[the] government . . . to procure bread for the *peuple* . . . "); and it could also indicate
(4) this class in the local sense ("*le peuple* . . . broke several windows").[68]
The possibilities of linguistic "sliding" and ambiguity were therefore
great, and it is often best to interpret the word's usage in a text as a
function of at least two meanings.

A portmanteau word so vast had to be qualified and subdivided at
times for the communication of meaning to be possible (though the
word's place in old-regime ideology in a sense stemmed from its power
to maintain confusion). First, it was a circumlocution for the poor—
which makes for the awkwardness of statements like "the permanent
committee of Château-Thierry was occupied the whole day of the seventh with the means of tranquillizing that which is not the *peuple* and of
appeasing the *peuple* properly speaking . . . "[69] The inclusiveness of the
term *peuple* impeded its use for designating clearly the lowest social
strata, which had to be qualified as "le petit peuple," "le bas peuple,"
"the poorest part of the *peuple*," "the least prosperous part of the *peuple*,
that part interested in the destruction of the salt tax . . . " *Peuple* in the
sense of "crowd" was used with intonations that varied from the simplicity of the police account ("*Le peuple* followed the carter to the market's
exit") to an attribution of dignity, vigilance, and citizenship ("*Le Peuple*
watched with inquietude the loading of 10,000 [kegs] of gunpowder . . . "; "*le Peuple* believed itself obliged to seize two of M. the
registrars . . . ").[70] Yet the writer who felt the need to socially qualify a
crowd might be constrained to use expressions such as "a crowd of the
peuple"; "many persons of the *peuple*." The usage of *peuple* for "crowd"
gave the word an urban connotation that slanted the meaning of *peuple* as
class and forced such long expressions as "[The press] spreads a multitude of impious writings as far as the class of *peuple* and into the countryside . . . "[71] *Le peuple* was also too large and diffuse a grouping to
receive moral condemnation, for instance from embattled municipalities; often the condemnation itself demarcated a subdivision of *le peuple*:

> . . . that part of the *peuple* which treats as an enemy all those whom they have
> not constituted. (Municipal officers of Douai, November 29)

> That part of the *peuple* easily embittered by misery, accustomed not to rea-
> son about its rights, and which readily forgets its duties . . . (Mayor of
> Compiègne, September)[72]

If a moral subdivision of *le peuple* were created in discourse, the entire class of those designated by *le peuple* taken alone would not be antagonized, nor did this subdivision break down the larger linguistic "class" in a way that would clarify social conflicts in the community.

In describing popular activities, *le peuple* would normally be the active subject of the sentence, especially in the reports of those in direct contact with rioters, such as military officers. But another construction was also current, which used *peuple* as a passive object, however labored the sentence need be:

> It is necessary to forget the unfortunate circumstances that carried the unreflecting *peuple* beyond its duties. (Municipal officers of Château-Thierry to the Keeper of the Seals, March 3, 1790)

> The spirit of inquietude and fermentation still reigns with so much empire over *le Peuple*, that we fear it is still not possible [for municipal officers] to make grain purchases . . . (General deputies of the Estates of Artois to the colonel inspector-general of provisioning, October 16, 1789)

> [The high prices] naturally should not cease, save by the return of abundance procured by the harvest. The impatient murmurs of the *peuple* do not permit it to await this much-desired return. (Municipal deliberations of Amiens, July 23)[73]

In these examples, *le peuple* is dominated either by its environment ("unfortunate circumstances") or by its passions ("inquietude," "murmurs"); the language occults the fact that *le peuple* are acting dynamically.

This brief discussion of the word *peuple* has only opened the question of its use. However, it is of interest that Montjoie, the royalist historian, also saw the problem—posed for him by a context in which *peuple* had been wrenched from an old-regime usage to a revolutionary constellation of usages. To his history of the Revolution he added an appendix— "in which is given the true and accepted meaning of words of which the innovators have made a pernicious abuse . . . "[74]—wherein he gave more than three pages to *peuple* and its cousins *multitude* and *populace*.

Montjoie begins by giving priority to the first meaning of *peuple*: "*Le peuple* taken in the mass is the very body of the nation . . . The Third Estate was, like the clergy, like the nobility, a portion of the *peuple français*."[75] Here he is attacking the famous argument of the abbé Sieyès that the Third Estate comprised a whole nation, as well as the bourgeois appropriation of the first meaning. Montjoie proceeds: "An assemblage of men, whatever their rank . . . is a multitude; it would be absurd to say that it is a *peuple* . . . he who . . . would say that he harangued the *peuple* français would speak rubbish."[76] Here he attacks the bourgeois assimilation of the third and fourth meanings to the first meaning.

However, Montjoie must also deal with the third meaning, *le peuple* as a social class, which is indeed typical of his own language elsewhere in his book. His inability to define this class is eloquent. He begins with the broad form—" . . . we call *peuple* the portion of society which is not composed of the great and the rich . . . ," defined in turn as "all those who gain their bread by the sweat of their brow . . . "[77] In this phrase Montjoie draws the line between those who labor under the Adamic curse and those who do not. "That class that one calls *peuple*, is not *le peuple*,"[78] he is constrained now to declare, keeping the third meaning separate from the first meaning.

The curse of work includes that of ignorance, for only undisturbed leisure can support education. And yet "it is in this class, which among us replaces that of slaves; it is in this class, made vile and kept in ignorance by its labor . . . that the chiefs of sedition search for dupes and instruments to execute their ambitious projects." This theme forces a new connotation of *peuple* on Montjoie, in which the word designates followers, of whatever social class. "Thus ignorant and credulous men are *peuple* . . . in this class . . . are included the great like the small, the rich like the poor. One seduces it easily; one leads it on with sophisms . . . " The word has now lost all social meaning and has wandered into the moral realm. "To be *peuple* is not to be *le peuple*; it is to be its least recommendable portion."[79]

Montjoie now staggers through a paragraph in which he attempts unsuccessfully to manage this moralizing contradiction between "very unjust and wicked men" and "very peaceable and mild men." He then appears to sense that he has lost the thread, for he begins a new section, entitled "Populace," and tries to cast his discourse in social terms again. He subdivides *peuple* somewhat, and evokes "le petit peuple, le bas peuple, le menu peuple" the only way he can, by naming their pitiable trades, which are so many images to suggest the human beings he means: "the men and women who peddle secondhand goods, the street porters, the cobblers, for to be clear I must name everything by its name, the water-carriers of Paris, the ones who collect rags in the gutters that we convert into paper. . . "[80]

Montjoie's circle around this word traces a little Hades of old-regime ideology. For he must at all costs separate the global meaning of *le peuple* as the "peuple français" from the social meaning: the greater, disadvantaged part of the Third Estate. However, to make this separation, he would have to sacrifice the classic old-regime meaning of *peuple*—the vast majority of society cursed by the need to work—because this meaning is too inclusive, too close to that of Sieyès' *Third Estate*. Montjoie needs to use *peuple* in a way that breaks the solidarity of the Third Estate, and he tries to do so, but the task requires an analytic approach to the many strata comprised by *peuple* which is beyond the capacity of old-regime ideology.

We have seen that the basic meanings of *peuple* were (1) the whole nation; (2) the peoples of the regions of France; (3) a (low) social class, very ill-defined; and (4) a crowd or mob. It is likewise clear that old-regime ideology relied on a confusion between the third and the fourth meanings. The revolutionary tactic, on the other hand, was to confuse the first and the third meanings. The pivot of the whole semantic field lies in the imprecision of the third meaning, *peuple* as a social class. If this imprecision helped the old regime to submerge specific social groups with particular needs and aspirations, it also helped the Revolution to preserve the Third Estate's political unity.

Aristocrate

This epithet had a diffusion that can be traced. Both a moral and a political expression, it was propagated in the provinces by visiting deputies of the National Assembly. On July 17, 1789, a general assembly of the Laon commune was addressed by the deputy of nearby La Ville aux Bois. The congratulatory address to the National Assembly drafted in the meeting did not fail to mention "a most perverse aristocratic coalition; the most formidable enemy of the *patrie* and of the King and the sole cause of our misfortunes. . . "[81] However, there are no other provincial sources in 28 occurrences of *aristocrate* that precede October 21, though Parisian manuscript documents, like the Parisian press, used *aristocrate* frequently.

L'aristocratie seems to have been either greater or smaller than, but not identical with, the *noblesse*; nor was it identical with *despotisme*, which was regarded as overthrown from July 14 onward. Its great attributes were silence and activity, which facilitated comparisons to a snake: "the serpent of *Aristocratie*, more dangerous than despotism, knows how to multiply its resources and assure the success of its maneuvers. . . "[82] *Aristocrates* were said to "act secretly," "practice secret maneuvers," "make their agents move," "secretly conduct despotism," "secretly mediate a second treachery." By January 1790, when the shift in power to the Third Estate was definitive, the *aristocrates* were accused of "sow[ing] the public with seditious libels and seductive and alarming discourses."[83] In two cases, *aristocrates* were also blamed for grain shortages: once in a September 4 letter from Babeuf in Paris to his wife, and once in an anonymous petition from Coucy-le-Château dated November 13—of which more shortly.[84]

Above all, the appellation *aristocrate* became an accusation, which in itself is an argument for its lack of clear relation to any social class: a precise class link would have limited its utility. Yet the heightening of rhetoric that launched the word *aristocrate* at someone's head was a very palpable phenomenon. The former municipal officers of Enghien, 10 kilometers north of Paris, passed on their distress to the National Assembly:

> . . . the assemblies that [the new municipal officers] hold in the church of Notre Dame every Sunday can only redouble our inquietude. There a dozen young people's heads are heated continuously by repeating to them that we are *aristocrates*, persons sold to the aristocratic party, and, according to certain reports made to us, monsters of aristocracy.[85]

In the rhetorical succession that the shivering former magistrates assembled secondhand, they were first simply *aristocrates*, then "gens vendus," and worst, "monstres." No less moral than social or political, these epithets primarily depict varying depths of rejection of the general good.

Enghien, however, lived in the shadow of the capital. For an inkling of the diffusion of *aristocrate* in the rural Soissonnais, we must turn to the anonymous petition of November 13 from Coucy-le-Château.[86] Addressed to the National Assembly by someone who claimed to write for "the inhabitants of the mountains and valleys for two leagues around the town of Coucy," it shows how the idea of *aristocrates* could be grafted onto an older tradition of remonstrance over grain provisioning.

The petition opens in a properly revolutionary manner; praise of the National Assembly is mingled with warnings against its enemies:

> What is known of the Assembly's operations in the provinces inspired the *peuple* with the greatest veneration and the most profound respect, and proves to it that the wish of this assembly is the good of all; yet the *peuple* fear that *aristocrates* who act in secret are still weaving plots to retard this good, or to prevent its complete achievement; up to now they have practiced all the means that can force *les peuples* to arm against each other by hoarding grains, by having them sent abroad, in a word, by occasioning a frightful general shortage in the Kingdom.[87]

Praise for the king immediately follows, for government assistance after the poor harvest of 1788 ("*Le peuple*. . . received with gratitude, with tenderness, the paternal aid that the best of kings lavished upon it"). This

was quite in keeping with the current constitutionalist rhetoric, probably expressed the author's genuine sentiments, and was also shrewd,
since one never knew where one's petition might be forwarded. But (the
letter proceeds) 1789 is different. The harvest has been good, and the
poor know it; yet its fruits are not appearing at market: "Why does the
farmer affect to send to market the worst or the least that he has? Why
do they still affect to carry there mixed grains including rye, barley, and
oats?" The petition continues that the ill-furnished markets are the fault
of the *aristocrates*.

> . . . the *aristocrates* send their agents from farm to farm to alert the farmers
> that if they cart their grains to the merchants of Soissons they will get the
> price they want for them, so in fact the farmers rush to finish threshing and
> travel to Soissons, where their grains are bought at 260, 265, 270 per *muid*
> containing eight sacks of Paris, which brings the price. . . to 33 per sack;
> thus attracted by the bait of this excessive price, the farmers no longer
> provision the markets. . . [88]

That old enemy the grain merchant from elsewhere is tentatively
presented in new dress. As an *aristocrate*, perhaps he can excite the distrust of the new bourgeois power, the National Assembly. The rest of the
letter shows how experimental this approach must have seemed to the
author, for the remedy he proposes is the renewal of the royal declaration
of 1723, which made sale of grain away from market punishable by a
fine. The last three pages of the petition are devoted to lauding the old
regulations, and the *aristocrates* are not mentioned again.

This petition provides some indication of the diffusion of the idea of
an "aristocratic plot" in the Soissonnais. The anonymous writer was
clearly a person of some education—a notary or a curé—but his geographic location, which incidentally he was at pains to identify ("2
leagues . . . from Coucy. . . which is 4 leagues from Soissons, 10 leagues
from La Fère and Chauny, 10½ leagues from Noyon,"[89] etc.), planted
him firmly in a rural milieu. Here the issues of grain sale and circulation
had been the burning topic in the spring and summer, and they were the
first subjects to which elements of the new political language were applied. Given the infrequency of the term *aristocrate* in Soissonnais documents of 1789, and the kind of diffusion suggested by the two examples
that have surfaced, it seems unlikely that the "aristocratic plot" played a
role in the region's Great Fear.

By way of conclusion, let us now attempt to deepen the reconstruction
of the Great Fear in the Soissonnais that was outlined in chapter 4.

The initial panics at St-Martin-de-Béthisy and Estrées-St-Denis were each spread by the tocsin through widening circles of villages before reaching a town of any importance. Judging by the variety of uses to which the tocsin could be put, it is likely that many village syndics rang the tocsin under severe pressure from their neighbors. The use of the tocsin ratified a community consensus about a sense of emergency more than it signified a decision taken by local officials, and this underlines the popular, mass nature of the Great Fear near its origins.

The social status of the Great Fear's "news" improved as the Fear spread. Beginning as a *bruit* that grew to encircle authorities and constrain them to active responses, the Fear turned into a *nouvelle* once towns began to dispatch couriers to other towns. As it extended in distance, the Fear ceased to "spread" and began to "arrive," until at its outer fringes the towns and villages that received it (such as Grandchamp and Jouarre along the Marne) treated the Fear's rumor, alarming though it was, as a piece of information yet to be confirmed, rather than as a process of information with its own social dynamic.

The overall pattern of transmission of the Fear was strongly marked by a social inclusiveness that took in poor and prosperous peasants, municipal oligarchies and their artisans, local notables, and partisans of the Third Estate: a phenomenon well described by the sociologist Edgar Morin's term *interclassism*. It was the portmanteau word *brigand* that carried the Great Fear between classes and estates and from country to town and back again. It would be too neat to think of *brigand* as signifying for each class its own distinct bugbear, and yet the word undeniably could make landed proprietors think of peasants in revolt, large farmers think of peasants forcing the sale of private grain stocks, smaller farmers think of harvest workers demanding their pay, still smaller farmers think of vagabonds and forest-dwelling poachers and smugglers, and so on. And who was so rich or so poor as to be indifferent to the Fear's central content, the report that "brigands" were destroying the standing crop, awaited for so long and with so much social tension? The concept of "brigands" was too confused for us to break down its meaning by social class, even if the sources were rich enough to permit it; but class-related connotations must have existed, intermingled in the vast common meaning of "outside": outside old-regime legality, outside the rigid, faltering, home-parish organization of society, or outside the physical and social limits of cultivation.

A comparison of *brigand* with another immense portmanteau word, *peuple*, makes the social roles of both words clearer. The term *brigand* was (so to speak) the term *peuple* turned inside out. Both words performed the same function in the ideology of the old regime: they obscured the structure of most of its population.

The idea of an "aristocratic plot" seems to have little power of explanation for the Soissonnais of 1789. The process of diffusion of the word *aristocrate*—emerging in Paris, transmitted to the Soissonnais through Parisian contacts, and taken up hesitantly in provincial usage later in the year—argues for a different rhythm of radicalization, in which the nobility was singled out more slowly as the enemy. This is not to say that the "aristocratic plot" was only a Parisian invention and that the pattern of diffusion in the Soissonnais would hold good for the rest of France in 1789. One might look for the "aristocratic plot" arising spontaneously in regions where the seigneur-cultivator relationship was more starkly central to peasant experience. But the existence of an influential class of large farmers in the Soissonnais created a situation of three-cornered conflict where a single adversary was less readily identifiable. The shape taken by the Great Fear in the Soissonnais thus partook of the region's movement toward an early capitalist agriculture.

PART III

Attitudes toward Authority

SIX ❧ THE PRACTICE OF PUBLIC ORDER IN 1789

Over the course of 1789, the very meaning of public order underwent a shift to which the National Assembly, ministerial bureaucrats, local authorities, and various elements of the population all contributed in different ways. Each of these groups sought to retain certain elements of what public order had meant in the old regime while introducing revolutionary novelties. No one group could see its own design in the outcome, which was the result of an interplay among them all.

Let us define "public order" at the outset as the social appearance of general obedience to law and respect for superiors. A breach of public order, accordingly, was a crime that injured this appearance, as well as transgressing the law. In the late old regime, crimes that caused no notorious disturbance were not viewed as affecting public order, and notorious disturbances were punished according to a perspective different from the modern one of "correction."

The question of public order is really a subdivision of the larger field of crime and justice. A wealth of new studies on old-regime criminality have appeared in recent years, and we can tap this new literature to design a schema of public order in the old regime. Several decrees of the National Assembly affected public order, but to understand how, we must consider the process of their diffusion into common knowledge. In various towns and villages of the Soissonnais, the post–Great Fear forms of public order were patched together out of the Assembly's decrees, popular activity, and local officers' wariness and prudence.

Gramsci pointed out that "everyone is a legislator" because even obedience can be inflected in many different ways: "[A person] continues to be a legislator even if he accepts directives from others—if, as he carries them out, he makes certain that others are carrying them out too."[1] Certainly France in 1789 was a milieu where both law and custom were open to personal and community interpretation, as the common people vied with national and local authorities in "legislating" a new public order. A multipolar dynamic of change altered the general sense of public order, and this change gave an inner meaning to the local struggles that arose as the consensus of the Great Fear broke down.

The Three Realms of Public Order

The development of old-regime justice is often portrayed as the progressive extension of the absolutist state, working its way into a backward, rural world that was hostile and even alien to it. While there is nothing inaccurate about this schema, it is not the only possible one. For the limited purpose of understanding the cohesion of old-regime society—a cohesion that was loose-knit but real—focusing on the state's development can be inapposite. Since the "unfinished state" lacked legal uniformity and adequate repressive force, it seems more to the point to consider the basis of mass "consent" (in the Gramscian sense) to the social rules that the "unfinished state" defended.

At least for the study of public order, there is heuristic value in viewing state and community as a continuum, not a manichean opposition. In this perspective, prerevolutionary public order can be described as consisting of three realms: the rural community, with its habits of (imperfect) internal regulation; the towns and their resident courts, here called the municipal-legal realm; and the state, making itself felt primarily through the intendant, his subdelegates, and the presence of military detachments, as well as the mounted police, who combined certain police and judicial functions. Eighteenth-century public order was differently ensured in different realms. While the relations among these three realms were full of contradictions, still on many occasions the gears did mesh; and to exaggerate the distances between different aspects of the same society may lead to an error of appreciation.

This eighteenth-century public order was also conceptually distinct from modern notions of public order, particularly in its relation to law. Yves Castan has written of the Languedocien's resistance to courts and preference for a locally mediated compromise: "The Languedocien does not wish to perceive this rent fabric of the general order, or rather, it is none of his business . . . Public order is not the gauge—both reassuring and rigorous—of the certainty of correction [of a wrong or injury]. Its true function is to assure by its presence, its threat, its terror, the appropriate compensation for—or prudent abstention from—the misdeed."[2] Public order deterred the wrongdoer or frightened him or her into making compensation, but it was not corrective.

The legal construct of graded crimes and penalties stood on a different level from public order understood as a practical equilibrium of human relations within the community. The restoration of this equilibrium in the present could be more important than the punishment at law of a transgression that was steadily receding into the past. The courts were not perfectly adapted to this mentality, but they did exist in coordination with it. Nicole Castan judges that "the apparatus of criminal justice [may have been] ideological in certain of its pretensions—a sterling representative of a Christian and hierarchical society . . . [however] the maintenance of these aspects does not seem to have obsessed its organizers or most of its magistrates. Like Montesquieu, they were preoccupied above all with maintaining security, in a conservative sense."[3] As a lawyer who was a Third-Estate deputy in the National Assembly expressed it, "The object of the laws is to maintain public tranquillity."[4] In short, justice was perceived as instrumental to the goal of public order. Once a disorder was concluded, "calm being perfectly reestablished" (in the stock phrase of local reports), to actively prosecute participants would require a detour back to the time of a disruptive event that was better treated as an aberration. "It is necessary to forget the unfortunate circumstances that misled the unreflecting people,"[5] wrote the municipal officers of Château-Thierry in such a situation. Public order was perceived as a continuity, while disorders were cyclical interruptions. Thus, to prosecute offenders was thought to give unwanted chronological extension to events that were "really" fleeting moments.

Public order in the realm of the rural community was primarily treated as an extension of the sphere of personal relations. Verbal abuse and physical assaults were put on the same plane and were often resolved in the same manner—through the mediation of the curé, for example— just as they had been classified together by the law in earlier centuries.[6] In her examination of Languedoc court records, Nicole Castan has been able to analyze 306 cases between 1779 and 1790 in which legal proceedings began and then a private settlement was reached (which did not necessarily preclude continued crown prosecution).[7] These cases included property and contract disputes, insults and blows, pregnancies and rapes, thefts, and even murders. Property case settlements were more frequent in the rural than in the urban milieu (29 percent versus 6 percent of Castan's sample), since rural property cases usually involved land under cultivation and the agricultural cycle could not await a judgment. Overall, cases involving insults and blows comprised almost one-fifth of the settlements recorded.

An incident from the Soissonnais is illustrative. In December 1788, the curé of Beaugies (10 kilometers northeast of Noyon) was beaten with a stick by a tavernkeeper, one Degrenier. The curé did not want to make a legal complaint, but the seigneur's fiscal attorney got wind of the matter and saw to it that proceedings were instituted. The curé's continued resistance appears to have brought the affair to the attention of the intendant Blossac. Writing to the Keeper of the Seals on February 8, 1789, Blossac conscientiously provided the village background to the case: "It remains true that Degrenier is seen as a violent and passionate character and that he is suspected of being the author of a fire that took place in the parish about two years ago . . . The curé is also reproached for having given Degrenier's animosity an opening by denouncing him to the excise collectors as a seller of untaxed drink." Blossac also mentioned Degrenier's excessive drinking as a mitigating circumstance and recommended a pardon. We learn from the curé's own letter of October 9, 1789, that he had served as rent collector in Beaugies for "Sr Debrie, bourgeois de Paris," and that Degrenier had beaten him in this capacity—another fact of which Blossac was probably aware.[8]

This little incident shows how the humiliation of an important village personage could be dealt with in different realms of public order. It seems evident that the community thought Degrenier something of a fool but was willing to tolerate him; that it felt the curé had been attacked not in his sacerdotal function but in his temporal sideline and should have had more sense than to provoke someone like Degrenier; and that in any case the curé was too close to the excise collectors and perhaps needed a lesson. The curé seems to have preferred consenting to this common assessment over entering legal proceedings. Most important, we learn all this from the state realm: from the intendant himself, the chief royal administrator of the Soissonnais, who in this case checked and ratified the community's internal regulation. Thus the community and state realms were in harmony on this occasion; the discord came from the seigneurial court, where the fiscal attorney may have pursued Degrenier for reasons of his own.

The village's internal regulation was no more a closed system than was its local economy. Once adequate conditions were united, the village accepted or even invited an outside force, typically the mounted police, to aid in restoring equilibrium. Timothy J. A. LeGoff and Donald M. G.

Sutherland cite a paradigmatic example from Brittany. A 50-year-old widow fell in love with a notary half her age. She could not gain his affections; after the failure of several ruses, the notary became engaged to another woman. In frustration, the widow "cut the ears and tail off his horse and nailed them to his fiancée's door. She also tried, unsuccessfully, to interrupt the marriage ceremony by hiding under the altar and making rude noises." Her harassment continued for a year without her victim informing outside authorities. At last she set fire to the notary's house, and the law was called in.[9] Since everyone recognized arson as a threat to the community, the village could support an intervention.

Robert Schwartz's study of the Caen intendancy suggests that such support was not unusual. About 4 of every 10 offenders in the Caen workhouse were turned in by public reporting between 1768 and 1776.[10] To judge from Schwartz's sample of the total workhouse population, perhaps nine-tenths of these were not native to their parish of arrest.[11] But this does not mean that those arrested were strangers, unknown to the villagers who reported them. Schwartz found that 67 percent of his sample were natives of the Caen intendancy, and describes in detail a case in which a village urged the arrest of a young beggar, imagined to be the leader of a robber band, who had been born in a parish nine kilometers away[12]—that is, about two and a half hours' walk.

In a different range of circumstances, legal intervention was perceived by the community as an intrusion that justified a violent solidarity. Iain Cameron's study of the mounted police in the Auvergne and Guyenne is rich in examples: "an attempt . . . to take a deaf-mute off to a monastery," a brigade's descent on beggars at a previously announced distribution of charity to commemorate a deceased seigneur, an act of strong-arm military recruitment—such scenes evoked large, determined crowds that freed the captives and drove the mounted police out of the village, walking backward toward their mounts with bayonets fixed.[13] Yet these dramatic reactions to external authority were not signs of manichean conflict between state and subjects. Rather, they were the temporary consequences of disputes between different realms of public order.

When we look beyond the rural community to consider the effectiveness of the municipal-legal realm in which the bailliage or *sénéchaussée* courts were situated, we are at once confronted, just as eighteenth-century prosecutors and plaintiffs were, with the problem of costs. The costs of a criminal prosecution varied widely and were also conditioned by the physical distance between the court and the scene of the crime; still, a range is suggested by examples of murder trials that cost between four hundred and six thousand livres.[14] In theory, these substantial sums were regained by a system of cost recovery from convicted defendants. Such a system, of course, required the defendants to be propertied.

The careful outlay of the limited funds available for crown prosecutions was the responsibility of the royal attorney. Julius Ruff has examined decisions to prosecute in the *sénéchaussées* of Libourne and Bazas, east of Bordeaux. The royal attorney was able to pursue just under one-quarter of the cases in which the plaintiff is known. Special attention was paid to homicide (90.6 percent of homicide cases were pursued at crown expense), offenses against the Catholic religion (82.7 percent), and vagabondage and military desertion (53.1 percent). Cases of assault, verbal violence, and crimes against morality (bestiality and rape of minors excepted) were generally not taken up. Only one-third of crimes against property were serious enough to warrant royal prosecution.[15] It is against this background that the infrequency of convictions for disruptions of public order must be understood.

Disorders came in many sizes, and legal language drew on an imprecise yet graded set of terms to describe them. Cameron has captured this vocabulary well:

> "Rebellion" in eighteenth-century France was much less serious than "riot," as it involved physical resistance to the authorities by only a handful of people or even a single individual. "Rebellion" in fact was as devalued a term as *assassinat* [which covered assault as well as murder], and was always supplemented in police reports and judicial charges with references to aggravated circumstances: "rebellion with insults and threats"; "rebellion with violence and assault"; "armed rebellion" even if the accused had only carried a pistol or shotgun. If at least four people had been involved in the resistance, it became "rebellion with *attroupement*." If so many had taken part that the authorities had seriously taken fright, it became a "sedition." A full-scale riot was usually described as a "popular emotion." For greatest effect, these various charges would be compounded, so that a grain riot became an "*attroupement* and popular emotion with insults, threats and violence likely to prevent the grain trade."
>
> Despite the apparent gravity of these charges, it is clear from the lenient, even trivial, sentences imposed by the magistrates that the eighteenth-century authorities were not so alarmed for the safety of the political and social fabric as their vocabulary suggested.[16]

The phrase "popular emotion" has a certain decriminalizing and psychologizing quality; it made a good linguistic counterpart to court practice, which was to drop such cases when they involved large numbers.

Ruff notes 10 cases of "collective, violent resistance against officials representing the crown" that found their way onto the docket. Eight of these cases were apparently abandoned; sentences can be found for 2, "and these involved the smallest numbers of rioters in any episodes included in this study."[17] In the aftermath of a particularly serious urban grain disturbance, alarmed municipal officers might press the provost of mounted police for punishments to serve as examples for the future. In this circumstance the police looked for someone who could be described as the inciting intelligence behind the whole event, the "motor" (*moteur*). Cameron mentions an instance in which the *moteur* of a grain disturbance was found by simply releasing the many women accused and prosecuting the only male on the suspect list.[18]

The courts' role in public order might be schematized as follows. Endowed with limited resources, court officers sought to prosecute significant crimes that were consensually condemned. Popular disturbances did not match this profile. Their frequency and the inconsequential status of those involved made them fundamentally insignificant, at least when one took the long view from the perch of a venal office. Their connections to rising prices, hunger, or patent injustice, and their tendency to involve most of the community ruled out a consensus for their condemnation. Their pursuit at law might evoke polarized and unpredictable situations, leading to further breaches of public order. In sum, most problems of public order implied poor relations between the municipal-legal realm and the realm of internal regulation, and the way to solve them was for the former realm to conciliate the latter. In a minority of cases, the disturbance left behind a continuing "fermentation" that had to be subdued by one or two exemplary punishments.

The third realm of public order, that of the state, made its day-to-day presence felt through army detachments and the mounted police (the *maréchaussée*). Garrisoned troops served very delimited police functions, largely supplying a visible armed reserve (*main-forte*) for the tactics and ruses of municipal or bailliage officers managing a crowd. The mounted police force was both an enforcement agency and a judicial institution; its cavaliers were the arm of the prevotal courts, which had their own area of competence. Troops were part of the urban scene, while the mounted police brigades largely functioned in a rural setting (in fact, they were barred from making arrests in their towns of residence).

The role of the troops is more readily comprehensible than that of the mounted police. The regular use of the army to restrain internal disorder was generic to eighteenth-century societies from Britain to

Russia.[19] The map of France was divided on the military plane into *gouvernements*, whose borders were not congruent with those of the intendancies. *Gouverneurs* were princes of the blood or marshals of France, but by the mid-eighteenth century these posts were honorific and their holders were absentees. The commandant, the *gouverneur*'s direct subordinate, was the resident military authority. Within the limits of the War Ministry's activities, the commandant allocated troops to towns of his circumscription. Barracks were rare and still essentially an innovation; soldiers were billeted on households, and municipal officers saw to the details of these arrangements.

When one considers the potential for disputes between soldiers and citizenry,[20] it is striking how desirable the presence of troops was to municipalities. Of course the frequency of requests for troops varied between years of shortage and years of abundance, but Nicole Castan finds demand exceeding supply in Languedoc from the late 1770s until the Revolution—and this despite the fact that all the expenses of transfer and lodging of troops fell on the requesting towns. A town generally lodged a detachment of only 30 to 50 men. At moments of high social tension, the pressure on the commandant to splinter regiments and scatter the fragments around his *gouvernement* was very great. Commandants were deeply concerned by this, as it increased the difficulties of reuniting a large, effective force at the very time when one might be required. But this point was lost on municipal officers, who had a psychological, not a military, use for soldiers. They sought "the tranquillity due to the fear that troops inspire when they are in force."[21] The troops were present to impress and cow the population: in contemporary language, *s'imposer*. If this tactic failed and the disturbance took on real magnitude, the municipality's first concern was often to make sure the troops did not use lethal force. Deaths or injuries might raise the ante in future crowd relations, putting the whole process into unknown territory.[22] It was better to let the disturbance run its course, retake control, punish a few participants as necessary, and again reserve the troops as an ultimate threat.

The mounted police force, composed though it was of old ex-soldiers, was a very different affair.[23] There was a system of special or "prevotal" courts to which the mounted police were appended. The prevotal courts were empowered to judge a specific set of offenses without appeal, including highway robbery, breaking and entering, un-authorized possession of firearms, riot (*sédition*), and sacrilege (usually, affronts to Church persons and property). Its competence also extended to any offenses committed by two classes of persons: soldiers away from their units, and *gens sans aveu* (defined as anyone unemployed for six months for whom no one in the community could vouch). The prevotal courts' area of competence was conceived primarily in terms of the roads and those people who used them too often. In times of grain shortage the mounted police brigades were especially active, coaxing or forcing grain to market and watching any movements of grain in a contrary direction—helping to enforce the moral economy from above. They also worked, with uneven success, to keep the peasantry disarmed, confiscating weapons at the request of seigneurs and other authorities. The brigades made regular patrols to seek and arrest a clientele that corresponded to this charter; however, just as often the mounted police acted at the service of other courts, of municipalities, of the military, of the intendant, and so on.[24] In daily practice their legal identity was rather fluid.

The forces of the mounted police were sparse. Their total personnel numbered 141 for the entire Soissonnais, of whom 92 were cavaliers. While clearly inadequate as a police force, they had a psychological impact beyond what their real strength warranted. To begin with, they were old soldiers, a widely feared category—indeed, one of the categories they were supposed to police. Second, they were judges as well as enforcers. Third, their court was a legal dead end. Once the presidial court had decided that a case was within prevotal competence, it remained there. No appeal was possible, a fact that could not fail to impress the mounted police's clientele. It is certain that, as a 1790 observer commented, the mounted police's effectiveness lay in "presenting to culprits at one and the same time the apparatus of justice and that of force, the dreadful uniform of the warrior, and the imposing apparel of the magistrate."[25]

The mounted police and the army presented different faces of the state's role in public order. The mounted police attempted to deal with the wide interstices in society into which the town-based courts could not reach, and in which rural communities could only signal the presence of "outsiders." Its emphasis on vagabonds and wayward soldiers had consensual support, to which the near-unanimous requests for more and larger brigades in the cahiers of 1789 bear witness. When the mounted police arrested an old inhabitant who happened to be begging, took muskets away from farmers, or walked into a village dispute in progress, it took its chances; but even though it intruded into the community realm at times, it had the great asset of a well-understood social role. Troops, on the other hand, had little such consensual grounding. By their nature as an extraordinary force, transients in their town of garrison, they had the appearance of imposing the unmediated power of the state. It was this appearance that so pleased municipal officers, but once a disturbance had gotten entirely out of hand this same appearance placed the small detachment at serious risk. And—as commandants understood but civilian authorities seldom did—this risk endangered the army's capacity to induce respect in general, with potential consequences for the state itself.

The state also made its presence felt through the practice of royal clemency. It has been shown above how infrequently public disturbances were pursued at law; but when a prosecution was undertaken and convictions resulted, the practice of clemency—an exclusive prerogative of the king, managed by the Keeper of the Seals—was available to brake repressive machinery in response to a changed local situation. Further, clemency had an ideological value: repression by example that was tactically based on the state's weakness could be transfigured by clemency into a display of mercy and forbearance, with the same quieting effect on the popular audience.

Subjects' appeals for clemency had a certain utility to the crown. Authority was confirmed when it was in the position of acceding to a plea; this looked better than simply letting people off on one's own initiative, as part of a rather obvious maneuver to facilitate the settling down of the community.

The intendancy of Soissons was not violent enough in 1789 to provide us with many documents relating to clemency, though one case— that of the tavernkeeper Degrenier of Beaugies, who beat his curé with a stick—has been touched upon. The more numerous and more distinctly revolutionary episodes in Hainaut, Flandre, and northern Picardy resulted in a number of appeals for clemency that are now preserved among the papers of the Keeper of the Seals.

The Keeper of the Seals' own formulation of clemency's role is illuminating. On August 28 he answered the comte d'Esterhazy, commandant of the *gouvernement* of Flandre, who had argued repeatedly for a greater number of "examples," saying that "the number of ill-intentioned people is prodigious and they cannot be contained except by examples—this town [Valenciennes] is full of them . . . "[26] The Keeper of the Seals replied:

> . . . I think like you, Monsieur, that only prompt justice can effectively remedy disorders, and that delays render punishments nearly useless. But it often happens that a single example of severity suffices, and once the initial moment has passed, humanity and clemency resume all their rights and

solicit the King's indulgence for a multitude of guilty persons, for whom it would be the last cruelty to wish them all severely punished. So it is best to give reprieves, pronounce amnesties, and grant pardon. Such are the principles I will always propose that His Majesty graciously adopt in these matters.[27]

The key to this passage is its notion of timing ("prompt . . . delays . . . once the initial moment has passed"). In the view of the Keeper of the Seals, punishments had to immediately follow (or even be concurrent with) the disturbance itself. The lapse of time necessary to punish a larger and more carefully chosen body of participants would have negated the punishments' psychological impact. Once the crest of disorder was behind, authority was best asserted by applying magnanimity to the collective fear of punishment that the examples should have evoked in the community. Thus clemency was just as necessary for maintaining public order as was repression itself. It allowed the state to override court procedure when this aided the management of the populace.[28]

The model of old-regime public order proposed here—an association of community, municipal-legal, and state realms—is also of value for understanding the Great Fear. Clearly the Fear was a moment of high coordination among all three realms. In the Soissonnais and elsewhere, the community realm expressed itself through impromptu militias, in many cases guided by municipal officers and local magistrates. The municipal-legal realm orchestrated joint forces of mounted police, militia, and even light calvary where these were unavailable; it allotted to the infantry the role of defending the town proper from marauders. It momentarily commanded forces of the state realm in harmony with those of the community. In this perspective the Fear was a moment not of disruption or breakdown, but of a triumph in the old regime's possibilities of organization. When the illusion of the "brigands" that had made this triumph possible faded away, the authorities were left with a new equilibrium among realms of public order that would be impossible to keep in balance.

National Decrees Affecting Public Order

In Soissonnais correspondence and petitions concerning public order in 1789, a handful of measures are mentioned again and again. These are the decrees reviewed in this section, all save one emanating from the National Assembly. Viewed on the national scale, these decrees were no masterpieces of Revolutionary legislation, but in the experience of the

Soissonnais they were significant. They fall into five areas: the competence of the mounted police; the grain trade; taxes, especially the salt tax
(*gabelle*); the popular use of forests; and the means of enforcing public
order.

A royal council decree of May 21 temporarily gave the prevotal court
full competence to try participants in public disturbances; the usual
requirement that the presidial court judge the competence of the
mounted police for each case was removed. This emergency measure had
been authorized before, in the bad harvest year of 1739–40. It created
elbow room for the mounted police and encouraged prosecutions.[29] The
measure soon became entangled with those of the National Assembly on
the grain trade, as we shall see. The resulting procedural confusion
widened the field for popular seizures and other moral-economic initiatives.

On the grain trade the National Assembly laid down an abstract
premise of a unified national market. Its decree of August 29 declared
that the sale and circulation of grain and flour was unrestricted throughout the kingdom; exportation was provisionally forbidden and transport
by sea required municipal certificates at the ports of embarkation and
arrival, but all other controls were removed.[30] Broad resistance to this
laissez-faire policy continued throughout France, bringing on the decree
of September 18. Those who either exported grain abroad or blocked it
at home were equally criminals to be prosecuted before the regular local
judges, that is, the bailliage or *sénéchaussée* courts in most cases. By putting the responsibility for prosecuting grain disturbances on the bailliage courts, the National Assembly distanced itself from the "judicial
despotism" attributed to exceptional tribunals such as the mounted police's prevotal court. In the process, however, it contradicted the royal
decree that had empowered the mounted police, and created a procedural conundrum.

The September 18 decree was important in other ways. It instituted
rules to prevent exportation across the country's land frontiers, creating
a three-league limit within which grain in movement that was not heavily
documented could be confiscated and sold locally. In other words, it set
out territory and conditions in which *entraves*—popular grain blockades—were legal. At the same time, it enjoined police, court, and municipal officers to "call upon the national militias, the mounted police, and
even other military troops if need be, to lend enforcing power" to the
law.[31] This phrasing is highly significant. It ratified the power of local
authorities to direct the armed forces of both the state and the community—which of course was precisely what had happened in the Great Fear.

However, there was a world of difference between the consensual base of the Great Fear, with its unity against "brigands," and the consensual base of a local altercation around a grain cart. The Great Fear had briefly created a unity that matched the discourse of harmonious, patriotic regeneration prevalent in the National Assembly. Unfortunately, the mechanics and psychology by which the Fear had achieved this unity belonged to the old regime, not to the Revolution.

October 5 brought a third decree that responded to the poor execution of the two prior ones. Recognizing that much of the resistance was coming from municipalities themselves, the National Assembly warned them that municipalities too could be declared "disturbers of public order." A last decree in 1789 (November 16) took another step toward condoning popular seizure by granting two-thirds of the profits of forced grain sales related to "exportation" to those who had stopped the grain.[32]

Tax collection had been in abeyance ever since the drafting of *cahiers de doléances* in the early spring. Especially in rural districts, people saw fit to await the work of the Estates-General before paying to support an order of things that now had an ephemeral look. On June 17, after taking the "tennis court oath" and naming themselves the National Assembly, the Third Estate deputies had voted their provisional consent to all existing taxes, so long as the Assembly was not dispersed by royal force. In the same act they described all current taxes as established without consultation and hence illegal and null, surviving only through the good graces of the representatives of the nation.[33] Though some old-regime officials would attempt to use this pathetic instrument to enforce tax collection, it quite properly fooled no one.

On September 23 the Assembly passed a more realistic decree on taxes. By now the political context was utterly different, marked by a developing royalist constitutionalism. The Assembly aligned itself with royal efforts to reconstruct the collection apparatus, shattered by popular attacks in many locales. It promised that the salt tax would disappear as soon as a substitute was worked out, and in the interim it reduced the price of salt to 6 sous per pound (from as high as 13 sous in the *pays de grande gabelle*, of which the Soissonnais was part). House searches for contraband salt and severe criminal punishments for smugglers were ended, and the salt tax was softened in other ways.[34] This law accepted the people's *fait accompli* against the salt tax, and it offered concessions in exchange for a breathing space in which tax collection could be reorganized.

Popular use of the forests exploded after the Great Fear, which had put arms in the hands of many and had annihilated the formal principle of a disarmed peasantry. The royal administration replied first with a proclamation from the king on November 3; the Assembly chimed in on December 11. The December decree barred communities from forcibly repossessing usurped commons, whether woods, pasture, or wasteland. It authorized mounted police, forest guards, or bailiffs to seize scavenged timber, but with one condition: the search and seizure had to be in the presence of a municipal officer, who could not refuse this obligation. Here again the Assembly sought to force a unity among different types of authorities—a unity contrary to old-regime forms of public order and unlikely in a revolutionary countryside. Equally problematic was the decree's permission for *maîtrises* (forestry jurisdictions) or judges of any type to borrow reinforcements from "the municipalities, National Guards, and other troops"—another burden that municipal officers were forbidden to refuse.[35]

The Assembly's tendency to throw disparate authorities together in awkward situations is epitomized by its decrees on public order. The first of these was passed on August 10 in reaction to the July peasant revolts and the Great Fear. The Assembly was serious about finding the "prime mover" of the Fear. It ordered that the sentencing of those caught spreading false alarms be postponed; records of these cases were to be sent to the Assembly, which would compare them in order to "work back to the source of disorders." Municipalities were made responsible for the maintenance of public order. The militia, mounted police, and troops were available to them on simple requisition. They were to control all "attroupements séditieux" in town and countryside. They were to draw up rolls of unvouched-for persons and disarm them. Finally, they were to preside over a public ceremony in which garrisoned troops swore fidelity to the nation, and the troops' officers swore in their men's hearing never to deploy force against citizens without orders from a civilian authority.[36]

The October 21 decree on martial law added sharp relief to this picture of municipal responsibility. Its first article held municipal officers answerable for negligence if they did not declare martial law when public order was in danger. They were to hang a red flag out the window of the town hall; assemble militia, mounted police, and troops as available; and march in force to the scene of the disturbance. The Assembly's scenario then unfolds as follows. The officers invite the crowd to choose a small delegation to present a petition, and disperse. If the crowd does not disperse, they are warned three times and then fired upon (which apparently closes the matter, instead of provoking a townwide uproar). The "*moteurs* and instigators" are tried and in most cases sentenced to death; militiamen or soldiers who switch sides are likewise sentenced to death.[37] One can only think that the Assembly conceived this fantasy of rigor in reaction to the tradition of bargaining and concessions that marked old-regime authorities' relations with crowds.

The immense weight put on municipalities by these decrees is evident. The Assembly intended to strip away the cocoon of royal administration, the subdelegates and the intendant, the intermediate bureaus and the provincial commission. All of that was too intimately linked to Versailles to be trustworthy in revolutionary circumstances. No longer would municipal officers blend into the florid old-regime environment, with its profusion of species of public authority. They now found themselves exposed at the center of a system—crude and impromptu, but a system nonetheless—in which they were prominently responsible for the exercise of force.

The Arrival of Decrees in the Village

The various decrees of 1789 were intended to enter the common knowledge of the population; so much is clear from their content. A decree to the effect that taxes must still be paid, for instance, requires some public awareness to be efficacious. It is well known how public transmission took place in the towns: through open-air readings after church, printed posters, and less formal discussion by municipal officers. But how did the decrees reach the rural-dwelling majority?

In the Soissonnais and other provinces without provincial estates, municipalities of a sort had been imposed on the smallest rural communities by the edict of June 1787, which bestowed new provincial assemblies on areas that lacked them. This edict augmented the intendancy's administrative framework. At the summit was the provincial assembly or, when it was not in session, its ongoing commission, which was supposed to work closely with the intendant and in the Soissonnais really did so. The intendancy was divided into departments, each with an intermediate bureau composed of local notables; the departments were subdivided into districts, and at the base were the communities. Communities without municipalities—and these were numerous—had to establish them. Inhabitants who paid at least 10 livres in taxes elected a restricted 'municipal assembly' of three, six, or nine members paying 30 livres or more. These were joined by the syndic and the clerk, elected under the same rules; by the curé (an automatic member); and by the seigneur (in the Soissonnais, most often absent).[38]

This imposition of stratified local control, an "oligarchization" in Gutton's phrase, was a far cry from customary village governance in the Soissonnais and much of the Parisian basin. Up to that time, general assemblies of heads of households had elected a syndic and one or two assistants to aid in tax collection. The syndic was not empowered to make decisions; any real problem had to be put before the assembly. Registers were not kept, and occasional paperwork was done on loose sheets. The ambitious June 1787 edict sought village institutions that could serve as relays for higher levels of authority, and hence required each village to come up with some "notables" by hook or crook. Many communities had no notables to display, and the fiscal qualifications were often circumvented in an effort to provide municipal officers. The beggar-clerk of Noyales, five kilometers west of Guise, illustrates the difficulties of villages throughout the Soissonnais. In the municipal deliberations of June 28, 1789,

> The syndic said that the clerk [was] in the habit of presenting himself every week at various houses to receive a certain quantity of bread due him in place of wages. He was sorry to see that most were powerless to give, since they lacked for themselves, and that the clerk could only live from his position. It would be appropriate for the municipality to make an arrangement with him so that he would be provided a lump sum paid once . . . The clerk will be required not to demand, or even ask for, bread in any house before [September 1].[39]

Many communities probably invented some compromise between their familiar methods and the new requirements. Because these were also compromises between the familiar oral and the new written styles of transacting business, few documents inform us about the compromises' content.

The village assemblies of spring 1789 to pick electors who would vote for deputies to the Estates-General broke all the rules of the 1787 edict. Property qualifications were irrelevant; all residents whose names were on the tax rolls could participate.[40] The impact of these spring assemblies tended to desiccate the municipalities of 1787. In the Soissonnais, some municipal registers fall silent in March 1789 and show no entries until 1791.[41]

In much of the countryside, only those faltering 1787 municipalities spread the news of national decrees. Official copies traveled from the intendant's seat in Soissons to the intermediate bureaus, which distributed them to rural municipalities. However, many of the latter were disintegrating for lack of financial support. For the needs of communities, as opposed to those of the state, the 1787 municipality was too costly an apparatus. The Noyon intermediate bureau was frank with Soissons in late May about the problem of expenses:

> The position taken by M. the intendant to [require municipal officers to pay] the expense accounts of municipalities . . . will result in the total disorganization of municipal assemblies . . . the greater part of these expenses [originated in] the sums advanced by the syndics . . . to buy (1) paper, ink, quills, wood, and candles; and (2) the two ledgers and the coffer that the municipalities must have; last, for the reimbursement . . . of packets addressed to municipalities, for which the syndics have paid. Only with a great deal of trouble have we gotten the syndics to decide to make the said advances, and we could make them consent only under the promise . . . that the total would be reimbursed them in the course of making up the roll for the cash payment that substitutes for the *corvée* [labor service]. Since today this roll cannot be drawn up . . . you must realize that, in the minds of the syndics and the municipality members, we are going to pass for men of bad faith who abused their credulity to deceive them, and for this reason they will refuse, not only to communicate with us, but even to exercise their functions.[42]

In many villages the reading of decrees grew desultory or simply ended. By September 18 Noyon reported this breakdown of transmission as an accomplished fact, referring to "the negligence that different syndics and a number of municipalities bring to conforming with the instructions sent to them, even to giving them a reading . . . "[43] Heightened political tension in the countryside accompanied an actual weakening of the link to the political center.

Those village municipalities that persisted give further hints why others fell silent. Venizel was too close to Soissons (just four kilometers to the east) for the municipality to evade its duties. The number and length of the decrees that were read aloud made for after-Mass sessions that listeners must have found mind-boggling. On August 30 the officers posted and read all the Assembly decrees originating in the night of August 4, the decree on public order of August 10, and the royal proclamation concerning "brigands" of August 9. On November 8 they conscientiously caught up with a month's business, including two letters from the provincial commission, the royal sanction of the September 23 Assembly decree that lowered the salt tax, royal regulations and proclamations on the same subject of October 2, 8, 14, and 16, and the Assembly's decree on martial law.[44] Contemporary audiences, inured to oral exposition and fresh from a sermon, may have retained more of the content than we would today if put in their place. Still, listeners must have reduced what they heard to a gist they could pass on to others, and this gist comprised the popular "final draft" of the National Assembly's texts.

The Results on the Ground

In the Soissonnais, the work of the National Assembly seriously disrupted the fragile world of provincial public order. This is a paradoxical statement to make about a revolutionary countryside that the Assembly was, after all, trying to calm. But old-regime public order was itself paradoxical: it could bounce back from any number of breakdowns, infractions, or disturbances, because its agenda was limited to the present. It punished not to "correct" criminals, but to inspire obedience from their neighbors; its concern was not with those individuals selected as examples, but with the mass of spectators that the examples instructed. Where concessions or pardons might serve public order better than exemplary punishments, trials, sentences, and penalties were simply dropped. The Assembly's labors tended to make this old order impossible before elements of a new order could be substituted.

From the August 10 decree on public order onward, confused provincial judges sent their queries to the Keeper of the Seals. Even before the grain circulation decree of September 18, court officers saw the contradiction between the free hand given the mounted police by the decree of May 21 and the new direction in which the Assembly was going.[45] By December, the contradiction had widened thanks to further legislation. The royal attorney of Laon wrote the prosecutor-general Joly de Fleury on December 14:

> A coalition seems to have developed throughout my jurisdiction to obstruct the circulation of grains and even their transport into the markets. A number of parishes feel free to block grain; the inhabitants set the price, always at half or less the actual value, and then there are those who do not pay at all. I wanted to bring formal complaints on these acts, but the judge did not want to accept it.

The mounted police regarded itself as competent and was investigating such cases, but the royal attorney knew well that the prevotal court was now in limbo and so appealed to his superior:

> It seems to me that popular emotions whose object is to trouble the general tranquillity are within the mounted police's competence, but the trouble

brought to grain circulation seems to me within the competence of regular judges, if I am to believe the decrees of August 29, September 18, and October 5 . . . and when the judge refuses to register my indictments, what am I to do?[46]

Joly de Fleury referred the letter to the Keeper of the Seals, who gave this problematic response:

> When the obstacle brought against grain circulation is the primary offense, its pursuit belongs to the regular judge; when, on the contrary, the offense . . . was riot and sedition, the provosts of the mounted police should have instruction and judgment, and they also hear facts relative to the grain trade as incidentals.
> Accordingly, the Laon judge's refusal is unfounded . . . [47]

To the Keeper of the Seals, a disturbance over grain could be treated as a disturbance per se or as an obstacle to the trade; because these types of offenses were in the purview of different courts, whichever aspect was most significant determined which judge heard the entire case. This exchange shows the degree of confusion at the top,[48] which allowed wary judges to take cover and judges sympathetic to the classic market regime to discreetly support the actions of communities. For the Assembly's decrees attacked not only popular grain regulation in the community realm of public order but also the activities of formal grain regulation in which the mounted police, as well as court and municipal officers, had all distinguished themselves in the past. Local regulation of the grain trade had consensual value and tended to bring the different realms of public order into harmony. The occasional trader might have suffered, but social peace in the Soissonnais had basically held—especially in comparison to neighboring Picardy and the Cambrésis, and the local authorities were less than eager to relinquish such a valuable tool.

Salt Smuggling and the Gabelle

The intendancy of Soissons was within the *pays de grande gabelle*, and so was most of the intendancy of Amiens. To the north, Artois, Flandre, and Hainaut were all exempt from the salt tax, creating an ideal smuggling ground that ran from Le Touquet on the coast through Arras and the Cambrésis and along the Soissons intendancy's northern border. If the *cahiers de doléances* can provide any indication, opposition to the salt tax in the Soissonnais was broad and reached into the clergy and the nobility.[49] Though it seems likely that salt tax enforcement progressively broke down over the spring, various documents give the impression of an eruption of disobedience in the days and weeks following the Great Fear.

From May through July, contraband salt and tobacco received little mention in administrative correspondence, which was preoccupied above all with grain questions. Then on July 30 (three days after the Great Fear) the intendant Blossac wrote this alarming assessment to the Maison du roi:

> Smugglers profit from the fermentation that reigns in all minds; they introduce themselves into the towns, force the toll barriers and, seconded by the people, who find their advantage in it, publicly sell salt and tobacco; the excise collectors and the mounted police dare not oppose these disorders, fearing that the populace that threatens them will knock them senseless. Yesterday, Monsieur, a wagon of white salt was sold in the heart of Soissons, there being no way of forbidding it . . . without much bloodshed; prudence did not permit undertaking this, given the disposition in which the people were found to be.[50]

In the Noyonnais, the intermediate bureau signaled to Soissons the complete collapse of salt tax and excise collections in a letter of August 7. Outside the intendancy, but within the current of the Fear that had originated in Estrées-St-Denis, there is evidence of a similar trend. In Aumale, 40 kilometers southwest of Amiens, the salt tax collector declared his task hopeless and put himself under municipal protection on August 21.[51] And in Doullens, 30 kilometers north of Amiens, a spectacular riot on August 16–17 burnt the archives of the director of excises and did 22,000 livres of property damage to his residence.[52] While the violence of this last example bespeaks the greater intensity of the Picard revolution, its post-Fear timing was synchronous with turmoil in the less flamboyant Soissonnais.

There is no evidence that the National Assembly's conciliatory decree of September 23 on the salt tax altered this situation. The forms of defiance against all indirect taxes grew only more acute in November. In Picardy, Cressy threw off the tax on sales in its livestock market; nonpayment of the tax was vigilantly enforced by the militia.[53] Roye put a stop to excise collections, and the collectors were threatened with violence.[54] On November 20 in Laon, the excise collectors arrested a man whose horse was loaded with contraband tobacco. Immediately a crowd formed and broke down the door of the official warehouseman, freeing man, horse, and tobacco. The municipal officers declared martial law and used dragoons and mounted police to restore order.[55]

On November 29 the salt tax collectors of Crépy-en-Valois got wind of a procession of five or seven wagons loaded with salt only three kilometers away from Crépy, traveling southwest. The collectors and the mounted police caught up with the smugglers, and a pitched battle ensued in which three collectors and two cavaliers were wounded. The forces of order retreated to Crépy and sent a messenger to Villers-Cotterets for dragoons and more cavaliers to join them. Thus reinforced, they overtook the smugglers again 16 kilometers further southwest, outside Le Plessis-Belleville (clearly the smugglers were taking a direct route to Paris). After another battle four smugglers were captured, with all the merchandise and equipage. The return of the troops and police with their prizes greatly provoked the people of Crépy. The smugglers escaped from prison—probably with popular assistance, though this is not certain—and on December 4 they returned, stormed the town hall, and retrieved their wagons. The municipal officers were alarmed by the mood and arguments of the townspeople on November 29:

> The people, who generally have shown only the greatest moderation at all times, has been suddenly carried away to a pitch of fury incredible to anyone not a witness. Despite our efforts to maintain order, the mounted police and dragoons have been exposed to the liveliest reproaches, and we ourselves to the gravest insults. Its general cry was, that salt was being seized lest it be available at a modest price, and that grain hoarding and clandestine circulation was being encouraged to make the people die of hunger.[56]

Indeed Crépy's inhabitants had discerned the hypocrisy of the Assembly's policies in 1789, which applied the doctrine of free trade selectively and at popular expense only, never at the expense of the state. In this area as in others, the Assembly hoped to reshape, not to dismantle, the ensemble of strictures and tacit permissions that made up the *police* of the old regime. However, these strictures and permissions were closely related; they were the result of a long dialectic between ruling and subordinated classes. It was impossible to change any element without causing repercussions through the entire fabric.

The Forest and the Right to Hunt

Popular incursions into the forest to hunt, forage, and collect timber increased greatly from July onward, changing from a small-group to a mass activity in some locales. The forests had always been significant to the economic life of the Soissons intendancy: roughly one-seventh of the intendancy was forested, and the five major forests (Villers-Cotterets or Retz, Le Nouvion, St-Michel, l'Arrouaise, and St-Gobain) were distributed with fair evenness across its territory. The southern forests were situated near rivers and their timber was readily transportable to Paris, while the northern forests either fed factories (as did the forest of St-Gobain) or were less fully exploited than those of the south.

We have already seen in chapter 4 that at the end of the Great Fear in Clermont-en-Beauvaisis, hundreds of peasants who had come to the defense of the town went off to hunt in the forest of La Neuville to its west. The game killed was publicly sold in the villages for days afterward.[57] The National Assembly's decree of August 11 abolished without indemnity the nobility's exclusive right to hunt, much to the alarm of Soissonnais notables and authorities. On August 14 the Noyon intermediate bureau wrote its colleagues in Soissons:

> If, at a time when the inhabitants of the countryside were still unarmed, they dared to proceed to such an extremity [trouncing a Soissons messenger who had told them that the National Assembly had ordered payment of the salt tax], how much more justified are we in fearing the results of the permission that is being accorded them to hunt with firearms; already they have begun to make use of this permission in a fashion that makes us expect calamities . . . [58]

The Compiègne forest, on the intendancy's western border, was cut indiscriminately by large groups from August onward.[59] In Coincy (16 kilometers north of Château-Thierry) the syndic reported on September 7 that he had been contending with "persons who shoot pigeons in the streets with impunity . . . bad subjects without property who hunt freely, though there is no game."[60] Near Crépy-en-Valois, a shot aimed at pigeons started a fire on a straw roof which consumed several houses, and the municipal committee attributed a number of recent injuries to inexperienced marksmen with old and unreliable firearms.[61]

However, the major popular use of the forest was not hunting but gathering. The forest had always been a daily source of wood—for fuel, for construction and patching-up, for vine supports, for barrel-staves—and there were always nuts and berries, grass and leaves for fodder, and animals let to graze.[62] The Revolution ended all effective limits to this rummaging, and the forest suffered for it over the next decade. Intensive exploitation was not limited to the poor. The purchasers of wooded national lands cut so indiscriminately that by 1801 the values of their properties were severely reduced.[63]

In 1789 inhabitants in many localities collectively entered the woods of an abbey or seigneur and cut enough fuel for the winter. The abbé of Bucilly reported on November 3 that "for over 10 days our woods have been devastated to the point that not one oak is left . . . these depredations are accompanied . . . with such threats and imprecations that I dare not leave the house lest I fear for my life . . . "[64] On the other hand, the same rapid exploitation was initiated by the abbey of St-Médard near Crouy, which had five hundred poplars cut on a single autumn day. Apparently anticipating either popular or national confiscation, the monks did not hesitate.[65]

On November 2 the National Assembly voted to put ecclesiastical lands "at the disposal of the nation." As word spread of this simple yet ambiguous statement, it probably heightened the popular sense of freedom in forest exploitation. According to the Maîtrise of Streams and Forests of Amiens, "many inhabitants of riverbank parishes in the forest . . . affect to believe, and proclaim, that by this decree . . . all the wood is at the disposition of those who want to cut it and take it away . . ."[66] Forest hunting appears to have increased again east of Crépy-en-Valois by January 1790. The syndic of Faverolles, seven kilometers east of Villers-Cotterets, complained not just of groups of poachers but of "an infinite number of hotheads who, under the pretext of hunting, form considerable troops and invade the woods . . ."[67]

This great expansion of popular hunting, poaching, and scavenging was one of the most significant results of peasant rearmament in the Great Fear. It had two meanings that must be explored: an economic meaning and a political symbolism.

In economic terms, the expansion was a natural consequence of the struggle of poor peasants to survive on inadequate land. The fields of communities near forests were generally less productive. The parish of La Chapelle-sur-Chezy declared in 1788, "One can rank among the obstacles [to prosperity in the parish] the woods that surround its lands, which do them harm by their shade . . ."[68] When an officer of the Orléans apanage went to evaluate similar land, he reported: "I found this piece of land in the heart of the forest more closed up than ever . . . [Its] product . . . could be fixed in truth at 10 to 11 livres, if these lands were not wedged in by the forest and exposed to shade and damage from game."[69]

Communities that worked such land were usually poor. They could enjoy extra revenue if they had the right to exploit the forest; but this could not come to much unless they were situated near decent roads. In Nogent l'Artaud, ". . . these woods, though situated near the port, result in great carting expenses for the merchant, and the merchant keeps the lumberjack's labor at a low price to compensate himself for these transport costs."[70] The presence of the forest made agriculture less rewarding, while always offering the fruits of hunting and forage. For peasants struggling to retain a tenuous link to the land, the prospect of a wider

use of the forest to supplement their subsistence was a precious opportunity to be seized.

The greatest holder of forests in the Soissons intendancy was the
Orléans apanage. The richness of its forest reserves can be seen in the
upkeep of the forest of Retz, part of the Orléans apanage near Villers-
Cotterets. The 1786 report of its administrator, the marquis de Limon,
outlines its varied wealth. Running game and pheasants were specially
raised in the forest for hunting by the nobility. The shooting of actual
"wild beasts," including rabbits, was an activity of stewards, perceived as
augmenting the value of the reserve. The neighboring peasantry were
required to cut the underbrush from the ditches between field and forest, where rabbits took refuge; if they did not, no complaint for damages
would be entertained.[71]

The long-term strategy of the apanage against poaching was to surround the forest with a belt of outlying properties through which
poachers would have to pass. In 1786 a list of 59 such desirable properties was drawn up. Some were purchased, others rented, still others fell
back into the apanage by seigneurial right (*retraite féodale*). They included fields, but also inns and hostels; proximity was the deciding
factor.[72]

The game reserve was compatible with light timber-cutting, though
nothing like that carried on in the apanage's nearby forest of Coucy
(141,230 livres worth in 1788). The considerable roadmaking in the
forest of Retz had less to do with timber than with the employment of
the population and consequent decrease in general use of the forest. De
Limon recommended the repair of all forest roads at once over the
winter of 1786–87, at an estimated expense of 40,000 livres; in May
1789 he suggested the diversion of this work force to the château of
Villers-Cotterets until the harvest. The apanage's solution to the problem of popular forest use was to convert neighboring villages into pools
of semiproletarian labor. It should be noted that in this regard the position of the apanage was quite different from that of the large farmers of
the Soissonnais, who (as discussed in chapter 1) wanted cheap agricultural workers fixed to the land by houses and gardens. For the apanage,
dominance over the local population, not over its labor, was the crucial
factor. Though its creation of a protective belt of properties around the
forest tended to depopulate the surroundings, this outcome preserved
the apanage's assets and was acceptable to it in a way that it could not be
to the major tenant farmers.[73]

The economic significance of hunting and foraging was matched in
importance by its political symbolism, rooted in images centuries old.

Until the night of August 4, hunting was an exclusive privilege of the nobility. When the Assembly abolished the hunting privilege and later restricted hunting to proprietors or possessors on their own lands, it took a position remote from existing jurisprudence and habits of land use.

In Roman law and Frankish practice, freedom of the chase was the universal rule, and game was a *res nullius*: it belonged to its finder. This freedom was gradually "enclosed" by the nobility, who appropriated the act of hunting the *res nullius*. First the large game was taken, leaving the general right to hunt small game. Then the creation of reserves left only the hunting of dangerous animals, such as wolves. The right to hunt was formally denied to commoners in the fourteenth century under Charles V. Jurisprudence gradually linked hunting more closely to the seigneurie until the ordinance of 1669 offered a complete feudal theory: the hunting privilege was an attribute of sovereignty, and the king permitted its exercise to the nobles as his vassals and forbade it to commoners anywhere in his kingdom. Game had been fully converted from a *res nullius* to an accessory to the fief, and formed part of feudal conceptions of property.[74]

In 1789 it was widely understood that the general destruction of feudal forms implied a new statute for hunting, but it was harder to agree on what the new statute would consist of. The solution that the National Assembly adopted in 1790 permitted proprietors (and renters) to hunt on their own lands exclusively, except when these lands bore unharvested crops. Game as accessory to the fief was turned into game as an aspect of the enjoyment of landed property by the law of April 28–30, 1790. But other solutions had seemed equally plausible. In March 1789 Vailly-sur-Aisne's deputy carried a working paper to the Soissons bailliage assembly that proposed "free hunting to the people during one month to be specified in the year."[75] And in the debate over the drafting of the 1790 law, Robespierre lucidly staked out a position contrary to the emerging bourgeois conception of property:

> I rise to speak against the principle that restrains the right to hunt to proprietors only. As soon as the land's surface has been stripped, the hunt should be open to all citizens without distinction. In every case, wild beasts belong to the finder. I therefore demand the unlimited freedom of the hunt, while taking measures at the same time for the preservation of harvests and public security.[76]

What the 1790 law, the Vailly-sur-Aisne proposal, and Robespierre's challenge all shared in common was a concern for the protection of agriculture on unenclosed terrain. What sharply divided them was the nature of the concept of property into which hunting would be integrated: a legalistic, "modern" concept; or a concept based on use rights and rooted in existing patterns of land use.

Just as the issue of hunting was a battleground between differing views of property, it was also an area of class antagonism. Either hunting was to remain a privilege—though organized on a new basis—or it was to become a common right, regulated along lines that applied equally to all. The documents offer glimpses of a deep dislike of plebeian hunting among petty officials, for whom hunting clearly retained its status as an activity of nobles, suited to an elite position only. The syndic of Coincy demanded testily of the Château-Thierry permanent committee in early September: "Indeed, Messieurs, is it in the order of things that Robert Hochard and his family—people who are quite suspect for all kinds of reasons, convicted a number of times for carrying arms . . . play the role of the noble by hunting with impunity . . . ?"[77]

A letter to the National Assembly from the royal attorney for the Laon Maîtrise of Streams and Forests gives an articulate rationale for the writer's horror of plebeian hunting. The use of firearms by the poor was not the only problem; the social basis of labor itself was supposedly undermined by the direct recourse to nature:

> The disgust that the passion for hunting leaves for any sort of work made the wise Solon forbid it to the people of his republic; this disgust actually augments the misery of the unfortunate who let themselves be borne off by this passion; and from the extremity to which such a man always finds himself reduced, there is often just a step to undertaking dishonest acts that alone can support the most pressing needs of himself, his wife, and his children.
>
> A hunter of this type is incapable of ever resuming the trade he has left, or of taking up another: he is a man lost to society . . .
>
> I do not even know if he is not more [lost]—because more incorrigible—than the smugglers . . . with which this region abounds, due to the frontier . . . [78]

This letter carries an inverted comment, conscious or unconscious, on the nobility. It describes hunting as a passion, the opposite of work. The thrill of the chase supposedly makes labor repulsive and drags the poor who are seized by it into even greater impoverishment, and thence to crime. But if this passion creates men who are "lost to society" and are given to desperate enterprises, what are its effects on persons at the top of the social scale? Hunting as a passion and (for wealthy nobles) as an occasion for conspicuous waste could only befit a group perceived as both idle and martial. The traditional image of the nobility as a warrior caste whose values limit its participation in social production is indirectly reinforced here. Since the attorney's account ignores the utility of hunting for the poor as a supplement to subsistence, it makes the motives and effects of plebeian hunting into a parody of those of noble hunting. Thus the poacher is posed as the noble's mirror image in the depths of society: a plebeian social type in whom the disdain for work tends to cultivate a martial spirit.[79] Of course such a martial spirit could seem quite desirable, even necessary, to commoners living in a revolutionary situation.

Officers of the Maîtrises of Streams and Forests sought for exemplary punishment hunters who matched this image. Punishment by solitary example was essential, since much poaching from June on was done in groups too large for officials to repress without personal risk. A perfect mark was the infantry sergeant Rasselet—on leave from his regiment in Brittany in autumn, staying in his father's house at Longpont near Villers-Cotterets: a soldier whose station was far away, fond of his gun and solitude. He hunted occasionally, not in the forest of Retz, on his doorstep, but in the forest of Coucy, 10 kilometers north. The lieutenant of the hunt, Duhal, extracted a denunciation of Rasselet from the Coucy municipality and had him arrested. After a month of prison, the Coucy attorney offered Rasselet his release if he would return to Brittany without traversing either Villers-Cotterets or Paris, but the sergeant refused and demanded that he be cleared unconditionally.

> I was not to be found in any assemblage [he wrote the National Assembly]. I hunted most often alone, or infrequently with one of my brothers . . . What then is my crime? An involuntary error. I hunted on the lands of M. the duc d'Orléans because I believed hunting was permitted. This imaginary offense, too rigorously punished by a fine, seemed an enormous crime to a powerful and vindictive man . . . To reach his goal he accused me of heading up a crowd . . . I was not a vagabond, I was at my paternal home . . .[80]

But Rasselet was a perfect screen for the image of social reversal projected by Duhal. A plebeian warrior without involvement in local production, he carried a kind of dignity that let Duhal cast him in the role of leader.

In the rural revolutionary situation of August onward, to hunt and to carry firearms was no less a badge of allegiance than the cockade— and arguably a more important one in the subpolitical atmosphere of the rural Soissonnais. Peasants who hunted defied not only the old-regime authorities of the present moment but also the old and formidable psychological structure that buttressed the division of society into estates.

The Public Order Decrees

Finally, let us turn to the local effects of the National Assembly's laws on public order: the decrees of August 10 and October 21. The August 10 decree spoke of "national militias" as though every town in France was already equipped with one, but this was far from being the case. In the Soissonnais, the municipalities of Chauny and Braine (and probably others as well) first felt the need for a militia upon receiving the text of the decree. The Assembly had not prescribed how a militia should be established, but it had been definite on the question of "unvouched-for persons, without trade or profession, and without a constant domicile"; municipalities should find them, register them, and disarm them, just as the National Guard had done in Paris in the second half of July. Chauny collapsed the two processes by selecting officers first and then developing a roll of citizens for the militia which excluded workers, artisans without domicile, and servants.[81]

The October 21 decree on the forms of martial law apparently had a stronger resonance. It is mentioned in the documents from the start of November on, sometimes in curious contexts. We know that Villers-Cotterets had at least one day of martial law on November 5, but we do not know why or what it consisted of in this well-controlled post of the Orléans apanage.[82] On November 7 the duc de Guise's fiscal attorney reported a shooting incident between a group of nine poachers and a party of armed peasants raised and led by their seigneur. The fiscal attorney did not neglect to mention that the seigneur "made to [the poachers] the interpellations prescribed by martial law." It is striking that this reference appears in a provincial letter only two weeks after the passage of the legislation in the Assembly.[83]

On November 20 Laon experienced its first public uproar of 1789, a riot over enforcement of the tobacco excise tax. The municipality responded by declaring martial law, which it left to garrisoned dragoons to enforce—a prudent and effective tactical choice, but one quite old-regime in character.[84] Compiègne on December 15 actually held a "general rehearsal" of martial law which presumably took advantage of all the elements of spectacle in the Assembly's scenario—the red flag hanging from the town hall, the massing of royal troops and militia formations, the procession, led by municipal officers, to the scene of the disturbance—on an opportune day when that scene was empty.[85] It is more than possible that "martial law" at Villers-Cotterets had a similar character.

To take a last example from farther north, a dispute between Dunkerque's municipality and its commune led an anonymous correspondent to urge the commune's president to demand martial law. The letter's language shows how the Assembly's decree on martial law could be inserted into an old-regime framework of governance through display:

> To avoid your demand, the magistrate will perhaps come say to you, "But Article 1 says that *martial law will be promulgated in the case where public tranquillity is in peril*" [emphasis in original].
>
> These words only concern its execution, but not its proclamation. Certainly one will not put it into execution when there is no assemblage, but is it necessary to wait until there is a dangerous sedition to proclaim it, and does the magistrate believe he has done enough by posting it up? No, the greater number of *gens du peuple* who are most to be feared and the most inclined toward revolt cannot read and are unaware [of martial law], or if they are aware of it by tradition, it is in a manner so distorted as to be unrecognizable. On the other hand . . . for the vulgar ignorant, the spectacle of the law's proclamation is much more imposing than the law's posted notice, because someone who mechanically reads a poster stuck to a wall will tremble at the aspect of a red flag planted at a window.[86]

By inventing a distinction between the proclamation of martial law and its execution, the writer converted the Assembly's police doctrine into a "spectacle," denaturing it completely and assimilating it to traditional forms of public order. It seems likely that the "general rehearsal" of Compiègne came from a similar inspiration.

The content of public order was indeed relegislated in 1789, but by multiple centers of power that affected each other dynamically. The National Assembly sought to create by fiat a form of public order congruent with bourgeois property relations. The subordinated classes embraced those aspects of the Assembly's work that they found liberating, while vetoing aspects that interfered with use rights or that granted immunity to commercial operations. Caught in the middle, local authorities cobbled together forms of public order that depended on the balance of forces in their jurisdictions, but that also owed something to their fund of conventional wisdom about social control.

The Assembly declared the existence of a unified national grain market to which any local hindrance was illegal. The subordinated classes accepted the "national" theme of the Assembly's project. At the northern border they defended the integrity of the national market against "exportation," combining traditional tactics with a new factor: militia activity. Throughout the Soissonnais they recast the market regime into a new, "national" mold, impugning the patriotism of grain merchants and confronting royal institutions such as the Company of Military Provisions. In frontier-related matters they were strong enough to bend the Assembly toward their own conception.

The Assembly regarded itself as the one legitimate source of national taxation and declared that the taxes enforced by the monarchy without the nation's consent were inherently illegal. However, these taxes were permitted to continue by the grace of the Assembly while it reorganized the national finances. In this way the Assembly tried both to break with the old order and to preserve it for the sake of convenience. However, the subordinated classes understood and agreed that the old taxes were arbitrary; hence they stopped paying them, and in some places they acted against the outposts of collection. Their consistent stance brought about a rapid softening of the Assembly's ambiguous position and foreclosed the (already faint) possibility of a revamping of existing indirect taxes.

In 1789 it was a foregone conclusion that the exclusive hunting privileges of nobles would be abolished. But the Assembly disagreed with most of the rural population over the future basis for hunting's legality. Not until April 1790 did the Assembly arrive at a text that framed hunting within the modern concept of landed property, with its concentration of all forms of "enjoyment" in one legal personage. By that time, a greatly extended popular practice that appropriated game and forest fruits as a subsistence reserve was well anchored and would remain through the 1790s.

The Assembly sought a base for enforcing public order outside the royal ministries, the *gouvernements*, and the nobles who commanded the army. It seized upon the civil officers of localities (mayors, municipal officers, and bailliage officers) and made them—on paper—the fulcrum for enforcement. In theory, the mounted police, troops, and militia were constellated around the civil officers, who could use each or all indifferently. Municipalities were to be direct agents of the law and directly responsible for its being followed. This meant that municipalities' familiar role as entities that bargained with outside power centers was undercut, leaving them in a fragile new position.

The inhabitants also saw their municipal officers as a fulcrum, but they sought to apply leverage in the opposite direction. Events had made the community realm of public order stronger than ever, and in many places this realm's concerns were now articulated by the commune or the new militia. The subordinated classes were active in enforcing a vision of public order congruent with their opinions on the grain trade, excise taxes, hunting, foraging, and other matters. The mounted police and garrisoned troops were not merely additional resources available to civil officers; they were symbols of the state realm and of the old order as well, and municipalities were often in no position to coordinate them with the militia. As we have seen, this entire predicament was born of responses to the Great Fear at local and national levels.

This, then, was the matrix in which attitudes toward authority evolved over the latter half of 1789. The next chapter attempts the closest approach possible to these attitudes in individuals by examining a single event: the peasant invasion of the château of Frétoy in the Noyonnais on July 27, the day of the Great Fear in the surrounding area. This incident can be reconstructed in the rich personal detail that only repeated interrogations by policemen or inquisitors leave to the historian, and it illustrates how revolutionary ideas interpenetrated with the long-tested tactics of peasant action from the old regime.

THE ART OF VISITING
CHÂTEAUX
(FRÉTOY, JULY 27, 1789)

On July 27, 1789, the inhabitants of five villages entered the château of
Frétoy near Noyon and carried away 60 *septiers* of grain. This was the only
attack on a château in the Soissons intendancy in 1789. Its participants
were oblivious to the Great Fear, which was going on around them that
very day. Four kilometers to the west, the village of Beaulieu-les-
Fontaines mobilized completely and marched toward Roye, but Frétoy
and its neighbors literally followed a different drummer. As the Noyon
intermediate bureau described it, "In the morning of the day when the
false reports of the devastated harvests were being spread, a considerable
troop of peasants, with a veteran at their head, arrived in Frétoy with
drums beating; once in that parish they broke down the doors of the
château [and] pillaged the grain to be found there, drank the wine and
the liqueurs, and pilfered various effects."[1]

The thoroughness of the prevotal inquiry that followed offers the
historian a rare opportunity to recreate an event in detail, down to the
words, gestures, and outbursts of feeling of many of the participants.
Because nine people gave accounts that are in considerable agreement, a
reliable composite narrative can be presented. The inquiry also permits
an analysis of individuals' attitudes toward authority.

On the basis of the narrative of the Frétoy incident that will be
presented in this chapter, five major issues will be analyzed. First, how
does the Frétoy incident compare to the Great Fear on the same day? The
Frétoy participants circulated rumors of their own, distinct from the

rumors associated with the Fear, and these give clues about the different forms of consciousness behind the two events.

Second, can the Frétoy incident be understood in terms of the model, proposed in chapter 6, of three realms of public order: community, municipal-legal, and state? At a first view, it appears that the course of the attack on the château was determined by internal community dynamics and that the municipal-legal and state realms came into play only in the wake of the event. However, a closer look reveals that the forms taken by the attack itself depended on the community's understanding of how the municipal-legal and state realms would react.

Third, the Frétoy incident offers an unusual opportunity to examine the internal authorities set up by peasants in revolt: the interaction between an ostensible leader and his followers, the leader's style of authority, and the degree of actual command ceded to him by the peasant troop. The comportment of the retired soldier Pierre Joly, who headed the Frétoy attack, was a mélange of elements borrowed from the mounted police on one hand and from revolutionary Paris on the other. His performance, and his followers' reactions to it, is suggestive of the kind of political consciousness available to the rural Soissonnais in 1789.

Fourth, how did the participants seek to protect themselves from arrest and arraignment? They cooperatively developed a whole network of defenses by evaluating specific acts for their legal consequences, imputing responsibility to the troop's leader, and denying acquaintance with persons from villages a short walk from their own.

Finally, how did the authorities assess the Frétoy incident and go about their repressive duties? The prevotal court's choice of culprits shows how, in practice, the philosophy of punishing "examples" shaped inquiries. Further, the court's strategy of interrogation reveals its expectations of a conspiracy engineered from Paris.

The Nature of the Source

All documents used in this chapter come from a single dossier that the mounted police in Clermont-en-Beauvaisis sent to the National Assembly on August 22, 1789. The Assembly had reacted to news of peasant revolts and the Great Fear by decreeing on August 10 that all persons arrested as instigators of troubles or panics be tried but not sentenced. The Assembly was to receive the records of these cases. A committee would assemble the evidence into a grand pattern so as to "work back to the source of the disorders." The documents on the Frétoy incident sent by the Clermont mounted police cover the full inquiry of the bailliage officials and the prevotal court. They begin with the record of the leader Joly's arrest and conclude with the final ordering of evidence prior to judgment.[2]

Cavaliers of the mounted police arrested Joly in Frétoy on July 27 and brought him that day to officials of the Noyon bailliage for questioning. The bailliage examined him on the twenty-seventh and again on the twenty-eighth, when it turned him back over to the mounted police. The bailliage had determined that Joly's case fell under the royal decree of May 21, which gave the prevotal court competence over public disturbances without need for the presidial court's approval.

On August 2 and 3, seven inhabitants of Frétoy made depositions about the events of July 27. These seven were Quentin Lamy, the village curé; Pierre Briet, the village syndic; Jean Cordier, the innkeeper and baker; Charles Magnier, the guard of the château; Charles-Louis Pailliart, the son of the local woodseller; Louis Caboche, the village surgeon; and Etienne Souplet, one of the two locksmiths in Frétoy (the other was the syndic Briet). All except the château guard had actively assisted in the attack, but all claimed that they had participated under duress.

The depositions are in the form of narratives unbroken by questions. The witnesses were apparently told only to recount the day in the fullest possible detail. Frétoy's curé, Quentin Lamy, gave the most ample description. The other six depositions are hardly cursory, but they primarily confirm Lamy's narrative and add further details. An eighth deposition was made by Joseph L'Herondelle, the syndic of Muirancourt, a village four kilometers away. He saw the peasant troop on the march before it arrived in the neighborhood of Frétoy, and his deposition provides our only glimpse of the troop early in its formation.

On August 10 and 16, the leader Joly was interrogated again, this time with the background of the witnesses' depositions (called the *information*). Over August 17–18, the eight witnesses came to Clermont. Each witness, with the exception of the syndic of Muirancourt, was presented to Joly (the *confrontation*). The witness's deposition was read to Joly, Joly was allowed to dispute its points, and the witness could modify his testimony. The *confrontation* was accompanied by a verification (the *recollement*) that offered each witness a last opportunity to add remarks or alter the deposition. The Frétoyards made some additions but no retractions—a common pattern in prevotal cases, perhaps inspired by a fear of perjury charges.[3]

To summarize, the Frétoy dossier includes the following documents: the police report of Joly's capture, July 27; four interrogations of Joly, on July 27, July 28, August 10, and August 16; the depositions of eight witnesses, including the curé and the syndic of Frétoy, taken over August 2-3, together with the court's formal charges; the confrontations between Joly and seven of the eight witnesses, August 17-18; the *recollement* of depositions, in which each witness made his final changes in testimony, August 17-18; and a cover letter addressed to the National Assembly, dated August 22.

The information provided by the witnesses is presented here as a composite narrative; the repetitiveness of the seven Frétoy depositions and their elaborate confirmation of detail lend themselves to this form. The Frétoy case bears out Iain Cameron's characterization of prevotal inquiries in general: "There does not seem to have been much prompting, or unrecorded suggestions the witnesses concentrate on one aspect or another, for the depositions are full of material irrelevant even by the lax standards of the eighteenth century, while witnesses were allowed to repeat each other to a soul-destroying degree."[4] This very repetition allows the building of a reliable composite narrative. The witnesses' accounts diverge only over the actual moment when the peasant troop decided to take the château's grain without paying any compensation. At this point our narrative compares the variants provided. On the one hand, concrete particulars that could have been confirmed by more than one witness, but were not, have generally been excluded. On the other hand, more delicate evidence, such as the leader Joly's gestures and facial expressions as described by the curé, seems too valuable to delete.

The Frétoy dossier is an excellent source for the activities of the peasant troop from the time it arrived in the village, through its attack on the château, to the moment of the leader's arrest by the mounted police. However, it tells us almost nothing about how the troop formed and what it did before it reached Frétoy. The prevotal court focused on the major offenses—forced entry and theft—and probably did not have the resources to pursue the origins of the disturbance. For the troop's appearance near Muirancourt we have the brief testimony of that village's syndic. For its arrival in the village of Rezavoine, where its leader Joly joined or was made to join it, we must rely primarily on Joly's testimony, though the curé of Frétoy made his own inquiries in Rezavoine after the event and communicated at least some of them to the court.

The court was obsessed with finding a leader, or *moteur*, on whom popular action could be blamed, and thus questioned Joly about his personal background at some length in three of his four interrogations. Joly supplied a self-description that is coherent and consistent, but without independent verification. The dossier, and consequently our narrative, displays this emphasis on the leader, which is a fundamental limitation of the source. The dynamics of a group of peasants in revolt appear as an accompaniment to a leader's acts because that was the only way in which the court could construe them.

The Frétoy Incident: A Composite Narrative

The investigators of the Frétoy incident were almost indifferent to the turmoil in the nearby villages of Crisolles, Muirancourt, Rezavoine, and Bussy on the previous day. They cared only for the thoughts and movements of the villagers' ostensible leader, a retired army sergeant named Pierre Joly.[5]

Joly was, as best he could remember, 53 years old. He had been born in Beaulieu. His father had been a servant at the château of Frétoy for almost 30 years, and he himself had grown up there. His father had served Mme. de Frétoy, the mother-in-law of the comtesse Destournelles. From 1751 to 1777 Pierre Joly served in the artillery and rose to the rank of sergeant. Then his unit was traded to the engineering corps, and he spent two years supervising road *corvées*. After his discharge Joly sought a place in the night watch (*garde*) of Paris. He waited on the comtesse Destournelles at her Paris residence, hoping to request her intercession, but he was turned away from the door. Nevertheless, by about 1786 he was serving in the Paris watch when he was offered a post at Mehun-sur-Yèvre, in the Artois apanage in Berry. Thus by 1789 Joly was an estate guard, like so many veterans in their fifties.

On July 16 Joly left his sinecure to head north for the Noyonnais. He had two reasons that we know of. First, his brother-in-law in Rezavoine had died and his sister needed help. Second, Joly believed he had discovered (on an earlier visit?) a "gold and silver mine" on the heights of Quincy, near Braine. (There are veins of yellow mica and iron pyrite throughout southern Picardy and the forest of Compiègne.)[6] This "discovery" was Joly's excuse to the police for lingering in Paris on his way north.

Joly entered Paris on July 20, one week after the fall of the Bastille. Hastily organized bourgeois of the 60 Paris districts—the embryo of the National Guard of August—stopped him to see his papers. They read the certificate from his municipality that stated his name and business and also mentioned his artillery experience. They grew excited: he could place himself to advantage in Paris, they told him. Joly replied that he was already engaged by the comte d'Artois as an estate guard, but that if he was needed he would gladly volunteer for the Third Estate. The Parisians let him pass, urging him for his safety's sake not to make so free with the name of Artois, for the comte d'Artois had already emigrated.

Joly lodged near the place St-Michel, under the roof of an old-clothes dealer named Meusiot, for 12 sous a night. He consulted goldsmiths about his mica samples (and claimed later they did not disabuse him). While out walking on the twenty-first, he saw the head of Foulon go by, but did not join the crowd. He visited old military friends and must have talked over the feverish succession of events with them. We shall see later what he made of it all.

Joly left Paris for Rezavoine on Friday, July 24, and arrived that Sunday evening. On the road to Noyon he heard rumors that the surrounding peasants might attack Noyon for its stores of grain.

The same evening that Joly arrived in his sister's house, the village of Frétoy one kilometer away was electrified by advance word of peasant activity. Several nearby villages were joining forces to pillage the château of the comtesse Destournelles. Quentin Lamy, the curé, told Jean Cordier, the innkeeper who doubled as a baker,[7] before dashing off to see Langlois, the concierge of the château. Langlois had already heard the news from his son and had alerted the servants and the guard, Charles Magnier. Lamy urged Langlois to remove money and documents from the château and stayed with him until after midnight.[8]

At three someone sighted the invaders and woke the village, but it was a false alarm. Lamy could not sleep. He dressed and went back to the château. The whole household was awake. The concierge could not bring himself to believe in the coming raid, yet precautions had to be taken, and the estate manager had to be written . . . the curé went back and forth between his house and the château another three times before morning.[9]

At seven o'clock, four kilometers to the east in Muirancourt (Figure 7.1), Joseph l'Herondelle, the tavernkeeper and syndic, spied two groups of peasants circling around the mill. The larger group set off for Rezavoine; the smaller entered the mill, emerged with grain, and started home, dispersing to take the road to Muirancourt or to Crisolles.[10]

In Rezavoine, Joly was asleep when his sister suddenly awakened him, "crying for mercy, and declaring that all was lost because of a horde of bandits ravaging the countryside." He leaped up, reached for his long hunting knife, and went outside. Twenty men and women surrounded him, demanding that he lead them to the château. He knew it well, they reminded him; his father had served there and he had grown up there. Joly insisted later that they had threatened him; certainly his sister felt

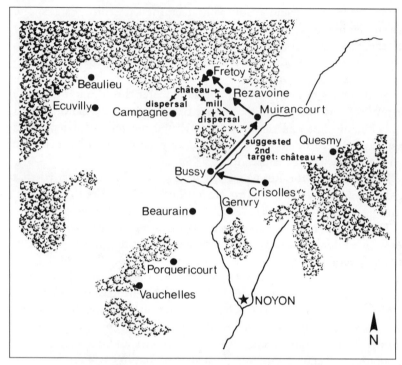

Figure 7.1. A Movements of peasant groups around Frétoy on July 27, 1789.

threatened by them. In any case, he agreed to lead them to the Frétoy château.[11] First, however, he demanded and got the surrender of firearms from those carrying them; the guns were left in Rezavoine.[12]

In Frétoy the news of the peasant troop's arrival came just ahead of the troop itself. Charles-Louis Pailliart, the woodseller's son, warned Magnier the guard that the "troop of brigands" was already at Rezavoine and preparing to descend on Frétoy.[13] Shortly afterward, the "brigands" commenced their work at Pailliart's own house. Joly and 15 others came inside and ordered Pailliart to join them. He demurred, saying that he was about to have breakfast and would join them soon. Joly accepted this and left Pailliart to his meal, muttering that if he did not show up they would kill him and burn down his house on the way back from the château.[14]

Marching down the main street of Frétoy, Joly encountered Louis Caboche, the village surgeon. Joly demanded whether he was of the Third Estate. Caboche replied flippantly, "It's a good bet I am." His tone put Joly off; he said he didn't understand all that, but that Caboche had

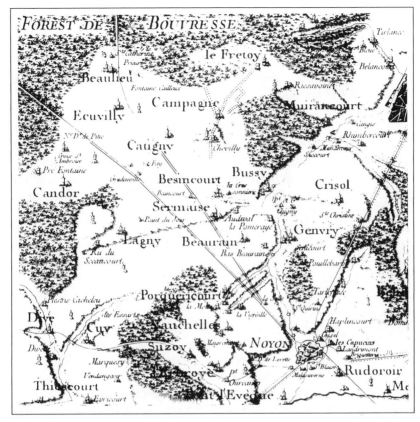

Figure 7.1. B The terrain of the Noyonnais in the eighteenth century. (Detail of the Cassini *Carte de France* [1744–60], Library of Congress, Washington, D.C.)

to follow him, and had to wear a tricolor cockade—"a thing he did right away, fearing a greater mishap."[15]

Jean Cordier, the innkeeper-baker, had been awaiting the troop since the previous evening. About eight o'clock he heard "a considerable noise from a troop of people" and walked outdoors. He saw perhaps 50 people led by an older man in uniform, carrying what Cordier thought was a saber.[16] The troop was armed with clubs, some paltry, some formidable, and a scattering of pikes. Many carried empty sacks. Joly detached himself and began to harangue Cordier. Was he of the Third Estate? Yes, Cordier replied. Then he must follow Joly or be hung: Joly's orders required him to hang all those who did not obey his first command. He had learned that Madame Destournelles had 1,200 *septiers* of grain, and this was grain that they all needed unless they wanted to die of hunger.

His sister in Rezavoine had neither grain nor bread—and at these words Cordier recognized the veteran: "It's you, M. Joly!" Joly confessed his identity as Cordier fell in and they all walked along, Joly giving Cordier news from Paris (of a sort): "Mme. the comtesse had refused the cockade of the Third Estate . . . she was a scamp and a wretch . . . she was locked up like a dog in her house . . . she would never return to Frétoy . . . in a few days she would lose her taste for bread [i.e., be killed] . . . "[17]

Quentin Lamy the curé lived in the house of Pierre Briet the syndic. Both saw the troop coming toward them, pausing here and there to accumulate their neighbors, and both started to retire into the house— a bit too late. Joly hailed the curé, who went to present himself to the "chef." Joly announced that he was empowered by the government to search the châteaux of the region for hoarded grain and to sell grain to those who lacked it. According to his commission, the curé of the parish had to accompany him at all times in order to certify that the search and sale had been orderly. The inhabitants of Frétoy had nothing to fear; he, Joly, had once been Lamy's parishioner and knew him to be a worthy man.[18] If the curé had to certify the leader, Lamy asked, shouldn't the syndic have to also?—for Briet was just about to disappear up the stairs. Joly agreed and called down Briet, who recognized him at once.[19]

The troop was now admixed with Frétoyards "constrained to follow Joly by threats on the part of the king."[20] They all set off for the château, Joly at the head, the curé on his right and the syndic on his left. Joly kept up a running commentary of threats, assurances, abuse, and justifications. He cursed the absent comtesse: "damned bitch . . . damned whore . . . she would never more be seen at Frétoy . . . she should soon, perhaps this very day, have her head cut off . . . in any case that would happen, or had happened already . . . all Paris had sworn her death, because she well deserved it." Ceaselessly he insisted that "he, Joly, was within regulations and well authorized for these kinds of expeditions." He told the curé that his commission derived from the Parlement. Lamy replied that Joly could make his ignorant parishioners believe that, but not him. Joly stumbled a bit and then said that it was not the old Parlement he meant, but the "parlement of the Third Estate."[21]

They entered the château courtyard by a little side gate and demanded the concierge. But Langlois had fled. Magnier the guard opened the door and asked their business. Joly declared that he had certain knowledge that the château hoarded 1,200 *septiers* of grain. The troop was still swelling with latecomers: Charles-Louis Pailliart had finished his breakfast;[22] the locksmith Etienne Souplet had got the news late . . . [23]

Plans for dividing the grain were already in the air. Some proposed leaving only 40 *septiers* behind—all the rest would be taken and paid for.[24] Perhaps they were discussing their "leader" too: according to Joly afterward, "the troop did not cease to menace him in case he might abandon them."[25]

A servant led Joly to the granary over the stable, and on the way the discussion between the curé and Joly grew heated. The curé insisted that there were not more than 60 *septiers* in the château. Joly told Lamy that he was misinformed. They entered the granary. The curé saw astonishment cross Joly's face: the heap of grain on the floor was not much over 60 *septiers*. Joly, recovering, cried out that "this was the proof that the grain had been hidden, that [the curé] was not to leave him for a single step in the search he would make of all the rooms, that no harm would be done anywhere, that after this he [Lamy] would be required to give him a certificate of his good conduct to be presented to the government."[26] He added that unless all his orders were followed to the letter, thousands of soldiers would come to destroy Frétoy before nightfall. Then he urged the curé to take responsibility for setting a price on the grain they would find. The curé demurred, but a miller's boy was present to suggest 36 livres per sack. Joly said it was too much and went down from the granary.

The troop went on to a second granary in the coach-house. The door was locked: Joly began to growl about breaking the door down. Jean Cordier quickly suggested a ladder, and they saw through the windows that the granary was empty.[27]

Raiding the château's secret hoard was clearly more work than the participants had hoped. Most people had had no breakfast and were getting hungry. Caboche the surgeon invited Poileau the gardener to join him for a meal at home: they left.[28] Joly mentioned to the curé that he was famished. Lamy took him home, warning Joly that there was bread and cider there, but no wine. Joly's visible disappointment spurred Lamy to borrow a bottle of wine from Jean Cordier, whom he saw going home likewise.

At the curé's Joly drank moderately—"only . . . two small glasses"— but soon the house was filled with people seeking something to eat and drink. Lamy repeated that there was very little bread in Frétoy: Briet had borrowed for last night's supper. But this was a special occasion, and somehow Briet came up with the real thing: "a loaf of new rye, dried in the oven, baked that morning." Lamy was moved: he broke into tears, entreating the visitors to refrain. After a pause, they each slowly, with restraint, broke off a small piece and washed it down with cider. Everyone wanted to pay and dug coins from their pockets, but Briet refused. They protested they "did not want to wrong anyone, whoever it might be." The curé intervened. Was not their real business at the château? And what was the rest of the troop doing while they were away?[29]

Everyone returned to the château together. They resumed their search in the pantry (where Lamy, lagging behind, did not see them) and then attacked the laundress's room. It was locked. Someone cried that a servant named Cotteau had the key. He was searched for, without result. A dispute arose: Joly and several others were ready to break down the door, but "the greater part . . . cried that they had not come to break down any doors . . . " The curé suggested a locksmith as a compromise. Joly agreed.[30] Conveniently, Briet the syndic was a locksmith as well; he went home for his tool basket, asking Charles Magnier and Poileau the gardener to note well that he was acting under constraint.[31] Briet returned and burst the lock, and the troop crowded into the room.[32] Lamy feared for the house linen, and at his request Joly chased everyone out: "No one is going to steal any linen . . . only grain is being searched for."[33]

Joly and Briet broke into all the servants' chambers in succession, finishing with that of the concierge. The crowd streamed in and out of each room in a cycle of hope and disappointment. There was yet another granary above the servants' rooms, but it contained only dirty linen.[34]

One Merlier from Crisolles concluded that the grain had been hidden in the village. He walked alone into the village carrying a stick and knocked at the door of Jean Cordier. He told Cordier that grain must have been moved from the château into the village during the night, and that he, Cordier, must have at least one hundred *septiers* of it. Cordier took Merlier by the hand and brought him to his granary, where he had to admit that "he saw well he had not been told the truth," and so returned to the château.[35]

A number of the troop began to observe that no matter how badly the search for grain was going, they were hungry. There were those who said that "they would not leave the château until they had been served bread with stew and something to drink." The curé insisted that this was impossible: the concierge himself bought from the baker. "He was answered that in any case, it would be found somewhere," which Lamy took to mean his own house.[36] One man took the curé aside. He said that he had not eaten for a very long time, that he was hungry and thirsty. Why not take me home, he suggested, and give me a little bread and a few glasses of cider? Lamy did so. In Briet's house the curé gave the man a piece of bread; he broke off a third and returned the rest.

On returning to the château, Lamy noticed that a tall, furious-looking young man who had stayed in the forefront throughout was picking himself a saber from the wall. Lamy discussed this with Joly. Joly held forth again on his own responsibilities: "He was commissioned to seize not only those arms that he found in the château, but even those that he might find in the houses of individuals, that visits to all the houses would be made later for this purpose . . . " Then Joly, with only a few others, headed for the room where the archives were kept. It was locked. Joly was ready to burst it as he had the locks of the servants' doors. Lamy was horrified. "He begged him with clasped hands, one knee almost to the ground . . . not to permit this room to be opened . . . one cannot eat papers, and the present lady of Frétoy had usufruct only; it would do far more harm to the owners of the land if their titles were taken away and torn up."[37] Joly submitted, and they all went down into the courtyard.

In the garden was a tempting wine cellar. Joly was close to it now, and his "followers," who had dispersed all over the château, returned and closed ranks around him. Lamy and Magnier conferred; they both feared drunkenness above all else. Then the curé took Joly aside and whispered in his ear, "Everything was lost if he permitted the pillage of the wine, he would no longer be master of his command . . ." Lamy pointed to Joly's old uniform, "the two swords in satin that decorated it . . . telling him not to tarnish in an instant the military merit he had acquired through long service . . ." Joly "let his sense of honor be piqued." He swore again that he was only looking for grain and had the syndic open the wine cellar. Joly peered inside, snatched a bottle, smashed off its neck with his knife, and let Briet lock the cellar immediately. The young man with a saber—a carpenter named Poule—raged at the curé and Joly, threatening to kill them both if he caught them whispering again.[38]

In the garden Joly passed among the orange trees. Suddenly he ordered a bouquet cut for himself.[39] Frétoyards were still drifting back from lunch, among them Caboche and Poileau, the château's gardener,[40] who found his son offering Joly a few tentative branches. " . . . He scorned them and said they were not enough for a man like him, and getting angry, gave an orange tree two blows with his cane." Poileau cut a handsome bouquet and handed it to Magnier the guard. Magnier handed it to Joly. The *chef* was mollified: "This is what I require—I am the master."[41]

By now liquor flowed at last. The biggest cellar was out of bounds, but drink had been discovered all over the château: wine in one of the concierge's rooms, some bottled cider in the pantry, a little cache of liqueurs below the staircase. People broke the bottles' necks and filled their hats. The curé looked through the crowd for Joly, found him in the pantry, and told him that he had to make the troop leave the château before people got too drunk. Joly agreed that "it was time to finish and go over to the grain because everything had been searched."[42]

Then suddenly Joly broke a pane of glass in the pantry window— from frustration? from anxiety over the coming division of so little grain? The curé trembled; this might be a signal to break every window in the château. But Joly had a quite different project. In his monologues to everyone and no one he had repeated that the little seigneurial prison must be opened. Joly located both Briet and Souplet and set them to work, telling them that "the nobles could no longer have either prisons or arms, that the Bastille had been well broken down and it could be just the same with the prisons of seigneurs . . . "[43] The prison was opened and its few inmates released.

Joly decided the time had come to divide the contents of the granary over the stable. The troop reassembled around him: everyone had found a sack somewhere or other. They entered the granary and stood around the mass of wheat. The little room filled up at once.

Until this point the accounts of the seven witnesses from whom we have depositions (Lamy the curé, Cordier the innkeeper, Magnier the guard, Caboche the surgeon, Briet the syndic of Frétoy, Souplet the locksmith, and Pailliart the woodseller) can be reconciled without difficulty. Here, however, the accounts of Lamy, Caboche, and Magnier diverge over the actual division of the grain. Probably all three had equal chances to see what was happening, packed together as they were in the granary, their views blocked only by the presence of their companions. The contradictions in their accounts may have arisen from the tension of the moment and their awareness that the legal guilt of the participants would hinge upon what happened next.

According to the curé Lamy's story, Joly called on the curé to set the price. Lamy said nothing. Joly seemed to reflect; then he priced the grain at 24 livres per sack, and ordered the curé to receive payments. Poule the carpenter, who had kept his saber, challenged Joly "that he, the carpenter, intended that those without money would get grain like those who had some . . . " The curé "trembled in all his members and saw that the grain and flour were about to be pillaged; having withdrawn a few paces, he was called back by Joly, who, pretending to cry, or crying, said, extending his joined hands toward the heap of grain, 'See, M. le curé, I am no longer the master, it is confiscated—give me a certificate saying that I priced this grain at 24 livres a sack, and that I am being forced to abandon it for nothing.'"⁴⁴

According to Caboche, Poule was the first to set a price: 30 livres per sack. Then Joly lowered it to 24 livres—and a saber was flung into the grain, but Caboche could not tell whether it was Poule's.⁴⁵ According to Magnier, the sequence began with Poule's casting his saber down into the grain and declaring to Joly that the two of them would settle the price. Joly suggested 30 livres per sack, and the carpenter said 24.⁴⁶ Caboche, Magnier, and the curé agreed on the fact of the pillage; but the curé's account damaged Poule the most.

Etienne Souplet said he saw Joly coming down from the granary, saying that "he had wanted to have the grain paid for at one louis [24 livres], but that he had not been the master."⁴⁷ When Joly was questioned on August 10, he explained: "At the moment of the pillage, one man of the band tossed a saber onto the heap of grain as he began to gather some up . . . in this moment he thought he perceived a half dozen men closing tightly around him, who seemed to want to profit from the moment . . . to fall upon him with their sticks, and then he left them."⁴⁸

The curé left the granary and went down into the courtyard, "broken-hearted with sorrow," followed by those who were frightened by the prospect of taking the grain without leaving compensation. Merlier of Crisolles (the one who had visited Jean Cordier) plucked at Lamy's sleeve, recruiting a character witness: "I'm going now, M. le curé, without grain, I never intended to have any for nothing, how can they take away grain without paying for it? . . ." Lamy, resigned, was reading from his breviary as his neighbors passed him with their loaded sacks when he heard that the very horses' oats were being carried off. He located Joly in the château, surrounded by women at the bottom of the staircase. Together, Lamy, Briet, Joly, and Magnier shamed the others away from the oats: "The land had to be cultivated, and it could not be done if the horses' nourishment was taken away."⁴⁹

Lamy, "seeing the tumult carried to its climax," decided to go home. When he got there he found that Briet and Joly had preceded him. Briet poured Joly a drink. Joly pulled out a chunk of bread taken from the château's pantry and made short work of it. Then he asked Lamy to write out a certificate of his (Joly's) good conduct, to be signed by both the curé and the syndic. Lamy asked Joly a bit testily what there was to certify. Joly told him "that having wanted to sell the grain at 24 livres, he had been forced to give it up for nothing by the carpenter's threats to cut his head off."⁵⁰ The curé replied that he hadn't heard Poule's threats nor had he seen anything to prove that the carpenter had wanted to cut Joly's head off. And so he would limit the certificate to stating that Joly had set a price of 24 livres per sack, but that someone bigger had decided that people would pay only if they wished to.

Lamy was not enthusiastic about the certificate, but he was also afraid to refuse to write it. Even though he had "slipped away several times," Joly, still drinking, kept reminding him. Finally Joly began to sob.[51] "It was terrible, terrible for him to be found in circumstances like these . . . ,"[52] he lamented: " . . . he had performed a wrong action, since they had not wanted to pay." Then, the curé asked him, you're not going to the château of Quesmy? (Quesmy, about five miles east of Frétoy, had been mentioned among members of the troop as a next target.) Joly answered, "No, I will go to Paris right away."[53] At that point they heard a noise outside: the dragoons had arrived with the mounted police of Noyon.

The curé cried, "Are they coming as friends or enemies?" (Remember that Joly had prophesied the doom of Frétoy by nightfall.) But Joly did not lose countenance. "Let's go talk to them together," he said, getting up.[54] It was eleven in the morning.

Lamy and Joly approached the soldiers and police riding up before the château.[55] Joly declared "publicly and loudly" that he was Joly, the "head of the troop."[56] Lamy, "still not knowing what to say," confirmed that Joly was the *chef*, but added that he had resisted "a thousand more outrageous wickednesses that several of his troop had wanted to commit."[57] Joly was arrested. While Lamy led the dragoons through the château, describing and displaying, Joly was removed to the royal prison of the bailliage of Noyon.[58] Everyone else had already gone home.

The Great Fear: Its Proximity and Absence

Of the many questions raised by the Frétoy incident, perhaps the most intriguing is this: where was the Great Fear? It was in Beaulieu, just four kilometers west;[59] and it was also in the mind of Catherine Joly, who woke her brother crying that "all was lost because of a horde of bandits ravaging the countryside." Her experience may have been shared by others in Rezavoine, because she told him that "already women have taken refuge in the woods."[60] However, these are the only indications we have of the Fear in the villages between Crisolles and Frétoy. The participants' testimonies showed instead an entirely different world of rumor, in which the grain of the region was being hoarded in châteaux by nobles or their stewards while peasants starved, and suggestions of a popular attack on Noyon itself were in the air. As Joly took on the role of "royal emissary," the threats he improvised drew on this world of rumor for their images of vengeance. A royal army of seven thousand was attacking Noyon on the same day that Joly's troop was searching the château, and any laxity in their search would be punished by yet other soldiers, who would raze the château and the village of Frétoy along with it.

The troop's identification of châteaux as centers of grain hoarding indicates a possible belief in a "famine pact"— the idea of a coordinated concealment of grain stocks by the rich and powerful. It also suggests a class antagonism toward the nobility. Yet the expression of this antagonism remained within the limited context of grain and subsistence for most of the troop, despite Joly's efforts to broaden it by falling upon the château's archive and prison. And while there are signs of a hostility to Noyon which was doubtless real, and which we know emerged more strongly in August and September,[61] the troop moved away from Noyon, not toward it (Figure 7.1). Bussy, the southernmost of the villages whose names appeared in the inquiry, is about four kilometers from Noyon, but the troop's objective of Frétoy put another four kilometers between them and the town. Quesmy, which was bruited as the next objective, was seven kilometers east of Frétoy (perhaps two hours' walk) and seven kilometers northeast of Noyon. The participating villages lived almost beneath the town's walls, and so it is no wonder that the troop's itinerary shows a desire for elbow room in which to operate. Any participants who might have seriously contemplated an eventual massing at Noyon surely realized that it would require a rapid crisscrossing of the region to raise many more villages,[62] and no one seems to have had the stomach for such an undertaking.

When Lefebvre studied the Great Fear in France as a whole, he was struck by the fact that "between the agrarian revolts and the Great Fear, there is so little interdependence that the two do not coincide, except in the Dauphiné . . . "[63] Chapter 4 of this study has shown the truth of this observation on the scale of the Soissonnais, and Frétoy and Beaulieu demonstrate it again on an amazingly small scale. The Great Fear missed Frétoy and the villages to its south not for any conceivable geographic reason, but because they were in the throes of a different type of social process. The fear of an attack on standing crops could fuel the Great Fear in a given locale only if social antagonisms there had not yet boiled over. In this corner of the Noyonnais, cheek by jowl with another corner where the Fear was already in progress, the minimum of social calm that the Fear required had somehow been lost. The possible economic reasons that could account for this have been discussed earlier:[64] the hilly terrain of the Noyonnais and the polyculture it supported; the somewhat greater prevalence of peasant proprietorship of quite small parcels; the advanced stage of breakdown in triennial rotation; the dominance of nonsubsistence cash crops over grain; and the irrelevance of begging in terrain with few large farmers. Yet such an explanation falls apart when villages within the sounds of each other's bells go entirely separate ways.

Despite the mystery involved here, two points can still be noted. One is simply the nature of the difference between the Frétoy attack and the Great Fear. The peasant action at Frétoy—grounded in beliefs about grain sale and circulation—was confined to a couple of dozen square kilometers and was rapidly broken up by forces from Noyon, the marketing center. In Beaulieu, on the other hand, the fear of an attack on grain production brought the village into a movement that extended on a single day from the juncture of the Oise and Seine in the Paris intendancy to Amiens and Arras in the north.

The second point is that the Great Fear was a structure of individual perception, as the reaction of Catherine Joly demonstrates. While her village was responding quite differently to its situation, she seems to have experienced the Great Fear virtually on her own, interpreting the arrival of her neighbors in arms as "a horde of bandits ravaging the countryside." We primarily think of the Great Fear as a collective phenomenon, but Catherine Joly's response shows us that it did not have to be. The Fear could also appear as an individual response to stress, a personal perception rooted in the "common sense" that elsewhere mobilized whole communities.

Frétoy and the Realms of Public Order

Does the Frétoy incident fit into the model of three realms of public order proposed in the last chapter? Clearly the troop's formation took place in the community realm, to which Frétoy's curé and syndic were native. The behavior of Quentin Lamy and Pierre Briet shows that their authority was internal to their community, not oriented to the law or to any outside source. They were carried along by the force of the troop's impact on their village, and while careful not to commit many infractions on their own account, they do not seem to have felt much legal vulnerability in this situation. The municipal-legal realm was represented by Noyon and its civil authorities, and by no one closer. Noyon dispatched the agents of the state realm, the mounted police and dragoons, who arrived too late to do anything but arrest Joly when he presented himself.

Joly was first questioned on July 27 by the municipal legal power, the royal counselor of the Noyon secondary bailliage (higher bailliage officers were absent at the time). A transcript of this interrogation was examined by the royal attorney, who decided that according to the royal decree of May 21 on the competence of the mounted police, Joly should be turned over to the Clermont prevotal court without more ado and kept in its jail. The rest of the inquiry took place within the state realm. By August 18 the case was ready for judgment, but the National Assembly's August 10 decree forestalled a sentence. A full copy of the testimony was sent to the Assembly so that it could be compared with other cases from all over France, in order to "work back to the source of disorders." Of course the Assembly was soon overwhelmed with other business. Joly languished in prison, where he died in 1791.[65]

Within the realm of the community, the relationship between Joly as a purported "leader" and the peasant troop that "followed" him was peculiar and convoluted. The evidence as a whole supports Joly's word that he was not the instigator of the march on Frétoy and that the troop sought him out to lead them. To what degree they coerced him into taking up this role is harder to assess. Catherine Joly's alarm speaks for there having been at least a menacing quality to the troop's presence.

Why did the troop want Joly? Joly stated to the royal attorney on the day of his arrest that the troop had told him, "With he the accused at their head, the gate [of the château] would be opened to them sooner."[66] In part, the troop picked up Joly simply for his utility. His knowledge of the château from boyhood and his status as a veteran qualified him for the most visible position in their enterprise.

But did high visibility mean leadership? It seems more likely that troop members saw Joly as a "leader" only insofar as he provided them with a form of legal insurance. Joly, once given "responsibility," was a scapegoat offered to the municipal-legal and state realms of public order; but the troop's ingenuity went well beyond this, for Joly was a perfectly chosen scapegoat, an ideal match for the prejudices of the authorities. Like that other sergeant, Rasselet—the NCO on leave who poached in the forest of Coucy and was arrested as a "leader of a troop" even though he hunted alone[67]—Joly was a plebeian warrior, native to the area yet separated from it by years of military service. Joly was just the type that the authorities could envisage as a *moteur* for the Frétoy affair, and his arrival in the neighborhood the night before was a great stroke of luck for his neighbors. Once the inquiry had added Joly's claims of orders from above to his military background, its attention was fixed on him thereafter, to the great benefit of all the other participants. A uniformed veteran alleging a commission from the king was impersonating the state realm, and few things disturbed the authorities more than being impersonated. Thus Joly served the troop primarily as a decoy, and in this function he was highly effective.

Joly's Style of Authority

Joly was not merely the troop's hostage; the relations between the two were more complex than Joly's value as a decoy might suggest. The threat of force against Joly—implied in the background, or asserted loudly by Poule the carpenter—was one aspect of these relations; but another aspect was the real cession of a degree of authority to Joly at the moment when the troop agreed to leave its guns behind in Rezavoine. In the château Joly seems to have been obeyed in various matters, especially in his ban on the theft of linen and household objects. Joly in turn conditioned much of his behavior in Frétoy on his hopes for certificates of good conduct from the curé and the syndic. In fact, Joly's "certifiers" constituted a third corner of a triangle, for Joly sought to use them as a counterweight against pressure from the troop. Joly hoped to keep the troop within the bounds of the sort of public order associated with the community realm: this is what he wanted Lamy and Briet to certify. Then, with luck, the higher-realm authorities would put Joly's actions in a community-realm perspective and go lightly on him.

Operating within these ambiguous constraints, Joly nevertheless managed to give his partial authority a personal stamp. To create his "image" (as we would say today) he borrowed elements from two sources, the mounted police and revolutionary Paris. When the troop consented to Joly's demand to leave their guns behind, they were accepting a form of control reminiscent of the cavaliers' disarmament of villages. The curé Lamy saw a significant mitigating circumstance in this act of Joly's and gave the inquiry the names of witnesses who could confirm it. But the disarmament appears to have counted for little with the mounted police, who may have seen it as only another insolence in Joly's impersonation of themselves. For Lamy, however, it was congruent with the way Joly had described his "commission": to visit locations that might be hoarding grain, search them thoroughly, and force the sale of any hidden grain that might be found. These were all actual mounted police functions in the preharvest months of 1789, with the difference that the police acted for the market center while Joly appeared to act for the rural inhabitants. Joly also claimed that he was empowered to visit all the homes in the village and confiscate arms, just as the mounted police sometimes did. Joly even found a place for his *maréchaussée* manner in his replies to his interrogators. As late as August 16 he told them that "he had not seen any harm in visiting the château, to inform the messieurs of Noyon about the grain it might hold . . . "[68]

At the same time, Joly made an effort to give his impersonation of state-realm authority a revolutionary form compatible with events in Paris. This concern seems to have been his alone. Joly's recurring saluta-tion, "Are you of the Third Estate?" was almost comic when heard in the dusty street of a hungry village at a forest's edge, and the surgeon Caboche's comeback—"It's a good bet I am"—must have been hard to resist making. Joly's insistence that Frétoyards wear cockades; his "news from Paris" and his pronouncement that the Parisians would soon kill Frétoy's *châtelaine*; his interest in the château's archive; and above all his opening of the seigneurial prison and release of its captives—Joly's per-sonal conquest of a miniature Bastille, which one imagines may have deeply satisfied him—all went unshared by most of the participants. They show the impact that four days in Paris had made on Joly. But they also show, no less than Joly's *maréchaussée* manner does, his concern with giving legitimate forms to his comportment. Those actions of Joly's that smacked most of the Revolution might justify him in the new order, just as the actions that echoed the mounted police might mitigate his punish-ment in the old order. This mixture of old regime and Revolution in Joly's behavior was perhaps calculated in part, but it also expressed the subjective medley inside him.

The Participants' Precautions against Arrest

Throughout the morning Joly kept up a discourse full of mingled threats and reassurances, with his "certifiers" hearing more of the reassurances and various participants hearing more of the threats. Both Lamy and Brict made ambiguous statements about the real meaning of what Joly said. The curé sought to minimize Joly's threats of violence: "The var-ious threats that are spoken of . . . were more the bluster of a soldier than the determined will of Joly the accused to put them into effect. He was not afraid of Joly, especially since the accused always assured him that he had nothing to fear . . . He embraced Briet and many of the village women of his acquaintance in reassuring them, or rather out of friendship."[69]

Joly's threats contrasted strangely with the rest of his discourse and with much of his conduct. Briet, the syndic, was less sympathetic to Joly, and his comment provides a better clue. He said, "The accused was not capable of putting his threats into execution, nor did he want to, but it is no less true that he made them . . . "[70] Briet's remark is intriguing because it implies that the mere existence of Joly's discourse should be more important to the court than what Joly actually meant. Since Briet had burst locks for the troop in the château, it was of course crucial for him to establish that he had acted under constraint, and the fact of Joly's threats allowed Briet to do this. From Briet's standpoint it was immaterial whether Joly had intended his threats, or whether they were even plausible.

Joly's verbal stream of menace and reassurance sounds a harmony when we grasp that the leader's threats were the alibis of his followers.[71] To be menaced was itself a reassurance. It was evidence of coercion before witnesses.

For the Frétoyards, Joly's hyperbole was indispensable for their participation. For those whose forte with the police was their show of ignorance and gullibility, here was the man in uniform prepared to claim that he was a royal emissary. For those with more education or position, he was a violent veteran who had best be humored. However, the creation of "mitigating circumstances" was reciprocal. Just as the troop menaced Joly into menacing them, he provided their excuses on the condition that excuses were developed for him. Joly sought his defense in the community that served as host for the troop. Hence his selection of Frétoy's curé and syndic to certify his probity, and the parade of the troop toward the château, Joly in the first rank with the curé on his right and the syndic on his left.

Joly never got his certificate, and yet the curé and the syndic did modify their depositions in his favor. All the witnesses were given this opportunity to revise their testimony. Lamy tried hardest to aid Joly, while Briet was more cautious. Louis Caboche shifted the blame where he could from Joly to Poule. Etienne Souplet recalled how Joly forbade petty thefts in the château. Others made no changes, yet no one made things worse for Joly. Mitigation was reciprocal, but sequential. Before Joly could be made a candidate for clemency, his guilt had to be established.

While Joly was the centerpiece of the participants' network of legal defenses, this network had other resources as well. One such resource was the distances between the villages that contributed members to the troop. The prevotal court asked Joly whom he had recognized in the troop when he first saw them in Rezavoine. He responded, "Having arrived the previous evening in the region, from which he had been absent so long, he did not recognize anyone."[72] However, as Lamy pointed out, it was remarkable how many of the women of Frétoy Joly seemed to remember. Jean Cordier and Pierre Briet recognized Joly at once. Joly reminded Lamy that he had once been Lamy's parishioner. How likely was it that the others in the troop were unknown to the Frétoyards?

All of the witnesses were asked to name names. The guard Magnier claimed he knew nobody, but had heard that the carpenter with the saber was from Cressy and was named Poule. He then remembered that he had seen the newly married son of Charles Grevin, the miller in Muirancourt, among those in the granary.[73] Jean Cordier said he had recognized no one except Merlier, who had made a one-man expedition to Cordier's house.[74] Etienne Souplet's answer spoke for all Frétoy: "that he knew by sight the greater part of those in Joly's band as being from Crisolles, Muirancourt, Rezavoine, and Bussy, but he did not know the names of those who had taken grain . . ."[75]

The four villages that Souplet named were not socially distant, but they were legally distant—in the sense that the presumption of mutual anonymity passed with the authorities. This was probably another reason (along with the need for greater distance from Noyon) that the troop began to collect several kilometers from its target, wound through a few villages collecting personnel, struck, and dispersed.

Above all, the participants shared a common legal sensibility that was expressed in their conduct. We have seen Briet, the syndic and locksmith, finding witnesses to his constraint as he went home for his toolbasket; and Merlier of Crisolles showing the curé that he had emerged from the granary without grain. The participants showed a finely graded sense of the seriousness of offenses committed along the way. The troop protested against Joly's desire to break down the servants' doors. The curé suggested a locksmith, and the syndic performed this office. When Joly attacked the archive and then the prison, he had little company. For most of the troop, objectives of a legal-political nature were taboo. We can gauge the tension the participants felt over the coming division of the grain by their breakfasting with Briet rather than at the château, and by their insistence on paying him for the little they took. All these gestures show a refined grasp of one's legal position, individually and as a group; a concern to participate not only in this affair, but in the next.

The Priorities of Repression

The documents allow us a glimpse of the mentality of the authorities as well as that of the participants. We know so little about the troop's formation before it arrived in Rezavoine because, for the prevotal court, these internal workings of communities were either insignificant or (in a sense) outside its competence. What mattered was to distinguish the active participants from the passive ones; to find those who led the troop astray and dismiss those who were swept along; and thereby to reduce the affair to punishable proportions. Consequently the court sought above all to establish that Joly had claimed a royal commission. Not only would this provide the inquiry with the *moteur* it sought, it would suit the entire logic of exemplary punishment. After all, if communities had been misled to the point of revolt by an impostor mimicking legitimacy, then legitimacy itself was fundamentally secure. It would be merely cruel to punish dozens of wretches who had fallen into error.

Within this logic, the court's attitude toward Poule the carpenter becomes explicable. The judge viewed Poule as a secondary figure because he did not impersonate authority. He did qualify as an agitator from outside because he came from Cressy, 8 kilometers north of Frétoy and 12 or 13 kilometers from the cluster of villages that provided the troop's personnel. By autumn Cressy would become markedly radical,[76] and Poule may have been a harbinger of this spirit. Briet the syndic testified that Poule had frequently repeated the story that a regiment of dragoons accompanied by thousands of men would raze Frétoy and its château if the troop was hindered in its work. The woodseller Pailliart even said that Poule, "who did not seem to be in any good humor . . . pushed along the said Joly," supporting Joly's claim that the carpenter had menaced him into taking extreme action. But when the prevotal judge Douviller gave the charges their final form, he slated Joly as "finally . . . the chief and author of the pillage that was carried out by his band," while Poule was charged only with having accompanied Joly, having made the same threats, and having opposed paying compensation for the grain.[77] Ultimately, Poule was a civilian, while Joly was a former part of the state apparatus; Poule wore no uniform, while Joly did; and the probability that Poule was an earlier participant, closer to the affair's origins, did not weigh with the court. Poule personified the community realm, and so there were limits to his culpability despite the evidence.

Both the bailliage and the prevotal court had two priorities in questioning Joly: to find confederates, especially Parisian ones, who might be behind him; and to get his confession that he had impersonated authority—that he had claimed to be a "carrier of the king's orders."[78] Although the Noyon authorities could not yet know the national scope of the events in late July, their expectations of conspiracy were no less keen. When Joly was arrested, a note was found in his pocket from a Parisian named Benoiste, inviting him to lunch on July 24. Benoiste turned out to be an inspector of guards for the comte d'Artois who had met Joly when the latter was on the Paris watch in 1786 or 1787. The counselor grilled Joly about his traveling companion on the way to Rezavoine. This person turned out to be a young man of 21 whom Joly had run into in Senlis and who was going home to his village of Villers-St-Cristophe, four kilometers north of Ham.⁷⁹ Among Joly's effects the mounted police found a sealed letter, addressed to a certain Jaget at Versailles, a postillion for the queen. Asked if he knew Jaget, Joly replied that he only knew Jaget's father in Mehun-sur-Yèvre. Did Joly correspond with the young Jaget? He denied this; the letter (still sealed) was shown to him, and he was asked if the address was in his handwriting. Joly said no; the letter had been given him by Jaget *père* to deliver to his son. The court broke the letter open. It was indeed personal, and not from Joly.⁸⁰ Unfortunately for the court's conspiracy theories, most of Joly's connections were with persons who served either the throne or a prince of the blood.

On the very day of the Frétoy incident, in Joly's first interrogation, the counselor took care to have written in the minutes: "Interrogated whether he had not said that he was carrying orders from the king, that he was supported by dragoons . . . said that he had effectively said that he was carrying orders from the king . . . "⁸¹ It is impossible to know what "effectively" really meant. The very turn of phrase suggests that this passage in the minutes was less than faithful to what Joly actually said. We can only note the haste with which the court nailed the point down. Joly was asked again on August 16 "if he had not said to the curé that he had the king's orders . . . [and] later, those of the Parlement?" He replied, "Only a fool could make such statements." When the judge told Joly that he had admitted as much in his first interrogation, Joly collapsed, saying that "he didn't know what he was saying." The minutes continue, "As he was even close to fainting, the judge graciously had him given a glass of wine."⁸² Joly knew that if he had confessed to this charge—which he thought he had not—he would probably go to the gallows.

The court was especially interested in Joly's threats and menaces, and the witnesses recounted as many as they could remember. On August 17 Joly was confronted with seven of the eight witnesses. His reply to Charles Magnier is a catalog of the threats most held against him:

> The accused said . . . that he did not threaten to cut the locksmiths' throats if they did not pick the locks fast enough; that he did not say he had the right to seize arms, both at the château and from individuals' houses; that it is not true that he threatened to hang or to have hung Mme. the comtesse Destournelles and her concierge from the iron gate of the château, and that he

was the master; that it is also false that he threatened to burn the château . . . ; that he did not threaten to kill the locksmith on the pretext that he was not fast enough at forcing the door of the cellar beneath the grand staircase, that the locksmith was fast enough and afraid enough without being threatened.[83]

How seriously had Joly's hearers taken him? On the morning of July 27, Pailliart did not leave his breakfast. A high tension of illegality coexisted with moments of relaxation; the Frétoyards felt free to go home to eat and return whenever they chose. This evidence of casualness does not seem to have entered into the court's thinking as it drew up the charges that would leave Joly in detention until his death.

The attack on the Frétoy château shows us how the old regime and the nascent Revolution interlaced in social practice. Revolutionary forms were present in the Soissonnais of 1789, but they were nested within older forms of community action; their power for rupture with the past had not yet manifested itself. The relationship between Pierre Joly and the other participants is emblematic of this nesting of new forms within old.

Joly has all the appearances of a recently radicalized man, profoundly affected by his passage through a Paris still reverberating from the shock of the fall of the Bastille. Superficially, he seems to evoke a classic image: the politically conscious revolutionary, leading a mass mobilized by its immediate needs and swayed by rumors of an aristocrats' "famine pact." Viewed in more depth, he appears as a recently arrived radical manipulated by a community in movement, its leader and its hostage, a red flag for the eyes of the authorities. The community's immediate goal was simple; yet this simplicity belies the art involved in long-term relations with authority—an art that anticipated not only the present action, but the legal riposte to it, the continuing freedom of the greatest number, and hence the possibility of the next action. Undeniably, Joly's outlook included revolution in the modern sense as an overthrow of existing power relations, while that of his "followers" may not have. But he, like them, also planned for the morrow and prepared to deal with the bailliage and the mounted police, those centers of legitimacy that seemed to span past, present, and future. In the incident at Frétoy, each approach needed and used the other as a vehicle for its ends.

EIGHT

THE RISE OF
REVOLUTIONARY
MILITIAS

In 1789 the thoughts, feelings, and actions of French people from all social classes showed a thorough interpenetration between old-regime and revolutionary characteristics. This does not mean, however, that we should regard the early Revolution as dominated by a hidden continuity with the old regime. Rather, we can conceive of France as a social field in flux, in which the deeds, gestures, and verbiage of communities and individuals were often purposely ambiguous because they had to convey meaning in both the old regime and the revolutionary contexts.

The revolutionary militias were above all new, open fields for local power struggles and conflicts over political symbols and substance. The fall of the Bastille on July 14 to a spontaneously organized Paris militia gave the militia as institution a new incarnation as an insurrectional force, but the militia also had a tradition that linked it to the communes of the Middle Ages and gave it its roots in ongoing social practice. The historian searches in vain for a town that in 1789 did not know how to put itself on a paramilitary footing. Significantly, this knowledge was common to both authorities and subjects. The questions raised by the creation of a new militia were of a different type: it was the militia's place in the broad pattern of public order that had to be worked out. Who would command and control the militia? What were its responsibilities and scope? Was it subject to, or a partner of, the municipality? What was its relationship to troops in garrison? After July 14, each of these questions had potentially two dimensions: one involving strictly local power, and the other involving the locality's degree of alignment with the Revolution in general.

Historians have typically viewed the Great Fear as closely connected with the sudden formation of new militias. The conspiracy theories prevalent in nineteenth-century discussions of the Fear often portrayed it as a ruse designed to bring about a general armament that would further the revolutionary cause. Lines from the local historian of Aumale typify this kind of explanation: "It is known that on July 27, 1789, the agitators, intending to obtain the armament of the whole population, spread the report throughout northern France that enemies had penetrated into the heart of the country; in spite of its absurdity, this report caused a terrible panic."[1] Lefebvre's work disposed of conspiracy theories and their assumptions of stage machinery behind the Fear's events; but it emphasized the political edge of these events. For Lefebvre, even though localities presented a myriad of exceptions, the overall sense of the Fear was to be found in a reaction against an imagined aristocratic plot, and the militias of 1789 foretold the graver mass mobilizations of 1792–93:

> There must be no exaggeration: when the brigands were announced, there were many whose first thought was to run away . . . However, from a national point of view, the reaction aroused by the panic was far from negligible. It was by and large a rough attempt at a mass levy of able-bodied men . . . If the people rose, it was to frustrate the conspirators, not the brigands or the foreign troops who were only the tools of the nobility: it was to complete the defeat of the aristocracy.[2]

As we have seen in earlier chapters, the "aristocratic plot" framework is not readily applicable to the Soissonnais; the evidence for such a mentality is lacking. Rather, the Great Fear's moment of panic is more comprehensible as a sudden closing of ranks in communities around deeply held consensual views, at a moment of extreme stress involving food shortages and economic, social, and political turmoil. However, the formation of militias created open fields for politicization, and this new process began as soon as the panic ended. In this sense, the Great Fear did propel the political development of many towns against the wills of their elites. The great paradox of the Fear is that it presented conditions in which the authorities could benefit from a wide, popular mobilization, and could easily integrate the mobilized citizens with troops and mounted police; and then, after a day, these conditions evaporated. The threat of "brigands" was gone, but the mobilized citizens remained— and this new predicament powerfully contributed to the politicization of local life during the remainder of the year.

The following pages concentrate on militia formations and their immediate aftermaths, from spring to fall 1789. Though events beyond October or November are highly relevant, they anticipate the 1790 elections of new municipalities, and to pursue them would unfortunately lead this study too far out of its temporal limits. Even within the compass of May through September 1789, three distinct phases, each with its own dynamics, must be accounted for: (1) the militia formations of May through early July; (2) the militia formations of July 15–25, when the Parisian example was available; and (3) the militia formations during the Great Fear (July 27–28) and in the weeks and months that followed.

The formation of militias during the first, spring phase was closely related to the subsistence situation. Villages sought to protect their fields, small towns their grain stocks, and larger towns their markets. The rural areas seem to have taken the lead, and they were encouraged by the authorities, notably the intendants of Soissons and Amiens. The birth of the Parisian militia altered the definition of what a militia should be and how it should relate to municipal authorities, the military, and new Third-Estate leaders such as local electors for the Estates-General. After July 14, new militias might take one of several possible stances toward the Parisian "model." The Great Fear gave a strong impetus to the formation of militias of the subsistence-oriented type, superficially similar to those of the spring; but the continuing resonance of July 14 now made it difficult for these new militias to keep this character for very long.

In order to follow these shifts in the nature of the militia as an institution, we must begin with a look at its prerevolutionary form. The excitement widely felt in 1789 for the idea of a "national militia" can only be understood by its contrast with the older, highly stratified, bourgeois militia.

The Nature and Context of the Traditional Town Militias

The bourgeois militia was originally a town's armed expression, its military and police organ.[3] Its beginnings in northern France stemmed from the eleventh and twelfth centuries, the heroic period of the communes' establishment. Militias were significant forces, which the king might call on in emergencies. This was particularly true in the valleys of the Aisne and the Oise, which were already integrated into the direct domain of the royal house by the time of Philippe I (1059–1108). In 1124 Louis VI confronted the German emperor Henry V near Reims with an army that included militias from Laon, Soissons, St-Quentin, Amiens, and Beauvais, according to Suger's chronicle.[4] However, in the medieval period as well as later, the militia was primarily used for policing the town and its hinterland.

The martial exploits of the early period remained in the institutional memory of the bourgeois militias centuries later, in their decadence. In the eighteenth century, quite a few traditional militias still existed—in Soissons, Château-Thierry, St-Quentin, Laon, Crépy-en-Valois, and Creil, for example. They were by then well-endowed ceremonial institutions that functioned somewhat like exclusive male clubs. The traditional militias are important to an understanding of the new militias of 1789 because their pronounced upper-class character made them so many enemies. Supporters of the Third Estate perceived the traditional militia companies as being everything that a new, "national" militia should not and would not be. The case of the arquebusiers of Soissons will suffice to indicate the nature of these companies and the tensions to which they gave rise.

In 1116, Louis VI ("le Gros") conceded to the commune of Soissons the right to enroll its citizens in militia companies. These companies were militarily active as late as 1651, when they defended the outskirts of Soissons from a Spanish incursion. Soissons, like many other towns of its size, had a militia divided into several companies: infantry, archers, and marksmen of the crossbow (later the arquebus). Arquebuses were costly weapons, and the volunteers who used them were well off and could afford them. The arquebusier's military services and their economic weight in the community led to an accumulation of privileges: exemption from direct taxation and from billeting, precedence for burial in the graveyard of the chapel of St-Crepin in Soissons, and so on. The arquebusiers accumulated ceremony also; their dress uniforms were dashing and their demeanor on public occasions carnivalesque. The company's symbol was the comic figure of an idler with eyes open wide in astonishment; the figure's face was pictured on the company's pennant, and in civic parades the arquebusiers were preceded by a clown dressed as the "idler of Soissons."[5]

In 1687, the arquebusiers of Soissons were described as "more than two hundred persons of quality and the most distinguished of the bourgeois."[6] This privileged fraction of the militia was resented by other, more plebeian companies, and the early years of the eighteenth century saw some near-brawls over precedence in civic parades. The newer companies, the "Grenadiers" and "Youth," largely made up of artisans and with a less glorious past, often took up advance positions at the cathedral door or the town steps and forced the arquebusiers to either take second place or make a scene over the matter. Similar disputes in Laon and Crépy-en-Valois brought the matter as high as the king's state council, which intervened on behalf of the arquebus companies of all three towns in 1715.[7]

Soissons had lost its status as an official fortified town in 1656, and France's expansion to a new northern border in the Low Countries brought a decline in the strategic importance of the intendancy of Soissons as a whole. The arquebus companies, now armed with muskets, were militarily irrelevant, and the king's council abolished those in Laon (in 1733) and in Soissons (in 1735). The Soissons company's sumptuous lodge was converted into an armory for regular troops. Its erstwhile members stuck together, however, and seized an opportunity for patronage when Soissons was integrated into the Orléans apanage in 1751. The arquebusiers' petitioning of the duc d'Orléans resulted in the reestablishment of their company and the return of its property.[8]

In the late 1760s, the War Ministry briefly attempted to reform the kingdom's bourgeois militias by making service in them universal and compulsory. In Soissons, well-to-do townsmen who were not arquebusiers cast about for a way to keep the militia's class pyramid inviolate. The means they hit upon was the creation of a new company, the "Company of the Town," which enrolled only themselves, but provided officers for the artisan companies. Its ceremonial rank was set out in its founding statutes: it was to march second on public occasions, behind the arquebusiers. In the 1780s, tension between the two elite companies was manifested in quarrels over precedence which interrupted public ceremonies. The king's council intervened again, but this time it demoted the arquebusiers and gave the Company of the Town public precedence and a monopoly over the officering of other companies.[9]

Such was the structure and internal discord of the Soissons militia by 1789: several companies with sharply differing histories, status, and class composition. It and many other traditional militias acted as a sharp reminder of social distinctions, not only between classes but also within the town's upper crust. Moreover, these reminders came primarily on festive occasions that gave pleasure to the general population: occasions when they were especially unwelcome. The utility of traditional militias was no longer apparent, because they had abdicated their peacekeeping role to professional troops in garrison. Indeed, even the old regime had tried to abolish arquebus companies in the Soissonnais as pointless, but had failed in the long run. In the perceived emergency of the Great Fear, the authorities in Soissons preferred to let a new, spontaneous militia organization confront the "enemy"; but then, with the emergency over, they tried to dissolve the impromptu militia and go on as if nothing had happened. We can readily understand the attractiveness of a "renewed" or "national" militia to its supporters in 1789. The term implied for them, at the very least, a unified and effective body not suffocated by internal class divisions.

The Great Fear brought the question of militia organization to the foreground of town life, either through the town's direct involvement in the panic, or two weeks later by fiat from the National Assembly. The Assembly's August 10 decree implied that every town should have an active militia, and so the municipal officers of towns without militias had to consider creating them. Since a militia was a potential source of independent power, the militia's formation and control offered a major test of the governing elite's capacity to retain its authority. The characteristics of these elites in northern France are precisely summarized by Lynn Hunt in her study of Troyes and Reims:

> Admission to their circle, though not closed, was carefully circumscribed. By the middle of the eighteenth century, wholesale merchants, lawyers, and doctors had been integrated into the ruling circle of royal officials and noblemen. Wealth and professional affiliation were not magic passwords, however; only family connection could definitely open the door to political position . . . Town elections did not occasion the arbitrary rotation of elites; the members of the political elite themselves chose their partners and successors, and they "naturally" chose the men who shared their family interests.
>
> . . . Nobles and non-nobles learned how to rule in tandem on the local level in order to defend a social system based on property and family. This accommodation was not possible everywhere . . . But in Reims and Troyes and towns like them, the political style usually associated with nineteenth-century French politics first took shape in the final decades of the Old Regime.[10]

Hunt's description rings true for municipal government in the Soissons intendancy and its surroundings. Whether an oligarchy operated in near-autonomy (as in Compiègne, Château-Thierry, and Noyon), or was ruled in turn by the Orléans apanage (as in Crépy-en-Valois, Soissons, and to a lesser degree Laon), it was always close-knit through blood ties, marriage alliances, and dovetailing landed and trading interests. These ties often linked all three Estates. The same figures who managed the lands of the clergy and hobnobbed with local nobility were also well situated to lead the Third Estate in the bailliage assemblies of March that selected deputies to the Estates-General. The fall of the Bastille and all the tumult of July and August did not disqualify them from leadership of the Third Estate. Municipal officers who could collect a few revolutionary credentials to embellish a self-confidence backed by decades of rule might manage the early Revolution quite well (as Hunt has shown for Reims). To do this, they had to skillfully co-opt two new institutions—the "permanent committee" of Third-Estate electors, and the new militia—to recreate a local polity that centered on themselves.

In towns where old elites showed vigor and intelligence, they might be able to include new members from among their peers and perpetuate a "rule of notables" through the Feuillant and Girondin phases of the Revolution, until the breaking point of 1793. In other towns, clumsier ruling groups might be pushed aside by "usurpers" with popular followings who would create seedlings of republican power as early as 1789. The militia's disposition was often enough to shift the balance. In a discussion of permanent committees, Lynn Hunt has put it well: "The committees' relation to the new militias was the key issue of the fall and winter of 1789. Where the committee kept a firm grip on the militia, it usually also managed to retain control of town politics. But where the militia broke away from the grasp of the committee, the urban revolution changed course."[11]

The Formation of Militias: May through Early July

The new militias of 1789 were not created all at once. Successive waves of militia formations can be distinguished in the Soissonnais: an early wave in May and June that responded to growing tension over subsistence and the future harvest; a second wave after July 14, when the Third Estate's anxiety to preserve its sudden Parisian victory was added to the food supply problem; and a third wave that began in late July in response to the Great Fear, and revived in the latter half of August once the National Assembly had made it clear that the "national militias" were intrinsic to the new pattern of public order. After August and well into 1790, new militias continued to appear as smaller towns caught up with larger ones and recalcitrant municipalities found themselves cornered by the march of events.

In the initial wave of May and June, militias were created not by the large towns but by villages and hamlets that feared for their standing crops. Since smaller communities took the lead, the evidence available to us almost certainly underrepresents the real frequency of militia formation. The documents point clearly to militia activity in the Thiérache, the northern half of the Soissons intendancy. Before June 4, the Laon inter-

mediate bureau had written the royal authorities to insist "how important [it is] to defend in advance against the depredations that are feared
for the moment of harvest; threats have been made to cut grains before
their maturity."[12] Noting that numerous communities had begun guarding themselves, the bureau discussed whether a circular proposing the
same course to other villages was a good idea. In the end they rejected
the circular because it might "sow alarms."[13] Though evidence is very
sparse for northern participation in the Great Fear seven weeks later, the
fear of brigands[14] was vivid and had already inspired the organization of
militias at the village level.

The source of anxiety in the Thiérache was probably the mid-May
peasant revolt to the north, in the Cambrésis. The village of Hargicourt,
14 kilometers northwest of St-Quentin, was outside the Soissons intendancy, yet no farther north than intendancy towns such as Guise. On
May 14, Hargicourt conducted a grain census and forbade all grain sales
without express permission (these would have been sales in private or in
other towns, since Hargicourt had no market). With control over grain
stocks established, the municipal officers created a "bourgeois guard" of
all males aged 17 to 70. Some residents refused to serve, and the municipality wrote the St-Quentin subdelegate and even the royal household in
Versailles for an order that would force all the men to mount guard.[15]
Hargicourt's municipal officers feared that "ill-intentioned people"
would pillage the community's grain supplies, but this danger did not
seem to worry all inhabitants equally. Presumably, community sympathies were divided over the grain sales at "just prices" that large troops
of peasants were forcing on abbeys and large farmers a little farther
north.

A few more early militia formations in larger towns also should be
noted. In the Amiens intendancy, Crèvecoeur-le-Grand (20 kilometers
north of Beauvais) formed a 30-man militia on June 24 to keep order at
market. As we have seen in chapter 4, Clermont-en-Beauvaisis received
an anonymous arson threat in June that aired the neighboring parishes'
discomfiture over Clermont's severe control of these parishes' grain
stocks. The town responded by activating part of its traditional militia
for a night watch. Compiègne had a night watch organized on similar
lines during June to guard the grain supplies under municipal control; it
was discontinued on July 6, when fresh supplies arrived thanks to the
intendant of Paris.[16]

In this first wave of militia formations, rural communities organized
to protect crops, while large villages defended grain stocks and towns
defended their markets. Militias at this stage lacked political coloring,

and it is important to realize that there was nothing inherently "revolutionary" about a new militia even in early July. Militia activity was generally initiated by municipalities confident of their ability to manage it; other municipalities that had reservations on this score did not propose militias, and their citizens rarely demanded them.

Intendants, who were familiar with the drawbacks of strewing small detachments of soldiers across a wide territory, actively proposed militias as solutions to local anxieties. Blossac, the intendant of Soissons, told members of the provincial commission in mid-May that each small town should engage "a dozen bourgeois patriots" to keep public order. The commission mentioned this idea in a letter to the intermediate bureau in Laon but added that "if . . . it is not expected that this bourgeois militia can replace true soldierly types," Blossac still might dispatch more shavings from the Swiss regiment in Soissons.[17]

In Amiens, at the same time, the intendant d'Agay pleaded strongly for new militias to an unresponsive royal household. D'Agay was receiving requests from "small towns and villages" for permission to organize militias; he had granted permission only to Boulogne and its hinterland, which kept a traditional privilege of mounting its own defenses against invaders (d'Agay explained that "the privilege has been interpreted as regarding as enemies the brigands who attack the properties of good citizens"). The intendant wanted a royal ordinance favoring militias which he could publicize throughout Picardy, but Villedeuil, secretary of the royal household, turned him down curtly after consulting the military commander of the province, the comte de Rochambeau. D'Agay wrote Villedeuil again and recounted the talk he had had with Rochambeau's second-in-command:

> M. the comte de Sommièvre . . . has sent me word that he believes it would be very useful for the communities to guard themselves, but that it would suffice to authorize them to arm themselves with sticks . . . [I] observed to him that if there were 10,000 more soldiers in Picardy than are present already, it would still not be possible to stop the pillage of harvests everywhere, and that . . . if one does not permit the peasants and farmers, who would not have regular troops nearby to defend them, to use more than sticks to push back troops of thieves, the arms will be equal on both sides . . . [18]

Both Blossac in Soissons and d'Agay in Amiens understood that the professional troops on hand could not possibly deal alone with social disturbances in the magnitudes that were then feared. Civilian participation was necessary, and the militia form was ready at hand, a familiar institution with a long pedigree. The royal household, out of touch with rural conditions, was loath to drop the basic policy of permitting as few firearms in general circulation as possible, and probably blocked new militias for this reason. However, this difference of perspective among administrators at the top only concerned the proper moment for using an instrument that was thought to be a known quantity.

This view of militias naturally changed after the Bastille fell to a force of at least 1,000 Parisian insurgents on July 14, of whom 98 died and 73 were wounded.[19] The great majority of assailants in the vanguard were members of the new militia that had been founded officially the day before. It is often assumed that Paris offered a model of mobilization and that the militias created in France afterward took the lines of this model. Again, the assumption is broadly true, but an important proviso must be added: the nature of the Parisian model was open to different interpretations from the start. Was the "real" Parisian militia the structure designed by La Fayette after July 15, or the unlikely yet formidable force that succeeded against all expectation on July 14? In a sense, each provincial town creating a militia had to find its own answer to this question.

La Fayette immediately took steps to scale down the militia, now called the "National Guard," to include no more than four hundred propertied men from each district, who would buy their own uniforms and receive no compensation. However, the *gardes françaises*—a regular army unit that had joined the insurrection—demanded to be enrolled in the militia. La Fayette had to accede to this request, which meant forming additional companies of paid, lower-class members. The effectiveness of his first efforts to make the National Guard a force for stability can best be judged from the "October days" (October 5-6), when 20,000 National Guards forced La Fayette to lead them in joining the women's march on Versailles, which forced the royal family to move to Paris. By October the Paris Commune had still not succeeded in using the National Guard to exert control over the assemblies of the 60 districts, which in fact administered Paris neighborhood by neighborhood.[20]

For provincial towns, then, Paris presented at least two conflicting "models" for militias of their own. One model suggested an armed force with broad participation, independent of the municipality, developing its own relationship with the soldiery through fraternization, and regarding itself as a new source of authority and legitimacy. Another model derived from La Fayette's efforts and the Commune's claims. It proposed a hybrid of the traditional bourgeois guard and a revolutionary militia—a restricted, yet not elitist, armed body at the command of municipal authorities, which could be trusted both to undertake police duties and to defend (not advance!) the Revolution.

The Formation of Militias: July 15–25

The origins of the militias created in the 10 days between the fall of the Bastille and the beginning of the Great Fear (July 15–25) are best examined geographically, starting with some examples nearest Paris and working northward into the Soissonnais and beyond. This approach lets us map different responses to the influence of Paris across regions of northern France. Each locale was affected by questions of subsistence and by the astonishing political news from Paris, but each locale was unique in the relative weight given to these two factors. It appears that a northern belt including Flandre, Hainaut, and much of northern Picardy resonated more strongly to the fall of the Bastille than did the Soissonnais and the northern part of the Paris intendancy. In the latter region, acute food supply problems exacerbated by the needs of Paris often reduced political affairs to a secondary role. This evidence tends to disprove the notion of a simple geographic diffusion of militancy from Paris, though our first example—Enghien-Montmorency, eight kilometers north of the capital—was a fine case of such diffusion.

Enghien organized a militia on July 22 at the behest of its municipality, which dated back only to the reform of 1787.[21] Enghien's syndic told its assembled inhabitants the reason: "The troubles which have agitated the capital for several days having given rise to a bourgeois guard, [and] the fear that wanderers and vagabonds may spread into this town, coming to make various ravages and disorders harmful to inhabitants of every type and quality in . . . this parish." The militia's purpose was to "watch, warn against, and stop . . . all dangerous incursions."[22] However, provisions in the statutes creating the new militia suggest that the municipality feared internal enemies as well. The militia began with no officers of its own. It was directly controlled by the municipality, of which at least one member always had to be awake and in control. After the first night's patrol (on the same night as the assembly, July 22, the municipality named a captain for the militia of 36 men (scaled down from a less trustworthy 48). At the same time it ordered an evening curfew, which it planned to extend at least to December. Violators of the curfew would be jailed for 12 hours.[23]

This unusual stringency must have contributed to the uproar on August 2, the night of the next village assembly. The municipality called the meeting to consolidate its new militia under a committee of five, but lost control of the agenda. The local attorney, one Leturc, rose and correctly pointed out that Enghien's municipality was. the work of Bertier, the intendant of Paris, who had been put to death by a Parisian crowd. Bertier's authority was now "without force or virtue," and Leturc claimed that the authority of Enghien's municipal officers had collapsed with it. The hall's enthusiasm for Leturc's argument intimidated the municipal officers into resigning, and a new municipality led by Leturc was elected at once.[24]

Thus the Revolution proper arrived in Enghien, whose new municipality had an entirely different social base (described by the ousted officers as "a number of inhabitants, primarily day-laborers, paying six livres in taxes at most") than did the old.[25] The old municipality had acted in accord with the warnings of the Paris Commune, which blamed the "excesses" of July on unvouched-for persons who were being driven from Paris and against whom surrounding communities were to be on guard. However, Enghien's community had been strained by the experience of mobilization under their unpopular leaders, and Leturc, a lawyer in his thirties with just one year's residence in Enghien, was the right man to transmit the missing, subversive half of the Parisian experience to his neighbors.

Pontoise was just a little farther from Paris than Enghien—30 kilometers instead of 8—yet its experience was vastly less political. Here a subsistence crisis dominated the process of militia formation. Pontoise was a significant market town that ordinarily supplied Paris; now it was under pressure from surrounding villages, the St-Germain area, the capital, and its own residents. Grain traveling down the Seine destined for Pontoise was being confiscated by municipalities upriver; on July 14, nearby Mantes had captured a shipment of rye meant for Pontoise.[26]

However, the municipal officers of Pontoise had certain cards to play. They enjoyed a cordial relationship with resident troops, and their crisis was at least defined in familiar terms—those of subsistence—and demanded resourcefulness of a type that they understood. The municipal officers called a restricted assembly of notables on July 17, at the suggestion of the commander of the dragoon detachment then in garrison. The commander, Langlois, had heard that the desperate countryfolk who had rioted in the market at St-Germain would soon come to Pontoise. Not only was a militia suggested by a military officer, but on July 24 another officer—major of a different regiment present for a few days—offered to loan the militia 60 muskets, which were accepted. Pontoise was also one of the towns that received a letter from the duc de Lévis, conveying the king's permission to arm a militia. The militia itself initially comprised only 21 men (later increased to 40): arquebusiers reinforced by a few citizens well trusted by the municipality.[27]

When the Great Fear arrived in Pontoise on July 27, the town's elite was well prepared. The tocsin rang and arms were handed out to a wide segment of the population, but militia officers were in place and the cooperation of Langlois's dragoons was exemplary. When the alarm was over, the town hall got all its arms back. The disarmed inhabitants remained to demonstrate for bread at two sous per pound, and got a promise of lower prices from the authorities.[28] While the tensions and anxieties of Pontoise's subsistence troubles were fierce (and too involved to be recounted here), its municipal officers were effective old-regime managers of these troubles, who made concessions skillfully and could rally the community against demands from outside. Despite Pontoise's nearness to Paris, its militia formation lacked a revolutionary quality.

Meulan, 35 kilometers northwest of Paris (about the same distance as Pontoise) created its "revolutionary" institutions in a mundane, pragmatic spirit. On July 19 the town learned that the new provisions committee of Mantes had seized grain bound for Meulan. Meulan's municipality decided simply to outfit itself with its own committee and militia, to put itself on a better footing for negotiations with the towns around it. A deputation from Meulan went to Mantes, came to terms with the committee of that town, and returned to Meulan with 150 sacks of grain, escorted by a detachment of militia from Mantes. The Meulan and Mantes militias fraternized amid general rejoicing, and Meulan sank into a calm that the Great Fear on the twenty-seventh could not interrupt. Couriers brought the Fear's rumor at ten o'clock that night, but the militia commander refused to mobilize at night. A brief reconnaissance the next morning dispelled such apprehension as there was. On August 9 Meulan's committee became the new municipality after an assembly in which it gained general approbation by displaying its accounts.[29] Meulan was well under a day's ride from Paris, but its immersion in the institutional market problems of its locale certainly overrode the capital's example. Its adoption of new institutions was a form of administrative streamlining in which no social transfer of power was involved.

In the Soissons intendancy there were only two notable militia formations in the 10 days between the fall of the Bastille and the Great Fear, and their stated motives were identical. In Clermont-en-Beauvaisis, municipal officers told a general assembly on July 21 that "an infinite number of unvouched-for persons chased out of the city of Paris" were spreading into the provinces, and that Clermont (situated on the road between Paris and Amiens) should take precautions.[30] The municipal officers succeeded in incorporating the town's higher social strata into a new, larger militia by renouncing their own exemption privileges and persuading others to do the same. The militia's officers were predominantly retired soldiers; nobles monopolized the top positions.

In Crépy-en-Valois, the Orléans-appointed municipality created a militia on July 22, citing "incursions of ill-intentioned people and brigands, the example of the capital and of surrounding towns." Arms were sought from Paris. When the Great Fear arrived on July 27, the municipality formed a permanent committee, primarily from its own members, and mobilized the militia. The following day the permanent committee ended guard duty and put the militia on ice for the time being.[31] Both in Clermont and Crépy, the creation of a militia was a highly controlled process in which the authorities took the lead. Parisian influence was indeed prominent, but it was the influence of the Commune and its efforts to contain the actions of the lower classes. (Acute harvest anxiety may have also played a part, since both Clermont and Crépy were situated near epicenters of the rural Great Fear: Estrées-St-Denis and St-Martin-de-Béthisy, respectively.)

If we continue north and away from Paris, we find the capital's influence paradoxically appearing to increase. Amiens experienced the Great Fear, while Valenciennes and Dunkerque did not. However, all three towns give evidence of a more political outlook and a stronger Parisian flavor than can be found south of them.

The municipality of Amiens relied on the town's garrison to offset rising social and political pressures throughout 1789. Here July 14 brought a confrontation between textile workers and the municipal officers who were in session. The workers demanded and got a sharp reduction in food prices; to avoid a riot, the municipality and the intendant, d'Agay, made this major concession without knowing how it would be financed. The next day an officer of the Berry cavalry regiment in garrison conferred with the municipal officers and urged them to "have the upper bourgeoisie take up arms." So here, as in Pontoise, the idea of a militia originated with the military, who proposed it to a municipality grasping to regain its equilibrium. Meetings to organize the militia were to be organized by quarter, not by trade (thus avoiding meetings of the trades most affected by the ongoing slump in textile manufactures). The military commandant promised that all troops would still mobilize "at the least movement." Troops were to remain the prime force for public order in Amiens, with the militia covering their flanks.[32]

That night (July 15–16) some of the poor of Amiens armed themselves with cudgels and attacked the homes of leading grain merchants,
members of a consortium called the "Civic Association," which had
purchased grain abroad for the city's relief—without, however, much
lowering its price to the poor. The military responded to the attacks on
its own initiative. The municipality armed a militia at the town hall
without further ado at 5:00 P.M. on July 16. This armament probably
extended deeper into the citizenry than the authorities preferred, but
since they named the new militia's officers themselves and the army
superintended the operation, they had effective control over the new
body. On July 20, municipal officers explained to an assembly of the
commune: "In concert with M. the commandant, we have taken the
resolution to arm all our fellow-citizens, and we can only applaud the
zeal . . . with which all have carried this out without exception . . . By
this provisional formation, we have not meant to infringe on rights of
any sort, nor to obstruct the liberty of citizens who would prefer another formation."[33] Despite their words, this question of the militia's
officering and regulations became a bone of contention between municipality and militia that would last through the year.

The Great Fear made a strong sensation in Amiens on July 27. The
Fear was the occasion for a second distribution of arms which widened
the effects of the first.[34] From this point the militia's growth appears to
have taken on its own momentum, though the municipality (reinforced
after August 5 with a body of electors from all three estates) kept control
of its general staff. By the end of September between 2,500 and 3,000
men were enrolled in 20 companies.[35]

As to the political tenor of Amiens in these days, the wearing of
cockades provides one index. By July 31 cockades were already widely
sported in Amiens; civilians pressed them on soldiers, just as was done
in Paris. The municipality observed that "in the circumstances of the
troubles that agitate France, it is only prudence to avoid all occasions for
division; . . . the cockade . . . offered to soldiers might occasion rumors
and even acts of violence." As a public safety measure, the magistrates
offered cockades to the military commanders, who accepted them.[36]
Thus another crack in the bloc of army-municipality-militia was sealed
up. The ability of the authorities of Amiens to keep integrating revolutionary institutions into an ensemble of old-regime power was well
above average, but not unique: many municipalities attempted to maintain and renew traditional public order by such cooptation.

In Valenciennes, the relations between troops and militia were
markedly different. Valenciennes was an important garrison town with a

declining commerce, seat of the military *gouvernement* of Hainaut. Since its annexation to France during the reign of Louis XIV, its municipality had been appointed by the crown, and was overshadowed in any case by the military authorities, to which the town paid large sums for barracks construction and upkeep.[37] The Great Fear never reached Valenciennes. Instead, a massive riot on July 24 altered the balance of forces in the town. No account could improve on the testimony of the *gouvernement*'s military commandant, the comte d'Esterhazy:

> In most towns [of my command] the prisons have been opened and the toll gates . . . destroyed; in several towns houses have been pillaged. The circumstances have deprived the military authority of the activity it should have kept up to repress these disorders, and they have ceased in the towns since the national militias have been established there; the royal troops have no longer [acted] except as auxiliaries. Even so, an individual here—leader of a riot which took place on July 24—was released at the absolute insistence of the bourgeois militia companies, and I was so little sure of my troops that I preferred the weakness of consenting over the danger there would have been in showing firmness.[38]

The situation in Valenciennes also shows a greater analogy to that in Paris than have our more southern examples. Disorder bordering on insurrection was contained by a militia with its own popular roots and sympathies. Both military and civil authorities found themselves relatively marginalized by their inability to control events.

Dunkerque's oligarchy was far stronger and more agile than that of Valenciennes, and kept a step ahead of the local fermentation. The magistrates of Dunkerque were named by the intendant of Flandre. They seemed to be the sole target available for popular anger, since there were almost no nobles in the town, and the clergy took orders from a foreign bishop who did not even collect tithes. When the town's *cahier de doléances* was drafted on March 24, the meeting was stormy and the magistrates, who presided without voting, received much abuse. However, the magistrates' solid links with Dunkerque's shipping and trading circles did offer them a social base of sorts, if they could only draw upon it.[39]

When the news of the fall of the Bastille arrived on July 18, it had immediate repercussions on Dunkerque's political culture. The magistrates removed Calonne's portrait from their meeting room to obviate any demand that they do so. After some reluctance, they agreed to the celebration of a Te Deum on the twenty-third in thanks for the king's capitulation to the National Assembly. After this ceremony, cockades blossomed throughout the town; and the municipality decided to form a militia at once, so that Dunkerque might "forestall the disorders ready to break out in its midst."[40] A meeting of notables and principal merchants produced the skeleton for a militia, officers were selected, and then a broad enrollment brought in artisans in large numbers. A new permanent committee to supplement the magistrates included three of their relatives and four of the new militia officers. Garrisoned troops were readied but kept in the background. Thus endowed with a new set of "revolutionary" institutions, Dunkerque's elite prepared to face the storm. These measures succeeded remarkably well. A degree of popular participation in the militia apparently worked in the municipality's favor in Dunkerque. The form of organization improvised on July 23 resisted challenges in the autumn by upper-class dissidents who could not gather a broad following. When the militia (like all militias in France) became a "Garde Nationale" in early 1790, its structure stayed basically the same. The Great Fear never arrived in Dunkerque, and so the militia never went through the intense mobilization and widening of ranks that had disruptive effects on militias in many other towns.[41]

From Enghien to Dunkerque, the examples just given show the dimensions of the historical problem posed by the formation of militias during the period between the fall of the Bastille and the Great Fear. The fall of the Bastille seems to have had more import for a northern belt including Flandre, Hainaut, and much of northern Picardy than it did for the Soissonnais and the northern part of the Paris intendancy. The variety of origins and political meanings of the new militias themselves is striking. However, three broad patterns can be distinguished among our examples. In the first pattern, a close coordination between municipality and garrison remained the real axis of power (as at Pontoise and Amiens). At times, a militia was even proposed to the municipality by army officers, and the project of creating it was executed by the two entities in tandem. In a second pattern, municipalities in towns without a dominant military presence (e.g., Meulan, Clermont, Crépy-en-Valois, and Dunkerque) formed militias roughly according to the prescriptions of the Paris Commune. Often in these cases the Commune's warnings about unvouched-for persons expelled from Paris tended to harmonize well with subsistence concerns and harvest anxiety. Valenciennes and Enghien represent extreme cases that fall into a third pattern. In Valenciennes the municipality was not strong enough to intercede in a direct confrontation between the military and the community; while in Enghien the municipality's sway over the community was too weak to support the strain of a mobilization, and it was actually driven from office.

In both towns the militia became a radical vehicle that looked to a different model also emanating from Paris: that of revolutionary autonomy.

In all cases, it is apparent that whether municipalities stood or fell depended on their capacity to make alliances. They could ally with the state via a garrison, if the town had one; or they could ally with the community via several possible strategies: consolidating the support of their own class, uniting most of the community around their efforts and concessions over subsistence (often a daring and costly task), or adopting parts of a popular agenda and symbolically embracing the Revolution.

The Formation of Militias during the Great Fear and Afterward

While the phase of July 15–25 saw the widespread creation of militias in the Paris suburbs and to the north and west of the Soissons intendancy, the Great Fear on July 27 provided the impetus for new militias within the Soissonnais. In the Soissonnais the actual moment of mobilization had a rural inspiration, grounded in the fear of an attack on agricultural production. Yet the new militia's role in public order, its class composition, and its political meaning were urban issues that came alive with the creation of the militia and remained either active or smoldering for as long as the militia continued to exist. A brief comparison of Verberie, Noyon, and Château-Thierry can illustrate some of the many forms this situation could take.

We know only a little about how the village of Verberie formed its militia, yet Verberie was clearly a model of controlled access to revolutionary energies. On July 28, the day after the Great Fear, Verberie created a militia that was restricted to 15 members. Not only their arms but even their cockades had to be deposited at the guardhouse at the end of their night patrol; in this way the municipality sought to hoard away the cockade's political potency.[42]

Because Noyon had a real, if minuscule, peasant revolt to deal with, its case is distinct from those of other communities that formed new militias at the time of the Great Fear. Noyon received the Fear's rumor hours after it had already sent its detachment of dragoons to deal with the peasant troop in the village of Frétoy. Responding to the Great Fear as well as to local troubles, the municipality of Noyon enrolled a large militia. Four days later, on July 31, Noyon's intermediate bureau wrote, "All the inhabitants of our town, without exception, are under arms and mount guard." The municipal officers were spurred to maintain full mobilization by the growing hostility of the countryside to Noyon's various authorities. The town's elite longed for a full infantry regiment in garrison, but lacking this it kept up a rigorous schedule of guard duty that seems to have involved every trustworthy male regardless of class. On October 7 the royal household in Versailles denied the municipality's request for support in its dispute with some weary militiamen seeking to avoid duty. In December municipal officers wrote the royal household again, this time to request four hundred rifles.[43] The quantity of arms they wanted speaks volumes about their confidence in Noyon's militia. A real and deepening antagonism between town and country was part of that militia's coherence, and it helped to keep a new, "national" militia within an old-regime framework.

In Château-Thierry, the mounted police and arquebusiers led different bodies of armed inhabitants on the day of the Great Fear, which implies that no new militia had yet been organized. Yet in the same week a large commercial shipment of gunpowder on its way from Metz to Rouen was stopped in Château-Thierry and brought to Paris under escort—a highly political event that may have stirred public opinion. The formal creation of a militia was probably under way between July 30 and August 5, because on the latter date the town's permanent committee accepted a youthful company of volunteers in their teens and twenties into the militia. In August the committee was at work on a plan to federate nearby rural militias with that of Château-Thierry; surviving village records indicate reception of the plan at the end of August.[44] This suggests the authorities' desire to create a rural peacekeeping role for the town militia. On September 7 the barracks of a cavalry detachment burned to the ground, climaxing a local crisis.

At the beginning of September, popular sentiment had rapidly developed for the departure of 16 "hussars": Austrian cavalrymen in French service. On September 6 the permanent committee was preparing to write the War Ministry to ask for the hussars' withdrawal, and a rumor was afloat that if the detachment did not depart the next day it would be burnt out of its quarters in the Hôtel de Verdun. That evening the detachment's officer, Lieutenant Keer, posted sentinels around the building and was then called away to pacify a dispute between a militia patrol and two hussars who had supposedly insulted it. Keer ordered the two taken to jail, purely to mollify the militia and the crowd. He then agreed to go report to the permanent committee, but refused a militia escort. The committee, Keer, militiamen, and people from the crowd were wrangling in the town hall when word arrived that the hussars' barracks were on fire.[45]

The crowd and the militiamen took the lieutenant with them to the barracks and tried to fight the fire, without success. After a time the idea caught on that the hussars had started the fire in revenge for the imprisonment of their comrades. While people argued over this theory, Keer slipped away and found his horse. Sympathizers urged him to leave town at once, and he took their advice, only asking them to tell his men, who were collecting the remains of their possessions, to join him on the road to Soissons. A militia patrol shot at him harmlessly as he galloped past. Four hussars did join Keer, and they rode to Soissons together. The remaining nine joined their two comrades in jail. On September 10 the town jailer appeared before the permanent committee to deny the latest rumor: that the hussars were receiving a bottle of wine each per day from the municipal officers as an apology for their predicament.[46]

This incident shows that by September the militia acted as an interlocutor in its own right with the other powers in the town. It clearly viewed troops in garrison as rivals for possession of the street, and was not particularly subordinate to the permanent committee either.[47] After the fire, a militia captain organized a general meeting of his neighborhood to discuss the fate of the jailed hussars, thus preempting a central role of the municipality. The permanent committee's attempt to investigate the fire met with resounding silence, as witnesses refused to come forward.[48]

That the hussars were not billeted on the population makes the sudden hostility toward them all the more noteworthy. According to Keer, his unit's relations with the townspeople had been excellent since its arrival on May 22,[49] and the evidence does indicate that the demand for the cavalry's removal took authorities by surprise. The motives for the shift in attitude seem to have been political: people "discovered" that troops of foreign provenance were ideologically incompatible with a national militia.

If a specific incident provoked this antipathy, it was unknown to the authorities. The abbé Hébert passes on a story that officers of the Parisian National Guard visited Château-Thierry. They noticed the cavalrymen in the street and twitted their hosts for their tolerance in permitting the foreigners to remain.[50] No evidence has been found to confirm this story; yet it does suggest how the air of revolutionary Paris might have seeped into the town. The Great Fear per se did not actuate this shift; rather, it established a general mobilization based on old-regime premises of unity, which soon overstrained the traditional pattern of public order.

Noyon, Verberie, and Château-Thierry all had to face the incorporation of a new militia into an existing structure of authorities. Soissons, Laon, and St-Quentin form a class apart, because the elites of these three major towns all resisted new militias fairly successfully through the end of 1789. The styles and contexts of their resistance tell us a great deal about the different dangers that elites could fear from a new militia. In Soissons, they feared the specter of popular participation in the elite's internal quarrels; in Laon, they feared interference in the strong cooperation between the municipality and the garrison; and in St-Quentin, they feared the rationalizing of a long-standing militia tax whose unfairness was embedded in the town's social pyramid.

The town of Soissons is particularly unusual, because the town mobilized strongly in the Great Fear, but this mobilization did not consolidate into an active militia. On this town of only seven to eight thousand people were superimposed the apparatuses of the intendant's seat, the bailliage court, and a garrison billeted on the population. The town's economy depended on prosperous officeholders and cathedral chapters; apart from these, its primary commerce was the grain trade. As we saw in chapter 4, the citizens of Soissons who armed themselves in the Great Fear were sent out into the countryside to respond to rural requests for aid. After the Fear a plan was formulated to keep an armed and active militia. The new permanent committee of Soissons proposed a bourgeois mounted patrol to accompany the mounted police and protect the harvest. Within a few days, however, these ideas were squelched. By July 31 the municipal authorities were already arguing that the political emergency in Paris was over, even if the harvest was not, and that life should now return to normal.[51]

In early September there was no active militia in Soissons, traditional or "national." After the barracks fire in Château-Thierry, Brayer, the new intendant (for Blossac had fled in August), composed a draft of a letter to Necker in which he welcomed the displaced hussars with alacrity:

> The officer and the four hussars who escaped have been welcomed and are lodged awaiting new orders in Soissons, where the service of regular troops is too useful and too agreeable to the inhabitants for [the soldiers] to fear discontent . . . we would see their removal with all the more regret, since it would be difficult and perhaps dangerous to seek to replace them with the bourgeois militia.
>
> The officers' attention to maintaining subordination and discipline, and that of the municipal officers . . . to procuring billets without fatiguing the

people, allow no pretext for the movements of some restless spirits, very few in number, who intrigue for innovations . . . [52]

Clearly Brayer intended to do without a militia indefinitely. Though the soldiers were billeted in private homes—a chronic source of tension between troops and civilians—he relied on the municipality to manage this skillfully, and worried only that the garrison's numbers might drop. On October 30 Brayer received assurances from the royal household that a contemplated transfer of the Armagnac regiment from Soissons would not take place after all.[53]

Some hints about the status of the militia issue can be drawn from an anonymous local pamphlet, *The Jeremiad of the Master Porters and Other Mercenaries of the Sad Estate of Soissons.* Like innumerable journalistic pieces of which *Père Duchesne* is only the most famous, the *Jeremiad* put words in the mouth of an imaginary common man; the degree to which the views it expressed were really popular ones is difficult to estimate. But let us first hear the *Jeremiad*'s views and then evaluate them. In the following passage, the writer is almost certainly referring to the Great Fear:

> I also heard who escaped our firm grip on that day that our town officers held back the order to mount a guard; if I could only be the least certain of that, ha, for that I would make them tumble down fast enough, and I too can make them give the salutation of de Launay, Foulon, Bertier, etc. [royal officials killed by the Parisian crowd after the fall of the Bastille], in spite of what I said about not liking bloodshed . . .
>
> I also ask you to put an end to all these humiliating distinctions and to require all these companies of amusements to rejoin their quarter's company when there is question of mounting the guard or the bourgeois parade [Sunday review of the militia].[54]

A later passage concocts material reasons for the day-laborers of Soissons to support an active militia: "How will we get through the winter, since the regiment here does all the little odd jobs, sawing, splitting wood, carrying it, etc.; if the bourgeois militia had been reestablished, that would have been a resource, we could have mounted the guard for others . . . "[55]

Judging from internal evidence, the *Jeremiad* probably dates from late August or September, and so confirms for us that Soissons's authorities had avoided an active militia up to that time. The unknown writer threatens these authorities with a popular rage that other documents tell us was unavailable in Soissons at this early point in the Revolution. The picture of soldiers monopolizing wood hauling to the locals' disadvantage is entirely plausible, fitting well with what is known about off-duty activities in Paris and other cities.[56] The idea of relieving the poor by paying them to serve as substitutes in the militia was decidedly traditional. In many new "national militias," paid substitutions were frowned upon; they were seen as a form of exemption privileges; they deprived the militia of the active presence of its best-off members and thus tended to weaken overall bourgeois control over the armed body. The *Jeremiad*'s proposal of militia substitutions shows well how distant the idea of a revolutionary militia was even from the mind of an adversary of the municipality of Soissons.

Laon was another apanage-dominated municipality that sought to avoid having an active militia. At the end of July, Laon was agitated not by rumors of "brigands" but by true (though garbled) reports of a shipment of arms traveling toward the town. The wagons carrying arms were intercepted by the mounted police and impounded by the municipality for a month. On August 2 the town's electors of Estates-General deputies met with the municipal officers and agreed that a militia was unnecessary and possibly dangerous. On October 19 a militia was formally organized, but it is unclear whether the traditional militia was reactivated or a new structure was created. In any case, the militia was not asked to quell a riot on November 20 over a seizure of untaxed tobacco; instead, the mounted police and dragoons performed the work.[57]

Laon was traditionally a garrison town; it had hosted troops since the twelfth century. In 1781 the queen's regiment of dragoons were stationed in Laon, and its titular commander was a prince of the blood, the duc de Polignac. The duc's position at court aided the vigorous lobbying by the municipality and the diocese for state funds to construct barracks, and the barracks were complete and in use on the eve of the Revolution.[58] So both tradition and convenience disposed the authorities to rely on troops to maintain public order. The Great Fear never brought its rural inspiration for a militia into Laon; thus, even after the militia was organized it lacked chances to demonstrate its usefulness. Whatever popular energies a more independent militia might have channeled instead found outlets in pranks against the garrison, such as throwing firecrackers near sentry boxes.[59]

A last significant variation remains to be touched upon: the difficulty of restructuring the traditional militia in a town where it was active and had deep social roots. This problem may also have been present to a lesser degree in Soissons and Laon, which both had dormant but prestigious bourgeois guards. In St-Quentin, just across the northwest boundary of the Soissons intendancy, the traditional militia's role was the crux of the situation.

In St-Quentin, as in many other towns, the militia duties of the upper bourgeoisie in the 1780s were entirely ceremonial. Yet here the militia itself was a functional, not a ceremonial, body. St-Quentin, a center of textile manufacturing, was near France's northern frontier and had provided its own defense for centuries by royal permission. It hosted a small command staff of military officers, but no regular troops. Day-laborers were paid to perform the endless guard duties on the town's walls and bridges, and this practice was embedded in the town's social structure. The situation's fundamentals were well stated in November 1789 by the town commune's committee on the militia:

> St-Quentin has always been, and should be regarded as, a border city. Its fortifications, the distribution of its bridges, its arsenal, [and] the powder magazines within its walls absolutely demand a continual surveillance. Its position therefore requires a garrison; the fidelity of its inhabitants has supplied one . . . But at the same time . . . [St-Quentin is also important] because of its type of industry . . . [which] occupies thousands of hands and is among the most productive in exportation.
>
> In a manufacturing town one cannot and must not subject the citizens to guard duty seven days a week; [yet] the fortifications and . . . bridges require a continuous guard. Hence the necessity of a paid guard.[60]

The institution of a paid militia was indispensable for three reasons. First, the town had to meet its military obligation to the state. Second, the labor time of merchants, producers, and skilled artisans in textile manufacture had to be safeguarded. Third, the lower classes needed the employment a militia could provide; as the committee put it, the town's militia tax was a "necessary levy to pay the unfortunates."[61]

The militia tax roll was riddled with exemptions for nobles, ecclesiastics, and the town's oligarchy (which consisted of about 30 families).[62] The complex controversy that erupted in St-Quentin over the future militia need not be recounted here; but let it be noted that the quarrel was above all over the sharing of the financial burden of the militia—a burden that was also a commercial cost of operation for local textile manufacturing. In addition, the militia tax also functioned as a charitable expense, and this fact made exemptions for the rich appear particularly onerous.[63]

The St-Quentin case is unique within this study's limits, and yet it also illustrates a general point: that the problem of militia organization could readily become a microcosm of a town's internal class and status relations. Depending on local conditions, a national militia might confirm and even celebrate these relations, or it might powerfully subvert them.

Clearly, these examples—the tumultuous Château-Thierry, the well-regimented Noyon and Verberie, and the reluctant Soissons, Laon, and St-Quentin—show the great diversity of possible attitudes toward, and results of, militia formation after the Great Fear. Much depended on the acumen and resources of municipalities as they made their own way in the bewildering new political environment of 1789. What the Great Fear did was to force locales that had remained on the fringes of the national upheaval to enter this environment. The panic created a nonpolitical ground on which new, inevitably political institutions had to be erected. They might even be dismantled once the panic was over, but the examples remained of other towns where they had persisted. It would be too much to say that after the Great Fear nothing could remain the same. But it is true that many municipalities exhausted all their forces in the effort to keep them the same.

One of the most astute and capable old-regime municipalities of the Soissonnais—the officers of Crépy-en-Valois, appointed by the Orléans apanage—was willingly preparing to leave office in December 1789. Their moves during the year had been sure and well-timed. They had created a militia on their own terms, a few days in advance (as it happened) of the Great Fear. On the day of the Fear they selected a permanent committee that served to reinforce their position. Their influence over the militia remained great enough that in late August they could direct it against the contraband trade in untaxed salt. After August there is no evidence of militia participation in such expeditions, but salt-tax employees aided by royal troops were able to continue their work through November—something of an accomplishment in itself. Yet on December 8 the municipality wrote the National Assembly, "It is impossible for us to keep our faces to the storm any longer, and to continue functions that are all the more dangerous for us as the people appear persuaded that we are the masters, able to obstruct the hoarding of grain."[64]

By their own account, townspeople still looked to the municipal officers for leadership—but to lead in a direction toward which they dared not go. The consensus that had originated in the Great Fear was gone—or rather it had been transformed into something quite different.

It was possible for the municipality and the militia to remain united with the community only by harmonizing with the latter's growing demands. Ironically, in the fall Crépy's municipality was lobbying the National Assembly for a legal limit on the size of tenant farms: the four-*charrue* (120- to 160-hectare) limit that many Soissonnais *cahiers de doléances* had requested in the spring. In this way the municipality struggled to shore up one face of the rural ideology that had kept the Soissonnais relatively quiet earlier in the year.[65]

The Crépy municipality's experience of "keeping our faces to the storm" can stand for the dilemma that the Great Fear had brought, in varying ways, to the Soissonnais. Even those municipalities that were rather successful in straddling the transition from the accustomed pattern of public order to the new one saw their insecurity rapidly increasing. They could preserve their sway only by one bold maneuver after another—or by taking the plunge and according completely with community demands, ceasing in effect to represent their own social class. The Great Fear put the early Revolution's institutional platform of permanent committee and new militia into an unpolitical context, and via the Fear this platform penetrated deeply into small town and village life. Once in place, the new institutions extended the public space that authorities were trying to control. The difficulties of containing participation were insurmountable in some places, and those towns where the effort of containment was more successful had to live in view of neighboring towns where it was less so. The old regime was dying, not from the single blow inflicted in Paris, but in a cellular fashion—community by community.

❧ *CONCLUSION*

Willingly or no, the preceding chapters have inevitably proposed a model of sorts for the range of provincial responses to the travail of July 1789. It would be pleasant, but evasive, to leave this model implicit and avoid making a contrast between the Soissonnais and the profuse variety of French regional life. The Soissonnais could then cast a longer shadow of suggested relevance—at least for the generous reader. The richness of the provincial Revolution would be ill served, however, so let us make the model explicit, the better to observe its breakdown.

The experience of the Soissonnais suggests that certain economic structures in rural life favored the reception of the Great Fear, yet it also shows how tensions that were properly social and political could override these favorable conditions. Let us postulate that in those rural economies where agriculture remained within some type of strong community framework, people were more likely to embrace the Fear. This does not mean only an agriculture bound to the "northern model" of triennial rotation; the national scope of the Fear belies this from the start. Nor does a community framework suggest any rough equality within the peasantry. Community agriculture may be dominated by a well-off few while remaining within a collective discipline that requires everyone to play a set role.

On the social and political levels, some types of popular activity made an area impervious to the Great Fear, while other types were neutral or even prepared the ground for it. Of the last class, those disturbances that remained inside the familiar, well-worn bounds of grain provisioning and prices on the regulated town market were the most consistent with receptivity to the Fear. As long as violence was contained within the theater of moral-economic relations between people and au-

thorities—and especially if antipathy between town and country remained important—then violence failed to rupture the social surface
that the Fear needed for its travels.

However, such ruptures did occur, and in rural economies apparently quite propitious for the Great Fear. Where conflicts grew to trans-
gress the bounds of moral-economic theater, particularly through a combined urban-rural rising, other favorable conditions for the Fear were
overridden. The rumor's current typically circumvented places where
people were already threatened or mobilized by a conflict that displayed
class divisions, and this held true not only for the disturbed area but
often for a neighboring zone as well.

Where the Fear's rumor did gò, its collective meaning did not en-
code a threat posed by one class to another. Though a class meaning may
have found its way into individual interpretations, this was not the meaning that was agreed upon and that mobilized communities. Rather, the
rumor encoded the imagined "outside" of the agrarian world as a source
of threat—an "outside" that was a staple of the parish-oriented ideology
of the old regime.

Community mobilization in the Great Fear was a subpolitical act.
Yet at the local level it created new political entities: the militias of 1789.
A subpolitical experience became the nucleus of politicization. A new
process then began in which the municipalities lost their traditional
place in public order as brokers between the powers of enforcement and
popular demands. From August onward, municipal officers' margin for
maneuver and ambiguity slowly melted away. Both local conditions and
the political requirements of the National Assembly demanded their
initiative and leadership. While some towns traversed this process via
sharp municipal revolutions, in more of France it was not conflict but its
very opposite—the Great Fear—that enlisted localities in a progression
of events linked to the national Revolution.

Such are the lessons we can draw from the experience of the Soissonnais if we extrapolate a model from it. Now let us watch this model bend
and alter during a quick tour of the situations in other regions. We can
divide these simply into some places where the Great Fear appeared
(western Provence, the Massif Central, and much of the southwest);
places where it did not (Brittany and much of Normandy); and problematic areas where the Fear appeared but did not thrive (the Orléanais
and northern Burgundy). In all these places we can compare Lefebvre's
research with fine regional studies.

Can we establish anything of substance in this way, by making a
survey of secondary materials without resort to local primary sources? I

think not. But we can learn how further study of the Great Fear—and of its absence—could illuminate a whole range of local responses to the early Revolution. At bottom, the issue is not to understand the Fear for its own sake. Rather, the Fear can be understood well enough to become an exploratory tool, a question that can be used to probe regional societies from multiple angles.

Thanks to the team that produced the *Atlas historique de Provence* under Michel Vovelle's direction,[1] the Great Fear in the southeast can be viewed in relation to other popular disturbances and in full geographic detail. From March 23 through mid-April, an urban-rural revolt spread from Marseilles and Toulon along strings of small towns running northeast of each city. On July 29 the Fear reached Avignon and moved eastward, through Aix and as far as St-Maximin; but apart from this current, the Fear left the region of the spring revolt untouched, avoiding the Mediterranean coast and most of lower Provence. Vovelle offers a social explanation: "Perhaps this pre-politicized France of urbanized *bourgs* lent itself poorly—if at all—to a collective panic that ran from village to village. The rising of spring 1789 was not a 'fear'; on the contrary, with its structure radiating from urban epicenters where the revolt began, it presents an example of a quite different type of rising."[2]

There was, however, a slender arrow of eastward penetration. The stretch from Aix to St-Maximin offers an intermediate zone of great interest, in which the Great Fear overlapped a region of earlier revolt. From Vovelle we also learn the ambiguity of Aix's role in the spring rising. Marseilles and Toulon rioted on March 23, Aix on March 25. In all three cases, the grain supply situation was the initial cause. Yet crowds in Marseilles and Toulon used this "platform" differently from those in Aix. In Marseilles and Toulon, crowds used the provisioning issue to attack the municipal government head-on: people stoned the town hall and the homes of municipal officers, and they assaulted the offices of collectors of a local flour tax (the *piquet de farine*). The rioters in Aix, on the other hand, were drawn to the grain, not to the administrators. They neglected civic buildings and besieged the granary instead.[3] This distinct intonation of the Aix riot may represent a different stage of politicization, one in keeping with Aix's greater receptivity to the Fear.

The Great Fear passed without hindrance across the Massif Central and much of the southwest. In this broad transregional zone, the many internal variations make evident the limits of strictly topographic and economic explanations. Only a few patches of the problem can be sketched out here; but we are fortunate to have P. M. Jones's work on the southern Massif, *Politics and Rural Society*,[4] which takes a village-based approach to a whole range of departments (especially Haute-Loire, Ardèche, Lozère, and Aveyron). The Massif appears a strong candidate for the discovery of new patterns in the Fear's diffusion and consequences—and this for two reasons.

First, the texture of community cohesion in the southern Massif was quite different from that in the Soissonnais. While concentrated village settlements existed in the Massif, they were counterbalanced by a profusion of hamlets of less than 10 households each; some villages "had as many as a hundred tiny satellites in watchful orbit around them."[5] The many implications of this for patterns of land use, sociability, and politics are readily imagined, though only a reading of Jones's book can do them justice.

Second, much of the southern Massif and the southwest was caught up in a powerful antiseigneurial revolt from November 1789 through March 1790,[6] in which peasants invaded over a hundred châteaux. Was this the outcome of a distinct pattern of politicization—one in which the Great Fear played a role quite different from the one we have seen in the North? The southwest could be compared closely with the Dauphiné, the only region where the Fear led directly to a peasant revolt. Could the influence of the Fear have been roughly analogous in the southwest, despite four months' delay? In any case, the use of the Fear as an exploratory tool in regional studies seems particularly attractive here.

A subset of the same problem is offered by Patrice Higonnet's village study of Pont-de-Montvert in the Cévennes.[7] For the Revolutionary period, Higonnet argues effectively that the solidarity of the Protestant poor with their Protestant notables allowed the community to both welcome the Revolution and avoid acting out its social conflicts. In Pont-de-Montvert, an army garrison that watched the "new Catholics" had been withdrawn for good only in 1755. Lefebvre reports that the Cévennes was highly receptive to the Great Fear; the rumor arrived from the Dauphiné as a fear of approaching "Piedmontese."[8] Could the wording in the Cévennes have served as a euphemism for Catholic troops? Certainly more light on the Fear would be valuable for testing Higonnet's picture of the Revolution's general impact on the Protestant hill country.

Now let us turn to two regions where the Great Fear was absent: Britanny and much of Normandy. In the West, Brittany was the largest area to be completely unaffected by the Fear. Like the strongly affected southern Massif, it diverged from the famous "northern model" of nucleated settlement in concentrated villages and triennial rotation.

In *Vannes and Its Region*, T. J. A. LeGoff paints a rural world of hamlets comparable to Jones's Massif, one that lived without the "rigorous communal practices" of the openfield.[9] Farmers seeded plots with alternate grains annually until fertility gave out, then dropped them from cultivation. For five or seven years these plots would join the waste (*landes*), to offer forage for livestock and turf for fertilizer (to be mixed with manure and seaweed). This type of intensive agriculture was anchored by a peculiar form of land tenure, the *domaine congéable*, in which, to oversimplify, tenants rented land but owned the structures on it. In this environment the middle peasantry was stronger, and grain less commercialized, than in the North.

The absence of the Great Fear in Brittany may not be the unitary phenomenon it appears to be on Lefebvre's map—different causes may prove more compelling for different districts—but we can ponder the strong presence of the factor that Lefebvre thought central to the Great Fear, the belief in an "aristocratic plot." Brittany was the home of the "Brest plot," a rumor that a British squadron was poised in the Channel to seize the port with the collaboration of its maritime authorities.[10] In the municipal politics of spring and summer, the "Brest plot" offered the revolutionary notables a splendid device for intimidating the clergy and nobility, who feared being implicated. In Vannes the revolutionaries on the town council organized a militia to facilitate their own takeover, on July 28–31; on July 29 a "nobles' plot" was reported at a nearby château, and an expedition to search it let the militia's youth brigade make its formal debut (they found two nobles and 13 hunting guns).[11] Yet it seems that the "aristocratic plot" did not support the Fear, but took its place.

In an area where a coalition between high bourgeoisie and liberal nobility never formed, the nobles remained outside the pale in 1789, and their conservative language preserved an oppositional vitality—admired and appropriated by Vannes's lower classes within a year's time. "Vive le roi, vive la noblesse, au diable le Tiers," chanted the Third Estate, led by drapers and wool-carders in an April 1790 riot over grain provisions and local excise taxes.[12] Could the "aristocratic plot" and the Breton municipal revolutions it served have set the political education of the modest classes on a different track? Perhaps a popular perception of bourgeois betrayal came clear and early here, because bourgeois leaders did not first have to be separated from their noble fellow-travelers under popular pressure. In the Soissonnais, where the Great Fear was prominent, the "aristocratic plot" was notably absent. In Brittany, the "aristocratic plot" not only was without any link to the Fear, but seems to have had effects far removed from those that Lefebvre expected.

Not far away—in the Norman setting studied by Jonathan Dewald in his *Pont-St-Pierre, 1398–1789*—we find another, different absence of the Great Fear.[13] Dewald presents a rural world that, like the Soissonnais, was evolving toward agrarian capitalism, but that (unlike it) was doing so outside a framework of community practice. Communal crop rotation had never been significant here, not even in medieval times;[14] *vaine pâture* had collapsed almost entirely by the mid-eighteenth century, because the prevalence of forest grazing rights offered room for individual control over the arable lands. As in the Soissonnais, tenancy, not ownership, was the prime form of peasant occupancy. Lefebvre characterizes this part of Normandy as overshadowed by an insurrection in Rouen on July 12–14,[15] but Rouen's violence did not spread to Pont-St-Pierre, which retained an almost gracious interplay at market between crowd and baronial officers throughout 1789. Not until autumn 1791, when some tenants refused to pay the full tithe, can Dewald detect a hint of trouble in the baronial archives.[16] The Norman case must be sharply distinguished from LeGoff's Breton one: though there was no Fear in either locale, in Pont-St-Pierre there was virtually no revolution either. Yet the Fear's absence here was part of a larger, cross-regional phenomenon. On Lefebvre's map, Pont-St-Pierre lies within a long stripe of inactivity running from Le Havre and Dieppe southeast almost to Bourges and Sancerre—all untouched by the Fear.[17]

Finally, we can examine regions where the reception of the Great Fear was ambiguous, among them the Orléanais and northern Burgundy. Let us focus on the Orléanais, at the stripe's southern end, to ponder briefly how a place could accept the Fear but not pass it on. Here we have the advantage of interrogating Lefebvre in his capacity as local historian. His *Etudes orléanaises*, two volumes written intermittently from 1918 until his sunset years, comprise in effect his second "state thesis." From his work on the Great Fear, we know that Orléans received the panic from the east, and that the Fear took the form of a fear of "brigands" in the forest of Orléans.[18] From the *Etudes* we also know that in this region of extensive noble property the arable land was actually regressing as seigneurs retired farms from tenancy, letting them revert to pasture and then to highly profitable forest. Could these densening woods to the town's north and east have conveyed a sense of threat and encirclement?[19]

Though Orléans responded to the Great Fear, it did not relay the rumor farther. Perched on the right bank of the Loire, it apparently did not even send the Fear across the river into the Sologne. Yet the Sologne's own character may have entered into this. It was a region notorious for its agricultural decline. Here a society that "in the fourteenth and fifteenth centuries . . . was . . . a region of small farms, well peopled and prosperous enough" had been altered by generations of noble proprietors into a more profitable mix of pasture, waste, woods, and fishponds—a mix that could only support a small, dispersed population, and that dropped the burden of the land tax squarely on the narrowing base of peasant subsistence farming.[20]

So much we can gather from the lay of the land, while the political circumstances of Orléans offer another lesson. In this town the conditioning event was a great riot on April 24; a conservatively officered militia was formed to aid its repression. However, this new, strictly bourgeois militia refused demobilization afterward, and the municipal officers' effort to use the militia after another market disturbance on July 18 led to their overthrow. Thus the arrival of the Great Fear on July 29 was greeted by a militia already fully formed.[21] Orléans accepted the Fear but did not pass it on, and this ambiguous response suggests that the Fear came too late to be crucial to the town's political education.

A last case: northern Burgundy, studied by Pierre de Saint-Jacob, Régine Robin, and Hilton Root.[22] Like the Orléanais, northern Burgundy was a complex intermediate region that the Great Fear entered but did not sweep. Lefebvre even says that "on this side there was no Great Fear properly speaking."[23] Instead we find separated urban alarms that did not link up, and around Dijon a "fear of brigands" (Lefebvre's psychological designation for apprehensiveness short of outright panic). Lefebvre explains northern Burgundy as a "zone of interference" in which three distinct sets of ripples cancelled each other out. The two separate revolts of the Franche-Comté and the Mâconnais each meant that neighboring areas would not prove receptive to the Fear (a situation analogous to the Cambrésis revolt's effect on the Laonnais in the present study). Third, a current of the Fear from the northwest ran into the sand south of Châtillon-sur-Seine.

However, in other regards the Burgundian experience challenges what we have found for the Soissonnais, for Saint-Jacob indicates important agricultural similarities. Burgundy too was well on the road to a capitalist agriculture; wheat was monetarized to such an extent that it had disappeared from the diet of adult peasants, who reserved it for their infants.[24] As in the Soissonnais, the middle peasant stratum was being pressured out of existence. It may be that in northern Burgundy the role of the great tenant farmers still lacked the historical depth it had attained in the Soissonnais by the mid-eighteenth century, and that consequently tensions between seigneur and community were sharper and more bipolar. Even so, a greater receptivity to the Fear might have been expected in the light of the patterns suggested by the Soissonnais.

To sum up, in 1789 four of the regions just discussed behaved in ways that are intelligible in terms of the patterns presented in this study. Parts of Provence accepted or were bypassed by the Great Fear, according to shades of earlier politicization that we can discriminate finely. The currency of the "aristocratic plot" in Brittany created a social fissure that may well have kept out the Fear. A looser, more individualized agriculture in Normandy's Pont-St-Pierre seems appropriate for a region that the Fear could not enter. In the Orléanais, a townspeople's fear of forest-dwellers could find no rural response in an area where peasant cultivation itself had become marginal.

On the other hand, the southern Massif and northern Burgundy offer exciting questions because they break out of the framework suggested by the Soissonnais. Might a Great Fear that could find its way through the dispersed settlement pattern of the Massif have stimulated the obscure social networks of peasant revolt, instead of draining them off? Might a microregional look at northern Burgundy reveal a universe of distinct rural configurations, partly corresponding to the intermittence of the Fear?

On these discordant notes we must leave this tantalizing problem. Ultimately, the value of reflecting on the Great Fear does not lie in an effort to conceive of it as a uniform, nationwide phenomenon. Rather, the Fear can be reintegrated into the many regional cells of the provincial Revolution that the vast majority of the French people experienced. In each locale where it appeared, the Fear was both a visitor and a native product; and a moment of transition as well in that place's dialectic with national events. The more we grasp the Great Fear in regional terms, the better we can understand the Revolution people lived.

When the Great Fear gave birth to new militias, it did not create a fixed institution so much as a dynamic—a kind of program in progress whose ultimate shape was still unknown. The original experience of the Fear reconciled unanimous participation in militias with noble-bourgeois leadership of those militias. Such a situation was possible only through a kind of alchemy of collective perception that was evanescent, even dreamlike. By late 1790, the separation of these two elements—universal membership and elite control—was quite complete, and the dynamism of the militia institution had split into two streams, each channeled by a separate program—one constitutional monarchist, and the other radical democratic.

In December 1790 Robespierre published a thick pamphlet—78 pages—containing a speech he had been unable as yet to give in the Assembly: the *Discourse on the Organization of National Guards*.[25] This extraordinary work of political analysis maps the extensive contradictions between the constitutional monarchist and the democratic visions of the militia. From village power-sharing to foreign relations, Robespierre connects all the levels on which the militia counted in 1790, and he does this for both the program he supports and the one he opposes.

The constitutional monarchist program had been formulated by two Assembly committees charged with devising a plan for the nation's future military and police forces. This program was founded on the fundamental division between "active" and "passive" citizens, the line drawn by the new, unratified Constitution between a propertied majority and a large, poor minority. Participation in the National Guard would be limited to active citizens. Not only elected municipal officers but also administrative authorities could give orders to the guard. Two important practices followed by many militias would be expressly forbidden: keeping arms at home when off duty, and free deliberation within the militia company.[26]

The National Guard—still according to the constitutional monarchists—would develop in liaison with the military, which would provide training, some officering, and a professional model for emulation. The Guard's table of ranks would be elaborated on the army's hierarchical pattern. Most significantly, an intermediate corps, the "auxiliary army," would be organized by drawing two men from each company. The auxiliary would serve alongside line army units. For the army, it would provide manpower; for the militias, a source of military training and a military outlook.[27]

This design was consonant with a certain understanding of the nation's total armed forces, and here Robespierre's critique was especially acute:

> The two committees have so mistaken the true object of the National Guards that they seem to regard the capacity to oppose outside enemies with immense military forces at all times as this institution's principal advantage.
>
> One must read in their report with what satisfaction they parade before the reader's eyes these armies, that they put in campaign at the first moment of invasion; how, after their auxiliary army, they detach new armies from the remainder of the National Guards, pressing them one upon another; how they congratulate the country on its grandeur and its power!—of course, it

is a question of all that—it is a question of constituting ourselves as if we wished to conquer Europe![28]

Robespierre saw at once—near the beginning of the long process to come—that the boundary between popular armament and popular militarization is terribly narrow. The intensity of the alternate program he proposed derived not only from his famous concern for first principles but also from his grasp of the stakes involved: mass mobilization may reinforce citizenship, but it may also slide into a new imperial schema.

Robespierre's program was rooted in the actual practice of the most autonomous militias that were familiar to all in 1790. His contribution was to integrate this practice into an overview that included the Revolution's prospects at home and the question of France's role in Europe.

Robespierre began by embracing universal male membership in the militia. Again, his democratic first principles were only half his argument. The other half was the reality of the sitting National Assembly's electoral base, for the deputies were chosen in spring 1789 through a process that involved the full male population. He hammered at the euphemistic designations of "active" and "passive" citizens: "These same men of whom we speak, are they (according to us) slaves, are they foreigners? or are they citizens? If they are slaves, outsiders, this should be declared openly . . . But no; in fact they are citizens; the French people's representatives have not stripped this title from the great majority of their constituents . . . they could not turn against them the same power that they received from them . . . and by that destroy their own authority."[29]

These political realities of 1789 were the basis for militias open to all adult males. They likewise supported Robespierre's incorporation of real militia practices into his program. We have already found them all in the historical record: the acceptance of youths down to the age of 18 (witness the many "youth companies" of town militias); the provision of weapons to those who cannot afford them; the retention of guns at home; the election of officers with short terms of office within neighborhood-based companies; a town-wide command staffed by rotating personnel; free deliberation within the company; and, as demanded by militias in countless petitions, the direct supply of arms by the War Ministry, with stepped-up arms manufacture to this end.

Robespierre was concerned to keep, even emphasize, these features because they safeguarded the contrast between the militia and the regular army. For him the two institutions had distinct purposes that had to be kept apart. The army was meant to deal with armies of other countries, while the militia expressed the civilians' defense of liberty—against the royal executive and the army when necessary. Consequently the militias should be, if anything, "civilianized"; profuse distinctions of rank should be pruned back; no mark of membership should be worn off duty; even royal awards or decorations should be prohibited. The militias should take orders from elected officials only, and they should be free to deliberate on those orders. The National Guards (Robespierre never puts them in the singular) should have sole responsibility for controlling riots because of their greater respect for human rights ("respect pour les droits de l'humanité");[30] and the military should be forbidden to assist them. Even the old mounted police should be integrated into a special militia unit paid to perform regular police duties.

Most striking of all, for Robespierre the existence of the National Guards imposed a complete review of French foreign policy. Otherwise the Guards' sheer numbers would be enlisted eventually by an expansionist project. The entire diplomatic corps should be recalled, examined, and replaced on a case-by-case basis, and the relevant committees of the Assembly should report on foreign affairs every three days. A drastic overhaul of foreign policy must proceed concomitantly with the immense buildup of civilian forces. The long-term goal of this double process was the abolition of the army. Ultimately, revolutionary France was to be an enormous Switzerland (whose example Robespierre cites): able to fully mobilize only for a defense of national territory, but then in numbers of several millions.

It would be a complete misunderstanding, and one typical of our own time, to see Robespierre's proposal as "utopian" and refuse to ponder it. What we might mistake for utopianism is really desperation, born of foresight. It was clear to Robespierre that the emerging reality of a "nation in arms" had to be profoundly democratized, localized, and demilitarized, because if it was not it would fall of its own weight into imperialism—as indeed occurred before the decade ended. Radical, communitarian self-defense might provide the means for France to avoid this path.

Robespierre's analysis thus stands at an early turning point in a long process that ended—or did it?—in 1815. The Great Fear, however, stands at its very beginning. Georges Lefebvre thought that the Fear played an important part in engendering the "nation in arms," and he was not mistaken. In the weeks that followed, as news of the extent of the panic accumulated in Paris and circulated through the provinces, the participants learned that they had played roles in a truly national event. But the actual moment when they took up arms was one of psychological suspension, a living social paradox in which many opposites in their lives—their town and country, their rich and poor, their elites and Third Estate—were briefly united. In that moment, those who marched were not yet militia companies of a nation in arms, but communities in motion, scattered across a world about to fade and disappear.

ᴥ *NOTES*

Abbreviations

AC   Archives communales
ADA   Archives départementales de l'Aisne, Laon
ADO   Archives départementales de l'Oise, Beauvais
AN   Archives Nationales
Arch. Parl.   J. Madival and E. Laurent, eds., *Archives Parlementaires de 1787 à 1860* (Paris: Société Paul Dupont, 1875-1914).
BN   Bibliothèque Nationale

Introduction

1. Georges Lefebvre, *La Grande Peur de 1789* (Paris: Armand Colin, 1970). Quotations in this study are from Joan White's English translation, *The Great Fear of 1789* (New York: Pantheon, 1973). In a few cases (indicated in the notes) I have amended the translation.

2. Soissons authorities to duc de Liancourt, July 27, 1789, AN C 89.

3. Volney proposed the formation of a correspondence committee (*comité des rapports*) on July 28; the motion was passed after considerable debate. The committee first reported to the Assembly on August 3. J. Madival and E. Laurent, eds., *Archives Parlementaires de 1787 à 1860* [Paris: Société Paul Dupont, 1875-1914], 8:292-93, 336).

4. Ibid., 8:345. All translations are mine unless otherwise indicated.

5. Lefebvre, *Great Fear*, 21. In this study, the spelling "Flandre" is used to denote the province acquired by France in the late seventeenth century before its transformation into the department of the Nord by Revolutionary legislation.

6. Ibid., 205-9. The Dauphiné revolt was the biggest of these incidents. It began on the morning of July 28, after a fruitless night of vigil by peasants from around Bourgoin. Concluding that the rumor was an aristocratic ruse against

them, they proceeded to attack and burn châteaux on both banks of the river Bourbre.

7. Six were located by Georges Lefebvre; Henri Dinet has found a seventh point of origin at Limours, between Paris and Chartres.

8. Lefebvre, *Great Fear*, 148–55.

9. For example, by Albert Mathiez: "The brigands whose imminent irruption haunted men's imaginations could not as a rule be distinguished from the artisans who burnt the toll-gates and fixed the price of wheat in the market, or the peasants who forced their lords to give up their title-deeds" (*The French Revolution*, trans. Catherine Alison Phillips [New York: Russell & Russell, 1962], p. 51). On occasion Georges Lefebvre wrote in the same vein: "The idea that there was 'brigands' in and around Paris was a fairly general one, and indeed the king had lent it support in order to justify his calling in troops . . . These brigands, whose existence was so desperately needed for political reasons, were in fact the floating population of Paris, mainly the local unemployed" (*Great Fear*, 125). Likewise Albert Soboul: "Unemployment and shortages multiplied beggars and vagabonds: in the spring, bands appeared. The *fear of brigands* reinforced the fear of an aristocratic plot" (*La Révolution française* [Paris: Editions sociales, 1962], 1:164).

10. "The agrarian revolts of the Normandy Bocage, Hainault, Franche-Comté, Alsace and even the Mâconnais preceded the Great Fear and only the outbreak in the Dauphiné can be put down to its influence. Between the agrarian revolts and the Great Fear, there is so little interdependence that the two do not coincide, except in the Dauphiné" (Lefebvre, *Great Fear*, 142).

11. The Great Fear's tendency to create unity—both between town and country, and across classes—was clearly noted by Lefebvre: "[The Great Fear] tightened the bonds of solidarity which linked the town and the countryside around it as well as the towns themselves . . . in the towns, the panic brought a strengthening of the communal defense system; it almost always suspended or diminished municipal disagreements instead of causing them." Speaking of Bresse, the peaceful region adjoining the Mâconnais in revolt, Lefebvre remarked that "when the Mâconnais rose in revolt all along the border, there is nothing to suggest that no one would have followed suit *if the Great Fear had not come along* [emphasis mine]" (ibid., 202–3).

12. Ibid., 133.

13. Lefebvre notes "the unexpected conjunction of nobles and bourgeois in an attempt to protect their property from the 'fourth estate' . . . The events in Versailles and Paris struck a hard blow at this union, but it managed to survive till 14 July: during the subsequent troubles it reappeared in the provinces far more frequently than is realized" (ibid., 49).

14. Most notably: Henri Dinet, "La Grande Peur en Hurepoix (juillet 1789)," *Paris et Ile-de-France: Mémoires* 18–19 (1967–68): 99–204, summarized in idem, "Les Peurs de 1789 dans la région parisienne: La Peur en Hurepoix (juillet 1789)," *Annales historiques de la Révolution française* 50 (1978): 34–44; and idem, "Les Peurs du Beauvaisis et du Valois, juillet 1789," *Paris et Ile-de-France: Mémoires* 23–24 (1972–73): 199–392.

15. Lefebvre, *Great Fear*, 210.

16. Ibid., 137.

17. Ibid., 168

18. Ibid., 91, 93.

19. Ibid., 66. For Hippolyte Taine's interpretation, see his *French Revolution*, trans. John Durand, (Gloucester, Mass.: Peter Smith, 1962). Taine's belief that criminals led most of the revolutionary crowds was largely based on his *a priori* notion that "in every mob it is the boldest and least scrupulous who march ahead and give the example in destruction" (*French Revolution* 1:14).

20. Lefebvre, *Great Fear*, 23.

21. The coherence of the boundaries of the new unit with those of the old, despite the shift in *chef-lieu* from Soissons to Laon, is demonstrated in René Hennequin, *La formation du département de l'Aisne en 1790: Étude documentaire de géographie politique* Soissons: Société académique de Laon, 1911).

22. Tamotsu Shibutani, *Improvised News: A Sociological Study of Rumor* (New York: Bobbs-Merrill, 1966); Edgar Morin, *La rumeur d'Orléans* (Paris: Editions de Seuil, 1969).

23. Shibutani, *Improvised News*, 14–16. For his comments on Lefebvre's work, see 105–6, 128, 147.

24. Morin, *Rumeur d'Orléans*, 67–77, 82.

Chapter 1. Cultivation and Its Consensual Base

1. Lefebvre, *Great Fear*, 44.

2. See Lefebvre's map, ibid., 4.

3. Dauchy [prefect], *Statistique du département de l'Aisne* Paris, Year X [1801–2]), 18.

4. Pierre Goubert, *Beauvais et le Beauvaisis de 1600 à 1730: Contribution à l'histoire sociale de la France du XVIIe siècle* (Paris: Université de Paris, 1958), 493–504; Gilles Postel-Vinay, *La rente foncière dans le capitalisme agricole* (Paris: Maspero, 1974), 17–20. Postel-Vinay's book takes the district around Soissons (its *pays*, not the whole intendancy), as a case study in the development of French capitalist agriculture.

5. Around Laon, the use of scythes to reap the harvest of 1788 (struck by a freakish July hail) required the permission of the *lieutenant général de police*. AC Laon HH 16 contains a sheaf of these authorizations for local farmers.

6. Cited by Postel-Vinay, *La rente foncière*, 45.

7. Bacquet of St-Quentin to National Assembly, July 21, 1789, AN C 89.

8. Cited by Postel-Vinay, *La rente foncière*, 46.

9. Lefebvre, *Great Fear*, 45. See also Georges Lefebvre, *Les paysans du Nord pendant la Révolution française* (Bari, Italy: Editori Laterza, 1959), 103–7.

10. Postel-Vinay, *La rente foncière*, 49–52.

11. This tendency of large farmers to expand through rent rather than through purchase extended through the Revolution and the sale of church lands. Rather than buying the parcels they had rented, they preferred to act as intermediaries for the new proprietors, who thus would be in their debt (ibid., 93).

12. Florence Gauthier, *La voie paysanne dans la Révolution française: L'exemple picard* (Paris: Maspero, 1977), 79–80. On the importance of this text, see David Hunt's "Peasant Politics in the French Revolution," *Social History* 9 (1984): 277–99, in which he states, "Gauthier fundamentally redirects the scholarly tradition in which she is working" (p. 294).

13. Postel-Vinay, *La rente foncière*, 70–71.

14. Pierre Brunet, *Structure agraire et économie rurale des plateaux tertiaires entre la Seine et l'Oise* (Caen: Caron, 1960), 338. A remarkable work of historical geography.

15. Referred to as *mouture économique*. E. Beguillet, *Traité de la connoissance générale des grains, et de la mouture par économie* (pt. 1, Paris: Pancoucke, 1775; pt. 2, Dijon: Frantin, 1778); also see César Bucquet, *Manuel du meunier, et du constructeur de moulins à eau et à grains* (Paris: Onfrey, 1790).

16. However, Guy-Robert Ikni's forthcoming thesis, *Crise agraire et révolution paysanne dans les campagnes de l'Oise: De la décennie physiocratique à l'An II*, is expected to document peasants' innovations in this part of the Soissons intendancy. In particular, the diffusion of the potato, a system of field drainage borrowed from Brie (Ikni, unpublished ms., 1981), the creation of "prairies artificielles," and the deflection of streams to irrigate meadows in springtime (parish cahier of Juvigny; see n. 26 below) indicate peasants' interest in change.

17. A society for Hainaut and the Cambrésis was created in 1763; the Picards successfully fought off several attempts to create a society, the last in 1789. See Emile Justin, *Les sociétés royales d'agriculture au XVIIIe siècle, 1757–1793* (Saint-Lô: Barbaroux, 1935), 55–132.

18. Bacquet of St-Quentin to National Assembly, July 21, 1789, A N C 89.

19. Camille Bloch and Alexandre Tuetey, eds., *Procès-verbaux et rapports du Comité de mendicité de la Constituante, 1790–1791* (Paris: Imprimerie Nationale, 1911), 47.

20. "Discours sur le commerce de grains par M. Sellyer" [November 1789], AN F11 221.

21. "Mémoire sur la suppression de la mendicité," in the working papers of the 1787 provincial assembly, AD C 989. This passage, unlike some others, stood in the printed minutes: *Procès-verbaux des séances de l'Assemblée provinciale du Soissonnais, tenue à Soissons en 1787* (Soissons: Waroquier, 1788), 228–48.

22. AN F11 294–95.

23. "Discours sur le commerce de grains par M. Sellyer" [November 1789], AN F11 221.

24. AN Dxxix 34; AN F11 221; AN Dxli 2.

25. Anonymous memorandum to Soissonnais provincial assembly of 1787, AD C 943.

26. Juvigny: Bibliothèque de Soissons, Collection Périn, ms. 1992; Trozy-Loire: Collection Périn, ms. 6089; Urvillers: AN Ba 70.

27. AC Nogent l'Artaud D1; AC La Chapelle-sur-Chezy D1.

28. Goubert, *Beauvais*, 115–16.

29. ADA 2 Mi 39 (1880s *instituteurs'* monographs, including excerpts from communal archives destroyed in World War I).

30. AN Ba 32.

31. AN Ba 46.

32. La Fère municipality to Guise municipality, April 3, 1789, AC Guise BB 14.

33. Register of intermediate bureau of Noyon, ADO C 358. For a detailed discussion of adjudication as seen at the intendant's level, see Gauthier, *La voie paysanne*, 86–94.

34. M. Melleville, *Histoire de la ville de Laon et de ses institutions* (Laon, 1846; reprint, Brussels: Editions culture et civilisation, 1976), 1:11.

35. R. Regnier, "Noyon port sur l'Oise: Le document Margerin (1786)," *Société archéologique, historique et scientifique de Noyon: Comptes-rendus et mémoires* 34 (1972): 39.

36. AN Ba 32.

37. Gauthier, *La voie paysanne*, 151–52.

38. For Fretin: *Rélation d'une partie des troubles de France, pendant les années 1789 et 1790* . . . (Paris, 1790), 27, on deposit in AN AD1 92. See also Lefebvre, *Paysans du Nord*, 379. For Petit St-Jean: commune to National Assembly, April 4, 1790, AN Dxxix 17.

39. See the assessments of both Postel-Vinay, *La rente foncière*, 107–9; and Brunet, *Structure agraire*, 310–15.

40. AN Ba 86, 35. The verbal formula varied little; here is the article from the nobles' *cahier* of Crépy-en-Valois: "Que pour perfectionner la culture et donner à un plus grand nombre de familles une subsistance plus facile, le même fermier ne puisse exploiter que quatre charrues, à moins qu'un nombre plus considérable n'appartienne au même propriétaire en composant le même corps de ferme" (AN Ba 35). A *charrue* was a local measure of the amount of land a single plow could cultivate: it varied between 30 and 40 hectares in the Soissonnais (Postel-Vinay, *La rente foncière*, 58–59).

41. AN Ba 70.

42. Cited by Brunet, *Structure agraire*, 289–90, who had it in turn from the local historian H. Luguet, *Villages et fermes du Valois* (Soissons, 1933).

43. "Discours sur la commerce de grains par M. Sellyer," [November 1789], AN F11 221.

44. See Postel-Vinay's discussion in *La rente foncière*, 59–72.

45. Ibid., 71–72. In his analysis, "il en va ainsi de ces machines à rente que sont les grands ensembles ecclésiastiques qui pratiquent à leur façon les deux rôles de la rente foncière à cette étape: l'extorsion du surproduit paysan étant complété par la fixation des paysans au moyen d'aumônes, surtout en temps de crise." But see chapter 3 below.

46. Maison du roi to Blossac, intendant of Soissons, January 28, 1790, ADA C 6.

47. "Mémoire sur la suppression de la mendicité," ADA C 989. This passage was one of many struck from the printed minutes for showing scratches in the assembly's Enlightenment varnish.

48. Jean Joseph d'Expilly, *Dictionnaire géographique, historique et politique des Gaules et de la France* (Paris: Desaint et Saillant, 1762–70), 1:53.

49. AN Ba 35, 86, 70.

50. AN F16 936. This carton is inventoried in Camille Bloch, *L'assistance et l'Etat à la veille de la Révolution: Généralités de Paris, Rouen, Alençon, Orléans, Châlons, Soissons, Amiens, 1764–1790* (Paris: Picard et fils, 1908), xvii–xviii.

51. Postel-Vinay, *La rente foncière*, 64.

52. For a full discussion of climate and geology, see Brunet, *Structure agraire*, 213–73.

53. Goubert, *Beauvais*, 99.

54. Lefebvre, *Paysans du Nord*, 197–208, 38.

55. Goubert, *Beauvais*, 94, 111–22.

56. Brunet, *Structure agraire*, 359–65, 284–88.

57. Postel-Vinay, *La rente foncière*, 56. These figures are based on the tax rolls of 1778 and an estate inventory of 1788.

58. Brunet, *Structure agraire*, 352, 217.

59. AN Ba 32.

60. Goubert, *Beauvais*, 118.

61. Postel-Vinay, *La rente foncière*, 57; Gauthier, *La voie paysanne*, 119–20; Lefebvre, *Paysans du Nord*, 94–96.

62. Brunet, *Structure agraire*, 310–11.

63. Vallerand, replying to an 1879 questionnaire on agricultural loans from the Chambre d'agriculture of Compiègne. Cited by Brunet (ibid., 367).

64. Postel-Vinay, *La rente foncière*, 56–57.

65. "Discours sur la commerce des grains par M. Sellyer," [November 1789], AN F11 221.

66. Including Georges Lefebvre, notably in the essay "La Révolution française et les paysans," in his *Etudes sur la Révolution française* (Paris: Presses universitaires de France, 1963).

Chapter 2. The Sale of Grain and the Managed Conflict between Town and Country

1. AN F11 210; Lefebvre, *Great Fear*, 163.

2. Entry of July 31, 1789, AC Guise BB 14.

3. Lefebvre, *Great Fear*, 203.

4. Provincial commission to comte d'Egmont, April 27, 1789, ADA C 930.

5. Provincial commission to de Montaran (*maître des requêtes*), June 14, 1789, ADA C 913; ADA C 14.

6. The commission informed the comte d'Egmont (noble deputy to the Estates-General for Soissons) on April 27, 1789, that "le ministre nous a répondu que nous devions trouver dans notre province de quoi la pourvoir abondant et sans nuire à l'approvisionnement de la Capitale" (ADA C 930).

7. Provincial commission to intermediate bureau of Laon, May 19, 1789, ADA C 941.

8. A *muid de Soissons* was about 1,200 liters; a Parisian *muid* was about 1,800 liters.

9. ADA C 913, 941. The quotation is from the commission's letter to the intermediate bureau of Laon, June 16, 1789, ADA C 941.

10. Provincial commission to intermediate bureau of Laon, June 16, 1789, ADA C 941. Note that the commission's powers allowed its agents to follow an itinerary like that of a troop of rural beggars: from farm to farm over whole districts, with special attention to the more prosperous-looking ones. This was precisely the type of legitimacy that a troop of beggars occasionally tried to counterfeit by claiming to act "de par le Roi." Brayer quotation: chief subdelegate Brayer to intermediate bureau of Laon, June 16, 1789, ADA C 941.

11. ADA C 913, 930, 14.

12. Provincial commission to comte d'Egmont, June 22, ADA C 930.

13. ADA C 1011.

14. Cited on p. 35 of Louise Tilly, "The Food Riot as a Form of Political Conflict in France," *Journal of Interdisciplinary History* 2 (1972): 23–57, from Norman Scott Gras, *The Evolution of the English Corn Market from the Twelfth to the Eighteenth Century* (New York: Russell & Russell 1967), viii, 95–99.

15. C.-E. Labrousse, *Esquisse du mouvement des prix et des revenus en France au XVIIIe siècle* Paris: Dalloz, 1933); Tilly, "Food Riot," 23–57.

16. Labrousse, *Esquisse*, 127, 130–32.

17. Tilly, "Food Riot," 44.

18. Ibid., 38.

19. Labrousse, *Esquisse*, 166.

20. Jean Meuvret, "Les oscillations des prix des céréales au XVIIe et XVIIIe siècles en Angleterre et dans les pays du bassin parisien," *Revue d'histoire moderne et contemporaine* 16 (1969): 551–52.

21. Bernard Vonglis, *Le commerce des céréales à Reims, au XVIIIe siècle* (Reims: Université de Reims, 1980), 188, 178; AC Guise BB 14.

22. Vonglis, *Commerce des céréales*, 203.

23. There are curious inconsistencies, however. It is probable that the 3,600 livres in relief accorded Guise by the ministry of finances in the first week of July was somehow part of the bargain struck with Soissons in mid-June.

24. AC Guise BB 14.

25. Ibid.

26. Massinot to the commission of the provincial assembly, April 24, 1789, ADA C 921.

27. AC Guise HH 11.

28. See above, p. 00.

29. ADA C 935. Eight hundred *sacs* weighed about 69 tons.

30. Provincial commission to comte d'Egmont, January 21, 1789, ADA C 930; Warlemont, abbé of Bucilly, to the intermediate bureau of Laon, May 19, 1789, ADA C 1018.

31. August 23, 1789, AN Dxli 2.

32. Voulpaix municipality to intermediate bureau of Laon, August 30, 1789, ADA C 1018.

33. September 15, 1789, AN Dxli 2.

34. Hennequin, *Formation du département de l'Aisne*, 25.

35. *Demande pour la conservation du chef-lieu de département dans la ville de Soissons* (Paris: D'Houry et Debvre, 1790), 4, BN Lk7 9378.

36. Cited in Hennequin, *Formation du département de l'Aisne*, 203–4.

37. Ibid., 92.

38. Ibid., 345.

39. E. P. Thompson, "The Moral Economy of the English Crowd in the Eighteenth Century," *Past and Present* 50 (1971): 129.

40. Jacques Necker, *Sur la législation et le commerce des grains*, vol. 2 of *Mélanges d'économie politique*, ed. Eugène Daire and Gustave de Molinari (Paris: Guillaumin, 1848), 2:345.

41. Ibid., 320–21.

42. Ibid., 266.

43. Ibid., 314–15.

44. It was through *Sur la législation et le commerce des grains* that Necker's reputation as a mature, moderate statesman first began to spread. Though denounced at once by the *économistes* and by Voltaire and Condorcet as well, it earned Necker European attention: the book was reviewed in Britain, the Netherlands, and Germany, and was translated into German in 1777. See Henri Grange, *Les idées de Necker* (Paris: Librairie C. Klincksieck, 1974), 25–33; also Robert D. Harris, *Necker: Reform Statesman of the Ancien Régime* (Berkeley and Los Angeles: University of California Press, 1979), 61–66. It is interesting to note that Harris presents Necker as a pragmatic liberal seeking only to modify Turgot's program, while Grange sees him as a frank interventionist, supporting "le droit et le devoir de l'Etat d'apporter à la liberté toutes les restrictions indispensables pour le bonheur des sujets" (*Les idées de Necker*, 25). Perhaps Necker's contemporaries experienced the same confusion of opinions.

45. Antonio Gramsci, *Selections from the Prison Notebooks of Antonio Gramsci*, ed. and trans. Quintin Hoare and G. N. Smith (New York: International Publishers, 1971), 91.

46. See p. 17, above.

47. AN F11 210; Maison du roi to de Latombelle, February 2, 1789, AN O1 485.

48. May 6, 1789, ADA C 14.

49. March 22, 1789, dossier 7, AN Ba 70.

50. Abbé Hébert, "Mémoires pour servir à l'histoire de Château-Thierry" (bound ms.), 2:202–5, in AD J 1054.

51. ADA C 1014.

52. ADA C 935. We know of Noyon's request for one hundred *muids* from the provincial commission's letter to the comte d'Egmont, May 13, 1789, ADA C 930.

53. May 22, 1789, ADA C 935.

54. June 5 and May 29, 1789, ADA C 935.

55. June 12, 1789, ADA C 935.

56. June 26, 1789, ADA C 935.

57. Actually, the orthography permits two possibilities: Licourt or Lihons, both within the Amiens intendancy, the Noyon diocese, and the Peronne *élection*. The great contemporary geographer Expilly puts Licourt two leagues south-southwest and Lihons three leagues southwest of Peronne.

58. June 26, 1789, ADA C 935.

59. July 17, 1789, ADA C 935. Noyon and Chauny were both seats of bail-liages that were involved in a jurisdictional dispute of obscure origins. Lieuten-ant-general of Noyon bailliage to *garde des sceaux*, March 6, 1789, dossier of Noyon secondary bailliage, AN Ba 46.

60. Lefebvre, *Great Fear*, 186–87. See also Dinet, "Les Peurs du Beauvaisis," map facing p. 384.

61. August 14, 1789, ADA C 935.

62. Ibid.

63. ADA C 935.

64. Lefebvre, *Paysans du Nord*, 367–68.

65. Four infantry batallions and four cavalry squadrons in all, according to the *prévôt* Bouchelet de Neuville (de Neuville to the *garde des sceaux* (Keeper of the Seals), May 12, 1789, Cambrai dossier), AN BB 30 87.

66. Desgaudières, the army lieutenant who worked with the *échevins* of Cam-brai to restore order, defended himself bitterly against the *échevins'* accusations of leniency in a long letter to the *garde des sceaux*. "Le magistrat cherche à me grever . . . lorsqu'il dit avoir fait des visites [des greniers], puisqu'elles n'ont été commencés qu'elles ont été arrêtées, et il n'a rien moins fallut que cette émeute pour les y determiner car peu de jours avant M. l'Intendant lui avoit écrit . . . J'aurois pu sans doute en emploiant la force que j'avois en mains dissiper ce groupe de femmes pour la plupart . . . mais, j'ai cru devoir ceder aux prières du prèvôt et d'un échevin qui m'ont observé que c'étoient des citoyens, et sujets du Roy, qu'il fallait les ménager ce qu'a été répété par ce même échevin à un dragon, en lui disant *doucement doucement* ce sont des citoyens . . ." (May 29, 1789, Cambrai dossier, AN Ba 87). In the village of Walincourt, seven kilometers to the southeast, the very next day the peasants "s'assemblèrent, et furent demander [*sic*] au seigneur du lieu, du bled pour le prix qu'il avoit été vendu la veille à Cambrai" (municipal officers of Walincourt to the National Assembly, July 15, 1789, AN C 89).

67. Lefebvre, *Grande Peur*, 102–103, 111–12, 116–17.

Chapter 3. Begging: The Central Channel of Noncommercial Distribution

1. Soboul, *La Révolution française*, 1:164.

2. Jean-Pierre Gutton, *La société et les pauvres en Europe, XVIe–XVIIIe siècles* (Paris: Presses universitaires de France, 1974), 95–96.

3. Jacques Depauw, "Pauvres, pauvres mendiants, mendiants valides ou vaga-bonds? Les hésitations de la législation royale," *Revue d'histoire moderne et contem-poraine* 21 (1974): 401–18.

4. Jean-Pierre Gutton, *L'Etat et la mendicité dans la première moitié du XVIIIe siècle: Auvergne, Beaujolais, Forez, Lyonnais* (St-Etienne: Centre d'études foreziennes, 1973), 124–26.

5. Depauw, "Pauvres, pauvres mendiants," 415.

6. Christian Paultre, *De la répression de la mendicité et du vagabondage en France sous l'Ancien Régime* (Paris: Larose et Tenin, 1906), 394.

7. "[Cinq pourcent] des mendiants affichent leur malheur en pleine rue, cette absence de vanité ne plaît pas trop aux commissaires qui s'empressent de noter dans leurs rapports les fantaisies vestimentaires des vagabonds" (Christian Romon, "Le monde des pauvres à Paris au XVIIIe siècle," *Annales: Economies, sociétés, civilisations* 37 [1982]: 750.)

8. "Dans l'optique de ce fonctionnaire, qui est le reflet de celle de son temps, il est indigne d'un homme ou d'une femme d'aller sans chapeau, sans bas et sans souliers. Quel que soit l'état de délabrement du reste de la mise, il précise toujours quand ces éléments essentiels font défaut . . . On peut affirmer que la majorité des renfermés tente au moins de rester conforme à la norme en vigueur, par tous les moyens" (Yvonne-Elisabeth Broutin, "Les mendiants et leur costume en Normandie avant la Révolution," *Ethnologie française* 12 [1982]: 41). One is inescapably reminded of Richard Cobb's discussion of the clothing of Directory suicides in his *Death in Paris* (Oxford: Oxford University Press, 1978), 71–86.

9. However, the results of police searches were noted in the *procès-verbal* in only 37 percent of Romon's total cases (Romon, "Le monde des pauvres," 754).

10. Gutton, *La société et les pauvres*, 81, 85, 81–92.

11. Gutton, *L'Etat et la mendicité*, 97–98.

12. Olwen H. Hufton, *The Poor of Eighteenth-Century France, 1750–1789* (Oxford: Oxford University Press, 1974), 223.

13. "La déclaration de mendiants occasionnaient de fréquentes erreurs, dont souffraient des journaliers et ouvriers allant de province au province, de ville en ville en quête de travail, particulièrement ceux qui venaient de la Normandie, du Limousin, de l'Auvergne, du Dauphiné ou de la Bourgogne à l'époque des moissons ou à d'autres moments" (Camille Bloch, *L'assistance et l'Etat en France à la veille de la Révolution: Généralités de Paris, Rouen, Alençon, Orléans, Châlons, Soissons, Amiens, 1764–1790* [Paris: Picard et fils, 1908], 53).

14. Gutton, *L'Etat et la mendicité*, 103, 231–40. Of the 28 beggars brought to La Charité of St-Etienne, 20 were arrested by the *maréchaussée*. The two arrests of able-bodied adults were also to their credit.

15. Paultre, *De la répression de la mendicité*, 489–91.

16. Marie-Odile Deschamps, "Le dépôt de mendicité de Rouen (1768–1820)," *Bulletin d'histoire économique et sociale de la Révolution française* 34 (1977): 83. Broutin, "Les mendiants et leur costume," 34.

17. Ibid.

18. Ibid.

19. Cited in Paultre, *De la répression de la mendicité*, 395–97.

20. Ibid., 397–98, quotation, 400–401.

21. Abbé Malvaux, ed., *Résumé des mémoires qui ont concouru pour le prix accordé en 1777 par l'Académie des sciences, arts et belles-lettres de Châlons-sur-Marne et dont*

le sujet était: Les moyens de détruire la mendicité en France, en rendant les mendiants utiles à l'Etat sans les rendre malheureux (Châlons: Seneuze, 1779), 103–4. This work was a pastiche of the dozen or so most notable essays from the 116 contestants (see also Bloch, *L'assistance et l'Etat*, 212). The editor provided footnotes every few pages to indicate the authors of the extracts used: for this passage Malvaux cited seven names, among them Leclerc de Montlinot.

22. Paultre, *De la répression de la mendicité*, 404.

23. Lefebvre, *Paysans du Nord*, 313.

24. Bloch and Tuetey, eds., *Comité de mendicité*, 514.

25. The deputies were Porcher and Chabot. Alan Forrest, *The French Revolution and the Poor* (Oxford: Basil Blackwell, 1981), 29.

26. Alexandre Vexliard, *Introduction à la sociologie du vagabondage* (Paris: M. Rivière, 1956), 19, n. 34.

27. Expilly, *Dictionnaire*, 6:164.

28. The document is undated, but is to be found in ADA C 938 among many other May grain censuses from the arrondissement of La Fère in the Laonnais.

29. Probably 50 to 80 households were not visited at all; the census shows 186, while AN Ba 46 gives 270 *feux* (though this is surely an inflated figure for "Ribemont et dépendances"). The unit of measure for grain is not given in the document, but internal evidence suggests a local variation on the *quartel* of Laon (32.5 lb.). The town had about 75 days to wait before the new rye; a *quartel* of Laon yielded 24 to 27 pounds of bread; and the consumption per person planned by the census is anything but stable, but clusters around 3 of the unknown unit. This would correspond to a local *quartel* of 35 to 40 pounds.

30. I have used 179 as my total number of households; the document lists 186 households. Seven entries were illegible.

31. This description of the commission's project is a reconstruction from several documents. A letter of April 20 from the Soissons intermediate bureau to the provincial commission (ADA C 921) gives some details. In the same dossier is the royal *maître des requêtes* La Millière's May 20 reply on Necker's behalf to a letter from the commission. The commission's expectations are discussed in its correspondence with the Laon intermediate bureau (entry of May 12, 1789, ADA C 1014). The commission's own minutes (ADA C 913) are fire damaged. Finally, no copy of the actual questionnaire has yet been found, though 184 replies are extant (ADA C 937–40). There is no evidence that the questionnaire was sent to any other intermediate bureau than that of Laon.

32. Entry of May 5, 1789, ADA C 1014.

33. ADA C 921.

34. Bailliages and *sénéchaussées* were required to give population figures by *feux* in their minutes of election of deputies to the Estates-General. The figures for the parishes of the Laonnais are in AN Ba 46.

35. These 16 parishes are examined case by case in the dissertation version of this study: Clay Ramsay, *The Ideology of the Great Fear: The Soissonnais in 1789* (Ann Arbor, Mich.: University Microfilms, 1990), 133–41.

36. Dossier of the arrondissement of Laon, ADA C 937.

37. Dossier of the arrondissement of La Fère, ADA C 938.

38. Ibid.

39. Dossier of the arrondissement of Vervins, ADA C 940.

40. Dossier of the arrondissement of Marle, ADA C 939.

41. Dossier of the arrondissement of La Fère, ADA C 938.

42. Ibid.

43. For Henry of Doeuillet and the anonymous curé of La Fère: dossier of the arrondissement of La Fère, ADA C 938.

44. Dossier of the arrondissement of Craonne, ADA C 937.

45. This is also evident from another source, the replies to the inquiries of the *élection* assembly of Guise in January: ADA C 989.

46. Dossier of the arrondissement of Laon, ADA C 937.

47. Dossier of the arrondissement of Craonne, ADA C 937.

48. Dossier of the arrondissement of La Fère, ADA C 938.

49. Dossier of the arrondissement of Laon, ADA C 937.

50. C.A.J. Leclerc de Montlinot, *Discours qui a remporté le prix à la Société Royale d'agriculture de Soissons, en l'année 1779; sur cette question proposée par le même société: Quels sont les moyens de détruire la Mendicité, de rendre les Pauvres valides utiles, et de les secourir dans la ville de Soissons?* (Lille: C. Lehoucq, 1779), 31, BN F 25592.

51. Dossier of the arrondissement of Vervins, ADA C 940.

52. Lerdun sent the circular to the parish assembly, whereupon it was lost from view (ADA C 937, dossier of the arrondissement of Laon).

53. True vagabonds are not under discussion here. They had broken with their original parish bases long before. Local beggars extending their rounds swelled the ranks of vagabonds on the road in bad years.

54. Dossier of the arrondissement of La Fère, ADA C 938.

55. Dossier of the arrondissement of Marle, ADA C 939. Godefroy refused to give names or figures, and so skillfully that one cannot guess his exact reasons.

56. Although one does: the letter of Gobert, curé of Clacy: dossier of the arrondissement of Laon, ADA C 937.

57. Dossier of the arrondissement of Craonne, ADA C 937.

58. Dossier of the arrondissement of Laon, ADA C 937.

59. Dossier of the arrondissement of Vervins, ADA C 940.

60. Dossier of the arrondissement of La Fère, ADA C 938.

61. Dossier of the arrondissement of Craonne, ADA C 937.

62. Dossier of the arrondissement of Laon, ADA C 937.

63. Flamant provided a list of names but opposed a tax; this was his suggested alternative (dossier of the arrondissement of Craonne, ADA C 937).

64. Dossier of the arrondissement of Vervins, ADA C 940.

65. Dossier of the arrondissement of Craonne, ADA C 937.

66. Dossier of the arrondissement of Laon, ADA C 937.

67. Ibid.

68. Dossier of the arrondissement of Sissone, ADA C 939.

69. Dossier of the arrondissement of Vervins, ADA C 940.

70. Dossier of the arrondissement of La Fère, ADA C 938.

71. Bloch and Tuetey, *Comité de mendicité*, xviii–xix; Forrest, *French Revolution and the Poor*, 24. Montlinot went on to serve as counselor to the *Comité de*

mendicité of the National Assembly in 1790; bureau chief of civilian hospitals for the Commission éxecutive des secours publics in Year II; division chief in the Interior Ministry in Year VI. He died in Paris in 1805.

72. Leclerc de Montlinot, *Quels sont les moyens de detruire la mendicité*, p. 31.

73. Ibid., 64, 88, 74, 65-66.

74. C.A.J. Leclerc de Montlinot, *Etat actuel du dépôt de mendicité de la généralité de Soissons, Vème compte, année 1786*, 2d ed. (Soissons, 1789), BN R 8041. I say that he attempted statistics because his figures are internally inconsistent and should be used with extreme caution. They are cited here only as a sign of how his thought was tending.

75. C.A.J. Leclerc de Montlinot, "Dépôts de mendicité," in *Encyclopédie méthodique: Économie politique et diplomatique*, ed. J.-N. Demeunier, (Paris: Pancoucke, 1786), 2:73-74, 77.

76. C.A.J. Leclerc de Montlinot, *Etat actuel du dépôt de Soissons, précédé d'un essai sur la mendicité* (Soissons, 1789) 34, 1-2, 13-14, BN R 8047.

Chapter 4. The Course of the Great Fear in the Soissonnais

1. Quoted by Henri Dinet in "Les Peurs du Beauvaisis et du Valois, juilliet 1789," *Paris et Ile-de-France: Mémoires* 23-24 (1972-73):339-40. The original is in AN F7 3690/2. "Les Peurs du Beauvaisis et du Valois" is a book-length (194-page) article that serves as an admirable document collection for the Great Fear in the northern Parisian basin.

2. Ibid., 340-41.

3. See chapter 1, above.

4. This last hypothesis is Dinet's ("Beauvaisis et Valois," 341-42).

5. Dinet goes a little further. He believes that the original panic in Estrées-St-Denis, which also reportedly originated in a poaching incident but which developed into a different set of currents enveloping the Beauvaisis, might be the same as the incident in the forest of Compiègne (ibid., 341).

6. This sharp geological division between forest and field is not the rule throughout the Soissonnais: the particularly high quality of Valois soil appears to have sharpened the contrast in the eyes of cultivators, affecting the course of reclamation (Brunet, *Structure agraire*, 458-59).

7. Gaspard Escuyer, *Histoire de Compiègne* (c. 1825), 6:30, archived as ms. 7 in the Bibliothèque municipale de Compiègne.

8. Jacques Bernet, "La crise des subsistances à Compiègne (1788-1789)," *Bulletin de la Société historique de Compiègne* 26 (1979): 118.

9. Dinet, "Beauvaisis et Valois," 346, 374.

10. Provincial commission of the Soissonnais to de Montaran, June 14 and 20 1789, AD C 913. De Montaran was a *maître des requêtes* involved in questions of grain trade regulation under the controller-general (Jean Egret, *The French Prerevolution, 1787-1788*, trans. Wesley D. Camp [Chicago: University of Chicago Press, 1977], 16-17, 227).

11. Provincial commission to its Guise bureau, July 18, 1789, AD C 1011.

12. Dinet, "Beauvaisis et Valois," 279.

13. Ibid., 374. Dinet quotes from AC Crépy-en-Valois BB 1.

14. Dinet, "Beauvaisis et Valois," 301–2.

15. Beatrice F. Hyslop, *L'apanage de Philippe-Egalité, duc d'Orléans, 1785–1791* (Paris: Société des Etudes Robespierristes, 1965), 246.

16. Dinet, "Beauvaisis et Valois," 346.

17. Ibid., 347.

18. It did not (ibid., 374–75). The original of the letter is in AN C 134.

19. Dinet, "Beauvaisis et Valois," 374.

20. AN Ba 35 is rich in complaints to Necker on this score, dating back to the months of advance work on the Estates-General.

21. Lefebvre, *Grande Peur*, 218.

22. Soissons notables to duc de Liancourt, July 27, 1789, AN C 89.

23. Michaux, *Histoire de Villers-Cotterets*, 84.

24. Ibid.

25. "La peur née au nord de Béthisy toucha Pierrefonds; celle qui regnait à Crépy-en-Valois s'avança jusqu'à Villers-Cotterets" (Dinet, "Beauvaisis et Valois," 375).

26. Ibid., 340.

27. Ibid., 275.

28. AN C 89.

29. G. Dumas, *Guide des archives de l'Aisne* (Laon, 1971), 246.

30. M. Leroux, *Histoire de la ville de Soissons* (Soissons, 1839), 2:360.

31. Hyslop, *Apanage*, 246.

32. AD C 930.

33. Dinet, "Beauvaisis et Valois," 277, 281.

34. Leroux, *Soissons*, 2:361.

35. Dinet, "Beauvaisis et Valois," 376. As Dinet indicates, the copies sent to Noyon (ADO 360) and to Guise (ADA C 1011) are virtually identical.

36. Soissons permanent committee to Rochefoucauld-Liancourt, August 5, 1789, Dossier C.II, no. 69, AN C 90.

37. AC Laon HH 16.

38. Entry of July 28, 1789, AC Venizel D1.

39. AC Braine D1.

40. Duc de Gesvres to duc de Liancourt-Rochefoucauld, July 28, 1789, AN C 89.

41. Hébert, *Mémoires pour servir a l'histoire de Château-Thierry*, 2:308–312.

42. Dinet, "Beauvaisis et Valois," 380.

43. Ibid., 381.

44. Ibid., 381–82.

45. Ibid., 382–84.

46. Lefebvre, *Grande Peur*, 218.

47. Escuyer, *Compiègne*, 6:20; AC Compiègne 1D1; Bernet, "La crise," 111.

48. Dinet, "Beauvaisis et Valois," 229.

49. June 30, 1789, ADA C 14. *Prévôtés* were anomalous police jurisdictions by the late eighteenth century, largely superseded throughout France by bailliage or *sénéchaussée* structures. The *prévôt* of Verberie had his own grudges against the

Crépy bailliage officers; at the March bailliage assembly to elect Estates-General deputies, he led other Verberiens in walking out of the meeting without signing the minutes, apparently because of the manipulations of de Limon, a high official of the Orléans apanage (anonymous correspondent to Necker, April 7, 1789, AN Ba 35).

50. Dinet, "Beauvaisis et Valois," 346. Dambry's letter appeared in the *Journal de Paris*, no. 211, July 30, 1789, p. 949.

51. Dinet, "Beauvasis et Valois," 347, 310–11.

52. Ibid., 228.

53. Lefebvre, *Great Fear*, 123.

54. Dinet, "Beauvaisis et Valois," 232. On July 28, the day after the Fear, Bedel (royal prosecutor) and Duchatellier (first town magistrate), traveled to Paris to request two hundred *septiers* of wheat.

55. Ibid., 307–8. It is possible that Pont reactivated its militia under the impulsion of the duc de Lévis, as did Senlis, Beaumont-sur-Oise, and Pontoise.

56. Lefebvre and Dinet both mention a memoir written by a woman of Creil during the Consulate: O. Boutanquoi, "Les souvenirs d'une femme du peuple: Marie-Victoire Monnard, de Creil, 1777–1802," *Comptes rendus et memoires de la Société d'histoire et d'archéologie de Senlis*, 6th ser., 1 (1925–26): 68–70. Dinet points to internal evidence of editorial tampering in Boutanquoi's rendering, however ("Beauvaisis et Valois," 348). Lefebvre quotes the memoir briefly in "Documents sur la Grand Peur de 1789 dans la région parisienne," *Annales historiques de la Révolution française* 11 (1934): 158.

57. Dinet, "Beauvaisis et Valois," 293.

58. Poissy and St-Germain (today St-Germain-en-Lay), neighboring towns, both on the Seine, both about 15 kilometers west of Paris, had little need of imported *malfaiteurs* to set off riots (Dinet, "Beauvaisis et Valois," 237, 251–52).

59. Ibid., 294.

60. Ibid., 296–97. Dinet's source here is AC Senlis.

61. Ibid., 372.

62. Ibid., 256.

63. Ibid., 372.

64. Hennequin, *Formation du département de l'Aisne*, 86.

65. G. Lefebvre, "Documents sur la Grande Peur: Clermontois, Valois et Soissonnais," *Annales historiques de la Révolution française* 10 (1933): 172–73. Or see Dinet, "Beauvaisis et Valois," 373.

66. Dinet, "Beauvaisis et Valois," 297–98.

67. A. J. Gorsas, ed., *Courrier de Versailles à Paris, et de Paris à Versailles* (Paris, 1789), 2:40–42. Or see Dinet, "Beauvaisis et Valois," 349–50.

68. Dinet, "Beauvaisis et Valois," 224.

69. AN C 134.

70. *Arrêté* of the Paris *hôtel de ville*, July 20, 1789, AN C 134; Bernet, "La crise," 116.

71. Dinet, "Beauvaisis et Valois," 343, 346, 289; Bernet, "La crise," 117.

72. Lefebvre: "[The Great Fear] also went up the Oise valley via Ribécourt and Noyon and indeed seems to have made good progress in this direction, for an

inquiry into the attack on the Château de Frétoy notes that it was in Muirancourt to the north of Noyon, at six o'clock on the morning of the 27th" (*Great Fear*, 186). The Muirancourt reference is more ambiguous than Lefebvre implies. It comes from the testimony of the syndic of Muirancourt, Joseph l'Herondelle, who was relating the seizure of grain from Muirancourt's mill by a peasant troop between 7:00 and 8:00 A.M. (AN C 92). Such peasant projects were known in advance to the whole neighborhood, and the language used later about them by witnesses was not always distinct form the words and imagery of the Great Fear. For a full discussion of the events at Frétoy and Muirancourt, see chapter 7, below. Also see Dinet, "Beauvaisis et Valois," 343.

73. AD C 935.

74. Dinet, "Beauvaisis et Valois," 343. The original of the quoted passage is in AN F7 3690/2.

75. See also the discussion of polyculture versus cereal culture, with the Noyonnais as one example, in chapter 1, above.

76. Brunet, *Structure agraire*, 360–62. There were five hundred hectares of vines in 1789 in the canton of Noyon (that is, within the canton boundaries drawn in 1790–91).

77. Ibid., 285; Guy Ikni, unpublished ms. (1981) and personal communication (1990). Guy Ikni's examination of municipal archive copies preserved in the Archives départmentales de l'Oise led him to an average figure of 27 percent of the land under peasant ownership in 1791, with sharp variations from parish to parish. Since the sale of national lands began here in December 1790, 27 percent represents a slight overevaluation for 1789. This slim share of land could support more small proprietors than it would on the plain, due to the different crops cultivated.

78. AC Chauny BB 33.

79. AN O1 486.

80. Lefebvre, *Great Fear*, 186.

81. Ibid., 187.

82. Intendant d'Agay to Versailles, May 13, 1789, AN F11 221.

83. The merchant Berleux actually wrote the royal household for an opinion as to whether the militia's royal statute of 1663 required him to march in the Sunday parade. Versailles concluded that it did not. It is indicative of the Maison du roi's baffling sense of priorities in this year of 1789 that its letter to the *lieutenant du roi* d'Estouilly (August 7) is one of the longest in the register (AN O1 486).

84. Bacquet of St-Quentin to the National Assembly, June 15, 1789, AN Dxli 2; Maison du roi to d'Agay, intendant of Amiens, June 14, 1789, AN O1 485.

85. Picardy's volatile state is referred to obliquely in the Third-Estate cahier of the Château-Thierry bailliage (AN Ba 32) and openly in the nobles' cahier of Crépy-en-Valois (AN Ba 35). The clergy's electors for the latter bailliage acted in concert with the nobles to warn Versailles that Picard troubles might cross intendancies.

86. Register entry of May 11, 1789, AC Guise BB 14; provincial commission

to the comte d'Egmont, May 13, 1789, ADA C 930; deliberations of the commission for May 23, 1789, ADA C 913.

87. AC Guise BB 14.

88. ADA C 1011.

89. AC Guise BB 14.

90. AC Laon BB 46.

91. Lefebvre, *Great Fear*, 71; AC Laon BB 46. The commune drafted a letter of support for the National Assembly that displayed its political sophistication, as well as the *dernier cri* in rhetoric. It lauded "la conduite . . . [des] . . . citoyens de Paris pour détruire les efforts combinés, réunis dans le nouveau ministère, du despotisme judiciaire, militaire et ministériel . . . une Coalition aristocratique des plus perverses" and declared that "dans un si grand danger, il ne faut écouter que le *solus Regis et populi* qui est la Suprême Loi." The commune's early picking up of *aristocratique* as a term of abuse is itself evidence of excellent Parisian connections.

92. AC Laon BB 46.

93. Ibid.

94. AC Parfondeval D1. The translation is literal and follows the original syntax in order to show the literacy level of the persons involved.

95. For Amiens, see *Documents pour servir à l'histoire de la Révolution française dans la ville d'Amiens* (Paris: Picard, 1894), 2:273–74. For Arras, see Louis Jacob, "La Grande Peur en Artois," *Annales historiques de la Révolution française* 13 (1936): 139–42.

96. Dinet, "Beauvaisis et Valois," 331. Dinet learned this from AC Pont-St-Maxence, deliberations of June 8, so apparently the Clermont *procureur* sent the Pont municipality a pointed note.

97. Dinet, "Beauvaisis et Valois," 313, 301.

98. Aisne dossier, AN F11 210. Emphasis in original. Dinet remarks that Clermont's municipal deliberations, otherwise complete, are silent about the Fear ("Beauvaisis et Valois," 329).

99. Lefebvre, *Great Fear*, 142.

Chapter 5. The Semantics of the Great Fear

1. George Rudé, "Ideology and Popular Protest," *Historical Reflections* 3 (1976): 69.

2. Gramsci, *Prison Notebooks*, 377.

3. Ibid., 376–77.

4. Ibid., 349.

5. A basic bibliography of works on Revolutionary vocabulary would begin with Régine Robin, *Histoire et linguistique* (Paris: A. Colin, 1973). Robin's book contains invaluable discussions on method along with examples of analyses by Geffroy, Guilhaumou, and others. For Robin's own work with language, see her *La société française en 1789: Semur-en-Auxois* (Paris: Plon, 1970), especially pp. 229–343; and her "Fief et seigneurie dans le droit et l'idéologie juridique à la fin du XVIIIe siècle," *Annales historiques de la Révolution française* 43 (1971): 554–

602, which is perhaps the best-realized work in this genre. A noteworthy article by Jacques Guilhaumou is "Idéologies, discours, et conjoncture en 1793," *Dialectiques*, no. 10–11 (1975): 33–58. A wide range of material by these and other authors can be found in the lithographed *Bulletin du Centre d'analyse du discours de l'Université de Lille III* and *Travaux de lexicometrie et de lexicologie politique* (Ecole normale supérieure de St-Cloud). For a different approach, inspired by cultural anthropology, see William H. Sewell, Jr., *Work and Revolution in France* (Cambridge: Cambridge University Press, 1980), especially pp. 62–142.

6. Régine Robin comments lucidly on Hébert in *Histoire et linguistique*, 41. Abstracts of Geffroy's work on Saint-Just and Guilhaumou's work on Hébert also appear in this volume.

7. Robin, *Histoire et linguistique*, 16.

8. Jacques Godechot, "Linguistique et la Révolution française," *Annales historiques de la Révolution française* 56 (1984): 301. Godechot is quoting his own 1972 comment on Robin's work.

9. This summary is from Charles Fillmore, "Types of Lexical Information," in *Semantics: An Interdisciplinary Reader in Philosophy, Linguistics, and Psychology*, ed. Danny D. Steinberg and Leon A. Jakobovits (London: Cambridge University Press, 1971), 370–92. For a more extensive discussion, see Charles Fillmore, "The Case for Case," in *Universals in Linguistic Theory*, ed. Emmon Bach and Robert T. Harms (New York: Holt Rinehart & Winston, 1968), 1–88.

10. In the village of Parfondeval, an altercation between curé and syndic continued through the spring of 1789: "Le syndic nous a représenté que malgré les plaintes par nous précédemment faites, à . . . maître Duguet notre curé à l'occasion de la sonnerie des cloches à l'issu de la messe paroissiale . . . laquelle interrompt entièrement les assemblées de paroisse qui se font au devant de l'église et empêchent d'entendre tant la lecture des ordres du roi que les propositions qui s'y fonts concernant la ditte communauté ledit Sieur Duguet continue ladite sonnerie, especialement le jour de la circoncision à l'issue de la messe ledit syndic qu'il l'avoit fait cesser et fait sonner l'assemblée pour nous . . . il en a été empeché par la reprise de ladite sonnerie ledit syndic a été une seconde fois faire cesser les sonneurs mais ledit Sr Duguet est accouru fort échauffé leur commander absolument de continuer ladite sonnerie ce qui a été forcée de se séparer et de remettre la lecture à un autre jour" (entry of January 17, 1789, AC Parfondeval D1). By May this question of turf had been resolved, though we do not know exactly how. Parfondeval was in the northeast corner of the Soissons intendancy, near Rozoy-sur-Serre.

11. Copy of Enghien-Montmorency's municipal deliberations for July 22, 1789 and *procès-verbal* of general assembly of August 2, 1789—both in AN Dxxix 37.

12. Dinet, "La Grande Peur en Hurepoix," 113–14.

13. Dinet, "Beauvaisis et Valois," 251.

14. *Procès-verbal* of Voulpaix municipality addressed to Laon intermediate bureau, August 30, 1789, ADA C 1018.

15. Comte d'Esterhazy to the *garde des sceaux*, August 22, 1789, AN BB30 79.

16. Dinet, "Beauvaisis et Valois," 266–67. Lefebvre also mentions the incident in *Great Fear*, 45.

17. Dinet, "La Grand Peur en Hurepoix," 142–45. The quotation is from the declaration of the bailiff Graville, July 27, 1789, in AN Y 15020.

18. Lefebvre, *Grande Peur*, 86 (my translation; White's is inadequate here).

19. See chapter 4, above.

20. Laon municipality, July 25, 1789, AC Laon BB 46.

21. Gorsas, *Courrier*, 2:132; Abbeville municipal officers and deputies of "ordres et corps," August 20, 1789, AN Dxli 2. Of 41 examples collected, 28 (68 percent) use *bruit* as either object or instrument in a sentence or phrase. The Fillmore case breakdown is as follows: agent, 6; counteragent, 2; object, 17; result, 1, instrument, 11; source, 3; goal, 0; experiencer, 1.

22. Some form of *répandre* appears with *bruit* in 22 out of 41 cases, or 54 percent of the time.

23. J.-P.-L. de Luchet, *Journal de la Ville*, August 27, 1789, quoted in Dinet, "La Grande Peur en Hurepoix," 189; intermediate bureau of Noyon, June 26, 1789, ADA C 935; Gorsas, *Courrier*, 2:109.

24. Gorsas, *Courrier*, 2:132; Maison du roi, August 5, 1789, AN O1 486.

25. Compiègne municipality to electors of Paris, July 20, 1789, AN C 134; entry of July 28, 1789, *Receuil des procès-verbaux de l'Assemblée des représentants de la Commune de Paris, du 25 juillet au 18 septembre 1789* (Paris, 1789), 9; Duc de Gesvres, July 28, 1789, AN C 89.

26. Royal proclamation of August 9, 1789, signed by comte de St-Priest, AN AD1 92; curés of Verchin to the *garde des sceaux*, received August 31, 1789, AN BB30 79.

27. *Arch. Parl.*, 8:311. The speaker was Mounier from the Dauphiné, later to resign.

28. Voulpaix municipality, August 30, 1789, ADA C 1018; Amiens militia officers [probably September 1789], AN Dxxix 17; testimony of an eau-de-vie excise tax collector in Hamel (near Douai), December 10, 1789, AN Dxxix 36.

29. Petition of "femme Dorimont" to *garde des sceaux*, received August 17, 1789, AN BB30 79.

30. Soissons provincial commission, August 1, 1789, ADA C 1011.

31. The sample includes 10 occurrences of *rumeur*. Four out of 10 describe persons in authority constrained to specific actions by *rumeur*; 9 out of 10 relate *rumeur* to popular action or the danger thereof. The Fillmore case breakdown is agent, 1; counteragent, 2; object, 6; result, 1.

32. Argenteuil municipality, about July 20, 1789, quoted in Dinet, "Beauvaisis et Valois," 316; lieutenant of hussars posted in Château-Thierry, September 7, 1789, ADA F2 354.

33. Unknown clerk in controller-general's office, October 1789, AN H1 1453; Douai municipality, August 31, 1789, AN C 89; Douai militia officers, December 10, 1789, AN Dxxix 36.

34. C.-F. Montjoie [Montjoye], *Histoire de la Révolution de France et de l'Assemblée Nationale* (Paris, 1792), 3:144; Soissons provincial commission, July 29, 1789, ADA C 1011.

35. Gorsas, *Courrier*, 1:309–10.

36. Duc de Nivernais in St-Ouen, July 15, 1789, quoted in Dinet, "Beauvaisis et Valois," 315; Montjoie, *Histoire de la Révolution*, 3:51.

37. The deputy Duport in the National Assembly, July 28, 1789, *Arch. Parl.*, 8:293; comte d'Esterhazy, August 22, 1789, AN BB30 79; Etampes municipality, July 23, 1789, quoted in Dinet, "La Grande Peur en Hurepoix," 157. The sample includes 15 occurrences of *nouvelle*, with a Fillmore case breakdown as follows: agent, 7; object, 8.

38. See n. 30 above.

39. Maison du roi, August 13, 1789, AN O1 486.

40. J. Le Scène Desmaisons, ed., *Feuille politique* (Paris), no. 20, July 28, 1789.

41. See n. 9 to Introduction, above.

42. D'Agay, intendant of Amiens, to Villedeuil, *sécrétaire d'état* of the royal household, May 13 and 28, 1789, AN F11 221.

43. *Rélation d'une partie des troubles de la France, pendant des années 1789 et 1790, suivie de réflexions sur le moyen d'en arrêter les progrès* (Paris, 1790), 27, AN AD1 92; Noyon intermediate bureau, August 7, 1789, ADA C 935.

44. Hébert, *Mémoires*, 2:202; *maître de la porte* (gatemaster) of Château-Thierry, July 30, 1789, AN Dxxix 32.

45. *Receuil des procès-verbaux de la Commune de Paris*, session of July 31, 1789, p. 3. The same source provides a quite parallel example: "Onze citoyens . . . animés par le seul sentiment de la Justice, ont conçu et éxécuté le projet de dissiper, à eux seules, quatre mille brigands, qui pilloient un bateau de blé, expédié pour la subsistance de Paris . . . mais . . . leur succès n'avoit pu empêcher la détention d'un de leurs concitoyens, qui . . . était exposé à la rage d'une populace reprimée dans son brigandage, et irritée de sa défaite" (session of August 4, 1789, p. 2).

46. Gachet de Sainte-Suzanne, *prévôt général de maréchaussée*, Paris intendancy, April 29, 1789; *maréchaussée* report of Fontainebleau brigade, July 31, 1789— both quoted by Dinet, "La Grande Peur en Hurepoix," 115–16, 184–85.

47. Dossier 57, AN C 89.

48. Letter to National Assembly, October 23, 1789, AN Dxxix 45.

49. Militia officers of Bailleul to the National Assembly, AN Dxxix 19.

50. Montjoie, *Histoire de la Révolution*, 1:102.

51. Savoyards were feared in the southeast, Spaniards in the southwest, and the English south of the Loire and at the port of Brest. The Moors were feared in Aquitaine, along with Poles and Croats (Lefebvre, *Grande Peur*).

52. *Rélation*, 64; Montjoie, *Histoire de la Révolution*, 2:144.

53. Provost of mounted police Duguey to intendant Blossac, July 28, 1789, Aisne dossier, AN F11 210.

54. AN C 134.

55. Hébert, *Mémoires*, 2:308.

56. Letter of *maréchaussée* brigadier Noël to the National Assembly, July 24, 1789, AN C 134; Jean-Pierre-Louis de Luchet, *Journal de la Ville*, August 27, 1789, quoted in Dinet, "La Grande Peur en Hurepoix," 189.

57. *Arch. Parl.*, 8:351.

58. Montjoie, *Histoire de la Révolution*, 1:91.

59. *Arch. Parl.*, 8:344.

60. Montjoie, *Histoire de la Révolution*, 1:56.

61. Ibid., 1:91.

62. Ibid., 4:63.

63. The *pacte de famine* was a current rumor under Louis XV; see Lefebvre, *Grande Peur*, 33. A 1789 version of the *pacte de famine* is presented in J. G. G. Le Prévôt de Beaumont, *Dénonciation d'un Pacte de Famine générale, au roi Louis XV; ouvrage manuscrit, trouvé à la Bastille le 14 juillet dernier, et contenant des découvertes fort intéressantes sur les malversations et les déprédations sécrètes de quelques hommes d'Etat* (Paris, [1789–90?]). Montjoie was familiar with this pamphlet and used it as a "source," though it is hardly royalist in inspiration.

64. Montjoie, *Histoire de la Révolution*, 3:136.

65. Ibid., 3:136.

66. Régine Robin, "Le champ sémantique de 'féodalité' dans les cahiers de doléances généraux de 1789," *Bulletin du Centre d'analyse du discours de l'Université de Lille III*, no. 2 (1975): 80.

67. Robin, *Histoire et linguistique*, 151.

68. *Arch. Parl.*, 8:344 (unnamed member); Douai militia, October 18, 1789, AN Dxxix 36; Maison du roi to duc de Gesvres, August 5, 1789, AN O1 486; Montjoie, *Histoire de la Révolution*, 3:37; the intendant d'Agay of Amiens, April 30, 1789, AN H1 1453.

69. Brayer (*délégué général*) to Necker, draft, September 7, 1789, AD C 6.

70. First quotation in sentence: the intendant d'Agay of Amiens, April 30, 1789, AN H 1453. Remaining two quotations: *Receuil des procès-verbaux de la Commune de Paris*, August 6, 1789, pp. 11, 13.

71. *Cahier* of the clergy, bailliage of Vermandois, AN Ba 46.

72. AN Dxxix 36; Escuyer, *Histoire de Compiègne*, 6:32 (copied here from AC Compiègne, 1D1).

73. AN BB30 79; Douai dossier, AN Dxxix 36; *La Révolution française dans la ville d'Amiens*, 2:259.

74. Montjoie, *Histoire de la Révolution*, 5:101.

75. Ibid., 5:105–66.

76. Ibid., 5:106.

77. Ibid.

78. Ibid., 5:107.

79. Ibid.

80. Ibid.

81. July 17, 1789, AC Laon BB 46.

82. Comité militaire d'Amiens, *Réflexions sur l'arrêté des officiers-municipaux et counseil permanent de la ville d'Amiens, du 11 décembre: Pour servir de suite à l'exposé de la conduite des membres composants ci-devant le Comité militaire de ladite ville* (Abbeville: L.-A. Deverité, 1789), 12, BN 4° Lk7 175).

83. Officers of the *garde nationale* of Bailleul (Flandre) to the National Assembly, January 15, 1790, AN Dxxix 19.

84. Robert Legrand, ed., *Babeuf avant 1790: Lettres à sa femme*, Aspects de la

Révolution en Picardie, no. 13 (Abbeville, 1970), 34; anonymous correspondent to National Assembly, AN Dxxix 34.

85. Letter of December 22, 1789, AN Dxxix 37.

86. AN Dxxix 34.

87. Ibid.

88. Ibid.

89. Ibid.

Chapter 6. The Practice of Public Order in 1789

1. Gramsci, *Prison Notebooks*, 265–66.

2. Quoted by Jean-Pierre Gutton in *La sociabilité villageoise dans l'ancienne France: solidarités et voisinages du XVIe au XVIIIe siècle* (Paris: Hachette, 1979), 150.

3. Nicole Castan, *Justice et répression en Languedoc à l'époque des Lumières* (Paris: Flammarion, 1980), 9.

4. The deputy was Prieur of Châlons-sur-Marne, speaking on July 31, 1789 (*Arch. Parl.*, 8:377).

5. The phrase is taken from the Château-Thierry municipal officers' letter to the *garde des sceaux* Champion de Cicé regarding the arson of a cavalry barracks, March 3, 1790, AN BB30 79.

6. See Michael R. Weisser, *Crime and Punishment in Early Modern Europe* (Brighton, England: Harvester, 1979), 14–15.

7. In the late eighteenth century, "la loi . . . stipule, en effet, qu'en matière criminelle la transaction vaut entre les parties, à condition de ne pas imposer silence à la partie publique . . . " (Castan, *Justice et répression*, 18).

8. Soissons dossier, AN BB30 69.

9. Timothy J. A. LeGoff and Donald M. G. Sutherland, "The Revolution and the Rural Community in Eighteenth-Century Brittany," *Past and Present*, no. 62 (1974):104.

10. Robert M. Schwartz, *Policing the Poor in Eighteenth-Century France* (Chapel Hill: University of North Carolina Press, 1988), 183–84.

11. Ibid., 22. Schwartz bases this finding on a sample of 271 cases drawn from the period 1768–88.

12. Ibid., 222, 179–81, 187–98. The *maréchaussée* captured the young man in question, who went by the nickname "Namur," and held him for 32 months while trying to substantiate the charges made by inhabitants of Trevières. Finally Namur was turned over to the *dépôt de mendicité*. Other than begging, vagrancy within a very narrow circuit, and the attitude of a *mauvais sujet*, no charges could be lodged against him.

13. Iain Cameron, *Crime and Repression in the Auvergne and the Guyenne, 1720–1790* (Cambridge: Cambridge University Press, 1981), 213–16.

14. The low figure is cited by Julius R. Ruff in *Crime, Justice, and Public Order in Old Regime France: The Sénéchaussée of Libourne and Bazas, 1696–1789* (London: Croom Helm, 1984), 47. The high figure comes from official correspondence in eastern Languedoc examined by Castan (*Justice et repression*, 116).

15. Ruff, *Crime, Justice, and Public Order*, 45–47.

16. Cameron, *Crime and Repression*, 212.

17. Ruff, *Crime, Justice, and Public Order*, 156–58.

18. Cameron, *Crime and Repression*, 238.

19. For a comparative view of this phenomenon across European societies, see Geoffrey Best, *War and Society in Revolutionary Europe, 1770–1870* (London: Fontana, 1982), especially 16–17. For an admirable study of the question in an English context, see Tony Hayter, *The Army and the Crowd in Mid-Georgian England* (London: Macmillan, 1978).

20. In Guise on September 25, 1789, a general assembly foundered on several issues, among them the mayor's arrangements for lodging a regiment that had arrived suddenly from Valenciennes. The mayor denied the charge that he had secretly requested the regiment. The assembly grew so heated that the municipal officers retreated to the mayor's house to draw up a *procès-verbal* (AN Dxxix 40).

In Soissons, a petition to the National Assembly from an imprisoned resident, Landieu, pungently expresses what billeting was like. "Je ne peux vous exprimer, Messeigneurs, la gêne que j'en éprouve, outre que je suis logé étroitement pour la famille nombreux dont je suis le chef, ayant trois enfans et ma femme enceinte du quatrième, c'est que l'un des deux soldats pourrit mes linges et matelas, ayant le malheur de lâcher ses eaux [au] lit. Ce soldat, compagnie de Saint-Jean, est déserté il y a dix jours, hier il a rejoint sa garnison; voulant reprendre le même logement chez moi, ma femme, sensible à la perte de notre mobilier, l'a refusée." A month earlier, the Landieu household had been left out of a general reshuffling of soldiers' quarters that they had counted on to free them of their guest. In a confrontation with the municipal officers, members of the permanent committee, and the company sergeant, Landieu lost his temper and was locked up. The National Assembly's correspondence committee was entirely sympathetic; its notation indicates that the reply should insist upon Landieu's release. October 27, 1789, AN Dxxix 76.

21. Castan, *Justice et répression*, 199. The quotation is from the consuls of Gignac in Languedoc in 1787.

22. The response of the *échevins* of cambrai to the riot of May 6–7, 1789, illustrates this concern well. The presence of four batallions of infantry and four cavalry squadrons may have made the *échevins* more, not less, indulgent toward the rioters. See chapter 2 above, particularly n. 66.

23. Very old soldiers: after 1778 brigadiers were required to have no less than 16 years of active service on their record. Exceptions were made for sons of brigadiers (called *enfants du corps*), who could enter the *maréchaussée* directly (Cameron, *Crime and Repression*, 43–44).

24. Ibid., 133–37.

25. This is particularly Cameron's argument *Crime and Repression*, 257).

26. Comte d'Esterhazy to *garde des sceaux* Barentin, August 12, 1789, AN BB30 87. A similar letter followed on August 12, 1789 (AN BB30 79), to which the *garde des sceaux* replied on August 28, 1789.

27. *Garde des sceaux* to comte d'Esterhazy, August 28, 1789, AN BB30 79.

28. The practice of clemency is a rich area for investigation whose possibilities

can only be hinted at here. Appeals for clemency were written by the kin, neighbors, or local administrators of those convicted. An unusual number may have been written by women, and the role of highly placed wives in pleading for pardons was not just a literary convention. The research for this study chanced upon seven appeals relating to events in Flandre, Hainaut, and northern Picardy. Three of these were written by women—a striking circumstance, despite the smallness of the sample. These include a letter from Mme. Necker to the mayor of Guise, describing her efforts to obtain pardons for smugglers (August 11, 1789, AC Guise BB 14); as well as a letter written by the grandmother of a young woman sentenced to hanging for her role in the Cambrai riot of May 6–7, addressed to the comtesse d'Esterhazy (wife of the *gouvernement's* commandant), and forwarded by her to the *garde des sceaux* Barentin (Agnes Arnould to comtesse d'Esterhazy, [probably late May 1789], AN BB30 87). These pleas are of great interest because they show men and women of different classes struggling to argue and persuade within the conceptual framework of old-regime public order.

29. Cameron, *Crime and Repression*, 234; *garde des sceaux* Champion de Cicé to the *procureur général* Joly de Fleury, defining the extent of the May 21 royal council decree, December 24, 1789, AN BB30 89.

30. Jean-Baptiste Duvergier, ed., *Collection complète des lois et décrets d'intérêt général, traités internationaux, arrêtés, circulaires, instructions, etc.* (Paris: Guyot et Scribe, 1824), 1:45.

31. Ibid., 1:46–47.

32. Ibid., 1:69.

33. Ibid., 1:27–28.

34. Ibid., 1:47–48.

35. Duvergier ed., *Collection*, 1:72–73.

36. Ibid., 1:62–63.

37. Ibid. For further evidence from royal household papers and Assembly debates of the conspiracy explanations that made the decrees of August 10 and October 21 plausible, see the dissertation version of this study, Ramsay, *Ideology of the Great Fear*, 299–302.

38. Egret, *The French Prerevolution*, 65.

39. Gutton, *Sociabilité*, 85. The quotation is from AC Noyales D1. The amount settled on was 24 livres.

40. Armand Brette, *Receuil de documents rélatifs à la convocation des Etats-Generaux de 1789* (Paris: Imprimerie Nationale, 1894), 1:76–77 (regulations of January 24, 1789, art. 25).

41. In Moussy-Verneuil, 11 kilometers west of Craonne, the king's proclamation to call the Estates-General was read on March 8, 1789; the next entry is on April 3, 1791 (AC Moussy-Verneuil D1). In Villeneuve-sur-Fère, 4 kilometers southwest of Fère-en-Tardenois, notes were kept of the receipt of decrees and official letters, but no municipal deliberations were recorded between March 1789 and November 1791 (AC Villeneuve-sur-Fere D1).

42. Noyon intermediate bureau to Soissons provincial commission, May 31, 1789, ADA C 935.

43. Noyon intermediate bureau to Soissons provincial commission, September 18, 1789, ADA C 935.

44. Municipal deliberations of Venizel, July 28 to November 8, 1789, AC Venizel D1.

45. For instance, de Fliscicourt of the Abbeville (Picardy) presidial court to the *garde des sceaux* Barentin on August 29, 1789, AN BB30 66. De Fliscicourt brought up the contradiction between the *maréchaussée*'s emergency authority and the stipulation in the August 10 decree that sentencing be delayed in cases related to peasant revolts and the Great Fear.

46. AN BB30 89.

47. *Garde des sceaux* Champion de Cicé to the *procureur général*, December 24, 1789, AN BB30 89.

48. Further evidence of this confusion in connection with the fear of grain exportation into the Austrian Netherlands is provided in the dissertation version of this study, Ramsay, *Great Fear*, 310–16. Another case of interest should be mentioned in this connection: that of the Third-Estate elector Dherbecourt of Eswars in Flandre. Dherbecourt encouraged inhabitants to flout the Parlement of Flandre at a village reading of one of its *arrêts* in September 1789. The prevotal court at Valenciennes took on the case with the Parlement's blessing, but this engendered criticism from elsewhere in the judiciary. The prevotal judge Demeaulx had to defend his initiative to the *garde des sceaux* in a letter of January 7, 1790 (AN BB30 79). There are several more documents concerning Dherbecourt in AN Dxxix 29. The case is mentioned by Lefebvre in *Paysans du Nord*, 373, 384, 389.

49. Articles demanding the suppression of the *gabelle* are to be found in the following *cahiers de bailliage*: Second and Third Estates of the baillage of Château-Thierry, AN Ba 32; First and Third Estates, Crépy-en-Valois (the second requested some "replacement", AN Ba 35; all three Estates of Vermandois, plus the *cahier réuni* (united *cahier* of all Estates) of the secondary bailliage of La Fère, AN (Ba 46), and strong remarks from the Laon municipality, AC Laon BB 46; First and Third Estates, Soissons, AN Ba 80; and Third Estate, Villers-Cotterets (the clergy asked only for a price reduction), AN Ba 86. Just outside the northwestern limits of the Soissons intendancy, the Second and Third Estates of St-Quentin and the parish *cahier* of Urvillers also rejected the *gabelle* (AN Ba 70).

50. ANF11 210.

51. ADA C 935; Ernest Semichon, *Histoire de la ville d'Aumale (Seine-Inférieure et de ses institutions depuis les temps anciens jusqu'à nos jours* (Paris and Rouen, 1862), 2:363.

52. Maison du roi to chief subdelegate Maugendre in Amiens, August 27, 1789, AN O1 486; notation on Doullens dossier of *garde des sceaux*'s office, AN BB30 79.

53. Cressy is nine kilometers northeast of Roye. Cressy also put carters under house arrest on market days. The mayor, the permanent committee, and the militia were of one mind in this well-organized community (D'Agay, intendant of Amiens, to the comte de St-Priest, November 21, 1789, AN F11 221).

54. The *droits d'aides* were applied primarily to alcoholic drinks; in Roye this meant cider above all (Maison du roi to Roye municipality, November 27, 1789, AN O1 486).

55. Though a militia had been established on October 19, there is no indication in the municipal register that the town's officers called it out. Even before the disturbance was over, the officers marked the scapegoats they would need for exemplary punishment: "Plusieurs des MM. auroient dit que la voix publique accusoit les nommés Tetis et Beauget dit 'trompette' d'avoir été les auteurs du tumulte . . . Considérant que ces deux particuliers déjà repris de justice inspirent aux bons citoyens de justes craintes, qu'il y a tout à appréhender qu'ils n'aient formé le funeste projet de troubler la tranquillité publique" (entry of November 20, 1789, AC Laon BB 46). See also Melleville, *Histoire de la ville de Laon*, 2:321.

56. Copy of minutes of *greffe du bailliage*, Crépy-en-Valois, December 4, 1789, AN BB30 89; the quotation is from a *mémoire* of Crépy's municipality to the National Assembly, December 8, 1789, AN Dxxix 34.

57. See the letter of *prévôt de maréchaussée* Duguey, quoted in full in chapter 4, above.

58. Noyon intermediate bureau to Soissons provincial commission, August 14, 1789, ADA C 935.

59. Escuyer, *Histoire de Compiègne*, 6:30.

60. Syndic of Coincy to Château-Thierry permanent committee, September 7, 1789, ADA F2 356.

61. Crépy-en-Valois municipal committee to correspondence committee of National Assembly, September 25, 1789, AN Dxxix 34.

62. See Arlette Brosselin, "Pour en histoire de la forêt française au XXe siècle," *Revue d'histoire économique et sociale* 55 (1977): 92–94.

63. Dauchy [prefect], *Statistique du départment de l'Aisne* (Paris; Year X [1801–02]), 16.

64. ADA C 1011.

65. Undated *mémoire* (October–November 1789] of Maîtrise des eaux et forêts to National Assembly, AN Dxxix 76.

66. *Procureur du roi* of Maîtrise to *lieutenant particulier* of Maîtrise, [between November 10 and 27, 1789], AN Dxxix 17.

67. Syndic and clerk of Faverolles, petition to unknown correspondent, January 17, 1790, AN Dxxix 38.

68. February 22, 1788, AC La Chapelle-sur-Chezy D1. These comments were part of a reply to an agricultural questionnaire from the Château-Thierry intermediate bureau.

69. The land described belonged to the abbey of St-Léger in Soissons. The apanage rented it anyway, consistent with its policy of "rounding off" the forest of Retz (*procès-verbal* of July 30, 1783, AN R4 236).

70. July 27, 1788, AC Nogent l'Artaud D1.

71. Hyslop, *Apanage*, 176–81; concerning ditches, printed notice of Orléans apanage, September 1787, AN R4 245.

72. Hyslop, *Apanage*, 178; various documents in AN R4 236.

73. Hyslop, *Apanage*, 176–81. Apanage policy was satirized in a pamphlet by Leonard Lebas, *Lettre d'un laboureur à Villers-Cotterets, à un laboureur au Raincy* (Soissons: 1788), BN 8° Lb³⁹ 496.

74. See Jehan de Malafosse, "Un obstacle à la protection de la nature: le droit révolutionnaire," *Dix-huitième siècle* 9 (1977): 91–100; and Paul Ourliac and Jehan de Malafosse, *Histoire du droit privé*, 2d ed. (Paris: Presses Universitaires de France, 1969), 204–6.

The legal context of the fief supported the phenomenon of hunting clerics who were fief-holders. The bailliage of Villers-Cotterets held some notorious cases of this. A fuming curé wrote Necker; ". . . j'ai d'un quart de lieu de ma paroisse une communauté de Prémontrés . . . quatre religieux qui jouissent de 4 mille livres par tête . . . qui se divertissent jusqu'a passer les bornes, qui se donne dans tous les plaisirs au grande scandale des paroisses voisines qu'en gemissent, ils sont tous les jours à la chasse, le qui est défendu par tous les canons . . ." (April 9, 1789, AN Ba 86). The Third Estate *cahier* of the St-Quentin bailliage called for clerical hunting to be legally forbidden (AN Ba 70).

75. "Abrégé des doléances aux Etats-Generaux, ou precis de mes sentiments pour la ville de Vailly-sur-Aisne à quatre lieues de Soissons," dated March 7, 1789, in AN Ba 80. Vailly-sur-Aisne is 14 kilometers east of Soissons.

76. Robespierre in the National Assembly, April 20, 1790, quoted in Malafosse, "Un obstacle," 97.

77. September 9, 1789, ADA F2 356.

78. Letter of December 23, 1789, AN Dxxix 45.

79. See also Octave Festy, *Les délits ruraux et leur répression sous la Révolution et le Consulat: Étude d'histoire économique* (Paris: Librairie Marcel Rivière et Cie, 1956), 35–39. Festy quotes one 1789 pamphlet, the anonymous *Réflexions sur la chasse et les capitaineries*, as follows: "Le plaisir de la chasse a un attrait presque irrésistible pour tout individu né avec de la force et du courage . . ." (*Les Delits ruraux*, 39).

80. Letter received March 21, 1790, Soissons dossier, AN BB30 79. In the upshot, Coucy sent the Assembly papers denying that it had requested Rasselet's arrest. The Minister of War ordered Rasselet's release on condition that he rejoin his regiment directly.

81. AC Braine D1; *Arch. Parl.*, 8:378; entry of August 23, 1789, AC Chauny BB 33.

82. Michaux, *Villers-Cotterets*, 86. The municipal archives of Villers-Cotterets were lost in World War I.

83. *Procureur fiscal* of duchy of Guise to Joly de Fleury, *procureur général*, November 7, 1789, AN BB30 89.

84. Entry of November 11, 1789, AC Laon BB 46.

85. Bernet, "La crise," 118.

86. Anonymous correspondent to Coppens, president of Dunkerque commune, November 24, 1789, AN Dxxix 36.

Chapter 7. The Art of Visiting Châteaux (Frétoy, July 27, 1789)

1. Noyon intermediate bureau to Soissons provincial commission, August 7, 1789, ADA C 935.

2. AN C 92, C.II 80. Quotation is from *Arch. Parl.*, 8:378.

3. For a general discussion of prevotal court procedure see Cameron, *Crime and Repression*, 141–54.

4. Ibid., 142.

5. This composite narrative is based on documents contained in the Frétoy dossier, AN C 92; C.II 80. Unless otherwise indicated, the details contained herein are confirmed by at least two of the seven witnesses' depositions. The five paragraphs that follow, which describe Joly's background, are derived from the third interrogation of Joly on August 10.

6. See C. Delattre, E. Miriaux, M. Waterlot, *Région du Nord: Guides géologiques régionaux* (Paris: Masson, 1973); also Expilly, *Dictionnaire géographique*, 6:829 (s.v. Soissonnais).

7. Deposition of Jean Cordier, August 2–3, 1789.

8. Ibid.

9. Deposition of the curé Quentin Lamy, August 2–3, 1789.

10. Desposition of Joseph L'Herondelle, August 2–3, 1789.

11. Joly, interrogations of July 27, August 10, and August 16, 1789.

12. According to the curé Lamy and Joly himself (Lamy: *recollement* of August 17–18, 1789; Joly: self-defense after confrontations, same date).

13. Deposition of Charles Magnier, August 2–3, 1789.

14. Pailliart did go to the chateau after breakfast according to his deposition (August 2–3, 1789), from which this exchange is taken.

15. Deposition of Louis Caboche, August 2–3, 1789.

16. The majority of witness-participants agreed with Joly that he had carried only his own hunting knife.

17. Deposition of Jean Cordier, Auust 2–3, 1789.

18. Deposition of the curé Lamy, August 2–3, 1789. Other participants provided variations on this encounter. According to Briet, the syndic, Joly began by reproaching the curé for his absent cockade. According to the surgeon Caboche, "Joly fit la rencontre de M. le Cure . . . où il lui a demandé pour qui il tenoit, il lui répondit qu'il étoit du Tiers Etat. En même temps le . . . Cure lui a demandé ce qu'il vouloit, il lui a répondu qu'il lui falloit le bled que étoit au château, que le . . . Curé a dit n'y a t'il que cela, je vais vous conduire" (deposition of Pierre Briet, August 2–3, 1789).

19. It was the curé who admitted that bringing the syndic into the affair was his own idea, while the syndic acknowledged that the leader of the troop was familiar to him (depositions of Lamy and Briet, August 2–3, 1789).

20. Deposition of the curé Lamy, August 2–3, 1789.

21. Ibid. This is Lamy's paraphrase of Joly's discourse.

22. Deposition of Charles-Louis Paillairt, August 2–3, 1789.

23. Deposition of Etienne Souplet, August 2–3, 1789.

24. Deposition of Charles-Louis Pailliart, August 2–3, 1789. The *septier* was a measure of volume, not of weight; it averaged 150 liters.

25. Interrogation of Joly, August 10, 1789.

26. Deposition of the curé Lamy, August 2–3, 1789.

27. Deposition of Jean Cordier, August 2–3, 1789.

28. Deposition of Louis Caboche, August 2–3, 1789.

29. Deposition of the curé Lamy, August 2–3, 1789.

30. Ibid.

31. Deposition of the syndic Pierre Briet, August 2–3, 1789.

32. Lamy stated that he did not know whether Pierre Briet or Etienne Souplet (another locksmith) had burst the locks: "La porte fût ouverte alors par la ministère d'un des deux maréchaux de ce lieu, qui sont le dit Briet et Etienne Souplet, mais le deposant ne sait lequel des deux, parce qu'il s'éloigna de l'endroit de l'indignation." Indignation was a frequent recourse of Lamy when his testimony verged on incriminating a friend. Briet admitted the work, however, and of course Souplet confirmed his story.

33. Deposition of the curé Lamy, August 2–3, 1789.

34. Ibid.

35. Deposition of Jean Cordier, August 2–3, 1789. Note (first) the modest amount that Merlier had in mind—only one hundred *septiers;* and (second) that Merlier was the only participant from outside Frétoy that Cordier would admit he had recognized—a sure sign that he had detested his behavior.

36. Deposition of the curé Lamy, August 2–3, 1789.

37. Ibid.

38. Ibid. According to Joly in his August 10 interrogation, "c'est lui accusé qui s'est emparé d'une bouteille, et que pendant le temps qu'il examinoit ce que le pouvoit être, un des hommes de la troupe porteur du sabre, en a fait sauter le goulot, ajoute l'accusé qu'il s'est des bouteilles de différentes espèces."

39. Deposition of the guard Charles Magnier, August 2–3, 1789. These were probably *orangers amers (citrus bigaradia)*, cultivated for their flowers only.

40. Deposition of the surgeon Caboche, August 2–3, 1789.

41. Deposition of Charles Magnier, August 2–3, 1789.

42. Deposition of the curé Lamy, August 2–3, 1789.

43. Deposition of the syndic Briet, August 2–3, 1789. In his August 10 interrogation, Joly denied both the actual lockbreaking and his own motivation: ". . . La porte étoit ouverte, qu'il n'a pu se refuser aux sollicitations de ceux qui le suivoient, de faire déceler les barreaux de la fenêtre . . ."

44. Deposition of the curé Lamy, August 2–3, 1789.

45. Deposition of Louise Caboche, August 2–3, 1789.

46. Deposition of Charles Magnier, August 2–3, 1789.

47. Deposition of Etienne Souplet, August 2–3, 1789.

48. Interrogation of Joly, August 10, 1789.

49. Deposition of the curé Lamy, August 2–3, 1789. Lamy's account is confirmed by Magnier's: both agreed that Joly lent his "authority" to the protection of the oats.

50. Deposition of the curé Lamy, August 2–3, 1789.

51. Ibid.

52. Deposition of the syndic Briet, August 2–3, 1789.

53. Deposition of curé Lamy, August 2–3, 1789.

54. Ibid.

55. Ibid.

56. Declaration of the *maréchaussée* cavalier Jean-Baptiste Rémy de Tailly, July 27, 1789.

57. Deposition of the curé Lamy, August 2–3, 1789.

58. Ibid; declaration of the cavalier Remy de Tailly, July 27, 1789.

59. See chapter 4, above.

60. Interrogation of Joly, August 17, 1789.

61. See the comments of Noyon's intermediate bureau cited above in chapter 2.

62. See Yves-Marie Bercé, *Croquants et nu-pieds: Les soulèvements paysans en France du XVIe au XIXe siècle* (Paris: Editions Gallimard/Julliard, 1974), 47–162. Without accepting Bercé's perspective, in which the mentality of peasant revolts supposedly remained changeless for three hundred years, one can appreciate Bercé's grasp of the tactical necessities faced by peasants confronting their urban center. It should be noted that Bercé's discussion of the Great Fear misconceives it as a process that ordinarily led to antiseigneurial revolt—something tht Lefebvre found only in the Dauphiné. Bercé even presents a document from the Dauphiné and claims it as typical of the Fear in general (*Croquants et nu-pieds*, 125–28).

63. Lefebvre, *Great Fear*, 142.

64. See chapter 4, above.

65. For the turnover of Joly to the prevotal court, Joly's interrogation of July 27, 1789; for the dispatch of testimony to the National Assembly, the cover letter of *maréchaussée* lieutenant Plansoy, August 22, 1789; for Joly's death, Guy Ikni, personal communication, April 1981.

66. Interrogation of Joly, July 27, 1789.

67. See chapter 6, above.

68. Interrogation of Joly, August 16, 1789.

69. Lamy's revision of his deposition, August 17–18, 1789.

70. Briet's revision of his deposition, August 17–18, 1789.

71. The term "alibi" is used loosely here, not in its specific legal sense (a plea that the accused was elsewhere when a crime was committed). The pleas of the Frétoyards were that they had been forced to participate.

72. Interrogation of Joly, August 10, 1789.

73. Deposition of Charles Magnier, August 2–3, 1789. Perhaps he found it shocking that the son of a miller should be after more grain than he could get in the course of his business.

74. Deposition of Jean Cordier, August 2–3, 1789.

75. Deposition of Etienne Souplet, August 2–3, 1789.

76. See chapter 6, n. 53.

77. Depositions of Pierre Briet and Charles-Louis Pailliart, August 2–3, 1789; formal statement of charges by prevotal judge Adrien Douviller, August 3, 1789.

78. The phrase first appears in the royal counselor's interrogation of Joly on July 27, 1789.

79. Interrogation of Joly, July 27, 1789.

80. Interrogation of Joly, July 28, 1789.

81. Interrogation of Joly, July 27, 1789.

82. Interrogation of Joly, August 16, 1789.

83. Confrontation between Joly and Charles Magnier, August 17–18, 1789.

Chapter 8. The Rise of Revolutionary Militias

1. Semichon, *Aumale*, 2:363.

2. Lefebvre, *Great Fear*, 203–4.

3. In the old regime the term *milice* was used with two major meanings. First, it designated the provincial militias that supplemented the professional troops of the royal army; their members were conscripted from villages, rarely from towns. The *cahiers de doléances* frequently demanded the abolition of provincial militias. The second meaning of *milice* was that of an urban or "bourgeois" militia, recruited from a town's citizens under the orders of its municipality. These institutions in their traditional and revolutionary versions form the topic of this chapter.

4. Alexandre Michaux, "Les milices du Soissonnais," *Bulletin de la Société archéologique, historique et scientifique de Soissons*, 2d ser., 14 (1883): 34.

5. Francis Biscuit, "L'Arquebuse de Soissons," *Bulletin de la Société archéologique, historique et scientifique de Soissons*, 2d ser., 4 (1872): 21–76.

6. Ibid., 36.

7. Ibid., 38–39.

8. Alexandre Michaux, "La milice, les garnisons et les camps de Soissons," *Bulletin de la Société archéologique, historique et scientifique de Soissons*, 2d ser., 14 (1883): 198.

9. Biscuit, "L'Arquebuse de Soissons," 44–45.

10. Lynn Avery Hunt, *Revolution and Urban Politics in Provincial France: Troyes and Reims, 1786–1790* (Stanford, Calif.: Stanford University Press, 1978), 37–38.

11. Ibid., 91.

12. Note in Laon intermediate bureau's deliberations of June 4, 1789, ADA C 1014.

13. Ibid.

14. See Lefebvre, *Great Fear*, 137, for his vital distinction between the Great Fear and the fear of brigands; or see introduction, above.

15. Hargicourt municipality to Villedeuil, secretary of the Maison du Roi, May 25, 1789, with enclosure of a May 14 extract from municipal deliberations, AN F11 210.

16. Dinet, "Beauvaisis et Valois," 289, 313, 281.

17. Letter of May 19, 1789, ADA C 941.

18. D'Agay to Villedeuil, May 20, 1789, AN F11 221; Villedeuil to d'Agay, May 25, 1789, AN O1 485; d'Agay to Villedeuil, May 28, 1789, AN F11 221.

19. Jacques Godechot, *The Taking of the Bastille, July 14, 1789*, trans. Jean Stewart (New York: Scribner's, 1970), 243.

20. George Rudé, *The Crowd in the French Revolution* (New York: Oxford University Press, 1972) 61–79; Georges Lefebvre, *The Coming of the French Revolution*, trans. R. R. Palmer (Princeton: Princeton University Press, 1971), 192–200.

21. For an account of the 1787 mass creation of village municipalities and its effects, see chapter 6, above.

22. Extract from Enghien-Montmorency's municipal deliberations of July 22, 1789, AN Dxxix 37.

23. Ibid. The issue of command is dealt with in art. 16 of the *règlement*. The curfew commenced at 10:00 PM and was moved to 9:00 PM for August, 8:00 PM for September, and so on.

24. The old municipal officers regretted their lack of firmness the next day and stuck together for the remainder of the year, writing petitions to the National Assembly; organizing their sympathizers; obtaining official mail from the postmaster; and continuing to keep their register of deliberations, on which the account given here of the August 2 assembly relies (extract addressed to the National Assembly, AN Dxxix 37).

25. The quotation about Leturc's base of support is from the old municipality's petition of September 27, 1789, AN Dxxix 37. In the fall Leturc fostered an atmosphere in Enghien-Montmorency worthy of 1791 or 1792. Wood from a nearby forest belonging to the duc de Condé was sold for the village's profit, and salt was sold publicly in the market with great *éclat*. Leturc went about in a Parisian National Guard uniform with buttons bearing the Montmorency arms.

26. Dinet, "Beauvaisis et Valois," 285, 318–319.

27. Ibid. For the duc de Lévis's letter (which must have reached Pontoise no sooner than July 19, two days after the decision to form a militia), see chapter 4, above.

28. Pontoise permanent committee to the Paris Commune, July 28, 1789, AN C 134, dossier C.III.

29. Raoul Rosières, *La Révolution dans une petite ville: Meulan (1789–1794)*, 2d ed. (Meulan: M. Lachiver, 1967), 18–22. Also see Lefebvre, *Great Fear*, 185.

30. Dinet, "Beauvaisis et Valois," 301.

31. For further detail on Clermont-en-Beauvaisis and Crépy-en-Valois in late July, see chapter 4, above.

32. The municipal deliberations of Amiens are published in *Documents pour servir à l'histoire de la Révolution française dans la ville d'Amiens* (Paris: Picard et fils, 1894). For the events of July 14–15, see vol. 2 of that collection, pp. 225–29. AN Dxxix 17 is also rich in materials, but its documents pick up the story after the formation of an expanded town council in Amiens' on August 5, 1789. This carton contains a retrospective account of July's events by the militia's vice

president and secretary in a petition to the National Assembly, [probably November 1789].

33. *La Révolution française dans la ville d'Amiens*, 2:230–32; the quotation is from 2:260.

34. Ibid., 2:273–74.

35. Collective petition of Amiens militia to National Assembly, [probably September 1789], minutes of meeting of deputies of militia companies, October 8, 1789, both AN Dxxix 17.

36. *La Révolution française dans la ville d'Amiens*, 2:280.

37. See Jean Baptiste Buvry, *Tableau de Valenciennes au XVIIIe siècle* (Valenciennes: Lemaître, 1887), 11–12, 24–26, 28, 31. The *Tableau* is a 1783 manuscript published a century later, that systematically describes the town on the eve of the Revolution.

38. Comte d'Esterhazy to the *garde des sceaux*, August 12, 1789, AN BB30 87.

39. See Louis Lemaire, *Histoire de Dunkerque des origines à 1900* (Brussels: Editions culture et civilisation, 1976), 314–26.

40. Petition by officers of the *garde bourgeoise* to the National Assembly in which they describe their militia's formation, October 28, 1789, AN Dxxix 36.

41. Lemaire, *Histoire de Dunkerque*, 314–26.

42. See chapter 4, above.

43. Entries of July 31 and August 7, 14, 21, and 28, 1789, ADA C 935; Maison du roi to Noyon municipality, October 7 and December 29, 1789, AN O1 486.

44. For details and sources on Château-Thierry on the day of the Fear, see chapter 4, above. The gunpowder shipment is reported in *Recueil des procès-verbaux de la Commune de Paris*, session of August 6, 1789, pp. 9–10, and in Gorsas, *Courrier*, 2:175. For the process of militia formation, see J. Rollet, "La Compagnie des volontaires de la jeunesse de Château-Thierry," *Annales de la Société historique et archéologique de Château-Thierry* (1884): 53–58. For attempts at federation, see entry of August 30, 1789, AC Nogent l'Artaud D1; August 26, 1789, AC Villeneuve-sur-Fère D1.

45. "Habitants" of Château-Thierry to National Assembly, September 7, 1789, AN Dxxix 32; statement of Lieutenant Keer, September 7, 1789, ADA F2 354.

46. Minutes of permanent committee meeting of September 10–11, 1789, ADA F2 354.

47. On October 1 the acting intendant Brayer urged the royal household to send troops, "peut-être même avec quelques pièces d'artillerie," to Château-Thierry and to forcibly disband the militia, "qui avoit d'abord été licenciée, que s'est rétablie contre le voeu du plus grand nombre des habitants et qui n'est aujourd'hui composée en grande partie que des séditieux de la populace" (ADA C6).

48. ADA F2 354, 356; Château-Thierry municipality to *garde des sceaux*, March 3, 1790, AN BB30 79.

49. Statement of Lieutenant Keer, September 7, 1789, ADA F2 354.

50. ADA J 1054, 2:315–16.

51. The municipality posted broadsides of a pacifying declaration from the Paris Commune and remarked that "M. Bailly, en rappelant que l'éloignement de M. Necker avoit été le signal du trouble et de la confusion, avoit ajoute que son retour étoit celui de l'ordre, du calme et de la paix." The letter of adherence from Soissons' to the National Assembly took the same tack. ("Extrait des déliberations prises par la Comité Municipale et la Comité Permanente," August 1, 1789, Bibliothèque de Soissons, Collection Périn, MS. 4801; "citizens of Soissons" to National Assembly, July 31, 1789, AN C 90.)

52. Intendant Brayer to controller-general Necker (draft), September 7, 1789, ADA C 6.

53. AN O1 486.

54. *La jérémiade des maîtres porte-faix et des autres mercenaires du triste état de la ville de Soissons . . . pour être presenté à Messieux les Etats-Généraux* (Soissons, 1789), 12–13, BN 8° Lb 39.7491.

55. Ibid., 16.

56. For an extreme example of off-duty behavior, see Richard Cobb's recounting of the life of Nicolas Guenot in *Reactions to the French Revolution* (London: Oxford University Press, 1972), 76–91.

57. See chapters 4 and 6, above.

58. Melleville, *Histoire de la ville de Laon*, 1:81–84.

59. Entry of August 21, 1789, AC Laon BB 46.

60. First paragraph: memorandum by the St-Quentin commune's committee on militia, November 25, 1789. Second paragraph: committee to National Assembly, November 27, 1789. Both documents are in AN Dxxix 72.

61. Memorandum of November 25, 1789, cited in n. 60, above.

62. St-Quentin municipal committee to National Assembly, received February 3, 1790, AN Dxxix 1. See also Charles Normand, *Etude sur les rélations de l'Etat et des communautés aux XVIIe et XVIIIe siècles: Saint Quentin et la royauté* (Paris: Champion, 1881), 29–32.

63. More documents on this dispute are to be found in AN O1 486; AN Dxxix 1; and AN Dxxix 72. On the traditional militia, see Georges Lecocq, *Histoire de la compagnie des canonniers-arquebusiers de la ville de Saint-Quentin, 1461–1790* (St-Quentin: Poette, 1874).

64. Memorandum of Crépy-en-Valois municipality to National Assembly, December 8, 1789, AN Dxxix 34.

65. Ibid. For a discussion of the widespread verbal opposition to the concentration of tenant holdings, see chapter 1, above.

Conclusion

1. This summary relies on Vovelle's essay treatment of this research in *De la cave au grenier: Un itinéraire en Provence au XVIIIe siècle—de l'histoire sociale à l'histoire des mentalités* (Quebec: Serge Fleury, 1980); 221–62.

2. Ibid., 237.

3. Ibid., 221–62.

4. Peter M. Jones, *Politics and Rural Society: The Southern Massif Central, c. 1750–1880* (Cambridge: Cambridge University Press, 1985).

5. Ibid., 21

6. Ibid., 173–79; Peter M. Jones, *The Peasantry in the French Revolution* (Cambridge: Cambridge University Press, 1988); 70–78.

7. Patrice L.-R. Higonnet, *Pont-de-Montvert: Social Structure and Politics in a French Village, 1700–1914* (Cambridge: Harvard University Press, 1971).

8. Lefebvre, *Great Fear,* 160.

9. T. J. A. LeGoff, *Vannes and Its Region* (Oxford: Clarendon Press, 1981), 166–70.

10. Lefebvre, *Great Fear,* 63.

11. LeGoff, *Vannes,* 146–47.

12. Ibid., 340.

13. Jonathan Dewald, *Pont-St-Pierre, 1398–1789* (Berkeley and Los Angeles: University of California Press, 1987).

14. Ibid., 87.

15. Lefebvre, *Great Fear,* 174.

16. Dewald, *Pont-St-Pierre,* 247–48, 269–70.

17. Lefebvre, *Great Fear,* 4.

18. Ibid., 189.

19. Georges Lefebvre, *Etudes orléanaises,* Commission d'histoire économique et sociale de la Révolution, mémoires et documents, no. 151 (Paris: Centre national de la recherche scientifique, 1962–63), 1:38–41.

20. Ibid., 1:40–47.

21. Ibid., 2:21-26.

22. Pierre de Saint-Jacob, *Les paysans de la Bourgogne du Nord au dernier siècle de l'ancien régime* (Dijon: Bernigaud et Privat, 1960); Robin, *La société française en 1789;* Hilton L. Root, *Peasants and King in Burgundy: Agrarian Foundations of French Absolutism* (Berkeley and Los Angeles: University of California Press, 1987).

23. Lefebvre, *Grande Peur,* 207. White's English translation is too loose here.

24. Saint-Jacob, *Les Paysans de la Bourgogne,* 539.

25. Maximilien Robespierre, *Oeuvres,* vol. 6, *Discours 1789-1790,* ed. Marc Bouloiseau, Georges Lefebvre, Albert Soboul (Paris: Presses universitaires de France, 1950), 616–46. Thanks to Florence Gauthier for bringing this important text to my notice.

26. This paragraph and the next summarize features of the report delivered by the National Assembly's committees on the military and on the Constitution, November 21, 1790 *(Arch. Parl.,* 20:592-98) and debated on December 5, 1790 *(Arch Parl.,* 21:235-38).

27. *Arch. Parl.* 20:592-98 and 21:235-38.

28. Robespierre, *Oeuvres,* 6:634.

29. Ibid., 624.

30. Ibid., 630.

❧ BIBLIOGRAPHY

Manuscript Sources

Archives Nationales, Paris

Séries anciennes

H1   Local administrations: *pays d'état, pays d'élection,* intendancies
       1438   Picardy, diverse local affairs, 1709–90
       1453   Diverse local affairs, 1789–90
O1   Correspondence of the Maison du roi in the old regime
       361   Diverse papers on grain provisioning, censorship, etc.
       485   Register of letters to officials in the provinces, January–June 1789
       486   Register of letters to officials in the provinces, July–December 1789
R4   Apanage of the duc d'Orléans
       236, 245   Administration of the forest of Retz, Villers-Cotterets

Séries modernes

Ba   Papers on the convocation of the Estates-General
       32   Château-Thierry bailliage
       35   Crépy-en-Valois bailliage
       46   Vermandois à Laon, including the secondary bailliages of Chauny, Coucy, Guise, La Fère, Marle, Noyon
       70   St-Quentin bailliage
       80   Soissons bailliage
       86   Villers-Cotterets bailliage
BB30   Later deposits by the Justice Ministry (1904–61)
       66   Correspondence with local judges and officers
       68–69   Correspondence with intendants
       79   Correspondence on matters under *maréchaussée* jurisdiction

       87   Correspondence on riots, etc., 1789–90
       89   Letters to Parlement of Paris regarding grain circulation, various disturbances

C   Documents of the Constituent Assembly
       86   Petitions, projects, etc., addressed to National Assembly, April–September 1789
       89–90, 92, 94   General correspondence to National Assembly
      134   Correspondence and minutes of the assembly of Paris electors, July 1789

Dxxix   Correspondence to Comité des rapports of the Constituent Assembly
       1   Aisne department, November 1789–August 1791
      16   Abbeville
      17   Amiens
      18   Aubenton
      19   Bailleul
      29   Calais, Cambrai
      32   Château-Thierry, Chauny
      33   Clatre
      34   Coucy-le-Château, Crépy-en-Valois
      36   Douai, Dunkerque
      37   Enghien
      38   Faverolles, Fontainebleau
      40   Guise, Guyencourt
      41   Hirson, Homblières, Ham
      45   Landifay, Landouzy-la-Ville, Laon
      72   St-Quentin
      76   Soissons
      84   Vauharie
      85   Correspondence on grain circulation near the northern frontier

Dxli   Correspondence to National Assembly subsistence committee
       1   *Mémoires,* petitions and projects
       2   Communities' subsistence reports (alphabetized)

F11   Papers on subsistence and provisioning, 1760–1815
       6   Grain purchases of controller-general Necker, 1789–90
      208   Grain trade: papers of controller-general's office, 1755–87
      210   Aisne department, subsistence matters, 1789–Year XII
      221   Somme department, subsistence matters, 1788–Year IV
      223   Grain importation and exportation, 1765–Year III
      294–95   Grain trade: papers of controller-general's office, 1768–71
      435–36   Accounts of northern grain exportation, 1772–88
      1179   Notes on provisioning of Paris, 1780–89

F16   Prisons and begging
      936   Papers on begging and poor relief (primarily of the National Assembly's *Comité de mendicité*), 1788–91

Séries divers

AD1 Printed archives: politics and administration
    92 Diverse publications (mostly official) on public disorders, 1789–Year VIII
ADxiv Printed archives: hospitals and public relief
    4 Pamphlets on begging and the poor
N III Maps of Aisne department, small format
NN Maps
    37 Maps of France, general
    201 Maps of Picardy

Archives départementales de l'Aisne, Laon

Séries anciennes

C   Provincial administration before 1790
    6 Correspondence of Soissons intendancy with ministries, 1782–90
    14–15 Intendancy correspondence on grain seizures, 1789
    913 Deliberations of provincial commission
    916 Deliberations of provincial commission: *atéliers de charité*, road work as poor relief
    921 Correspondence of provincial commission with intendant and with ministries in Paris
    930 Correspondence of provincial commission to the comte d'Egmont, noble Estates-General deputy for the Soissons bailliage
    935 Correspondence of intermediate bureau of Noyon to provincial commission
    937–40 Papers of intermediate bureau of Laon: curés' letters on parish poor, municipal grain censuses
    941 Correspondence between provincial commission and intermediate bureau of Laon
    943 Correspondence of provincial commission: *vaine pâture*, draining of marshlands, communal lands
    989 Provincial commission: various papers on begging and poor relief
    1001 Register of correspondence between Soissons and Château-Thierry bailliage
    1011 Correspondence between provincial commission and intermediate bureau of Guise
    1014 Deliberations of the Laon intermediate bureau
    1018 Correspondence to the intermediate bureau of Laon
F2   Diverse papers deposited by private parties
    354–56 Papers of Château-Thierry permanent committee, September 7–11, 1789
J   Diverse papers deposited by private parties since 1944
    1054 Hébert, abbé, "Mémoires pour servir à l'histoire de Château-Thierry" (1806); bound manuscript in two volumes

Séries diverses

2Mi   35-mm microfilm
       39   Manuscript monographs of *instituteurs* on the histories of their
            communes, written 1884–88 (Some of these contain extracts from
            communal archives since destroyed.)

Deposited Municipal Archives

AC Artonges
   D1   Municipal deliberations, 1788–Year III
AC Audignicourt
   D1   Municipal deliberations, 1788–1843
AC Barenton-sur-Serre
   D1   Municipal deliberations, 1788–Year II
AC Berny-Rivière
   D1   Municipal deliberations, 1788–Year VI
AC Braine
   D1   Municipal deliberations, April 27, 1788–August 28, 1791
AC Chauny
   BB 33   Municipal deliberations, 1765–90
AC Guise
   BB 14   Municipal deliberations, 1789
   HH 11   Subsistence matters, 1789
AC La Chapelle-sur-Chezy
   D1   Municipal deliberations, 1788–Year V
AC Laon
   BB 46   Municipal deliberations; matters related to the Estates-General, 1789
   HH 8   Grain circulation
   HH 16   Grain and subsistence matters
AC Mareuil-en-Dole
   D1   Municipal deliberations, 1788–1808
AC Montigny-Lengrain
   D1   Municipal deliberations, 1788–Year II
AC Moussy-Verneuil
   D1   Municipal deliberations, 1788–1843
AC Nogent l'Artaud
   D1   Municipal deliberations, February 3, 1788–December 30, 1791
AC Noyales
   D1   Municipal deliberations, 1788–91
AC Ohis
   D1   Municipal deliberations, March 16, 1788–March 5, 1793
AC Parfondeval
   D1   Municipal deliberations, 1788–Year IV
AC Ressons-le-Long
   D1   Municipal deliberations, 1788–92
AC Venizel
   D1   Municipal deliberations, 1789–93

AC Vesles-et-Caumont
  D1   Municipal deliberations, 1788–Year XIII
AC Villeneuve-sur-Fère
  D1   Municipal deliberations, 1788–Year II

Archives départmentales de l'Oise

Séries anciennes

C   Provincial administration before 1790
        318   Papers of intermediate bureau of Crépy-en-Valois
        357–58   Extracts from register and correspondence of intermediate
             bureau of Noyon
        756   *Greffe* of Clermont-en-Beauvaisis *élection*

Archives communales de Château-Thierry

Deliberations on fairs and markets of intermediate bureau, 1788 (unclassified)
Primary assembly of Château-Thierry, May 3–7, 1790 (unclassified)

Archives communales de Compiègne

1D1   Deliberations of municipal bureau, 1788–90

Bibliothèque municipale de Compiègne

Ms. 7   Escuyer, Gaspard, "Histoire de Compiègne" (c. 1825), vol. 6; bound
        manuscript

Bibliothèque de Soissons

Manuscripts

Ms. 238   Fiquet, M. [deputy of the Legislative Assembly and the Convention],
          "Mémoires pour servir à l'histoire de Soissons depuis son origine
          jusqu'à nos jours," vol. 3; bound manuscript
Ms. 251   Latte, M. [notary], "Comparaison des anciens poids et mesures du
          Soissonnais à ceux de la République française" (Year X [1802])

Collection Périn

Ms. 767   *Cahier de doléances* of Ambleny, March 8, 1789
Ms. 843   *Cahier de doléances* of Barizil-au-Bois, March 1789
Ms. 1992   *Cahier de doléances* of Juvigny, March 5, 1789
Ms. 4801   "Extrait des délibérations par le Comité municipal et le Comité per-
          manent" (August 1, 1789)
Ms 4806   "Observations importantes par M. Gouillart, procureur du roi au
          bureau des finances de la généralité de Soissons" (October 8, 1789)
Ms. 6089   *Cahier de doléances* of Trozy-Loire, March 1, 1789

Printed Primary Sources

"Adresse des electeurs des districts de Château-Thierry et Soissons à l'Assemblée Nationale." [1790]. BN 4° Lk⁵.26.

Amiens [Commission municipale des archives], ed. *Documents pour servir à l'histoire de la Révolution française dans la ville d'Amiens*. 5 vols. Paris: Picard, 1894.

Beguillet, E. *Traité de la connoissance générale des grains, et de la mouture par économie*. Part 1, Paris: Pancoucke, 1775. Part 2, Dijon: Frantin, 1778. BN 15404–15405; S.4465.

Bloch, Camille, and Alexandre Tuetey, eds. *Procès-verbaux et rapports du Comité de mendicité de la Constituante, 1790–1791*. Paris: Imprimerie Nationale, 1911.

Brette, Armand. *Receuil de documents rélatifs à la convocation des Etats-Généraux de 1789*. Paris: Imprimerie Nationale, 1894.

Brun, Felix. "Lettres et documents divers concernant Soissons et le Soissonnais (1599–1792), copiés aux Archives historiques du Ministère de la Guerre." *Bulletin de la Société archéologique, historique, et scientifique de Soissons*. 4th ser., 4 (1924): 119–93.

Bucqet, César. *Manuel du meunier, et du constructeur de moulins à eau et à grains*. Revised by E. Beguillet. Paris: Onfrey, 1790. BN Vz.1688.

Buvry, Jean Baptiste. *Tableau de Valenciennes au XVIIIe siècle*. Valenciennes: Lemaître, 1887.

"Cahiers et procès-verbaux du bailliage de Soissons, pour les Etats-Généraux de 1789." *Bulletin de la Société archéologique, historique et scientifique de Soissons* 20 (1866): 249–449.

Comité militaire d'Amiens. *Réflexions sur l'arrêté des officiers municipaux et conseil permanent de la ville d'Amiens, du 11 décembre: Pour servir de suite à l'exposé de la conduite des membres composans ci-devant le Comité militaire de ladite ville*. Abbeville: L.-A. Deverité, 1789. BN 4° Lk⁷ 175.

Dauchy [prefect]. *Statistique du département de l'Aisne*. Paris, Year X [1801–2].

Demande pour la conservation du chef-lieu de département dans la ville de Soissons. Paris: D'Houry et Debvre, 1790. BN Lk⁷. 9378.

Durand, M. *Observations et réflexions politiques sur le commerce et les finances du royaume . . . Précédé de réflexions rélatives au commerce en Picardie*, 2d ed. Paris: Godefroy, 1789. BN 8° Lb³⁹.11391.

Duvergier, Jean-Baptiste, ed. *Collection complète des lois et décrets d'intérêt général, traités internationaux, arrêtés, circulaires, instructions, etc.* Vol. 1. Paris: Guyot et Scribe, 1824.

Expilly, Jean-Joseph d'. *Dictionnaire géographique, historique et politique des Gaules et de la France*. 6 vols. Paris: Desaint et Saillant, 1762–70.

Gorsas, A. J., ed. *Courrier de Versailles à Paris, et de Paris à Versailles*. Paris, 1789.

Jousse, Daniel. *Traité du gouvernement spirituel et temporel des paroisses: Ou l'on examine tout ce qui concerne les fonctions, droits et devoirs des marguilliers, dans l'administration des fabriques, des biens des pauvres et des écoles de charité*. Paris: Debuse père, 1773. BN E 6246 [12°].

La jérémiade des maîtres porte-faix et des autres mercenaires du triste état de la ville de Soissons . . . pour être presentée à Messieux les Etats-Généraux. Soissons, 1789. BN 8° Lb³⁹.7491.

Lebas, Leonard. *Lettre d'un laboureur à Villers-Cotterets, à un laboureur au Raincy.* Soissons, 1788. BN 8° Lb³⁹.496.

Leclerc de Montlinot, C.-A.-J. *Discours qui a remporté le prix à la Société Royale d'agriculture de Soissons, en l'année 1779; sur cette question proposée par la même société: Quels sont les moyens de détruire la Mendicité, de rendre les Pauvres valides utiles, et de les secourir dans la ville de Soissons?* Lille: C. Lehoucq, 1779. BN F 25592.

⸻. *Etat actuel du dépôt de mendicité de la généralité de Soissons, Vème compte, année 1786.* 2d ed. Soissons, 1789. BN R 8041.

⸻. *Etat actuel du dépôt de Soissons, précédé d'un essai sur la mendicité, V. compte, année 1786.* Soissons, 1789. BN R 8047.

⸻. "Dépôts de mendicité," in *Encyclopédie méthodique: Économie politique et diplomatique,* edited by J.-N. Demeunier, 2:71–79. Paris: Pancoucke, 1786.

Le Prévôt de Beaumont, J. G. G. *Dénonciation d'un Pacte de Famine générale, au roi Louis XV; ouvrage manuscrit, trouvé à la Bastille le 14 juillet dernier, et contenant des découvertes fort intéressantes sur les malversations et les déprédations sécrètes de quelques hommes d'Etat.* [Paris, 1789–90?]. BN 8° Lb³⁹.1963.

Le Scène-Desmaisons, Jacques, ed. *Feuille politique.* Paris, July 1789.

Limon, marquis Geoffroy de. [Circulaire adressée aux curés, au nom du duc d'Orléans, sur les demandes à faire insérer dans les cahiers des assemblées des bailliages]. BN 4° Lb³⁹.1378.

Limon, marquis Geoffroy de, and abbé Emmanuel-Joseph Sieyès. *Instruction donnée par S. A. S. Mgr. le duc d'Orléans à ses représentans aux bailliages, suivie de déliberations à prendre dans ces assemblées.* 3d corr. ed. 1789. BN 8° Lb³⁹ 1380.C.

Luchet, J.-P.-L., ed. *Journal de la Ville.* Paris: Nyon, August-September 1789.

Madival, J., and E. Laurent, eds. *Archives Parlementaires de 1787 à 1860,* Paris: Société Paul Dupont, 1875–1914.

Malvaux, abbé, ed. *Resumé des mémoires qui ont concouru pour le prix accordé en 1777 par l'Académie des sciences, arts et belles-lettres de Châlons-sur-Marne et dont le sujet était: Les moyens de détruire la mendicité en France, en rendant les mendiants utiles à l'Etat sans les rendre malheureux.* Châlons: Senueze, 1779.

Montjoie [Montjoye], C.-F. *Histoire de la Révolution de France et de l'Assemblée Nationale.* Paris: Gattey, 1792.

Necker, Jacques. *Sur la législation et le commerce des grains,* in *Mélanges d'économie politique.* Edited by Eugène Daire and G. de Molinari. Vol. 2. Paris: Guillaumin, 1848.

Observations sur la dîme à la quatorzième gerbe dans le Soissonnois, province de grande culture. [1789?] BN 4° Lk² 1747.

Procès-verbaux des séances de l'Assemblée provinciale du Soissonnais, tenue à Soissons en 1787. Soissons: Waroquier, 1788.

Recueil des procès-verbaux de l'Assemblée des représentants de la Commune de Paris, du 25 juillet au 18 septembre 1789. Paris: J. R. Lottin de St-Germain, 1789. BN Lb⁴⁰ 20.

Résultat du Conseil de S. A. S. Mᵍʳ le duc d'Orléans, premier prince du sang, concernant l'approvisionnement de grains de plusieurs marchés de son apanage, et la remise de différens droits dû à S. A. S. [1789]. BN 4° Lb³⁹.1706.

Robespierre, Maximilien. *Oeuvres,* vol. 6, *Discours 1789–1790.* Edited by Marc Bouloiseau, Georges Lefebvre, and Albert Soboul. Paris: Presses universitaires de France, 1950.

Saint-Priest, comte F. E. G. de. *Mémoires.* Paris: Calmann-Levy, 1929.

Tables des rapports entre les mesures républicaines et les mesures anciennes. Paris: Comité d'instruction publique, Year III [1794–95]. BN V. Pièce. 11718 [8°].

Secondary Works

Adamson, Walter L. *Hegemony and Revolution.* Berkeley and Los Angeles: University of California Press, 1980.

Afanassiev, Georges. *Le commerce des céréales en France au 18e siècle.* Translated by Paul Boyer. Paris: Picard et fils, 1894.

———. *Tableau des mesures pour les grains qui étaient en usage en France au XVIIIe siècle.* Odessa, Russia: Odessky wiestnik, 1891.

Allport, Gordon, and Leo Postman. *The Psychology of Rumor.* New York: H. Holt, 1947.

Bercé, Yves-Marie. *Croquants et nu-pieds: Les soulèvements paysans en France du XVIe au XIXe siècle.* Paris: Editions Gallimard/Juilliard, 1974.

Bernet, Jacques. "La crise des subsistances à Compiègne (1788–1789)." *Bulletin de la Société historique de Compiègne* 26 (1979): 99–118.

Best, Geoffrey. *War and Society in Revolutionary Europe, 1770–1870.* London: Fontana, 1982.

Biscuit, Francis. "L'Arquebuse de Soissons." *Bulletin de la Société archéologique, historique et scientifique de Soissons,* 2d ser., 4 (1872): 21–76.

Bloch, Camille. *L'assistance et l'Etat en France à la veille de la Révolution: Généralités de Paris, Rouen, Alençon, Orléans, Châlons, Soissons, Amiens, 1764–1790.* Paris: Picard et fils, 1908.

Brosselin, Arlette. "Pour un histoire de la forêt française au XIXe siècle." *Revue d'histoire économique et sociale* 55 (1977): 92–111.

Broutin, Yvonne-Elisabeth. "Les mendiants et leur costume en Normandie avant la Révolution." *Ethnologie française* 12 (1982): 31–44.

Brunet, Pierre. *Structure agraire et économie rurale des plateaux tertiaires entre la Seine et l'Oise.* Caen: Caron, 1960.

Cahen, Leon. "Une nouvelle interprétation du traité franco-anglais de 1786–87." *Revue historique* 185 (1939): 257–85.

Cameron, Iain. *Crime and Repression in the Auvergne and the Guyenne, 1720–1790.* Cambridge: Cambridge University Press, 1981.

Castan, Nicole. *Justice et répression en Languedoc à l'époque des Lumières.* Paris: Flammarion, 1980.

Church, Clive H. *Revolution and Red Tape: The French Ministerial Bureaucracy, 1770-1850.* Oxford: Clarendon Press, 1981.

Clark, Martin. *Antonio Gramsci and the Revolution That Failed.* New Haven: Yale University Press, 1977.

Cobb, Richard. "L'Armée Révolutionnaire parisienne dans le département de l'Aisne, vendémiaire-germinal an II (septembre-octobre 1793-mars-avril 1794)." *Revue du Nord* 33-34 (1951-52): 242-52, 51-70.

———. *Death in Paris.* Oxford: Oxford University Press, 1978.

———. *Reactions to the French Revolution.* London: Oxford University Press, 1972.

Delattre, C., E. Meriaux, and M. Waterlot. *Region du Nord: Guides géologiques régionaux.* Paris: Masson, 1973.

Depauw, Jacques. "Pauvres, pauvres mendiants, mendiants valides ou vagabonds? Les hésitations de la législation royale." *Revue d'histoire moderne et contemporaine* 21 (1974): 401-18.

Deschamps, Marie-Odile. "Le dépôt de mendicité de Rouen (1768-1820)." *Bulletin d'histoire économique et sociale de la Révolution française* 34 (1977): 81-93.

Dewald, Jonathan. *Pont-St-Pierre, 1398-1789.* Berkeley and Los Angeles: University of California Press, 1987.

Dinet, Henri. *La Grande Peur dans la généralité de Poitiers: juillet-août 1789.* Paris: by the author, 1951.

———. "La Grande Peur en Hurepoix: Juillet 1789." *Paris et Île-de-France: Mémoires* 18-19 (1967-68): 99-204.

———. *Les milices nationales en Poitou, 1789-1790, avec divers documents inédits sur la Grande Peur.* Paris: by the author, 1952.

———. "Les Peurs de 1789 dans la région parisienne: La Peur en Hurepoix (juillet 1789)." *Annales historiques de la Révolution française* 50 (1978): 34-44.

———. "Les Peurs du Beauvaisis et du Valois, juillet 1789." *Paris et Ile-de-France: Mémoires* 23-24 (1972-73): 199-392.

Dommanget, Maurice. "Les grèves des moissonneurs du Valois sous la Révolution." *Annales historiques de la Révolution française* 1 (1924): 507-44.

Doyle, William. *Origins of the French Revolution.* Oxford: Oxford University Press, 1984.

Dumas, Georges. *Guide des archives de l'Aisne.* Laon, 1971.

Jean Egret, *The French Prerevolution, 1787-1788.* Translated by Wesley D. Camp. Chicago: University of Chicago Press, 1977.

Festy, Octave. *Les délits ruraux et leur répression sous la Révolution et le Consulat: Etude d'histoire économique.* Paris: Librairie Marcel Rivière, 1956.

Fillmore, Charles. "Types of lexical information." In *Semantics: An Interdisciplinary Reader in Philosophy, Linguistics, and Psychology.* Edited by Danny D. Steinberg and Leon A. Jakobovits, 370-92. London: Cambridge University Press, 1971.

———. "The case for case." In *Universals in Linguistic Theory.* Edited by Emmon Bach and Robert T. Harms, 1-88. New York: Holt Rinehart & Winston, 1968.

Fleury, Edouard. *Famines, misères et séditions: Études révolutionnaires.* Laon: Fleury et Chevergny, 1849.

——. *Vandales et iconoclastes: Études révolutionnaires.* Laon: Fleury et Chevergny, 1849.

Forrest, Alan. *The French Revolution and the Poor.* Oxford: Oxford University Press, 1981.

Furet, François, and Denis Richet. *La Révolution française.* Paris: Fayard, 1973.

Gauthier, Florence. "Sur les problèmes paysans de la Révolution." *Annales historiques de la Révolution française* 50 (1978): 305–14.

——. *La voie paysanne dans la Révolution française: L'exemple picard.* Paris: Maspero, 1977.

Gauthier, Florence, and Guy-Robert Ikni, eds. *La Guerre du blé au XVIIIe siècle: La critique populaire contre le libéralisme économique au XVIIIe siècle.* Montreuil: Les Editions de la Passion, 1988.

Godechot, Jacques. "Linguistique et la Révolution française (revue de presse)." *Annales historiques de la Révolution française* 56 (1984): 301–2.

——. *La prise de la Bastille, 14 juillet 1789.* Paris: Gallimard, 1965.

Goubert, Pierre. *Beauvais et le Beauvaisis de 1600 à 1730: Contribution à l'histoire sociale de la France du XVIIe siècle.* Paris: Université de Paris, 1958.

Gramsci, Antonio. *Letters from Prison.* Edited and translated by Lynne Lawner. New York: Harper & Row, 1973.

——. *Selections from the Prison Notebooks of Antonio Gramsci.* Edited and translated by Quintin Hoare and G. N. Smith. New York: International Publishers, 1971.

Grange, Henri. *Les idées de Necker.* Paris: Librairie C. Klincksieck, 1974.

Guilhaumou, Jacques. "Idéologies, discours et conjoncture en 1793." *Dialectiques,* no. 10–11 (1975): 33–58.

Gutton, Jean-Pierre. *La sociabilité villageoise dans l'ancienne France: Solidarités et voisinages du XVIe au XVIIIe siècle.* Paris: Hachette, 1979.

——. *La société et les pauvres en Europe, XVIe–XVIIIe siècles.* Paris: Presses universitaires de France, 1974.

——. *L'Etat et la mendicité dans la première moitié du XVIIIe siècle: Auvergne, Beaujolais, Forez, Lyonnais.* St-Etienne: Centre d'études foreziennes, 1973.

Harlé d'Ophove, Monique. *La forêt de Compiègne de la Réformation de Colbert à la Révolution.* Compiègne: Société historique de Compiègne, 1968.

Harman, Chris. *Gramsci versus Reformism.* London: Socialist Workers Party, 1983.

Harris, Robert D. *Necker: Reform Statesman of the Ancien Régime.* Berkeley and Los Angeles: University of California Press, 1979.

Hayter, Tony. *The Army and the Crowd in Mid-Georgian England.* London: Macmillan, 1978.

Hennequin, René. *La formation du département de l'Aisne en 1790: Étude documentaire de géographie politique.* Soissons: Société académique de Laon, 1911.

——. "Le Soissonnais à la fin du XVIIIe siècle: Son état agricole, commercial et industriel." *Bulletin de la Société archéologique, historique et scientifique de Soissons,* 3d ser., 18 (1911): 206–48.

Higonnet, Patrice L.-R. *Pont-de-Montvert: Social Structure and Politics in a French Village, 1700–1914.* Cambridge: Harvard University Press, 1971.

Hufton, Olwen H. *The Poor of Eighteenth-Century France, 1750-1789.* Oxford: Oxford University Press, 1974.

Hunt, David. "Peasant Politics in the French Revolution." *Social History* 9 (1984): 277-99.

Hunt, Lynn Avery. *Revolution and Urban Politics in Provincial France: Troyes and Reims, 1786-1790.* Stanford: Stanford University Press, 1978.

Hyslop, Beatrice F. *L'apanage de Philippe-Egalité, duc d'Orléans (1785-1791).* Paris: Société des études robespierristes, 1965.

Jacob, Louis. "La Grande Peur en Artois." *Annales historiques de la Révolution française* 13 (1936): 123-48.

Janrot, Léon. "La Révolution en Seine-et-Oise." *Recherche des documents rélatifs à la vie économique de la Révolution: Comité de Seine-et-Oise,* 12th fasc. (1932): 79-145.

Jones, Peter M. *Politics and Rural Society: The Southern Massif Central, c. 1750-1880.* Cambridge: Cambridge University Press, 1985.

———. *The Peasantry in the French Revolution.* Cambridge: Cambridge University Press, 1988.

Justin, Emile. *Les sociétés royales d'agriculture aux XVIIIe siècle, 1757-1793.* Saint-Lô: Barbaroux, 1935.

Kropotkin, Pierre. *La grande Révolution, 1789-1793.* 1909. Reprint. Paris: Stock, 1976.

Labrousse, Camille-Ernest. *Esquisse du mouvement des prix et des revenus en France au XVIIIe siècle.* Paris: Dalloz, 1933.

Laclau, Ernesto, and Chantal Mouffe. *Hegemony and Socialist Strategy: Towards a Radical Democratic Politics.* London: Verso, 1985.

Lancelin, Michel. *La Révolution en Province: Saint-Omer de 1789 à 1791.* Saint-Omer: Imprimerie de l'Indépendant, 1972.

Lecocq, Georges. *Histoire de la compagnie des canonniers-arquebusiers de la ville de Saint-Quentin, 1461-1790.* Saint-Quentin: Poette, 1874.

Lefebvre, Georges. *The Coming of the French Revolution.* Translated by R. R. Palmer. Princeton: Princeton University Press, 1971.

———. "Documents sur la Grande Peur: Clermontois, Valois et Soissonnais." *Annales historiques de la Révolution française* 10 (1933): 167-75.

———. *Etudes orléanaises.* Commission d'histoire économique et sociale de la Révolution, mémoires et documents, no. 15. Paris: Centre national de la recherche scientifique, 1962-63.

———. *Etudes sur la Révolution française.* Paris: Presses universitaires de France, 1963.

———. *La Grande Peur de 1789.* Paris: Armand Colin, 1970.

———. *The Great Fear of 1789.* Translated by Joan White. New York: Pantheon, 1973.

———. *Les paysans du Nord pendant la Révolution française.* Bari, Italy: Editori Laterza, 1959.

LeGoff, Timothy J. A., *Vannes and Its Region.* Oxford: Clarendon Press, 1981.

LeGoff, Timothy J. A., and Donald M. G. Sutherland, "The Revolution and the

Rural Community in Eighteenth-Century Brittany." *Past and Present,* no. 62 (1974): 96-119.

Legrand, Robert, ed. *Babeuf avant 1790: Lettres à sa femme.* Aspects de la Révolution en Picardie, no. 13. Abbeville, 1970.

Lemaire, Louis. *Histoire de Dunkerque des origines à 1900.* Brussels: Editions culture et civilisation, 1976.

Le Roy Ladurie, Emmanuel. "Pour un modèle de l'économie rurale française au XVIIIe siècle." *Mélanges de l'École française de Rome: Moyen age—temps modernes* 85 (1973): 7-29.

Leroux, M. *Histoire de la ville de Soissons.* 2 vols. Soissons, 1839.

Luguet, H. "Soissons pendant la Révolution." *Mémoires de la Féderation des sociétés savantes du département de l'Aisne* 1 (1953-54): 68-87.

Malafosse, Jehan de. "Un obstacle à la protection de la nature: Le droit révolutionnaire." *Dix-huitieme siècle* 9 (1977): 91-100.

Malicet, Pierre. *Les institutions municipales de Peronne sous l'ancien régime.* Paris: Recueil Sirey, 1912.

Mathiez, Albert. *La Révolution française.* 2 vols. Paris: Armand Colin, 1922.

Melleville, M. *Histoire de la ville de Laon et de ses institutions.* Laon, 1846. Reprint. Brussels: Editions culture et civilisation, 1976.

Meuvret, Jean. "Les oscillations des prix des céréales au XVIIe et XVIIIe siècles en Angleterre et dans les pays du bassin parisien." *Revue d'histoire moderne et contemporaine* 16 (1969): 540-54.

Michaux, Alexandre. *Histoire de Villers-Cotterets: La ville, le château, la forêt et ses environs.* Soissons, 1886.

———. "La milice, les garnisons et les camps de Soissons." *Bulletin de la Société archéologique, historique et scientifique de Soissons,* 2d ser., 14 (1883): 194-256.

———. "Les milices du Soissonnais." *Bulletin de la Société archéologique, historique et scientifique de Soissons,* 2d ser., 14 (1883): 25-53.

———. "Quelques notes sur le dernier intendant de la généralité de Soissons." *Bulletin de la Société archéologique, historique et scientifique de Soissons,* 2d ser., 19 (1988): 136-43.

Morin, Edgar. *La rumeur d'Orléans.* Paris: Editions de Seuil, 1969.

Mouffe, Chantal, ed. *Gramsci and Marxist Theory.* London: Routledge & Kegan Paul, 1979.

Nemeth, Thomas. *Gramsci's Philosophy: A Critical Study.* Brighton, England: Harvester, 1980.

Normand, Charles. *Etude sur les rélations de l'Etat et des communautés aux XVIIe et XVIIIe siècles: St-Quentin et la royauté.* Paris: Champion, 1881.

Ourliac, Paul, and Jehan de Malafosse. *Histoire du droit privé.* 2d ed. Paris: Presses universitaires de France, 1969.

Paultre, Christian. *De la répression de la mendicité et du vagabondage en France sous l'Ancien Régime.* Paris: Larose et Tenin, 1906.

Plaisance, Georges. *Guide des forêts de France.* Paris: La nef de Paris, 1961.

Postel-Vinay, Gilles. *La rente foncière dans le capitalisme agricole.* Paris: Maspero, 1974.

Regnier, R. "Noyon port sur l'Oise: Le document Margerin (1786)." *Société archéologique, historique, et scientifique de Noyon: Comptes-rendus et mémoires* 34 (1972): 38–46.

Rigby, [Dr.]. *Dr. Rigby's Letters from France, &c., in 1789.* Edited by Lady Eastlake. London: Longmans, Green, 1880.

Robin, Régine. "Fief et seigneurie dans le droit et l'idéologie juridique à la fin du XVIIIe siècle." *Annales historiques de la Révolution française* 43 (1971): 554–602.

———. *Histoire et linguistique.* Paris: A. Colin, 1973.

———. *La société française en 1789: Semur-en-Auxois.* Paris: Plon, 1970.

———. "Le champ sémantique de 'féodalité' dans les cahiers de doléance généraux de 1789." *Bulletin du Centre d'analyse du discours de l'Université de Lille III,* no. 2 (1975): 61–86.

Rollet, J. "La Compagnie des volontaires de la jeunesse de Château-Thierry." *Annales de la Société historique et archéologique de Château-Thierry* (1884): 53–58.

———. "Les compagnies d'arquebusiers de l'arrondissement actuel de Château-Thierry au prix général de l'arquebuse à Châlons-sur-Marne en 1754." *Annales de la Société historique et archéologique de Château-Thierry* (1881): 55–60.

Romon, Christian. "Le monde des pauvres à Paris au XVIIIe siècle." *Annales: Economies, sociétés, civilisations* 37 (1982): 729–63.

Root, Hilton. *Peasants and King in Burgundy: Agrarian Foundations of French Absolutism.* Berkeley and Los Angeles: University of California Press, 1987.

Rosières, Raoul. *La Révolution dans une petite ville: Meulan, 1789–1794.* 2d ed. Meulan: 1967.

Rudé, George. *The Crowd in the French Revolution.* New York: Oxford University Press, 1972.

———. "Ideology and Popular Protest." *Historical Reflections* 3 (1976): 69–78.

Ruff, Julius R. *Crime, Justice, and Public Order in Old Regime France: The Sénéchaussées of Libourne and Bazas, 1696–1789.* London: Croom Helm, 1984.

Saincir, J. *Histoire de Montigny-Lengrain.* Compiègne, 1931.

Saint-Jacob, Pierre de. *Les Paysans de la Bourgogne du Nord au dernier siècle de l'ancien régime.* Dijon: Bernigaud et Privat, 1960.

Schmidt, Charles. "La crise industrielle de 1788 en France." *Revue historique* 97 (1908): 78–94.

Schwartz, Robert M. *Policing the Poor in Eighteenth-Century France.* Chapel Hill: University of North Carolina Press, 1988.

Semichon, Ernest. *Histoire de la Ville d'Aumale (Seine-Inférieure) et de ses institutions depuis les temps anciens jusqu'à nos jours.* Paris: A. Aubry, 1862.

Sewell, William H., Jr. *Work and Revolution in France.* Cambridge: Cambridge University Press, 1980.

Shibutani, Tamotsu. *Improvised News: A Sociological Study of Rumor.* New York: Bobbs-Merrill, 1966.

Soboul, Albert. *The French Revolution, 1787–1799: From the Storming of the Bastille to Napoleon.* Translated by Alan Forrest and Colin Jones. New York: Vintage, 1974.

———. *La Révolution française.* 3 vols. Paris: Éditions sociales, 1962.

Taine, Hippolyte. *Les origines de la France contemporaine.* 11 vols. Paris: Hachette, 1904.

Thompson, E. P. "The Moral Economy of the English Crowd in the Eighteenth Century." *Past and Present,* no. 50 (1971): 76–136.

Tilly, Louise. "The Food Riot as a Form of Political Conflict in France." *Journal of Interdisciplinary History* 2 (1972): 23–57.

Vexliard, Alexandre. *Introduction à la sociologie du vagabondage.* Paris: M. Rivière, 1956.

Vonglis, Bernard. *Le commerce des céréales à Reims, au XVIIIe siècle.* Reims: Université de Reims, 1980.

Vovelle, Michel. *De la cave au grenier: Un itinéraire en Provence au XVIIIe siècle— de l'histoire sociale à l'histoire des mentalités.* Quebec: Serge Fleury, 1980.

Weisser, Michael R. *Crime and Punishment in Early Modern Europe.* Brighton, England: Harvester, 1979.

Woloch, Isser. *The French Veteran from the Revolution to the Restoration.* Chapel Hill: University of North Carolina Press, 1979.

৯ৼ *INDEX*

Abbeville, 11
Abbeys, 5, 17, 68-69, 76, 140, 180-181;
  and hunting, 279; religious houses, 43,
  50
Adjudication (of communal lands), 14, 67
Agay, d' (intendant of Amiens), 111, 139,
  216, 223
Agriculture, 3-24, 183-84, 240; commu-
  nity system of, 4, 18, 241, 245-47; fal-
  low, 5, 11, 19-20; of poor, 7, 10, 16-18,
  109-10, 181; royal societies of, 9, 73;
  technical progress in, 8-9, 16; triennial
  rotation, 5, 21, 23, 120, 241. *See also*
  Land, concentration of
Aiguillon, duc d', 144
Aippe, 65
Aisne, department, xxv, 26, 38
Aisne river and valley, 19-20, 31, 46, 217
Aix, 243
Alsace, xvi, 254
Amienois, 19, 21
Amiens, 9, 15, 115, 133, 149, 206,
  228-29, 231; intendancy of, 6, 111,
  115, 177, 222-23; militia, 217
Ardèche, department, 244
Argenteuil, 134
Aristocrate, term, 151-53, 155
"Aristocrats' plot," fear of, xx, xxiii, 52,
  152-53, 155, 216, 245, 248
Arms, 118, 121-22, 233, 249-50; and
  Frétoy, 196, 201-3, 208, 213; and Laon,
  113-14, 131, 237; and peasants,

166-67, 172, 180-81, 184, 186. *See
  also* Mobilizations
Arras, 115, 177, 206
Arrouaise, forest of, 179
Arson, 6, 117, 134, 140, 142-43, 162-63,
  222, 233-34, 274
Artois, xviii, xxv, 81, 115, 149, 177
Artois, comte de, 143, 194-95, 212;
  apanage of, 194
Attichy, 90-92
August 4 (1789), night of, xvii, 121, 144,
  183
Aumale, 178, 216
Austrian Netherlands, xxv-xxvi, 141, 277
Auvergne, 163
Averdy, controller-general, 57
Aveyron, department, 244
Avignon, 243

Bailly, 109
Bailly, J.-S. (mayor of Paris), 38
Bakers, 28, 34, 69, 192, 200
Barbançon, comte de, 91
Barley, 20, 46, 101
Barzy-sur-Marne, 13
Bastille, fall of, xvi, xxi, 101-2, 194,
  214-15; provincial reception, 50, 106-7,
  117, 130, 202, 217, 224-25, 230-31,
  236
Beaugies, 162
Beaulieu [-les Fontaines], 84, 109, 190,
  194, 204, 206

303

The Ideology of the Great Fear

Designed by Ann Walston

Composed by Blue Heron, Inc.
in Galliard text and display

Printed by Thomson-Shore, Inc.
on 50-lb. Glatfelter B-16

DATE DUE
